AMERICA
DURING THE
COLD WAR

AMERICA
DURING THE
COLD WAR

Steven M. Gillon

Yale University

Diane B. Kunz

Yale University

HARCOURT BRACE JOVANOVICH COLLEGE PUBLISHERS

Fort Worth   Philadelphia   San Diego   New York   Orlando   Austin   San Antonio
Toronto   Montreal   London   Sydney   Tokyo

Publisher	Ted Buchholz
Acquisitions Editor	Drake Bush
Project Editor	Karen Anderson
Production Manager	J. Montgomery Shaw
Senior Book Designer	John Ritland

E743
.A566
1993
0284 07609

Address for Editorial Correspondence: Harcourt Brace Jovanovich College Publishers 301 Commerce Street, Suite 3700, Fort Worth, TX 76102.

Address for Orders: Harcourt Brace Jovanovich, Publishers 6277 Sea Harbor Drive, Orlando, FL 32887. 1-800-782-4479, or 1-800-433-0001 (in Florida).

ISBN: 0-15-5004158

Library of Congress Catalogue Number: 92-073125

Printed in the United States of America

2 3 4 5 6 7 8 9 0 1   016 0 9 8 7 6 5 4 3 2 1

Preface

From Stettin in the Baltic to Trieste in the Adriatic, an iron curtain has descended across the Continent.

— WINSTON CHURCHILL, MARCH 5, 1946

Due to the situation which has evolved as a result of the formation of the Commonwealth of Independent States, I hereby discontinue my activities at the post of President of the Union of Soviet Socialist Republics.

— MIKHAIL GORBACHEV, DECEMBER 25, 1991

These two events–Winston Churchill's dire warning about a descending Iron Curtain in 1946 and Mikhail Gorbachev's resignation in 1991 signifying the collapse of the Soviet Union–provide approximate markers for the distinct period of American history known as the Cold War Era. Americans emerged from World War II with nearly unbounded confidence in the government's ability to promote economic growth and peaceful social change, and with unquestioned faith in America's power to influence events abroad. There was reason for optimism. The enormous wartime economic expansion had diminished fears of recurring depression and convinced many economists of the healthy state of the American economy. Many groups—especially African-Americans and women—who had made gains during the war, hoped to sustain that momentum into the postwar period. In 1945, *Reader's Digest* captured this sense of expectation when it predicted that in the postwar period, Americans had the "chance to make a second start."

Foreign affairs inescapably dominated the Cold War Era. At the end of the Second World War, Americans confidently expected the world to regain its pre-war configuration. Only slowly did both Washington leaders and public opinion accept the fact that the United States was one of the dominant world powers and could no longer absent itself from foreign affairs. Unfortunately the world we had irrevocably joined proved not to be a pacific one. Within two years, the fragile post-war coalition had been replaced by the Cold War. This bifurcated world order with two major super-powers dominating their respective spheres cast the shape of international affairs throughout the decades that followed. While the temperature of the Cold War oscillated dramatically, its tension never completely dissipated until Christmas Day 1991 when Mikhail Gorbachev, the first and last President of the Soviet Union, announced his resignation and the dissolution of his country.

Events at home also challenged the heady optimism that followed World War II. The Cold War spawned an atmosphere of anxiety and mistrust that stymied attempts for social change. But many groups, their appetite wetted by past accomplishments and their expectations raised by political rhetoric, persistently attempted to secure new rights. In the 1950s and 1960s, African-Americans challenged one of the central tenets of postwar liberal thought: that American institutions were sound and could be changed by working though the system. Women, inspired by the civil rights struggle, also battled many of the failings of contemporary society.

Protest groups were not alone in their efforts to correct social wrongs. In the 1960s, President Lyndon Johnson pushed through Congress legislation designed, among other things, to reduce poverty, protect civil rights, and beautify the environment. While many of these reforms improved the quality of life for millions of Americans, these legislative changes fell far short of expectations. In the 1970s and 1980s, public frustration with expanded government programs, rising taxes, and the vocal demands of disenfranchised groups created a powerful conservative backlash.

Abroad, the disintegration of the Soviet Union abruptly ended the Cold War. But optimism proved illusive as Americans focused on their weak economy and the crippling budget deficit which robbed the government of resources that could fund domestic programs. Indeed, by 1991 apathy and apprehensiveness seemed to characterize American public opinion. At a time when fledgling democracies around the world looked to the United States for inspiration, Americans seemed disdainful about their political institutions. "I get so embarrassed when I see elections in Central America where you can get shot by either the left or the right for voting, and yet they vote at twice the rate we do in this country," observed one congressman.

This book consists of selected readings on major topics in American history between the years 1945 and 1991. We have not tried to be comprehensive. Many events and issues are not included in this reader. We have, however, endeavored to present students with a manageable and readable collection of important essays. Along with selections on foreign policy and national politics, we have also included sections dealing specifically with the plight of African-Americans and women.

The authors wish to thank John Morton Blum, who has been an inspiring teacher and a good friend, for making this book possible.

Contents

AMERICA
DURING THE
COLD WAR

THE ORIGINS OF THE
COLD WAR

The Cold War defines the period 1945–1991. Japanese forces had brought the United States into the war in the Pacific by attacking Pearl Harbor on December 7, 1941. With Adolf Hitler's declaration of war four days later, the United States joined the war in the west as well, allying itself with Great Britain and the Soviet Union. During the war the American government, led by President Franklin D. Roosevelt, walked a tightrope trying to keep the "Grand Alliance" together. Interestingly, the Roosevelt administration often seemed more at odds with the British government led by Prime Minister Winston Churchill than Josef Stalin's Soviet regime.

The wartime euphoria eroded quickly after the German and Japanese surrenders on May 7 and September 2, respectively. In part, this result followed naturally as the parochial concerns of each country replaced the shared objective of defeating the Axis powers. More important, certain insurmountable obstacles soon dominated discussions among the "Big Three."

One of the biggest roadblocks was the question of European borders. While the Second World War had begun over the German invasion of Poland, Stalin was determined not to allow the Polish pre-war government, blatantly hostile to his regime, to return to Poland, which he viewed as a necessary buffer between the Soviet Union and Germany. Furthermore, Stalin intended to retain control over the Baltic states (Lithuania, Latvia, and Estonia), absorbed into the Soviet Union in 1940, and to push the borders of Poland westward with the Soviet Union retaining the third it had sliced off in 1939 and Poland receiving East Prussia from Germany in compensation.

The United States and Britain felt distinctly uncomfortable about this scenario. The United States had fought, in the words of historian John Morton Blum, a "necessitarian war," putting military victory above post-war concerns.[1] With no American soldiers east of Berlin, Stalin could not readily be dissuaded from his goals by military measures. But explaining these realities to the American people proved another task, one which both Roosevelt and his successor, Harry S. Truman flunked.

The realities of the American monopoly over the atomic bomb, first used militarily against Japan in August 1945, and over world economic resources, also influenced post-war geopolitical developments. Possessing overwhelming explosive and economic strength encouraged American policymakers to believe that they could automatically have their way in the world. It came as a rude shock to realize that neither monopoly would prove decisive.

Other rude shocks soon followed. Nineteen hundred forty-six brought a growing American perception that a confrontation with the Soviet Union was no mere nightmare. Conflict over the withdrawal of Soviet troops from Iran and Stalin's belligerent speech in February persuaded many in the United States that Churchill was correct when he proclaimed that an "iron curtain" had descended over Europe. George Kennan, an American diplomat stationed in Moscow, for one, needed no convincing. In February 1946, he sent to the State Department the now-famous "long telegram" setting out Kennan's pessimistic view of the possibility of cooperation with the Soviet government.

Within one year the American government publicly confronted the Soviet Union. In March 1947, Truman addressed Congress and asked for $400 million to defend Greece and Turkey. The central point of what would become known as the Truman Doctrine was the American pledge "to support free peoples who are resisting attempted subjugation by armed minorities or by outside pressures." Political and military programs proved insufficient. The winter of 1946–47 registered as one

---

[1]John Morton Blum, *V Was For Victory* (New York, Harcourt Brace Jovanovich, 1976), 177.

of the worst on record. European economies desperately needed aid to survive. Without aid Washington policymakers feared that not only economic but political chaos would ensue. And chaos could prove the fertile breeding ground for Communist takeovers. In response, motivated by enlightened self-interest, the administration unveiled the Marshall Plan. Donating $13.5 billion over four years, the United States rescued the economies and governments of Western Europe and laid the basis for the prosperity which was to follow. The Soviet Union did not participate nor did Stalin permit Eastern European countries, now all firmly tied to the Soviet orbit, to join either.

Each year that followed brought fresh confrontations. In 1948, Soviet forces blocked all land routes to the western sectors of Berlin, leaving the American, British and French sectors to starve. The American army went on complete alert but a full-scale conflict was avoided. Instead, after almost a year during which Anglo-American forces airlifted all supplies into the western sections of the city, Stalin lifted the blockade. But 1949 also brought the Soviet explosion of an atomic weapon which, as much as any other factor, put fear into the hearts of the American public.

Oddly, the first American military conflict with the Communists came in Asia. Korea, long a Japanese colony, had been haphazardly divided between the Soviet Union and the United States in 1945. Five years later, North Korean forces invaded the southern part which had allied itself with the United States. A United Nations force led by an American commander fought back. After three years of increasingly frustrating warfare, both sides acquiesced in a cease-fire which virtually restored the *status quo ante*. The Korean War was not only the first war the United States had not won in 140 years, it also set the scene for the creation of the national security state, which was with us for the next four decades.

The Sources of Soviet Conduct

GEORGE KENNAN

George Kennan has long occupied the role of dean of Sovietologists. Having first begun to study the Soviet Union during the nineteen twenties, he used his position as an American diplomat to devise the seminal theory explaining post-war Soviet conduct, expounded first in his long telegram. In this article, published anonymously in the influential journal *Foreign Affairs* in July 1947, Kennan sets forth the basic principles of the policy of containment which would guide American policy vis-à-vis the Soviet Union for the next forty-five years. Was the Cold War a reflection of Kennan's ideas or a result? Why does Kennan think that Soviet leaders differ from those of other countries?

The political personality of Soviet power as we know it today is the product of ideology and circumstances: ideology inherited by the present Soviet leaders from the movement in which they had their political origin, and circumstances of the power which they now have exercised for nearly three decades in Russia. There can be few tasks of psychological analysis more difficult than to try to trace the interaction of these two forces and the relative rôle of each in the determination of official Soviet conduct. Yet the attempt must be made if that conduct is to be understood and effectively countered.

It is difficult to summarize the set of ideological concepts with which the Soviet leaders came into power. Marxian ideology, in its Russian-Communist projection, has always been in the process of subtle evolution. The materials on which it bases itself are extensive and complex. But the outstanding features of Communist thought as it existed in

4

1916 may perhaps be summarized as follows: (a) that the central factor in the life of man, the factor which determines the character of public life and the "physiognomy of society," is the system by which material goods are produced and exchanged; (b) that the capitalist system of production is a nefarious one which inevitably leads to the exploitation of the working class by the capital-owning class and is incapable of developing adequately the economic resources of society or of distributing fairly the material goods produced by human labor; (c) that capitalism contains the seeds of its own destruction and must, in view of the inability of the capital-owning class to adjust itself to economic change, result eventually and inescapably in a revolutionary transfer of power to the working class; and (d) that imperialism, the final phase of capitalism, leads directly to war and revolution.

The rest may be outlined in Lenin's own words: "Unevenness of economic and political development is the inflexible law of capitalism. It follows from this that the victory of Socialism may come originally in a few capitalist countries or even in a single capitalist country. The victorious proletariat of that country, having expropriated the capitalists and having organized Socialist production at home, would rise against the remaining capitalist world, drawing to itself in the process the oppressed classes of other countries."[1] It must be noted that there was no assumption that capitalism would perish without proletarian revolution. A final push was needed from a revolutionary proletariat movement in order to tip over the tottering structure. But it was regarded as inevitable that sooner or later that push be given. . . .

II

So much for the historical background. What does it spell in terms of the political personality of Soviet power as we know it today?

Of the original ideology, nothing has been officially junked. Belief is maintained in the basic badness of capitalism, in the inevitability of its destruction, in the obligation of the proletariat to assist in that destruction and to take power into its own hands. But stress has come to be laid primarily on those concepts which relate most specifically to the Soviet régime itself: to its position as the sole truly Socialist régime

---

[1]"Concerning the Slogans of the United States of Europe," August 1915. Official Soviet edition of Lenin's works.

in a dark and misguided world, and to the relationships of power within it.

The first of these concepts is that of the innate antagonism between capitalism and Socialism.[2] We have seen how deeply that concept has become imbedded in foundations of Soviet power. It has profound implications for Russia's conduct as a member of international society. It means that there can never be on Moscow's side any sincere assumption of a community of aims between the Soviet Union and powers which are regarded as capitalist. It must invariably be assumed in Moscow that the aims of the capitalist world are antagonistic to the Soviet régime, and therefore to the interests of the peoples it controls. If the Soviet Government occasionally sets its signature to documents which would indicate the contrary, this is to be regarded as a tactical manoeuvre permissible in dealing with the enemy (who is without honor) and should be taken in the spirit of *caveat emptor*. Basically, the antagonism remains. It is postulated. And from it flow many of the phenomena which we find disturbing in the Kremlin's conduct of foreign policy: the secretiveness, the lack of frankness, the duplicity, the wary suspiciousness, and the basic unfriendliness of purpose. These phenomena are there to stay, for the foreseeable future. There can be variations of degree and emphasis. When there is something the Russians want from us, one or the other of these features of their policy may be thrust temporarily into the background; and when that happens there will always be Americans who will leap forward with gleeful announcements that "the Russians have changed," and some who will even try to take credit for having brought about such "changes." But we should not be misled by tactical manoeuvres. These characteristics of Soviet policy, like the postulate from which they flow, are basic to the internal nature of Soviet power, and will be with us, whether in the foreground or the background, until the internal nature of Soviet power is changed.

This means that we are going to continue for a long time to find the Russians difficult to deal with. It does not mean that they should be considered as embarked upon a do-or-die program to overthrow our society by a given date. The theory of the inevitability of the eventual fall of capitalism has the fortunate connotation that there is no hurry about it. The forces of progress can take their time in preparing the *coup*

[2]Here and elsewhere in this paper "Socialism" refers to Marxist or Leninist Communism, not to liberal Socialism of the Second International Society.

de grâce. Meanwhile, what is vital is that the "Socialist fatherland"—that oasis of power which has been already won for Socialism in the person of the Soviet Union—should be cherished and defended by all good Communists at home and abroad, its fortunes promoted, its enemies badgered and confounded. The promotion of premature, "adventuristic" revolutionary projects abroad which might embarrass Soviet power in any way would be an inexcusable, even a counter-revolutionary act. The cause of Socialism is the support and promotion of Soviet power, as defined in Moscow.

This brings us to the second of the concepts important to contemporary Soviet outlook. That is the infallibility of the Kremlin. The Soviet concept of power, which permits no focal points of organization outside the Party itself, requires that the Party leadership remain in theory the sole repository of truth. For if truth were to be found elsewhere, there would be justification for its expression in organized activity. But it is precisely that which the Kremlin cannot and will not permit.

The leadership of the Communist Party is therefore always right, and has been always right ever since in 1929 Stalin formalized his personal power by announcing that decisions of the Politburo were being taken unanimously.

On the principle of infallibility there rests the iron discipline of the Communist Party. In fact, the two concepts are mutually self-supporting. Perfect discipline requires recognition of infallibility. Infallibility requires the observance of discipline. And the two together go far to determine the behaviorism of the entire Soviet apparatus of power. But their effect cannot be understood unless a third factor be taken into account: namely the fact that the leadership is at liberty to put forward for tactical purposes any particular thesis which it finds useful to the cause at any particular moment and to require the faithful and unquestioning acceptance of that thesis by the members of the movement as a whole. This means that truth is not a constant but is actually created, for all intents and purposes, by the Soviet leaders themselves. It may vary from week to week, from month to month. It is nothing absolute and immutable—nothing which flows from objective reality. It is only the most recent manifestation of the wisdom of those in whom the ultimate wisdom is supposed to reside, because they represent the logic of history.

The accumulative effect of these factors is to give to the whole subordinate apparatus of Soviet power an unshakeable stubbornness and steadfastness in its orientation. This orientation can be changed at will by the Kremlin but by no other power. Once a given party line has been laid down on a given issue of current policy, the whole Soviet governmental machine, including the mechanism of diplomacy, moves inexorably along the prescribed path, like a persistent toy automobile wound up and headed in a given direction, stopping only when it meets with some unanswerable force. The individuals who are the components of this machine are unamenable to argument or reason which comes to them from outside sources. Their whole training has taught them to mistrust and discount the glib persuasiveness of the outside world. Like the white dog before the phonograph, they hear only the "master's voice." And if they are to be called off from the purposes last dictated to them, it is the master who must call them off. Thus the foreign representative cannot hope that his words will make any impression on them. The most that he can hope is that they will be transmitted to those at the top, who are capable of changing the party line. But even those are not likely to be swayed by any normal logic in the words of the bourgeois representative. Since there can be no appeal to common purposes, there can be no appeal to common mental approaches. For this reason, facts speak louder than words to the ears of the Kremlin; and words carry the greatest weight when they have the ring of reflecting, or being backed up by, facts of unchallengeable validity.

But we have seen that the Kremlin is under no ideological compulsion to accomplish its purposes in a hurry. Like the Church, it is dealing in ideological concepts which are of long-term validity, and it can afford to be patient. It has no right to risk the existing achievements of the revolution for the sake of vain baubles of the future. The very teachings of Lenin himself require great caution and flexibility in the pursuit of Communist purposes. Again, these precepts are fortified by the lessons of Russian history: of centuries of obscure battles between nomadic forces over the stretches of a vast unfortified plain. Here caution, circumspection, flexibility and deception are the valuable qualities; and their value finds natural appreciation in the Russian or the oriental mind. Thus the Kremlin has no compunction about retreating in the face of superior force. And being under the compulsion of no timetable, it does not get panicky under the necessity for such retreat. Its political action is a fluid stream which moves constantly, wherever it is permitted to move, toward a given goal. Its main concern is to make sure that it has filled every nook and cranny available to it in the basin of world power. But if it finds unassailable barriers in its path, it accepts these philosophically and accommodates itself to them. The main thing is that there should always be pressure, unceasing constant pressure, toward the desired goal. There is no trace of any feeling in Soviet psychology that that goal must be reached at any given time.

These considerations make Soviet diplomacy at once easier and more difficult to deal with than the diplomacy of individual aggressive leaders like Napoleon and Hitler. On the one hand it is more sensitive to contrary force, more ready to yield on individual sectors of the diplomatic front when that force is felt to be too strong, and thus more rational in the logic and rhetoric of power. On the other hand it cannot be easily defeated or discouraged by a single victory on the part of its opponents. And the patient persistence by which it is animated means that it can be effectively countered not by sporadic acts which represent the momentary whims of democratic opinion but only by intelligent long-range policies on the part of Russia's adversaries—policies no less steady in their purpose, and no less variegated and resourceful in their application, than those of the Soviet Union itself.

In these circumstances it is clear that the main element of any United States policy toward the Soviet Union must be that of a long-term, patient but firm and vigilant containment of Russian expansive tendencies. It is important to note, however, that such a policy has nothing to do with outward histrionics: with threats or blustering or superfluous gestures of outward "toughness." While the Kremlin is basically flexible in its reaction to political realities, it is by no means unamenable to considerations of prestige. Like almost any other government, it can be placed by tactless and threatening gestures in a position where it cannot afford to yield even though this might be dictated by its sense of realism. The Russian leaders are keen judges of human psychology, and as such they are highly conscious that loss of temper and of self-control is never a source of strength in political affairs. They are quick to exploit such evidences of weakness. For these reasons, it is a *sine qua non* of successful dealing with Russia that the foreign government in question should remain at all times cool and collected and that its demands on Russian policy should be put forward in such a manner as to leave the way open for a compliance not too detrimental to Russian prestige.

III

In the light of the above, it will be clearly seen that the Soviet pressure against the free institutions of the western world is something that can be contained by the adroit and vigilant application of counter-force at a series of constantly shifting geographical and political points, corresponding to the shifts and manoeuvres of Soviet policy, but which cannot be charmed or talked out of existence. The Russians look forward to a duel of infinite duration, and they see that already they have scored great successes. It must be borne in mind that there was a time when the Communist Party represented far more of a minority in the sphere of Russian national life than Soviet power today represents in the world community.

But if ideology convinces the rulers of Russia that truth is on their side and that they can therefore afford to wait, those of us on whom that ideology has no claim are free to examine objectively the validity of that premise. The Soviet thesis not only implies complete lack of control by the west over its own economic destiny, it likewise assumes Russian unity, discipline and patience over an infinite period. Let us bring this apocalyptic vision down to earth, and suppose that the western world finds the strength and resourcefulness to contain Soviet power over a period of ten to fifteen years. What does that spell for Russia itself?

The Soviet leaders, taking advantage of the contributions of modern technique to the arts of despotism, have solved the question of obedience within the confines of their power. Few challenge their authority; and even those who do are unable to make that challenge valid against the organs of suppression of the state.

The Kremlin has also proved able to accomplish its purpose of building up in Russia, regardless of the interests of the inhabitants, an industrial foundation of heavy metallurgy, which is, to be sure, not yet complete but which is nevertheless continuing to grow and is approaching those of the other major industrial countries. All of this, however, both the maintenance of internal political security and the building of heavy industry, has been carried out at a terrible cost in human life and in human hopes and energies. It has necessitated the use of forced labor on a scale unprecedented in modern times under conditions of peace. It has involved the neglect or abuse of other phases of Soviet economic life, particularly agriculture, consumers' goods production, housing and transportation.

To all that, the war has added its tremendous toll of destruction, death and human exhaustion. In consequence of this, we have in Russia today a population which is physically and spiritually tired. The mass of the people are disillusioned, skeptical and no longer as accessible as they once were to the magical attraction which Soviet power still radiates to its followers abroad. The avidity with which people seized upon the slight respite accorded to the Church for tactical reasons during the war was eloquent testimony to the fact that their capacity for faith and devotion found little expression in the purposes of the régime.

In these circumstances, there are limits to the physical and nervous strength of people themselves. These limits are absolute ones, and are binding even for the cruelest dictatorship, because beyond them people cannot be driven. The forced labor camps and the other agencies of constraint provide temporary means of compelling people to work longer hours than their own volition or mere economic pressure would dictate; but if people survive them at all they become old before their time and must be considered as human casualties to the demands of dictatorship. In either case their best powers are no longer available to society and can no longer be enlisted in the service of the state.

Here only the younger generation can help. The younger generation, despite all vicissitudes and sufferings, is numerous and vigorous; and the Russians are a talented people. But it still remains to be seen what will be the effects on mature performance of the abnormal emotional strains of childhood which Soviet dictatorship created and which were enormously increased by the war. Such things as normal security and placidity of home environment have practically ceased to exist in the Soviet Union outside of the most remote farms and villages. And observers are not yet sure whether that is not going to leave its mark on the over-all capacity of the generation now coming into maturity.

In addition to this, we have the fact that Soviet economic development, while it can list certain formidable achievements, has been precariously spotty and uneven. Russian Communists who speak of the "uneven development of capitalism" should blush at the contemplation of their own national economy. Here certain branches of economic life, such as the metallurgical and machine industries, have been pushed out of all proportion to other sectors of economy. Here is a nation striving to become in a short period one of the great industrial nations of the world while it still has no highway network worthy of the name and only a relatively primitive network of railways. Much has been done to increase efficiency of labor and to teach primitive peasants something about the operation of machines. But maintenance is still a crying deficiency of all Soviet economy. Construction is hasty and poor in quality. Depreciation must be enormous. And in vast sectors of economic life it has not yet been possible to instill into labor anything like that general culture of production and technical self-respect which characterizes the skilled worker of the west.

It is difficult to see how these deficiencies can be corrected at an early date by a tired and dispirited population working largely under the shadow of fear and compulsion. And as long as they are not overcome, Russia will remain economically a vulnerable, and in a certain sense an impotent, nation, capable of exporting its enthusiasms and of radiating the strange charm of its primitive political vitality but unable to back up those articles of export by the real evidences of material power and prosperity.

Meanwhile, a great uncertainty hangs over the political life of the Soviet Union. That is the uncertainty involved in the transfer of power from one individual or group of individuals to others.

This is, of course, outstandingly the problem of the personal position of Stalin. We must remember that his succession to Lenin's pinnacle of preëminence in the Communist movement was the only such transfer of individual authority which the Soviet Union has experienced. That transfer took 12 years to consolidate. It cost the lives of millions of people and shook the state to its foundations. The attendant tremors were felt all through the international revolutionary movement, to the disadvantage of the Kremlin itself.

It is always possible that another transfer of preëminent power may take place quietly and inconspicuously, with no repercussions anywhere. But again, it is possible that the questions involved may unleash, to use some of Lenin's words, one of those "incredibly swift transitions" from "delicate deceit" to "wild violence" which characterize Russian history, and may shake Soviet power to its foundations.

But this is not only a question of Stalin himself. There has been, since 1938, a dangerous congealment of political life in the higher circles of Soviet power. The All-Union Congress of Soviets, in theory the supreme body of the Party, is supposed to meet not less often than once in three years. It will soon be eight full years since its last meeting. During this period membership in the Party has numerically doubled. Party mortality during the war was enormous; and today well over half of the Party members are persons who have entered since the last Party congress was held. Meanwhile, the same small group of men has carried on at the top through an amazing series of national vicissitudes. Surely there is some reason why the experiences of the war brought basic political changes to every one of the great governments of the west. Surely the causes of that phenomenon are basic enough to be present somewhere in the obscurity of Soviet political life, as well. And yet no recognition has been given to these causes in Russia.

It must be surmised from this that even within so highly disciplined an organization as the Communist Party there must be a growing divergence in age, outlook and interest between the great mass of Party members, only so recently recruited into the movement, and the little self-perpetuating clique of men at the top, whom most of these Party members have never met, with whom they have never conversed, and with whom they can have no political intimacy.

Who can say whether, in these circumstances, the eventual rejuvenation of the higher spheres of authority (which can only be a matter of time) can take place smoothly and peacefully, or whether rivals in the quest for higher power will not eventually reach down into these politically immature and inexperienced masses in order to find support for their respective claims? If this were ever to happen, strange consequences could flow for the Communist Party: for the membership at large has been exercised only in the practices of iron discipline and obedience and not in the arts of compromise and accommodation. And if disunity were ever to seize and paralyze the Party, the chaos and weakness of Russian society would be revealed in forms beyond description. For we have seen that Soviet power is only a crust concealing an amorphous mass of human beings among whom no independent organizational structure is tolerated. In Russia there is not even such a thing as local government. The present generation of Russians have never known spontaneity of collective action. If, consequently, anything were ever to occur to disrupt the unity and efficacy of the Party as a political instrument, Soviet Russia might be changed overnight from one of the strongest to one of the weakest and most pitiable of national societies.

Thus the future of Soviet power may not be by any means as secure as Russian capacity for self-delusion would make it appear to the men in the Kremlin. That they can keep power themselves, they have demonstrated. That they can quietly and easily turn it over to others remains to be proved. Meanwhile, the hardships of their rule and the vicissitudes of international life have taken a heavy toll of the strength and hopes of the great people on whom their power rests. It is curious to note that the ideological power of Soviet authority is strongest today in areas beyond the frontiers of Russia, beyond the reach of its police power. This phenomenon brings to mind a comparison used by Thomas Mann in his great novel "Buddenbrooks." Observing that human institutions often show the greatest outward brilliance at a moment when inner decay is in reality farthest advanced, he compared the Buddenbrook family, in the days of its greatest glamour, to one of those stars whose light shines most brightly on this world when in reality it has long since ceased to exist. And who can say with assurance that the strong light still cast by the Kremlin on the dissatisfied peoples of the western world is not the powerful afterglow of a constellation which is in actuality on the wane? This cannot be proved. And it cannot be disproved. But the possibility remains (and in the opinion of this writer it is a strong one) that Soviet power, like the capitalist world of its conception, bears within it the seeds of its own decay, and that the sprouting of these seeds is well advanced.

IV

It is clear that the United States cannot expect in the foreseeable future to enjoy political intimacy with the Soviet régime. It must continue to regard the Soviet Union as a rival, not a partner, in the political arena. It must continue to expect that Soviet policies will reflect no abstract love of peace and stability, no real faith in the possibility of a permanent happy coexistence of the Socialist and capitalist worlds, but rather a cautious, persistent pressure toward the disruption and weakening of all rival influence and rival power.

Balanced against this are the facts that Russia, as opposed to the western world in general, is still by far the weaker party, that Soviet policy is highly flexible, and that Soviet society may well contain deficiencies which will eventually weaken its own total potential. This would of itself warrant the United States entering with reasonable confidence upon a policy of firm containment, designed to confront the Russians with unalterable counter-force at every point where they show signs of encroaching upon the interests of a peaceful and stable world.

But in actuality the possibilities for American policy are by no means limited to holding the line and hoping for the best. It is entirely possible for the United States to influence by its actions the internal developments, both within Russia and throughout the international Communist movement, by which Russian policy is largely determined. This is not only a question of the modest measure of informational activity which this government can conduct in the Soviet Union and elsewhere, although that, too, is important. It is rather a question of the degree to which the United States can create among the peoples of the world generally the impression of a country which knows what it wants, which is coping successfully with the problems of its internal life and with the responsibilities of a World Power, and which has a spiritual vitality capable of holding its own among the major ideological currents of the time. To the extent that such an impression can be created and maintained, the aims of Russian Communism must appear sterile and quixotic, the hopes and enthusiasm of Moscow's supporters must wane, and added strain must be imposed on the Kremlin's foreign policies.

For the palsied decrepitude of the capitalist world is the keystone of Communist philosophy. Even the failure of the United States to experience the early economic depression which the ravens of the Red Square have been predicting with such complacent confidence since hostilities ceased would have deep and important repercussions throughout the Communist world.

By the same token, exhibitions of indecision, disunity and internal disintegration within this country have an exhilarating effect on the whole Communist movement. At each evidence of these tendencies, a thrill of hope and excitement goes through the Communist world; a new jauntiness can be noted in the Moscow tread; new groups of foreign supporters climb on to what they can only view as the band wagon of international politics; and Russian pressure increases all along the line in international affairs.

It would be an exaggeration to say that American behavior unassisted and alone could exercise a power of life and death over the Communist movement and bring about the early fall of Soviet power in Russia. But the United States has it in its power to increase enormously the strains under which Soviet policy must operate, to force upon the Kremlin a far greater degree of moderation and circumspection than it has had to observe in recent years, and in this way to promote tendencies which must eventually find their outlet in either the break-up or the gradual mellowing of Soviet power. For no mystical, Messianic movement—and particularly not that of the Kremlin—can face frustration indefinitely without eventually adjusting itself in one way or another to the logic of that state of affairs.

Thus the decision will really fall in large measure in this country itself. The issue of Soviet-American relations is in essence a test of the over-all worth of the United States as a nation among nations. To avoid destruction the United States need only measure up to its own best traditions and prove itself worthy of preservation as a great nation.

Surely, there was never a fairer test of national quality than this. In the light of these circumstances, the thoughtful observer of Russian-American relations will find no cause for complaint in the Kremlin's challenge to American society. He will rather experience a certain gratitude to a Providence which, by providing the American people with this implacable challenge, has made their entire security as a nation dependent on their pulling themselves together and accepting the responsibilities of moral and political leadership that history plainly intended them to bear.

The Making of the Marshall Plan

ROBERT A. POLLARD

Robert Pollard, a diplomatic historian, has written extensively about the economic/security nexus that underlay the Cold War. Having traced the origins of the interventionist economic policy increasingly promulgated by the Truman administration, in this excerpt he discusses the origins of the Marshall Plan and its relationship to the reconstruction of West Germany. What were the arguments against the Marshall Plan? What made the Marshall Plan succeed, both with the American public and as a revolutionary form of foreign aid?

The European Recovery Program (ERP) grew out of an increasing sense of anxiety among American officials that Western Europe was nearing political and economic collapse. The surprising recovery of 1946 had been followed by a sharp drop in production and trade during the bitter winter of 1947. These problems worsened in the spring. Western Europe faced a huge balance-of-payments deficit with the outside world, particularly the United States (an estimated $4.25 billion in fiscal 1948) and raw materials suppliers. British insolvency caused special problems, for that country's traditional import surplus with the continent had supplied the foreign exchange earnings necessary to pay for European imports from the Americas and other areas. Factories shut down when stocks of raw and semifinished materials, notably coal, ran out, while inflation, inconvertibility, and the proliferation of protectionist commercial agreements crippled intra-European trade.

In April 1947, a SWNCC subcommittee reported that the European dollar gap required a vast infusion of American aid. A new program of U.S. assistance was imperative because existing relief programs were tapering off at the time of greatest European need. The State Department estimated in May 1947 that while aid by the U.S. government, including IBRD and IMF disbursements, would finance the export of $6.2 billion of goods and services in 1947, this figure would shrink to $4.6 billion in 1948 and $2.7 billion in 1949. Neither the World Bank nor private American banks could meet West European deficits, explained Bank President John J. McCloy in an April 1947 speech. The sums were too large, and financial institutions refused to extend what they considered economically unsound loans to accomplish political objectives.

Following his return from the Moscow Council of Foreign Ministers at the end of April, Secretary of State Marshall instructed George F. Kennan, then teaching at the National War College in Washington, to establish a Policy Planning Staff (PPS) that would formulate the principles for a European reconstruction program. (Marshall created the PPS, he told the Cabinet, because there had been a "notable lack of central planning on American policy.") Kennan's group contributed its preliminary report on European reconstruction on May 23. The PPS felt that the root of European instability lay in the after-effects of war rather than in Communist activities. While Europe itself must initiate a new cooperative recovery program, the United States could help by using aid to open up major production bottlenecks, such as the German coal industry. The Soviet bloc countries could participate, but only if they agreed "to abandon the exclusive orientation of their economics." The PPS concluded with a plea for a deemphasis of anti-Communism in U.S. policy.

On May 8, 1947, Under Secretary Dean Acheson defined the principles of a new aid program in a major address on the European economic crisis before the Delta Council at Cleveland, Mississippi. To answer domestic and foreign criticism of the Truman Doctrine's allegedly single-minded anti-Communism, Acheson stressed the positive U.S. commitment to European reconstruction. Acheson first described in vivid detail the destruction wrought by the war in Europe and the consequences of its inability to pay for desperately needed American goods. Just to maintain current imports, the European countries needed about $5 billion per year in additional hard currency. International institutions were incapable of handling the crisis, he explained, and only the United States had sufficient resources to help. But even with its impressive assets, America needed to concentrate its "emergency assistance in areas where it will be most effective in building world political and economic stability . . . [and] in fostering liberal trade policies . . . ," notably in Western Europe and Germany. "European cooperation," he stated, "cannot await 'compromise through exhaustion,' and . . . we must take whatever action is possible immediately, even without full Four Power agreement, to effect a larger measure of European, including German, recovery."

In a May 27 memo, Under Secretary for Economic Affairs William Clayton, recently returned from Europe and shaken by the deteriorating conditions there, argued that the United States had seriously understated European recovery problems. He recommended a three-year program of aid at $6–7 billion per year. But Clayton, remembering the negative public and Congressional reaction to UNRRA, believed the United States should carefully supervise the program. "*The United States must run this show,*" he wrote.

At this point, the administration had not decided such important matters as the size and duration of a recovery program or the scope of European participation in it. In his famous speech at Harvard University on June 5, Secretary of State Marshall simply called for a European initiative in a joint recovery effort and pledged American assistance. As of yet, there was no "Marshall Plan," for policymakers had not resolved the differing approaches among the various proposals for European reconstruction. The countries that the SWNCC subcommittee had identified as most deserving of American aid in its report on April 21, for example, did not correspond closely with the eventual ERP recipients. Similarly, the preliminary, hastily prepared PPS report of May 23 dealt with principles for European reconstruction rather than a concrete program, and had only a limited impact upon Marshall except for its recommendation of a European initiative. Indeed, the PPS did not deliver a final version of the report until late July 1947, and by then it was superceded by events. Finally, in stressing European self-help, Marshall seemed to reject Clayton's suggestion for direct U.S. control over the recovery program.

If they lacked a specific plan to rescue Europe, American officials at least shared the conviction that drastic action was necessary to secure American multilateralist aims on the continent. Already in early 1947, key European countries were turning to bilateral treaties and other restrictive measures to hold down imports from the dollar area. In preliminary discussions with Clayton in late June 1947, for instance, British

Cabinet officials threatened to pursue bilateral trade agreements—which on the scale they mentioned would have doomed the Marshall Plan—if they did not receive special interim aid and other concessions. In the American view, rescuing Europe required more than just another injection of dollar aid; it called for the full integration of the European economy.

THE SOVIET RESPONSE TO THE MARSHALL PLAN

In time, the Marshall Plan would polarize Europe into hostile blocs, but American policymakers were at first undecided about the roles of the Soviet Union and Eastern Europe in a recovery program. To be sure, Washington wished to contain Soviet power and influence. Yet both American and European planners were accustomed to thinking of the continent as an economic unit and viewed East-West trade as a key element in West European reconstruction.

U.S. officials did not welcome, but nevertheless did not entirely rule out, Soviet participation in the Marshall Plan. American aid, they reasoned, could perhaps counteract the Soviet hold over the East European countries; at the very least, the West would retain access to their raw materials and markets. On May 24, 1947, George Kennan advised Secretary Marshall to "play it straight" with the Russians. If the Russians responded favorably, the West could "test their good faith." If not, the Russians would exclude themselves. Most importantly, Kennan recalls arguing, "we would not ourselves draw a line of division through Europe." In a meeting of State Department heads of offices on May 28, Clayton contended that the inclusion of the East European countries was unnecessary, for they needed Western goods so badly that they would export coal and grain to Western Europe no matter what. Yet the group, siding with Kennan's PPS, decided to permit East European participation, "provided the countries would abandon [the] near-exclusive Soviet orientation of their economies."

The prospect of reconstruction aid must have tempted the Kremlin. By June 1947, the Soviets knew that heavy reparations from western Germany and credits from the United States would not be forthcoming. The Soviets had already stripped eastern Germany, and the capacity of the war-ravaged East European countries to provide reparations and trade was limited. Only the United States could offer critical supplies of machinery, technology, and food. Some administration officials fully expected Soviet participation. Secretary of the Navy James Forrestal, an outspoken anti-Communist who chafed at the thought of aid to Russia, exclaimed at a Cabinet luncheon shortly after Marshall's speech that "there was no chance of Russia's *not* joining in this effort."

Despite some initial skepticism, Moscow on June 22 accepted the Anglo-French invitation to confer in Paris and promised to cooperate as long as the United States did not intervene in its internal affairs. Yet in the opening meeting on June 27, Soviet Foreign Minister V. M. Molotov instantly aroused the suspicions of his British and French counterparts, Ernest Bevin and Georges Bidault. Molotov suggested that the three ministers should test the seriousness of Marshall's proposal by boldly asking Washington the exact sum of money that it was prepared to offer the European countries. On the next day, Molotov added that rather than investigate the prospects for European self-help, the needy countries should simply forward their aggregate aid request to Washington and await a reply. This procedure, Bevin and Bidault protested, fell far short of the coordinated European plan envisaged by Marshall. As a French diplomat privately put it, "The Soviets want to put the United States in a position where it must either shell out dollars before there is a real plan or refuse outright to advance any credits." On June 30, Molotov rejected a compromise offered by the British and French and reiterated his demands of the previous meetings, whereupon Bevin accused him of demanding a "blank check" from the United States. Unwilling to make any concessions for American aid, the Kremlin apparently had instructed Molotov to pull out of the conference. During the last session on July 2, Molotov denounced the Western ministers and warned of a division of Europe into two camps. Subsequently, the Soviets forced the East European representatives to leave Paris.

Why did the Soviets quit the Paris talks? Undoubtedly the Russians would have had to release economic statistics and allow some American inspection of their country. But Moscow rarely furnished candid data, and American probing would only have confirmed what almost everyone already knew: the Soviet Union was weak. Also, even if, as Molotov predicted, the U.S. Congress had rejected the plan because of Soviet participation, the Americans would then have taken the blame and the plan might have failed. If Congress had approved the plan, on the other hand, the Soviets would have gained reconstruction aid for themselves and their dependencies.

Some historians stress the economic vulnerability of the Russian sphere in Eastern Europe. Thomas G. Paterson, for instance, argues that the Soviets rejected the Marshall Plan because it would have signified a return to the *status quo ante bellum* in which Eastern Europe traded food and raw materials for Western machinery and consumer goods. Given the precarious Soviet hold over the region, he adds, "a massive influx of American dollars would certainly have challenged the Soviet position."

Yet neither side in 1947 anticipated or desired an interruption of the mutually profitable East-West trade. There is little evidence that American capitalists hungered after this market, and U.S. planners cared most about Eastern Europe as a source of trade and raw materials for *Western* Europe. Nor did the Russians have good reason to disrupt the traditional pattern of intra-European trade. Foreign trade had never figured largely in Soviet planning, and the East European economies did not complement Moscow's needs well. Czechoslovakia excepted, most specialized in agricultural and unprocessed goods of which the Soviet Union usually enjoyed a surplus. The Soviet satellites, on the other hand, depended upon Western trade for recovery. Thus, Western trade with, and investment in, Eastern Europe would not have necessarily conflicted with Soviet *economic* goals in the region, certainly not to the point of warranting Soviet rejection of the Marshall Plan.

Strategic and political needs, on the other hand, help explain Soviet fears of American influence in Eastern Europe. Moscow was determined to create a buffer zone against invasion from the West, but it had yet to secure allegiance from its dependencies when Marshall proposed a new recovery program. The anxious men in the Kremlin, Adam Ulam and Isaac Deutscher have speculated, may have interpreted the increasingly militant rhetoric of American spokesmen following the Truman Doctrine as the first step in a campaign to lure the East European countries out of the Soviet bloc. Indeed, the Poles and Czechoslovaks at first resisted Soviet pressure to withdraw from the Paris conference.

Ideology also militated against Soviet participation in the Marshall Plan. Obviously, the Kremlin did not want to help save capitalism in Western Europe. The Soviets, who equated economic control with political mastery of Eastern Europe, probably regarded the American goal of an open, free-trading, economically integrated Europe as a thinly disguised challenge to their sphere of influence.

In an "economic defense of Stalin's autarky," the Soviets gradually sealed off Eastern Europe and set up self-sufficient, "nationalist" economies and a bilateral trading system. During the 1930s, when the terms of trade had turned against primary goods and made imported machinery prohibitively expensive, Soviet planners had concentrated on the extraction of natural resources and the production of capital goods over consumer commodities. By the time the Red Army pushed into Eastern Europe, the Soviet experiment had become locked into an iron law of "Marxist"—or rather, Stalinist—economics, and Soviet and local Communist authorities began to apply the now orthodox operating procedures to the satellites. Ideological and bureaucratic imperatives thus overrode economic rationality and the specialization of labor. Countries as small as Albania constructed expensive and inefficient steel mills in deference to Stalin. In the mid-1950s, Comecon, the Soviet bloc's counterpart to the Marshall Plan, would finally abandon the irrational Stalinist model in favor of increased competition and trade with the West. But in 1947 the Marshall Plan probably seemed to challenge the Soviet promise of industrial growth and economic autonomy for the underdeveloped East European states.

A combination of strategic, political, and ideological factors led to the Soviet repudiation of the Marshall Plan. Economic issues played a smaller role. The Soviet withdrawal from the Paris talks was inevitable only in the sense that the absence of a general political settlement in postwar Europe, notably in Germany, precluded economic cooperation between East and West.

THE GERMAN QUESTION REVISITED, 1947–1948

Solving the German problem was an essential requisite for European recovery. By early 1947, several factors—the desire to lower occupation costs, the dependence of Western Europe upon German recovery, the failure of quadripartite control, and the decision to contain Soviet power and influence in Europe—all had committed the United States to the reconstruction of western Germany. But this prospect alienated France and other friendly European countries, not to mention the Soviet Union and the East European countries, which had suffered so grievously at the hands of Nazi Germany. Moreover, the State Department still expected France to act as the centerpiece of a new continental balance of power. The Truman administration needed to find a solution to the German problem that would serve simultaneously to resolve disagreements within the American government over occupation policies, reduce West European opposition to German reconstruction, and integrate the industrial giant of Europe into the U.S. orbit.

At first, American efforts focused upon raising the permitted level of industry in the Bizone. This was largely a symbolic political gesture designed to boost German morale and appease Congressmen disgruntled with the high cost of the occupation. In February 1947, for example, a presidential mission chaired by Herbert Hoover blamed the March 1946 limits on German industry for high occupation costs and European stagnation and warned, "We can keep Germany in these economic chains but it will also keep Europe in rags." Actually, German production had not even reached the March 1946 ceiling when Hoover issued his report.

Nonetheless, the British and Americans agreed in July 1947 to raise the German level of industry to roughly 1936 (as opposed to 1932) levels of production. The total ceiling on German steel *capacity* (not to be confused with actual *production*, which was lower) rose from 7.5 to 11.5 million tons, of which 10.7 million tons lay in the Bizone. Anglo-American agreement was achieved only after long and acrimonious negotiations over the Ruhr and German coal during the spring and summer of 1947. In the end, the United States picked up most British occupation costs in exchange for American predominance in the Bizone, which meant among other things the end of efforts to nationalize the German coal industry. In July 1947, the administration also replaced JCS 1067 with a new directive (JCS 1779) that reaffirmed the first-charge principle, Clay's halt to reparations deliveries, and other measures designed to revive the German economy.

The French forced the British and Americans to delay announcement of the Bizonal agreement. Bidault complained in July 1947 that the Anglo-American *fait accompli* seemed to confirm Communist charges that the United States favored German over French reconstruction. Paris demanded the internationalization of Ruhr industries, guaranteed access to German coal (at prices below the prevailing market rate), and the restoration of reparation deliveries. French petulance sorely tested the patience of Secretary of State Marshall, who told the French Ambassador in July 1947 that a Soviet-dominated Germany— the likely consequence of indefinite stagnation—posed a greater danger to France than did a reconstructed Germany linked to the West. The United States, Marshall made clear, intended to revive German production in order to cut Bizonal imports and occupation costs.

Under Secretary Clayton later voiced suspicions, with some basis in fact, that the French were using the security argument to suppress

German competition. In tripartite exploratory discussions in London during August 1947, John Gimbel observes, the French revealed that "their main objection to the bizonal level-of-industry plan was that it threatened the Monnet Plan's projected steel production figures." The French hoped that control of German coal and limits on the Ruhr would translate into industrial supremacy in Europe. In August 1947, Paris finally approved the higher production levels in the Bizone after the Americans agreed to reconsider the French position on the Ruhr in later negotiations.

In the meantime, the State Department again faced formidable opposition to its plans from General Lucius Clay and the Army. The policymakers at Foggy Bottom believed that the United States needed to meet the French halfway on the Ruhr if the pro-Western Paris government were to remain in power. State's seeming appeasement of the French infuriated the mercurial Clay, who threatened to resign in July 1947. Marshall and Under Secretary of War (later named Army Secretary) Kenneth C. Royall reassured Clay that his hard-won agreement with the British on Bizonal production would remain intact although some concessions would be necessary to win French participation in the fledgling European recovery program.

In early August, Royall himself caused a major flap by publicly suggesting that the United States was not obliged to consult with the French on the Bizonal plan, a rebuke that the Quai d'Orsay did not take lightly. Under Secretary of State Robert Lovett, among others, thought that the time had now come for the State Department to take over the occupation duties in Germany from OMGUS and the War Department. In Lovett's opinion, they were blocking State's plan for the balanced use of German resources for European recovery as a whole.

Yet as State Department officials further contemplated assuming Clay's job in Germany, they became increasingly sympathetic toward the OMGUS head. "Faced with the financial responsibilities that accompanied administrative responsibilities in Germany," John Gimbel notes,

> the State Department moved toward a position it had prevented the Army from taking for more than two years: it became more critical of France's aims and objectives regarding Germany and the future of Europe, and it finally concluded that France's territorial and economic demands were, in fact, incompatible with any program that would have Germany achieve a viable economy in the future.

Evidence of Washington's growing dissatisfaction with the French surfaced in the summer of 1947, as the Conference on European Economic Cooperation (CEEC) opened at Paris. Amid indications that the CEED was about to "produce little more than 16 'shopping lists' for which the United States would be expected to pay the bill," Lovett informed French Ambassador Henri Bonnet that the Europeans would have to show a greater willingness to help themselves before the Congress would appropriate more foreign aid. In particular, he warned that the American people would not support an expensive new aid program if France and other potential beneficiaries of U.S. largesse sought to impose a punitive peace on Germany.

From Washington's perspective, it seemed terribly wasteful for France to build new steel mills when the smokestacks of the Ruhr remained dormant. Lovett instructed American representatives in Paris to put "primary emphasis on efficient utilization of existing capacity rather than on capital development." Since the largest amount of idle capacity by far lay in Germany, the Truman administration had pinned its hopes for European recovery on the restoration of German industry. Thus, the State Department's revised position paper on the aid program in late August 1947 stressed European self-help through "elimination of bottlenecks" and "full use of existing or readily repairable capacity." Long-term capital development would receive secondary consideration. The State Department would "not agree to system of allocations of German resources or U. S. aid which would postpone German recovery until full recovery [of] other countries has been assured."

The French reluctantly came to accept the American viewpoint. When the Council of Foreign Ministers reconvened in London (November–December 1947), the Western allies had already given up on a quadripartite German settlement. As Communist-led strikes rocked France, Paris' representatives secretly expressed interest in the formation of a West German state and a western security alliance. Not surprisingly, Molotov's pleas for reparations and a unified Germany fell on deaf ears, and the conference ended amid bitter recriminations between the Russian minister and his three Western counterparts. With the Russians finally out of the picture, the way lay open for a fusion of the three western zones.

During the first session (February-March 1948) of the tripartite London Conference on Germany, however, the French refused to merge their zone with the Bizone until the British and Americans approved international control of the Ruhr and a security pact against Germany. Marshall felt that French fears of aggression from that corner were unfounded. "As long as Germany is occupied," the Secretary of State argued, "it will not be able to develop the prerequisites of military power."

But to win French agreement to trizonal unification, Washington in early March submitted a draft plan for an international control agency for the Ruhr. Ambassador Douglas also quietly assured British, French, and Dutch officials that the United States would pledge itself to a security arrangement against German aggression. The U.S. Ambassador told the Europeans that "it was very unlikely that American forces would be withdrawn from Germany for a long time—until the threat from the east had disappeared." On March 6, 1948, the first session concluded with an agreement by the participants to reconstruct the western zones of Germany under ERP.

Upon resumption of the London Conference during April and May 1948, American negotiators rejected French proposals for permanent limits on German industrial capacity. But the French received assurances that U.S. troops would remain indefinitely in Germany and that Washington would soon associate itself with the Brussels Pact (ratified in March 1948). In a final conference report on security, the United States reiterated its pledge to maintain occupation forces in Germany until peace was secured in Europe.

Due to steadfast opposition by Clay and the Army, the French won fewer concessions on the Ruhr. As Army Secretary Royall complained to Marshall in May 1948, the proposal for an International Authority for the Ruhr (IAR) violated the Bizonal fusion agreement, under which General Clay had won supreme authority over the resources of the Bizone. The Congress would rebel, Royall shrewdly intimated, if the Ruhr authority, the Economic Cooperation Administration (ECA), or some other interloper were to infringe upon Clay's domain. The State Department agreed that the United States must control the Ruhr in order to ensure the self-sufficiency of the Bizone. But, Lovett chided Royall, the Bizonal agreement was subordinate "to the subsequent and overriding policy of the President and Congress" as expressed in ERP, "which covers the [European] economic problem as a whole."

In discussions on the IAR in late May, the State Department again struck a careful balance between the French and the War Department. State officials managed to soothe French feelings without committing the United States to anything more than a supervisory body, as opposed to international ownership and management of Ruhr industries. As Paul Nitze later instructed Ambassador Douglas during the London Conference on the Ruhr (November–December 1948), the chief American aim in the IAR was not so much the containment of Germany as a "larger degree of Western European cooperation and economic integration" and a "more effective utilization of the Ruhr resources . . . for the common good."

The State Department used the Marshall Plan as a means both to win French (and other allied) consent to German reconstruction and to break the deadlock in the American government over German policy. In that sense, John Gimbel is correct in defining the Marshall Plan as a "crash program to dovetail German economic recovery with a general European recovery program in order to make German economic recovery politically acceptable in Europe and in the United States." Yet Gimbel is only partially correct, for the domestic debate over the Marshall Plan focused more on the Soviet threat than on Germany.

Implementing Containment

JOHN LEWIS GADDIS

In four major books Professor John Lewis Gaddis of Ohio University has established his position as one of the leading historians of the Cold War. In this excerpt he discusses NSC-68, a far-reaching statement of American defense policy, and the Korean War; the outbreak of which helped propel the United States into taking an ever harder stance against the Soviet Union. To what extent did external events justify the tone of NSC-68? What kind of price did the American public pay for the eternal vigilance stressed by NSC-68?

It seems odd, at first glance, that George Kennan, the most graceful prose stylist to serve in Washington in modern times, never took the trouble while in an official capacity to put his complete concept of containment in writing. Much of his thinking found its way into policy papers, to be sure, and the Truman administration did implement many of Kennan's recommendations between 1947 and 1949. But one had to glean the elements of his strategy from pronouncements delivered in a variety of forms before a variety of audiences. Kennan undertook no systematic exposition of his program.

This aversion to written policy guidelines was no accident: "I had no confidence," Kennan later recalled, "in the ability of men to define hypothetically in any useful way, by means of general and legal phraseology, future situations which no one could really imagine or envisage." Issues of international relations were too subtle and evanescent to be reduced to paper without oversimplification; once papers had been agreed upon it was too difficult to get bureaucracies to reconsider them in the light of changing circumstances. But because Kennan found it either impossible or unnecessary to convey to the bureaucracies charged with implementing his strategy the way in which its parts related to the whole, there never developed that sense of direction at all levels of government that alone ensures perpetuation. As a result, Kennan found the administration committing itself to moves that seemed reasonable enough in themselves—NATO, the creation of a West German state, the decision to retain military bases in postoccupation Japan, the development of a hydrogen bomb—but inconsistent with the ultimate objectives of his strategy. By the time he got around to detecting and pointing out the discrepancies, it was too late to make changes.

It was precisely this need for greater coherence in policy formulation following the shocks of 1949—the "loss" of China, the Soviet atomic bomb, persistent interservice debates over strategy, and the dilemma of how to meet expanding responsibilities with what appeared to be limited resources—that caused President Truman, early in 1950, to authorize just the sort of study Kennan had resisted: a single, comprehensive statement of interests, threats, and feasible responses, capable of being communicated throughout the bureaucracy. But Kennan was not there to direct it. He had resigned as director of the Policy Planning Staff at the end of 1949, and the task of drafting the new document, which came to be known as NSC-68, fell to a small *ad hoc* committee of State and Defense Department officials under the chairmanship of Kennan's successor, Paul H. Nitze.

NSC-68 was not intended as a repudiation of Kennan. He was consulted at several stages in the drafting process and the final document—of some sixty-six single-spaced typed papes—reflected his views at several points. The objective rather was to systematize containment, and to find the means to make it work. But the very act of reducing the strategy to writing exposed the differences that had begun to develop between Kennan and the administration; the search for means, together with the generous way in which the drafting committee construed its mandate, accentuated these. The result, like that more prominent product of a broadly construed mandate, the United States Constitution,[1]

---

[1] The drafting of NSC–68 also resembled the drafting of the Constitution in that both were done independently of the agencies nominally responsible for such matters—in the case of the latter, the Confederation Congress; in the former, the National Security Council.

was a document more sweeping in content and implications than its originators had intended.

I

The differences between Kennan's conception of United States interests and that of NSC-68 are not immediately apparent. The document proclaimed as the nation's "fundamental purpose" assuring "the integrity and vitality of our free society, which is founded on the dignity and worth of the individual." It went on to announce "our determination to create conditions under which our free and democratic system can live and prosper." It associated American interests with diversity, not uniformity: "the prime reliance of the free society is on the strength and appeal of its idea, and it feels no compulsion sooner or later to bring all societies into conformity with it." And it appeared to rely on the balance of power as the means of ensuring that diversity; the opening paragraph recalled with apparent approval the international system that preceded World War I, in which "for several centuries it had proved impossible for any one nation to gain such preponderant strength that a coalition of other nations could not in time face it with greater strength."

But there the similarity ended. Kennan had argued that all that was necessary to maintain the balance of power, and thereby safeguard diversity, was to keep centers of industrial-military capability out of hostile hands. Unfriendly regimes elsewhere, though not to be desired, posed little threat to global stability so long as they lacked means of manifesting their hostility. NSC-68 took a very different point of view: "any substantial further extension of the area under the domination of the Kremlin would raise the possibility that no coalition adequate to confront the Kremlin with greater strength could be assembled." And, again: "the assault on free institutions is worldwide now, and in the context of the present polarization of power a defeat of free institutions anywhere is a defeat everywhere."[2] The implication was clear: Kennan's strategy of defending selected strongpoints would no longer suffice; the

---

[2]The wording here suggests that Kennan's strategy might have been considered appropriate for less trying times, but that the balance of power had swung so far in favor of the Soviet bloc that no further losses could be tolerated.

emphasis rather would have to be on perimeter defense, with all points along the perimeter considered of equal importance.

NSC-68's endorsement of perimeter defense suggests several major departures in underlying assumptions from Kennan. One of these had to do with the nature of effective power in international affairs. Kennan had taken the view that only industrial-military power could bring about significant changes in world politics, and that as long as it was kept in rough balance, international stability (though not necessarily all exposed positions) could be preserved. But Kennan himself had been forced to acknowledge, by 1949, that things were not that simple. Insecurity could manifest itself in psychological as well as physical terms, as the Western Europeans' demands for American military protection had shown. And psychological insecurity could as easily develop from the distant sound of falling dominoes as from the rattling of sabres next door. This was the major unresolved dilemma in Kennan's thinking—how could the self-confidence upon which his strategy depended survive the making of distinctions between peripheral and vital interests? As far as the authors of NSC-68 were concerned, it could not.

From their perspective, changes in the balance of power could occur, not only as the result of economic maneuvers or military action, but from intimidation, humiliation, or even loss of credibility. The Soviet Union, Nitze reminded his colleagues, made no distinction between military and other forms of aggression; it was guided "by the simple consideration of weakening the world power position of the US." NSC-68 added that "[s]ince everything that gives us or others respect for our institutions is a suitable object for attack, it also fits the Kremlin's design that where, with impunity, we can be insulted and made to suffer indignity the opportunity shall not be missed." The Soviet Union was out "to demonstrate to the free world that force and the will to use it are on the side of the Kremlin [and] that those who lack it are decadent and doomed."

The implications were startling. World order, and with it American security, had come to depend as much on *perceptions* of the balance of power as on what that balance actually was. And the perceptions involved were not just those of statesmen customarily charged with making policy; they reflected as well mass opinion, foreign as well as domestic, informed as well as uninformed, rational as well as irrational. Before such an audience even the appearance of a shift in power relationships could have unnerving consequences; judgments based on such

traditional criteria as geography, economic capacity, or military potential now had to be balanced against considerations of image, prestige,
and credibility. The effect was vastly to increase the number and variety of interests deemed relevant to the national security, and to blur
distinctions between them.

But proliferating interests could be of little significance apart from
the means to defend them, and here NSC-68 challenged another of the
assumptions that had informed Kennan's strategy of containment: the
perception of limited resources, which had made distinctions between
vital and peripheral interests necessary in the first place. On this point
there had been no divergence of viewpoint between Kennan and the
administration. President Truman had continued to insist on holding
down defense expenditures in order to avoid either higher taxes or budget deficits; his guidelines for the fiscal 1951 budget, drawn up in the
summer of 1949, proposed increased spending for domestic programs as
well, and hence limited the military to a ceiling of $13 billion. "We
realize . . . that our Nation's economy under existing conditions can
afford only a limited amount for defense," General Omar Bradley,
chairman of the Joint Chiefs of Staff, had told the House Armed Services Committee later that year, "and that we must look forward to diminishing appropriations for the armed services." But Bradley added
that his reference to existing conditions had been deliberate, "because
obviously, if war is thrust upon us, the American people will spend the
amount necessary to provide for national defense, and to carry out their
international obligations."

What NSC-68 did was to suggest a way to increase defense expenditures without war, without long-term budget deficits, and without
crushing tax burdens. Only 6–7 percent of the gross national product
was then being devoted to military expenditures, it pointed out;[3] adding investment in war-related industries brought the figure to around
20 percent. Comparable statistics for the Soviet Union were 13.8 percent and 40 percent. But the Soviet economy was operating at nearly
full capacity; the American economy was not. The President's January
1950 economic report to the Congress had noted that with a higher
level of economic activity, the gross national product could be raised
from the 1949 level of $255 billion to as much as $300 billion in five
years. This increment could be used to finance a substantial build-up in

---

[3]Actually, the figure was closer to 5 percent.

Western military and economic strength without decreasing the domestic standard of living. Civilian consumption might actually rise as a result, since such a program could well push the gross national product beyond what was required for new military and foreign assistance programs. "One of the most significant lessons of our World War II experience," NSC-68 pointed out, "was that the American economy, when it operates at a level approaching full efficiency, can provide enormous resources for purposes other than civilian consumption while simultaneously providing a higher standard of living."

Despite their obvious implications for military spending, these ideas did not originate in the Pentagon, where doctrines of fiscal orthodoxy had become more strongly entrenched than usual with the appointment of Louis Johnson as Secretary of Defense. They came instead from a group of liberal civilian advisers eager to apply Keynesian techniques to the management of the domestic economy. The most influential of these was Leon Keyserling, soon to become chairman of the Council of Economic Advisers, who had begun to argue that the nation could sustain more vigorous growth rates if the government would stimulate the economy and tolerate short-term budget deficits until tax revenues from increased economic activity began to roll in. The idea, as Keyserling put it, should be to expand the pie, not argue over how to divide it. Keyserling of course had the President's domestic program in mind in advancing that argument, and to that end had persuaded Truman to endorse the eventual feasibility of a $300 billion gross national product.

The committee drafting NSC-68 was thus able to incorporate Keyserling's viewpoint with some semblance of presidential sanction, but to adapt it to purposes very different from its original objectives. Nevertheless, after reading NSC-68, Keyserling expressed "full agreement" with its economic conclusions, warning only of the need to undertake educational efforts to correct the widespread impression that "increased defense must mean equivalently lowered living standards, higher taxes and a proliferation of controls.[4] The implications were as startling as the idea that interests were indivisible: if the government would only take it upon itself to "manage" the economy, then the

---

[4]"Keyserling and I discussed these matters frequently; though he wanted to spend the money on other programs, he was convinced that the country could afford $40 billion for defense if necessary." (Paul Nitze, "The Development of NSC 68," *International Security*, IV [Spring 1980], 169.)

means of defense could be expanded as needed to protect those interests. As Robert A. Lovett, former under-secretary of state, Wall Street banker, and no Keynesian liberal, told the drafting committee, "there was practically nothing that the country could not do if it wanted to do it." To its earlier assertion that there *should* not be distinctions between peripheral and vital interests, NSC-68 had now shown with seductive logic that there *need* not be.

But if expandable means made possible larger ends, did it follow that these ends justified a larger *variety* of means than had previously been thought appropriate? The authors of NSC-68 took an ambivalent position on this point. On the one hand, they argued that "the responsibility of world leadership . . . demands that we make the attempt, and accept the risks inherent in it, to bring about order and justice by means consistent with the principles of freedom and democracy." They noted further that whereas "the Kremlin is able to select whatever means are expedient in seeking to carry out its fundamental design," democracies enjoyed no such freedom of choice:

> The resort to force, to compulsion, to the imposition of its will is . . . a difficult and dangerous act for a free society, which is warranted only in the face of even greater dangers. The necessity of the act must be clear and compelling; the act must commend itself to the overwhelming majority as an inescapable exception to the basic idea of freedom; or the regenerative capacity of free men after the act has been performed will be endangered.

But then they added:

> The integrity of our system will not be jeopardized by any measures, covert or overt, violent or non-violent, which serve the purpose of frustrating the Kremlin design nor does the necessity for conducting ourselves so as to affirm our values in actions as well as words forbid such measures, provided only they are appropriately calculated to that end and are not so excessive or misdirected as to make us enemies of the people instead of the evil men who have enslaved them.

This was a sweeping mandate indeed, difficult to reconcile with the self-denying ordinance that had just preceded it.

The reconciliation the authors of NSC-68 probably had in mind (although it is nowhere explicitly stated in the document) was this: that while in principle a democracy should choose its methods selectively when confronted with an absolute threat to its survival anything was fair game. The same reasoning could be applied to the problems of differentiating interests and providing means as well: considerations of priority and economy might be appropriate in normal times, but in the face of a threat such as that posed by the Soviet Union, preoccupations of this sort had to go by the board. The world crisis, as dangerous in its potential as anything confronted in World Wars I or II, rendered all interests vital, all means affordable, all methods justifiable. For the authors of NSC-68, American interests could not be defined apart from the threat the Soviet Union posed to them: "frustrating the Kremlin design," as the document so frequently put it, became an end in itself, not a means to a larger end.

II

But just what was the Kremlin design, and how did perceptions of it reflected in NSC-68 differ from Kennan's? "The fundamental design of those who control the Soviet Union and the international communist movement," the document argued, "is to retain and solidify their absolute power, first in the Soviet Union and second in the areas now under their control. In the minds of the Soviet leaders, however, achievement of this design requires the dynamic extension of their authority and the ultimate elimination of any effective opposition to their authority." This much Kennan would have found unexceptionable. Nor did Nitze and his colleagues see Soviet expansion as motivated primarily by ideological considerations; like Kennan they saw Marxism-Leninism as more the instrument than the determinant of Soviet policy: "the Kremlin's conviction of its own infallibility has made its devotion to theory so subjective that past or present pronouncements as to doctrine offer no reliable guide to future action." Rather, Soviet hostility stemmed simply from the inability of a totalitarian system to tolerate diversity: "The existence and persistence of the idea of freedom is a permanent and continuous threat to the foundations of the slave society; and it therefore regards as intolerable the long continued existence of freedom in the world."

The authors of NSC-68 also agreed with Kennan that this inability to live with diversity was a weakness, certain eventually to create problems for the Kremlin, but they differed with him as to how soon. Kennan took the position that the U.S.S.R. was already overextended; that it was finding it difficult to control areas it had already absorbed; and that the resulting strains, revealed vividly in the Titoist heresy, offered opportunities the United States could exploit. NSC-68 took a more pessimistic view. Soviet expansion, it argued, had so far produced strength, not weakness; whatever the liabilities of Titoism they were more than counter-balanced by the victory of communism in China, the Soviet atomic bomb, and Moscow's continued military build-up at a time when the United States was rigorously limiting its own comparable expenditures. Given this situation, it seemed imprudent "to risk the future on the hazard that the Soviet Empire, because of over-extension or other reasons, will spontaneously destroy itself from within."

Neither Kennan nor NSC-68 questioned the Russians' superiority in conventional forces or their ability, in time, to develop sufficient atomic weapons to neutralize the American advantage in that field as well. Rather, their conflicting assessments of the existing power balance hinged on the issue of whether or not the U.S.S.R. would deliberately risk war. Kennan, reasoning from an evaluation of Soviet intentions, argued that disparities in military power could be tolerated because the Russians had little to gain from using it. The Soviet leadership was cautious, prone to seek its objectives at minimum cost and risk without reference to any fixed timetable. The United States could therefore content itself with an asymmetrical response—reinforcing its own strengths and those of its allies, but with no effort to duplicate Soviet force configurations. NSC-68 emphasizing Soviet capabilities, argued that the Russians had not provoked war so far only because they had lacked the assurance of winning it. Once their capabilities had expanded to the point where they could reasonably expect to win—NSC-68 estimated that this would occur in 1954, when the Russians would have enough atomic bombs to devastate the United States—then the intentions of Kremlin leaders, if Washington did nothing in the meantime to build up its own forces, might well be to risk war, probably in the form of a surprise attack.

Until then, the most significant danger was that of war by proxy. Kennan himself had come to acknowledge the possibility that the Soviet Union might authorize limited military action by its satellites, but such maneuvers would be designed, he thought, precisely to achieve Soviet objectives without setting off a general war. Since not all of its interests were equally vital, the United States could still choose whether and how to respond: "world realities have greater tolerances than we commonly suppose against ambitious schemes for world domination." NSC-68, on the other hand, saw "piecemeal aggression" as an instrument of war, aimed at exploiting the Americans' unwillingness to use nuclear weapons unless directly attacked. Operating from the very different assumption that interests were indivisible, it warned that any failure to respond could lead to "a descending spiral of too little and too late, of doubt and recrimination, [of] ever narrower and more desperate alternatives." The result would be a series of "gradual withdrawals under pressure until we discover one day that we have sacrificed positions of vital interest."

Even without war the Soviet Union could use its armed forces—which NSC-68 described as "far in excess of those necessary to defend its national territory"—to erode the position of the United States and its allies: such strength provided the U.S.S.R. "with great coercive power for use in time of peace . . . and serves as a deterrent to the victims of its aggression from taking any action in opposition to its tactics which would risk war." The objective was "to back up infiltration with intimidation." It was true that the United States itself had greater military forces than ever before in peacetime, but the measure of effectiveness in such matters was comparison with present adversaries, not past economies. When balanced against increasing Soviet military power and the commitments the United States had undertaken to contain it, "it is clear that our military strength is becoming dangerously inadequate." If Kennan shared this concern, he said nothing about it; his sole recommendations for increasing peacetime military forces during this period were confined to the development of elite, highly mobile, compact units, capable of responding quickly and effectively to limited aggression, but in no way designed to counter Soviet capabilities he was convinced would not be used.

At the heart of these differences between Kennan and the authors of NSC-68 was a simple inversion of intellectual procedure: where Kennan tended to look at the Soviet threat in terms of an independently established concept of irreducible interests, NSC-68 derived its view of American interests primarily from its perception of the Soviet threat. Kennan's insistence on the need to deter hostile combinations of industrial-military power could have applied as well to the adversaries of World Wars I and II as to the Soviet Union. No comparably general statement of fundamental interests appeared in NSC-68. The document paid obeisance to the balance of power, diversity, and freedom, but nowhere did it set out the minimum requirements necessary to secure those interests. Instead it found in the simple presence of a Soviet threat sufficient cause to deem the interest threatened vital.

The consequences of this approach were more than procedural: they were nothing less than to transfer to the Russians control over what United States interests were at any given point. To define interests in terms of threats is, after all, to make interests a function of threats—interests will then expand or contract as threats do. By applying pressure in particular areas Kremlin leaders could, if they were astute enough, force the United States and its allies to expend resources in parts of the world far removed from Kennan's original list of vital interests. The whole point of NSC-68 had been to generate additional means with which to defend existing interests. But by neglecting to define those interests apart from the threat to them, the document in effect expanded interests along with means, thereby vitiating its own intended accomplishment.

2

THE COLD WAR
AT HOME

In September 1945, when the Japanese formally surrendered to the allies, the United States was a much different nation than it had been just four years earlier. Skyrocketing production and an expanding economy eased fears of an impending depression; the extraordinary government-business cooperation established a precedent for some degree of federal intervention in the economy; and the allied victory propelled the United States into the position of global superpower. Perhaps, most of all, America emerged from the war confident in its ability to solve pressing social problems at home, while also defending freedom and democracy abroad.

That optimism infected liberals as well. The liberalism that emerged after the war was skeptical of the need for radical change and more confident that a revitalized economy with limited state intervention could guarantee social and economic justice. "Keynes, not Marx is the prophet of the new radicalism," Arthur Schlesinger, Jr. wrote. Rejecting the simplistic ideological appeals of the Old Left, liberals were committed to piecemeal reform working through the established institutions of government.

Arthur Schlesinger, Jr., a brilliant Harvard-educated historian, provided the most concise statement of the new liberalism with publication of *The Vital Center* in 1949. Like many liberals of his generation, Schlesinger was influenced by the writing and teachings of the Protestant theologian Reinhold Neibuhr, who emphasized that the existence of individual sin and social evil required society to proceed cautiously toward the goal of social justice. In his book, Schlesinger called for a "new radicalism" that would discard progressive sentimentality and utopian schemes in favor of a sober recognition of the inevitability of social conflict and human weakness and the necessity of human progress.

But, as the British journalist Godfrey Hodgson points out, the new liberalism may not have been so "vital" after all. The liberalism that Schlesinger espoused, Hodgson argues, rested on flawed assumptions that economic growth would banish class divisions; that pluralism would guarantee the rights of all Americans; and that the public could distinguish between responsible and irresponsible anti-communism. Hodgson believes that by failing to recognize the persistence of class divisions, and by rejecting more radical means to redress structural inequities, the liberal ideology was bound to fail.

Inevitably, the post-war world also produced new anxieties and tensions. Perhaps Joseph McCarthy, and the Red Scare which he helped create, remain the most enduring symbol of the Cold War at home. Though he never uncovered a single communist, McCarthy became a powerful force of fear and intimidation. As Richard Fried shows, McCarthy gave his name to the period, but the anti-communist crusade was deeper and broader than any one man. Widespread public acceptance of the anti-communist cause forced McCarthy to compete with other Senate committee chairmen eager to expose communist influence in America. The oppressive atmosphere, Fried argues, limited intellectual debate and stifled artistic expression.

The Vital Center

ARTHUR SCHLESINGER JR.

Arthur Schlesinger Jr. was an important participant in the effort to redefine American liberalism in the years after World War II. After 1945, liberals divided into two camps. One group, which formed the Progressive Citizens of America (PCA) and later gravitated around the presidential candidacy of Henry Wallace, rejected the growing Cold War fervor and hoped to continue the wartime alliance with communists. Another group, which created the Americans for Democratic Action (ADA) and rallied around Harry Truman in the 1948 election, supported the administration's hard line with the Soviets and fought to banish communists from Democratic organizations. As a founding member of the ADA and a leading intellectual of the time, Schlesinger led the assault against the ideological extremes of reactionary conservativism and "doughfaced" progressivism, and suggested a "middle way" for American liberalism. Why is Schlesinger so critical of the Left in America? What in his mind are the differences between liberals and Progressives?

Since progressives, on the whole, create our contemporary climate of opinion, the impression exists that the present perils to free society result exclusively from the failure of the conservatives. In a sense, this is true—in the sense that the conservatives have had the power, notably in the period between the wars, and have failed to use it intelligently. Yet one reason for their failure, as D. W. Brogan has reminded us, is the failure of their critics, whose hearts were in the right place, but whose heads were too often "muddled, full of sentiment, empty of knowledge, living on slogans and clichés, unwilling to realize how complicated is the modern world and that the price of liberty is eternal intellectual vigilance." Compared with the conservatives, the progressives were indeed innocent; but is innocence enough?

During the years of plutocratic stagnation, why did not progressivism have strong faith and lucid purposes? And, in the cases where progressives were sure of their diagnosis and of their remedy, why has that certitude now vanished? Let us concede at once the relative superiority in practice of left-wing governments—at least of the pragmatic left, though not of the doctrinaire left. The New Deal government of Franklin D. Roosevelt, for all its confusions and defects, kept its eye more steadily on the ball than any other government of our time, conservative, socialist, Communist or fascist. Yet history has discredited the hopes and predictions of doctrinaire progressivism about as thoroughly as it has those of conservatism. The progressive "analysis" is today a series of dry and broken platitudes, tossed out in ash-heaps (where they are collected and dusted off by the editors of the liberal weeklies).

What is the progressive? The defining characteristic of the progressive, as I shall use the word, is the sentimentality of his approach to politics and culture. He must be distinguished, on the one hand, from the Communist; for the progressive is soft, not hard; he believes himself genuinely concerned with the welfare of individuals. He must be distinguished, on the other, from the radical democrat; for the progressive, by refusing to make room in his philosophy for the discipline of responsibility or for the danger of power, has cut himself off from the usable traditions of American radical democracy. He has rejected the pragmatic tradition of the men who, from the Jacksonians to the New Dealers, learned the facts of life through the exercise of power under conditions of accountability. He has rejected the pessimistic tradition of those who, from Hawthorne to Reinhold Niebuhr, warned that power, unless checked by accountability, would corrupt its possessor.

The type of the progressive today is the fellow traveler or the fellow traveler of the fellow traveler: see the Wallace movement or (until fairly recently) the columns of the *New Republic* and the *Nation*.[1] His sentimentality has softened up the progressive for Communist perme-

---

[1]Both journals began to show healthy schizoid tendencies in 1948. The *Nation* is now in good part liberated from the Soviet mystique, except for the devotional essays of Señor Del Vayo and pious genuflections by Miss Kirchwey herself. The *New Republic*, after waiving Mr. Wallace out of the league, has shown increasing evidence of waking up to realities. [In 1962, the *New Republic* is once again an excellent liberal magazine. The *Nation* still shows Doughface tendencies.]

ation and conquest. For the most chivalrous reasons, he cannot believe that ugly facts underlie fair words. However he looks at it, for example, the USSR keeps coming through as a kind of enlarged Brook Farm community, complete with folk dancing in native costumes, joyous work in the fields and progressive kindergartens. Nothing in his system has prepared him for Stalin.

This is not a new breed in American history. A century ago, after Jacksonian democracy had split over the slavery question, one wing of northern Jacksonians under Martin Van Buren went into the Free Soil Party. The other wing refused to turn against the South. Many of this prosouthern group retained a Jacksonian desire for social reform; they certainly held no brief for slavery; yet as men implicated in the industrial evils of the north, who were they, they would cry, to pronounce judgment on the social system of the South? "The only difference between the negro slave of the South, and the white wages slave of the North," as one member of this group put it, "is, that the one has a master without asking for him, and the other has to beg for the privilege of becoming a slave. . . . The one is the slave of an individual; the other is the slave of an inexorable class."[2]

The members of this group were known as Doughfaces—that is, "northern men with southern principles." The infiltration of contemporary progressivism by Communism had led to the same self-flagellation, the same refusal to take precautions against tyranny. It has created a new Doughface movement—a movement of "democratic men with totalitarian principles."

The core of Doughface progressivism is its sentimental belief in progress. The belief in progress was the product of the Enlightenment, cross-fertilized with allied growths, such as science, bourgeois complacency, Unitarianism and a faith in the goodness of man. It dispensed with the Christian myths of sin and atonement. Man's shortcomings, such as they were, were to be redeemed, not by Jesus on the cross, but

---

[2] The speaker was Mike Walsh, editor of the fiery radical weekly *The Subterranean* and one of the first authentic proletarian characters in American political history. He went on to challenge the abolitionists to produce "one single solitary degradation" heaped on the slave which a northern worker was not liable to suffer through poverty. "It is all very well for gentlemen to get up here and clamor about the wrongs and outrages of the southern slaves; but, sir, even in New York, during the last year, there have been over thirteen hundred people deprived of their liberty without any show or color of offense, but because they were poor, and too honest to commit a crime." Walsh speaking in the House of Representatives, May 19, 1854, *Congressional Globe*, 33 Congress 1 Session, 1224. Clearly the false comparison, which Arthur Koestler has called the Fallacy of the Unequal Equation, is no invention of the modern Doughface.

by the benevolent unfolding of history. Tolerance, free inquiry and technology, operating in the framework of human perfectibility, would in the end create a heaven on earth, a goal much more wholesome than a heaven in heaven.

The nineteenth century, with its peace and prosperity, supplied protective coloration for the enthronement of history and for the rejection of the dark and subterranean forces in human nature. Darwin furnished the scientific underpinnings, Spencer the philosophical superstructure, and even Marx accepted the psychological assumptions. At times one cannot but wonder at what psychic cost the Victorians purchased their optimism. How else to explain the fantasies of violence—the poorhouses and the madhouses, the public cruelties and the secret insanities—which run through the Victorian novel like a deep stain of fear?

Yet the official optimism triumphed. Only a few disreputable aesthetes, a few obstinate Christians dared openly to compute this psychic cost. The nineteenth century had, indeed, its underground movements—its doubters and skeptics, shaken by nightmares which we have come to see as often only too exact probings into reality, but which their respectable contemporaries dismissed as bad dreams. While the sum of optimism was still high in the sky, Dostoievsky, Kierkegaard, Nietzsche, Sorel, Freud were charting possibilities of depravity. Then, slowly the sun sank in the twentieth century, and practical men, like Hitler, Stalin, Mussolini, began to transform depravity into a way of life. Progress had betrayed the progressives. History was abandoning its votaries and unleashing the terror.

Why was progressivism not prepared for Hitler? The eighteenth century had exaggerated man's capacity to live by logic alone; the nineteenth century sanctified what remained of his non-logical impulses; and the result was the pervading belief in human perfectibility which has disarmed progressivism in too many of its encounters with actuality. As the child of eighteenth-century rationalism and nineteenth-century romanticism, progressivism was committed to an unwarranted optimism about man.

Optimism gave the progressives a soft and shallow conception of human nature. With the aggressive and sinister impulses eliminated from the equation, the problem of social change assumed too simple a form. The corruptions of power—the desire to exercise it, the desire to increase it, the desire for prostration before it—had no place in the progressive calculations. As a result, progressivism became politically inadequate: it could neither persuade nor control the emotions of man. And it became intellectually inadequate: it could not anticipate nor explain the tragic movements of history in the twentieth century. Ideologies which exploited the darker passions captured men by appeals unknown to the armory of progressivism.

Doughface progressivism—the faith of the present-day fellow traveler—may be defined briefly as progressivism kept alive by main force in face of all the lessons of modern history. It is this final fatuity of progressivism which has turned it into, if not an accomplice of totalitarianism, at least an accessory before the fact. For its persistent and sentimental optimism has endowed Doughface progressivism with what in the middle of the twentieth century are fatal weaknesses: a weakness for impotence, because progressivism believes that history will make up for human error; a weakness for rhetoric, because it believes that man can be reformed by argument; a weakness for economic fetishism, because it believes that the good in man will be liberated by a change in economic institutions; a weakness for political myth, because Doughface optimism requires somewhere an act of faith in order to survive the contradictions of history.

The weakness of impotence is related to a fear of responsibility—a fear, that is, of making concrete decisions and being held to account for concrete consequences. Problems are much simpler when viewed from the office of a liberal weekly than when viewed in terms of what will actually happen when certain ideologically attractive steps are taken. Too often the Doughface really does not want power or responsibility. For him the more subtle sensations of the perfect syllogism, the lost cause, the permanent minority, where he can be safe from the exacting job of trying to work out wise policies in an imperfect world. Politics becomes, not a means of getting things done, but an outlet for private grievances and frustrations. The progressive once disciplined by the responsibilities of power is often the most useful of all public servants; but he, alas, ceases to be a progressive and is regarded by all true Doughfaces as a cynical New Dealer or a tired Social Democrat.

Having renounced power, the Doughface seeks compensation in emotion. The pretext for progressive rhetoric is, of course, the idea that man, the creature of reason and benevolence, has only to understand the truth in order to act upon it. But the function of progressive rhetoric is another matter; it is, in Dwight Macdonald's phrase, to accomplish "in fantasy what cannot be accomplished in reality." Because politics is for the Doughface a means of accommodating himself to a world he does not like but does not really want to change, he can find ample gratification in words. They appease his twinges of guilt without committing him to very drastic action. Thus the expiatory rôle of resolutions in progressive meetings. A telegram of protest to a foreign chancellery gives the satisfaction of a job well done and a night's rest well earned. The Doughfaces differ from Mr. Churchill: dreams, they find, are better than facts. Progressive dreams are tinged with a brave purity, a rich sentiment and a noble defiance. But, like most dreams, they are notable for the distortion of facts by desire.

The progressive attitude toward history is sufficiently revealing. The responsible conservative, we have seen, finds in history a profound sense of national continuity which overrides his contemporary fears and trepidations. The Doughface, less humble in his approach, is like the neanderthal conservative, looking at history long and wistfully until it reassembles itself in patterns which support his current vagaries. Mr. Wallace and his followers, for example, have proclaimed repeatedly that they are doing more on behalf of the Russian Revolution than Thomas Jefferson did on behalf of the French: it is their support of social change that exposes them to the same reactionary persecutions as those which harried Jefferson in the nineties. It is quite true that Jefferson was an enthusiast for the French Revolution. But he was too intelligent a man and too profound a believer in human freedom to let his enthusiasm survive the transformation of the Revolution into an aggressive military despotism. Napoleon, Jefferson observed, was "the Attila of the age . . . the ruthless destroyer of ten millions of the human race, whose thirst for blood appeared unquenchable, the great oppressor of the rights and liberties of the world . . . a cold-blooded, calculating, unprincipled usurper, without a virtue." Mr. Wallace, who restrained his passion for Soviet Russia in its revolutionary days and opposed its recognition as late as 1933, became a great enthusiast for the Soviet Union only after it was embarked on its Napoleonic phase.[3]

In life one must make a choice and accept the consequences; in Doughface fantasy, one can denounce a decision without accepting the consequences of the alternative. Ask a progressive what he thinks of

---

[3]The Morgenthau Diaries document Wallace's opposition to the recognition of Russia; see Henry Morgenthau, Jr., "How F.D.R. Fought The Axis," *Collier's*, October 11, 1947. Wallace's comment is characteristic: "That was in 1933 and if I opposed it at that time it was because I was not thoroughly familiar with it." *Boston Herald*, October 4, 1947.

the Mexican War, or of our national policy toward the Indians, and he will probably say that these outbursts of American imperialism are black marks on our history. Ask him whether he then regrets that California, Texas and the West are today part of the United States. And was there perhaps some way of taking lands from the Indians or from Mexico without violating rights in the process? Pushed to it, the progressive probably thinks that there is some solution hidden in the back of his fantasy; but ordinarily he never has to push the question that far back, because he never dreams of facing a question in terms of responsibility for the decision. For him it is sufficient to dissociate himself from the Mexican War so long as he is not required to dissociate himself from the fruits of victory.[4]

Or take the question of the "robber barons." The phrase itself suggests the attitude of disfavor with which the progressive regards the industrialists of the second half of the nineteenth century.[5] The robber baron, of course, used to sally forth from his castle and steal the goods of innocent travelers. His war was a thoroughly nonproductive form of economic enterprise. Does even the most unregenerate Doughface consider this to be analogous to the achievements of Andrew Carnegie or John D. Rockefeller? And, to save the nation from the "robber barons," would the Doughface reduce our industrial capacity to the point where it was when the "robber barons" came on the scene? Or has he some other formula for industrialization in a single generation? The fact is, of course, that this nation paid a heavy price for industrialization—a price in political and moral decadence, in the wasteful use of economic resources, in the centralization of economic power. But the price we paid, though perhaps exorbitant, was infinitely less in human terms than the price paid by the people of Russia; and it is not clear that the managers who charged more have done the better job.

Everyone has seen the ignorant dogmatism of Doughface progressives at work on current issues. People who had barely heard of Spain in 1934 became world champion Spanish experts by 1937, though if you asked them what a Carlist was they would have been hard pressed for an answer. They did not know anything about history, but they knew what

[4]This discussion could be pushed further. Progressives, in pronouncing dogmatic judgments about the Mexican War, will undoubtedly refer to it as a slaveholders' conspiracy. Why then was John C. Calhoun opposed to it? . . . But ignorance is never any bar to certitude in the progressive dreamworld.
[5]Matthew Josephson, whose admirable book bears this unfortunate title, actually errs much less in this respect than the Doughface.

they liked. The system of falsification operated on contemporary lines, too, so that the average American progressive got the impression that the Spanish Republicans were a united group undone by the wicked fascists. Dreams are better than facts. Books like Franz Borkenau's *Spanish Cockpit* and George Orwell's *Homage to Catalonia* were simply not published in America; it was left to Mr. Hemingway and Mr. Dos Passos a few years later to report the savage political differences in the Loyalist ranks and, in particular, the unsavory rôle of the Communists in delivering Spain to fascist tyranny.

The belief that man is perfectible commits the progressive to the endless task of explaining why, in spite of history and in spite of rhetoric, he does not always behave that way. One favorite Doughface answer, borrowed from the Communists, is that contemporary man has been corrupted by the system of private ownership; let us change all this, they say, and our problems will be solved. This form of economic fetishism can be seen nakedly in the Webbs' dreamlike *Soviet Russia: a New Civilization*, where the nationalization of the means of production is believed to have liquidated injustice in society and evil in man.

But is private ownership the root of all evil? Private property, Reinhold Niebuhr has reminded us, is "not the cause but the instrument of human egotism." It is only one embodiment of the will to power. "By abolishing private property," as Freud puts it, "one deprives the human love of aggression of one of its instruments, a strong one undoubtedly, but assuredly not the strongest." Some social arrangements pander more than others to the human love of aggression; but aggression underlies all social arrangements, whether capitalist or Communist, and it remains a question whether aggression is more checked and controlled by Russian totalitarianism than by American pluralism. In any case, the root remains man.

At the bottom of the set of Doughface illusions is a need for faith. As the gap has widened between the sentimental abstractions of Doughface fantasy and the cruel complexities of life, the need has increased for mythology to take up the slack. One myth, to which the Doughface has clung in the face of experience with the imperturbable ardor of an early Christian, is the mystique of the proletariat. This myth, given its classical form by Marx, himself so characteristically a bourgeois intellectual, states that the action of the working class will overthrow capitalist tyranny and establish by temporary dictatorship a classless society. Its appeal lies partly in the progressive intellectual's sense of guilt over living pleasantly by his skills instead of unpleasantly by his hands, partly in the intellectual's somewhat feminine fascination with the rude and muscular power of the proletariat, partly in the intellectual's desire to compensate for his own sense of alienation by immersing himself in the broad maternal expanse of the masses. Worship of the proletariat becomes a perfect fulfillment for the frustrations of the progressive.

At one time perhaps there was *prima facie* support for the myth. Before capitalism raised mass living standards, the working classes had a genuinely revolutionary potential. This was visible in Britain and America in the early days of the nineteenth century and in France as late as the Paris Commune. In countries like Spain and Yugoslavia, where industrialization and its benefits have been delayed, the revolutionary potential existed well into the twentieth century. But, contrary to Marx's prediction of increasing proletarian misery, capitalism, once it has had the chance, has vastly increased the wealth and freedom of the ordinary worker. It has reduced the size of the working class and deradicalized the worker.[6]

As a result, workers as a mass have decreasingly the impulses attributed to them by Marxism. They too often believe in patriotism or religion, or read comic strips, go to movies, play slot machines and patronize taxi dance halls. In one way or another, they try to cure their discontent by narcotics rather than by surgery. The general strike is in principle the most potent weapon in the world, but it always remains potent in principle. The last great moment for the general strike was perhaps 1914, when syndicalist agitation had at least kept alive mass revolutionary emotions. But, even had Jaurès survived and led the call, the working classes would probably have succumbed to the bugle, the flag and the military parade. Marx recognized that many workers were not Marxists and so invented a classification called the *Lumpenproletariat* in which were dumped those who did not live up to theory. Lenin recognized this too and so invented a disciplined party which announced itself as the only true representative of the proletariat, reducing non-Communist workers to political non-existence.

[6]In the United States, between 1910 and 1940, the common laborer dropped from 38 per cent of the labor force to 25.9 per cent; whitecollar workers increased from 10.2 per cent to 17.2 per cent.

[7]Communists do not have any such illusions except for propaganda purposes. "Trade unionism," wrote Lenin, "signifies the mental enslavement of the workers to the bourgeoisie." David Shub, *Lenin*, New York, 1948, p. 54.

Progressives defending their belief in the proletariat sometimes cite the trade-union movement.[7] Yet the trade union has, in fact, surely been the culminating agency in the deradicalization of the masses. As an institution, it is as clearly indigenous to the capitalist system as the corporation itself, and has no real meaning apart from that system. Thus trade unions, while giving the working masses a sense of having an organization of their own, insure that the goals of this organization are compatible with capitalism. And, as unions become more powerful, they increase their vested interests in the existing order. Labor leadership acquires satisfactions in terms of prestige and power. Only acute mass disaffection could radicalize the union leadership; and, up to this point, at least, the increase in capitalist productivity has enabled the labor movement to bring the rank-and-file steady benefits in the shape of higher wages, reduced hours and better working conditions.

What operational meaning, indeed, does the conception of the proletariat as an agency of change have? Can it mean anything more than the proletariat as a pool of discontent from which leaders can draw recruits for a variety of programs? The technical necessity for organization, as Robert Michels showed long ago, sets in motion an inevitable tendency toward oligarchy. The leadership after a time is bound to have separate interests from the rank-and-file. A working-class organization will soon stand, not for the working class, but for the working class plus the organization's own instincts for survival plus the special bureaucratic interests of the organization's top leadership. No loopholes have yet been discovered in the iron law of oligarchy.

For these various reasons, the mystique of the working class has faded somewhat since the First War. In its place has arisen a new mystique, more radiant and palpable, and exercising the same fascinations of power and guilt: the mystique of the USSR. Each success of the Soviet Union has conferred new delights on those possessed of the need for prostration and frightened of the responsibilities of decision. In a world which makes very little sense, these emotions are natural enough. But surrender to them destroys the capacity for clear intellectual leadership which ought to be the progressive's function in the world. In an exact sense, Soviet Russia has become the opiate of the progressives.

"The facts of life do not penetrate to the sphere in which our beliefs are cherished," writes Proust; "as it was not they that engendered those beliefs, so they are powerless to destroy them; they can aim at them continual blows of contradiction and disproof without weakening them; and an avalanche of miseries and maladies coming, one after another, without interruption into the bosom of a family, will not make it lose faith in either the clemency of its God or the capacity of its physician." The Soviet Union can do very little any more to disenchant its believers; it has done about everything in the book already. I remember in the summer of 1939 asking a fellow traveler what the USSR could possibly do which would make him lose faith. He said, "Sign a pact with Hitler." But two months later he had absorbed the pact with Hitler; and so the hunger to believe, the anxiety and the guilt, continue to triumph over the evidence.[8]

Conservatism in its crisis of despair turns to fascism: so progressivism in its crisis of despair turns to Communism. Each in a sober mood has a great contribution to make to free society: the conservative in his emphasis on law and liberty, the progressive in his emphasis on mass welfare. But neither is capable of saving free society. Both, faced by problems they cannot understand and fear to meet, tend to compound their own failure by delivering free society to its totalitarian foe. To avoid this fate, we must understand as clearly as possible the reasons for the appeal of totalitarianism.

---

[8]The pact with Hitler might have been justified at the time on the ground that Stalin did not know the West would fight. But the more determined fellow travelers now argue that Stalin was right in any case—even if he had known the West would resist. Cf. Henry Wallace: "If Stalin were doing it all over again, in the light of his present knowledge of Hitler, France and England, he could hardly act differently than [sic] he did." *New Republic*, February 9, 1948.

Nightmare in Red

RICHARD FRIED

Richard Fried, an Associate Professor of History at the University of
Illinois, is the author of *Men Against McCarthy* and *Nightmare in Red*.
In the excerpt that follows, adapted from *Nightmare in Red*, Fried at-
tempts to place McCarthyism in a broader historical perspective.
What impact does he believe the Red Scare had on American society?

Even independent of [Senator Joseph] McCarthy, the years 1950–
1954 marked the climax of anti-communism in American life. The Korean stalemate generated both a bruising debate over containment and
a sourness in national politics. Korea's sapping effect and a series of
minor scandals heightened the Democratic Party's anemia. In addition,
the 1950 congressional campaign, revealing McCarthyism's apparent
sway over the voters and encouraging the GOP's right wing, signaled
that anti-communism occupied the core of American political culture.
"These," said liberal commentator Elmer Davis in January 1951, "are
bitter days—full of envy, hatred, malice, and all uncharitableness."

Critics of these trends in American politics had scant power or
spirit. Outside government, foes of anti-Communist excesses moved
cautiously lest they be redbaited and rarely took effective countermeasures. Liberals seldom strayed from the safety of the anti-Communist
consensus. Radicals met the hostility of the dominant political forces in
Cold War America and fared poorly. In government, anti-communism
ruled. Senate resistance to McCarthy was scattered and weak. In the
House, HUAC did much as it pleased. Truman upheld civil liberties
with occasional eloquence, but he remained on the defensive, and his
Justice Department often seemed locked in near-alliance with the

Right in Congress. Eisenhower, when not appeasing the McCarthyites, appeared at times no more able to curb them than had Truman.

Even at his peak, McCarthy was not the sole anti-Communist paladin, though he cultivated that impression. As McCarthyism in its broader sense outlived the personal defeat of McCarthy himself, so, in its prime, it exceeded his reach. Its strength owed much to the wide acceptance, even by McCarthy's critics, of the era's anti-Communist premises. Along with McCarthy, they made the first half of the 1950s the acme of noisy anti-communism and of the ills to which it gave birth.

Soon after the 1950 campaign, skirmishing over the Communist issue renewed in earnest. In December Senator Pat McCarran joined the hunt for subversives by creating the Senate Internal Security Subcommittee (SISS). As chairman of that panel (and the parent Judiciary Committee), the crusty Nevada Democrat packed it with such likeminded colleagues as Democrats James Eastland and Willis Smith and Republicans Homer Ferguson and William Jenner. While McCarthy darted about unpredictably, McCarran moved glacially but steadily to his objective, crushing opposition.

McCarran's panel spotlighted themes that McCarthy had raised giving them a more sympathetic hearing than had the Tydings Committee. In February 1951, federal agents swooped down on a barn in Lee, Massachusetts, seized the dead files of the Institute of Pacific Relations (IPR) and trucked them under guard to Washington. After sifting this haul, a SISS subcommittee opened an extended probe of the IPR, which led to a new inquest on "who lost China" and resulted in renewed loyalty and security proceedings, dismissals from the State Department and prosecution—all to McCarthy's greater, reflected glory.

The subcommittee acquired a reputation—more cultivated than deserved—for honoring due process. SISS was punctilious on some points: evidence was formally introduced (when an excerpt was read, the full text was put in the record); hearings were exhaustive (over 5,000 pages); witnesses were heard in executive session before they named names in public; their credentials and the relevance of their testimony were set forth; and some outward courtesies were extended.

The fairness was only skin-deep, however. Witnesses were badgered about obscure events from years back and about nuances of aging reports. Diplomat John Carter Vincent was even asked if he had plans to move to Sarasota, Florida. When he termed it a most "curious" question, counsel could only suggest that perhaps the Florida Chamber of

Commerce had taken an interest. The subcommittee strove to ensnare witnesses in perjury. One China Hand called the sessions "generally Dostoyevskian attacks not only on a man's mind but also his memory." To have predicted Jiang's decline or Mao's rise was interpreted as both premeditating and helping to cause that outcome.

A product of the internationalist do-goodery of YMCA leaders in the 1920s, the IPR sought to promote peace and understanding in the Pacific. It had both national branches in countries interested in the Pacific and an international secretariat. Well funded by corporations and foundations in its palmier days, the IPR had more pedigree than power. McCarran's subcommittee insisted that IPR's publications pushed the Communist line on China. Louis Budenz testified that the Kremlin had assigned Owen Lattimore the job of giving the IPR journal, *Pacific Affairs*, a Party-line tilt. Budenz claimed that when he was in the Party, he received "official communications" describing Lattimore (and several China Hands) as Communists.

McCarran's panel spent a year grilling Lattimore, other IPR officials, and various China experts and diplomats as it tried to knit a fabric of conspiracy out of its evidence and presuppositions. McCarran claimed that, but for the machinations of the coterie that ran IPR, "China today would be free and a bulwark against the further advance of the Red hordes into the Far East." He charged that the IPR-USSR connection had led to infiltration of the government by persons aligned with the Soviets, of faculties by Red professors, and of textbooks by pro-Communist ideas. He called Lattimore "a conscious and articulate instrument of the Soviet conspiracy."

The hearings revealed naiveté about communism, showed that IPR principals had access to important officials during the war, and turned up levels of maneuvering that sullied IPR's reputation for scholarly detachment. Proven or accused Reds did associate with the IPR and may well have sought leverage through it. There were tendentious claims in IPR publications, as in one author's simplistic dichotomy of Mao's "democratic China" and Jiang's "feudal China." Lattimore was a more partisan editor of *Pacific Affairs* than he conceded. However, in political scientist Earl Latham's measured assessment, the hearings "show something less than subversive conspiracy in the making of foreign policy, and something more than quiet routine." Nor was it proven that IPR had much influence over policy. Perhaps the China Hands had been naive to think that a reoriented policy might prevent China's Communists from falling

nists from falling "by default" under Soviet control and thus might maintain American leverage. Yet those who argued that unblinking support
of Jiang could have prevented China's "loss" were more naive still.

Unable to prove, in scholarly terms, its thesis of a successful pro-
Communist conspiracy against China, SISS could still carry it politically. The loyalty-security program helped enforce it. New charges,
however stale, motivated the State Department Loyalty-Security Board
to reexamine old cases of suspected employees, even if they had been
previously cleared. Moreover, nudged by the Right, Truman toughened
the loyalty standard in April 1951, putting a heavier burden of proof
on the accused. Thus under Hiram Bingham, a Republican conservative, the Loyalty Review Board ordered new inquiries in cases decided
under the old standard.

Amid the growing acrimony, the careers of the China Hands with-
ered. John Stewart Service was a case in point. He had been swept up in
the 1945 *Amerasia* arrests. (The episode reminded a colleague of
Heaven's My Destination, Thornton Wilder's 1930s version of *Candide*:
"Jack Service went into a bawdy house thinking it was still a girls'
boarding school.") In fact, Service had known of the magazine's radical
orientation and was using it to disseminate materials that discredited
Jiang Jieshi's regime. Though cleared of any crime, Service was a
marked man, subject to recurrent loyalty and security probes. By 1950
his career seemed back on track. He was slated to be consul-general in
Calcutta, but the China Lobby's ongoing attack prompted a down-
grading to consul (to avoid Senate confirmation). Even this looked
provocative, so he was switched to a job in the embassy at New Delhi.

On ship for India when McCarthy accused him, Service was ordered home. The Tydings Committee cleared him, but the Loyalty-
Security Board took another look. George Kennan, intellectual father
of containment, declared Service's China reports free of pro-communism. The Board heard new evidence, probably routed by the Chinese
Nationalists through the FBI, but cleared Service in October. The Indian assignment was by now long gone. In 1951 the Loyalty Review
Board called Service for a post-audit of his latest (eighth!) clearance.
After the hearing, the Board added a new charge based on the *Amerasia*
case: "intentional, unauthorized disclosure" of confidential documents
"under circumstances which may indicate disloyalty." In December Service was deemed a security risk, and Secretary of State Dean Acheson
fired him.

John Carter Vincent was another casualty. He once headed the State Department's Far Eastern Division, but his China connection led his superiors to ease him from the spotlight, sending him first as minister to Switzerland, then as consul-general to Tangier. In 1951 the Loyalty-Security Board called him to answer charges, including one that he had held "pro-Communist . . . views and sympathies" from 1940 to 1947. SISS quizzed him too. By convoluted reasoning, the Loyalty Review Board found him to be a loyalty risk. Acheson named a select panel to review the decision, but his successor, John Foster Dulles, bypassed the panel and gave Vincent a choice: quit or be fired. He quit.

The McCarran panel also grilled John Paton Davies, Jr., another China Hand, and pressed the Justice Department to indict him for perjury. He was not prosecuted, but in 1954 he was summoned from his post in Peru for a security hearing. John Foster Dulles implemented a recommendation for Davies's dismissal on the basis of "lack of judgment, discretion, and reliability."

By late 1954, the chief China Hands had been cashiered from service, and others were scattered in a sort of diplomatic diaspora. Vincent retired to tend his garden and lecture occasionally. In Lima, Davies entered the furniture business. Service worked for a firm that made and sold steam traps, eventually patenting a lucrative improvement. But while the China Hands, their loyalty slurred, were exiled from their chosen field, the China Lobby rode high. At a fete thrown by Nationalist China's ambassador after the 1952 election, Senators Knowland, McCarran, McCarthy, and other allies of the Nationalists raised glasses in a triumphal if unrealistic toast: "Back to the mainland."

By that point, the fate of Owen Lattimore had also been determined by SISS. In fact, the high point of McCarran's IPR inquiry was Lattimore's testimony in 1952. The committee questioned him for twelve days (on nine of which McCarthy attended), so peppering him with questions that his opening statement consumed three days. It pitted his memory against the massive IPR files and his word against those of ex-Communists like Budenz, whose testimony about Lattimore even the FBI doubted, and Harvey Matusow, who later confessed to perjury.

Often Lattimore's memory was hazy. The questions meandered over many years, he complained, "and it is getting increasingly difficult for me to remember what I remembered when." He denied knowing that one contributor to the journal he edited was a Communist or Marxist—only to be confronted with his 1937 statement that the author was reputedly at least a Marxist. Similarly, he dismissed the claim that he once answered mail for an absent aide to FDR, but his own correspondence contradicted him.

SISS also found it odd that, while claiming vindication from the Tydings inquiry and disclaiming any impact on policy, Lattimore had never told that panel of his meeting with Truman in 1945 to discuss China policy. "He visited the President once and forgot it," McCarran commented acidly. Another senator thought the fact that Lattimore had not mentioned giving Truman a memo after their meeting smacked of concealment. Lattimore was once asked to prove a negative: "can you say that the IPR and you had no influence upon the far-eastern experts of the State Department?" McCarran used post-hoc argument to rebut Lattimore's denial of any leverage. What else would explain the fact that, soon after his talk with Truman, State Department hardliners had been ousted and China Hands appointed, or that Marshall's policy while in China was "substantially the same" as Lattimore's memorandum had recommended? Exonerated by the Tydings Committee in 1950, Lattimore was not so fortunate in 1952. McCarran gave him a tongue-lashing. The witness was "so flagrantly defiant," so discourteous, and "so persistent in his efforts to confuse and obscure the facts, that the committee feels constrained to take due notice of his conduct." "That he has uttered untruths stands clear in the record."

That aftermath of the Lattimore inquiry showed McCarran's power and malice. The committee's report charged that Lattimore had lied a number of times. Subsequently, McCarran's ragging of James Mc-Granery, whose confirmation as Truman's Attorney General he held hostage, had the right effect: Lattimore was indicted for perjury in December 1952. Most of the seven perjury counts dealt with Lattimore's denials that he had known certain people were Reds or that he had published articles by authors he knew to be Communists. One count charged that he falsely denied being "sympathetic" to communism. When Herbert Brownell, Ike's Attorney General, took office, McCarran made sure that he put a zealous prosecutor on the case.

Federal Judge Luther Youngdahl heard the case and saw its flimsiness. He threw out as hopelessly vague the charge that Lattimore lied in denying pro-communism. The judge also weeded out three more counts and expressed doubt about the rest. The Appeals Court reinstated two counts, and in 1954 a grand jury added two new ones. Youngdahl struck down the two new counts, and the Appeals Court upheld him. The case was further dented when one witness, Harvey Matusow, confessed to perjury in *his* SISS testimony. The Justice Department dropped the case in 1955.

Critics, including some liberals, warned that Lattimore did not merit martyr status. He had defended the Soviet purges of the 1930s and romanticized the Chinese Communists and Soviet influence on Asia. Still, faulty or debatable views are rarely a crime. This nicety did not faze McCarran, whose power enabled him to define new crimes. Indeed, creation of new categories of illicit behavior was a salient feature of the era. Lattimore had a close call. Unlucky as he was to attract the enmity of the potent McCarran, he was fortunate to benefit from the "rule of law"—or the luck of the draw in having Judge Youngdahl preside over the case. It was not the last time the judiciary saved the country from McCarthyism's worst ravages.

The purge of the China Hands had long-term impact. American attitudes toward China remained frozen for two decades. Battered by McCarthyite attacks, the State Department's Far Eastern Division assumed a conservative bunkerlike mentality. Selected by President John F. Kennedy to shake the division up, Assistant Secretary of State Averell Harriman found it "a disaster area filled with human wreckage." Personnel who did not bear wounds from previous battles were chosen to handle Asian problems. Vincent's successor on the China desk was an impeccably conservative diplomat whose experience lay in Europe. JFK named an ambassador to South Vietnam whose prior work had been with NATO. In the 1950s, the field of Asian studies felt the blindfold of conformity as the momentum of U.S. foreign policy carried the country toward the vortex of Vietnam.

The IPR investigation was but one of many inquiries during the early 1950s that delved into Communist activities. The Eighty-first Congress spawned 24 probes of communism; the Eighty-second, 34; and Eighty-third, 51. HUAC busily sought new triumphs. In 1953, 185 of the 221 Republican Congressmen asked to serve on it. But HUAC faced the problem all monopolies meet when competitors pour into the market. Besides McCarran and McCarthy, a Senate labor subcommittee probed Red influences in labor unions, two committees combed the U.N. Secretariat for Communists, and others dipped an oar in when the occasion arose.

In part HUAC met the competition with strenuous travel. Hearings often bore titles like "Communist Activities in the Chicago Area"—or

Los Angeles, Detroit, or Hawaii. The Detroit hearings got a musician fired, a college student expelled, and UAW Local 600 taken over by the national union. In 1956 two Fisher Body employees were called before a HUAC hearing in St. Louis. When angry fellow workers chalked such slogans as "Russia has no Fifth amendment" on auto bodies and staged a work stoppage, the two men were suspended. The impact of junketing congressional probers was often felt in such local fallout rather than in federal punishments (though many witnesses were cited for contempt of Congress). That indeed was the point. A witness might use the Fifth Amendment to avoid perjury charges, but appearing before a committee of Congress left him open to local sanctions.

Lawmakers fretted over communism in the labor movement. The presence of left-wing unionists in a defense plant offered a frequent pretext for congressional excursions. HUAC addressed the issue often; McCarthy, occasionally; House and Senate labor subcommittees paid close heed. The liberal anti-Communist Hubert Humphrey held an inquiry designed both to meet the problem and to protect clean unions from scattershot redbaiting. Lest unions be handled too softly, in 1952 Pat McCarran, Herman Welker, and John Marshall Butler conceived the formidably labeled "Task Force Investigating Communist Domination of Certain Labor Organizations."

Attacks on radical union leadership from both within and without the labor movement proliferated in the early 1950s. During 1952 hearings in Chicago, HUAC jousted with negotiators for the Communist-led United Electrical Workers just as they mounted a strike against International Harvester. In 1953 McCarthy's subcommittee also bedeviled UE locals in New York and Massachusetts. Such hearings often led to firings and encouraged or counterpointed raids by rival unions. They hastened the decline of the left wing of the labor movement.

The UE was beset on all sides. When the anti-communist International United Electrical Workers Union (IUE), led by James Carey, was founded, Truman Administration officials intoned blessings. The Atomic Energy Commission pressured employers like General Electric to freeze out the UE; IUE literature warned that plants represented by the UE would lose defense contracts. The CIO lavishly funded Carey's war with the UE. Three days before a 1950 election to decide control of a Pittsburgh are a local, the vocal anti-Communist Judge Michael Musmanno arrived at a plant gate to campaign for the IUE. Bedecked in naval uniform, he was convoyed by a detachment of National Guardsmen, bayonets fixed and flags unfurled. Many local Catholic clergy urged their flocks to vote for the IUE on the basis of anti-communism. Carey's union won a narrow victory.

These labor wars sometimes produced odd bedfellows. Carey criticized McCarthy, but the latter's 1953 Boston hearings helped the IUE keep control of key GE plants in the area. GE management declared before the hearings that it would fire workers who admitted they were Reds; it would suspend those who declined to testify and, if they did not subsequently answer the charges, would dismiss them. Thus besieged, the UE often settled labor disputes on a take-what-it-could basis.

Where left-wing unions maintained reputations for effective bargaining, anti-communism had limited effect. The UE's tactical surrender of its youthful militancy probably eroded its rank-and-file support more than did any redbaiting. Yet the Longshoremen's Union, despite Smith Act prosecutions against its leaders in Hawaii and the effort to deport Harry Bridges, kept control of West Coast docks. (Indeed, having come to tolerate Bridges by the 1950s, business leaders had lost enthusiasm for persecuting him.) Similarly, the Mine, Mill and Smelter Workers Union held onto some strongholds despite recurrent redbaiting. Weaker leftist unions like the United Public Workers or the Fur and Leather Workers succumbed to raiding and harassment.

In an era when mainline labor was cautious, organizing initiatives often did originate with more radical unions and so fell prey to anti-Communist attack. In 1953 a CIO retail workers' union, some of whose organizers were Communists, struck stores in Port Arthur, Texas. A commission of inquiry named by Governor Allen Shivers (then seeking reelection) found "clear and present danger" of Communist sway over Texas labor. Shivers claimed he had foiled a Communist-led union's "well-laid plans to spread its tentacles all along the Gulf Coast and eventually into *your* community." Other Southern organizing drives succumbed to redbaiting too.

By the 1950s, labor's assertiveness had waned; where it persisted, it met defeat; and new organizing drives were few. Internal dissent—indeed, debate—was virtually stilled. Its momentum sapped and its membership reduced by over a third, the CIO merged with the AFL in a 1955 "shotgun wedding." Having won a place within the American consensus, labor paid a dear price to keep it.

Conservatives feared Communist influence in the nation's schools as well as in its factories. The influence of the "Reducators" and of subversive ideas that ranged, in various investigators' minds, from outright communism to "progressive education" perennially intrigued legislators at the state and national levels.

The Communists' long-running control of the New York Teachers Union alarmed the Senate Internal Security Subcommittee. Previously, the 1940–41 Rapp-Coudert inquiry had led to the dismissal of a number of New York City teachers. In 1949 the Board of Education began a new purge. From 1950 to early 1953, twenty-four teachers were fired and thirty-four resigned under investigation. By one estimate, over three hundred New York City teachers lost their jobs in the 1950s. SISS thus served to reinforce local activities with its 1952–53 hearings in New York City. The refusal by Teachers Union leaders to testify about their affiliations established grounds for their dismissal under Section 903 of the city charter.

Ultimately, the probers failed in their aim to expose Marxist-Leninist propagandizing in Gotham's classrooms. Bella Dodd, a former Communist and Teachers Union leader, claimed that Communist teachers who knew Party dogma "cannot help but slant their teaching in that direction." A Queens College professor said he knew a score of students whom the Communists had "ruined" and turned into "misfits." Yet aside from a few parents' complaints and "one case where I think we could prove it," the city's school superintendent had no evidence of indoctrination. Though Communists had obviously acquired great leverage in the Teachers Union, SISS located its best case of university subversion in a book about *China*.

HUAC quizzed educators too, but its scrutiny of the movie industry earned higher returns when it resumed its inquiry into Hollywood in 1951. By then the Hollywood Ten were in prison, the film industry's opposition to HUAC was shattered, and the blacklist was growing. Fear washed through the movie lots. The economic distress visited on Hollywood by the growth of television further frazzled nerves. Said one witness, the renewed assault was "like taking a pot shot at a wounded animal." When subpoenaed, actress Gale Sondergaard asked the Screen Actors Guild for help, its board rebuffed her, likening her criticism of HUAC to the Communist line. The Screen Directors Guild made its members take a loyalty oath.

Yet few secrets were left to ferret out: the identity of Hollywood's Communists had long ceased to be a mystery. Early in the 1951 hearings, Congressman Francis Walter even asked why it was "material . . . to have the names of people when we already know them?" For HUAC, getting new information had become secondary to conducting ceremonies of exposure and penitence. Would the witness "name names" or not?

Of 110 witnesses subpoenaed in 1951, 58 admitted having had Party involvements. Some cogently explained why they had since disowned communism. Budd Schulberg recalled that while he was writing *What Makes Sammy Run*, the Party told him to submit an outline, confer with its literary authorities, and heed its artistic canons. The *Daily Worker* received his book favorably, but after being updated on Party aesthetics, the reviewer wrote a second piece thrashing the novel. One screenwriter recalled how the Party line on a studio painters' strike shifted perplexingly in 1945: we "could walk through the picket lines in February, and not in June."

Witnesses seeking to steer between punishment and fingering coworkers faced tearing ethical choices. Naming known Reds or those previously named might stave off harm, but this ploy was tinged with moral bankruptcy. Some soured ex-Communists did resist giving names, not wanting, in actor Larry Parks's phrase, to "crawl through the mud to be an informer." Some named each other; some said little, ducking quickly behind the Fifth Amendment. Others told all. The 155 names that writer Martin Berkeley gave set a record. Others gabbed freely. Parrying with humor the oft-asked question—would he defend America against the Soviets?—actor Will Geer, already middle-aged, cheerfully agreed to fight in his way: growing vegetables and entertaining the wounded. The idea of people his vintage shouldering arms amused him; wars "would be negotiated immediately."

In this as in all inquiries, witnesses trod a path set with snares. The courts disallowed the Hollywood Ten's use of the First Amendment to avoid testifying, so a witness's only protection was the Fifth Amendment guarantee against self-incrimination. Even this route crossed minefields. *Blau v. U.S.* (1950) ruled that one might plead the Fifth legitimately to the question of Party membership. However, the 1950 case of *Rogers v. U.S.* dictated caution: one had to invoke the Fifth at the outset, not in the middle, of a line of questions inching toward incrimination. Having testified that she herself held a Party office, the court ruled, Jane Rogers had waived her Fifth Amendment privilege and could not then refuse to testify about others.

HUAC tried to quick-march Fifth-takers into pitfalls. One gambit was a logical fork: if answering would incriminate him, a witness might use the Fifth; but if innocent, he could not honestly do so. Thus, the committee held, the witness was either guilty or lying—even though the courts did not accept this presumption of guilt. However, a new odious category, the "Fifth-Amendment Communist," was born. Such witnesses, whether teachers, actors, or others, rarely hung onto their jobs.

Legal precedent also demanded care in testifying about associations. One witness pled the Fifth in response to the question of whether he was a member of the American Automobile Association. HUAC members enjoyed asking if witnesses belonged to the Ku Klux Klan, hoping to nettle them into breaking a string of refusals to answer. On their part, witnesses devised novel defenses like the so-called "diminished Fifth." A witness resorting to the "slightly diminished Fifth" would deny present CP membership but refuse to open up his past or that of others; those using the "fully diminished Fifth," on the other hand, testified about their own pasts but no one else's. (The "augmented Fifth" was like the slightly diminished Fifth, but the witness also disclaimed any sympathy for communism.)

The question of whether to testify freely or take the Fifth convulsed the higher precincts of American arts and letters. Writer Lillian Hellman, subpoenaed in 1952, took the bold step of writing HUAC's chairman that she would take the Fifth only if asked to talk about others. She realized that by answering questions about herself, she waived her privilege and was subject to a contempt citation, but better that than to "bring bad trouble" to innocent people. She simply would not cut her conscience "to fit this year's fashions." When she testified, she did invoke the Fifth but scored a coup with her eloquent letter and managed to avoid a contempt citation. In 1956 the playwright Arthur Miller also refused to discuss other people but, unlike Hellman, did not take the Fifth. (His contempt citation was later overturned.)

Art came to mirror politics. Miller had previously written *The Crucible*, whose hero welcomed death rather than implicate others in the seventeenth-century Salem witch trials. Admirers stressed the play's relevance to modern witch-hunts. In contrast, Elia Kazan, who had named names, directed the smash movie *On the Waterfront*, whose hero (Marlon Brando), implored by a fighting priest (Karl Malden) to speak out, agreed to inform against criminals in a longshoremen's union. None of these works dealt with communism, but their pertinence to current political issues was not lost. Among the arbiters of American culture, these moral choices prompted heated debate, which still reverberated in the 1980s.

The issues were not only philosophical. The sanctions were real. Noncooperative witnesses were blacklisted, their careers in Hollywood shattered. Many drifted into other lines of work. Many became exiles, moving to Europe, Mexico, or New York. Some suffered writer's block. Some families endured steady FBI surveillance and such vexations as sharply increased life insurance premiums (for an assertedly dangerous occupation). Being blacklisted so dispirited several actors that their health was impaired, and premature death resulted. Comedian Philip Loeb, blacklisted and unemployable, his family destroyed, committed suicide in 1955.

Even though several hundred members of the entertainment industry forfeited their livelihoods after HUAC appearances, the studios, networks, producers, and the committee itself did not admit publicly that a blacklist existed. (Privately, some were candid. "Pal, you're dead," a soused producer told writer Millard Lampell. "They told me that I couldn't touch you with a barge pole.") In this shadow world, performers and writers wondered if their talents had indeed eroded. Had one's voice sharpened, one's humor dulled?

For blacklisting to work, HUAC's hammer needed an anvil. It was duly provided by other groups who willingly punished hostile or reluctant witnesses. American Legion publications spread the word about movies whose credits were fouled by subversion; Legionnaires (and other local true believers) could pressure theatre owners, if necessary, by trooping down to the Bijou to picket offending films. The mere threat of such forces soon choked off the supply of objectionable pictures at the source. Indeed, Hollywood, responding to broad hints from HUAC and to its own reading of the political climate, began making anti-Communist potboilers. These low-budget "B" pictures did poorly at the box office. They provided insurance, not profits.

Though entertainment industry moguls justified screening employees' politics by citing the threat from amateur censors, usually professional blacklisters made the system work. Blacklisting opened up business vistas on the Right. In 1950 American Business Consultants, founded by three ex-FBI agents, published *Red Channels*, a compendium listing 151 entertainers and their Communist-front links. *Counterattack*, an ABC publication started in 1947, periodically offered the same type of information. In 1953 an employee left ABC to establish Aware, Inc., which sold a similar service. Companies in show biz subscribed to these countersubversive finding aids and paid to have the names of those they might hire for a show or series checked against "the files." Aware charged five dollars to vet a name for the first time, two dollars for rechecks. It became habit for Hollywood, radio and TV networks, advertisers, and stage producers (though blacklisting had its weakest hold on Broadway) not to employ entertainers whose names cropped up in such files.

A few found ways to evade total proscription. Writers could sometimes submit work under pseudonyms. Studios asked some writers on the blacklist to doctor ailing scripts authored by others. The blacklisted writers received no screen credits and were paid a pittance, but at least they were working. Ostracized actors did not have this option. Said comedian Zero Mostel: "I am a man of a thousand faces, all of them blacklisted." A TV producer once called a talent agent to ask, "Who have you got like John Garfield?" He had Garfield himself, the agent exclaimed; but, of course, the blacklisted Garfield was taboo.

Unlike actors, blacklisted writers could also find work in television, which devoured new scripts ravenously. As in film, some used assumed names. Others worked through "fronts" (whence came the title of Woody Allen's 1976 movie). They wrote, but someone else put his name to the script (and might demand up to half of the income). Mistaken-identity plot twists worthy of a Restoration comedy resulted. One writer using a pseudonym wrote a script that he was asked, under a second pseudonym, to revise. Millard Lampell submitted a script under a phony name; the producers insisted that the script's writer appear for a consultation; told that he was away and unavailable, they went for a quick fix: they asked Lampell to rewrite his own (unacknowledged) script.

The obverse of blacklisting was "clearance." Desperate actors or writers could seek absolution from a member of the anti-Communist industry. Often, not surprisingly, the person to see was one who had played a part in creating the blacklist. Roy Brewer, the chief of the International Alliance of Theatrical Stage Employees, had redbaited the leftist craft guilds, but helped rehabilitate blacklistees, as did several conservative newspaper columnists. The American Legion, which issued lists of Hollywood's undesirables, also certified innocence or repentance. A listee might get by with writing a letter to the Legion. Or he might be made to list suspect organizations he had joined and to tell why he joined, when he quit, who invited him in, and whom he had enticed. Thus the written route to clearance might also require naming names.

To regain grace, some sinners had to repent publicly, express robust patriotism in a speech or article, or confess to having been duped into supporting leftist causes. Typically, a blacklistee had to be willing to tell all to the FBI or to HUAC. Even liberal anti-Communists were "graylisted," and some had to write clearance letters. Humphrey Bogart had bought trouble by protesting the 1947 HUAC hearings against the Hollywood Ten. In his article, "I'm No Communist," he admitted he had been a "dope" in politics. Actor John Garfield, whose appearance before HUAC sent his career and life into a tailspin, was at the time of his death about to publish an article titled "I Was a Sucker for a Left Hook."

Like teachers and entertainers, charitable foundations also triggered the suspicion of congressional anti-Communists. These products of capitalism plowed back into society some of the vast wealth of their Robber Baron founders, but conservatives found their philanthropic tastes too radical. In 1952 a special House committee led by Georgia conservative Eugene Cox inquired into the policies of tax-exempt foundations. Did not "these creatures of the capitalist system," asked Cox, seek to "bring the system into disrepute" and to assume "a socialistic leaning"?

Foundations had dipped their toes in swirling currents by focusing on such subjects as Soviet studies, improved race relations, education, and peace, and by subsidizing writers and artists. Grants that had occasionally gone to those who turned up on "lists" would return to haunt the donor. Cox bridled at the Rockefeller Foundation's twenty-five years of support for the IPR, at a Carnegie grant to Owen Lattimore, and at a Rockefeller stipend to Hanns Eisler, the left-wing composer and brother of reputed Comintern "rep" Gerhard Eisler. And why, the committee wondered, had the Carnegie Endowment hired Alger Hiss?

Foundation officers apologized for such "mistakes" but argued that they could avoid error only by never taking risks. None of them sounded radical. One claimed he knew the Attorney General's list by heart; others swore they never knowingly gave to groups on the list and never funded Communists. Paul Hoffman seconded a description of his Ford Foundation program as "somewhere near the middle of the road." Another witness soothed Cox's fears of radicalized college students, noting that the young liked to "shock" their elders, but five years out of school, with jobs, they "are all over" such youthful ailments.

Cox's probe drew no blood, but in the next four years the conflict sharpened. In 1953 conservative Tennessee Republican B. Carroll Reece aggressively renewed the inquiry. Based solely on the testimony of critics of the foundations, his panel's 1954 report damned much of recent history, including the New Deal and the "moral relativism" that went back to William James and John Dewey, and attacked the foundations that subsidized such trends.

The Fund for the Republic, incorporated in 1952, was a special goad to conservatives. Spun off by the parent Ford Foundation, the Fund owed its independence partly to Henry Ford II's wish to distance himself from a program so controversial that it sparked boycott threats against Ford showrooms. The Fund had a commitment to enhance American freedoms and fifteen billion dollars to carry it out. Paul Hoffman was its chairman; in 1954 Robert M. Hutchins became its president. The Right loathed Hoffman; he had run the Marshall Plan (Socialist globaloney), backed Ike (not Taft) in 1952, and opposed McCarthy. The presence of Hutchins, who when president of the University of Chicago in 1949 had defended civil liberties and tweaked the noses of clumsy anti-Communists on the Broyles commission, further guaranteed trouble from the Right.

The Fund for the Republic supported such projects as sober academic studies of communism, inquiries into the loyalty-security programs, efforts to build racial tolerance, studies of blacklisting and censorship, and a program to stimulate public discussion of the nation's "basic documents." Not all awards were so schoolish. An Iowa town got $10,000 after it found housing for a black Air Force officer who had moved to the all-white community.

The Fund gave a particularly controversial grant in 1955 to the Plymouth (Pennsylvania) Monthly Meeting. In 1953 that Quaker body hired a librarian named Mary Knowles, who had lost her previous job in Massachusetts by pleading the Fifth before the Internal Security Subcommittee. FBI informant Herbert Philbrick had named her as a Red, and she had once worked for an agency named on the Attorney General's list. She refused to take a state loyalty oath or to revisit her past but stated that she had had no link with any left-wing or subversive groups since 1947 and that she adhered to her country and the Constitution. Further she would not budge.

Her stance stoked anger in the community. After the Plymouth Meeting hired her, local governments cut off funds to the library; schools halted class trips there. The American Legion, the Daughters of the American Revolution, and other pressure groups agitated, and petitions circulated. A group called Alerted Americans claimed that to keep Mrs. Knowles at the library "poses a possible future threat to our security." When the Plymouth Meeting refused to jettison her, the Fund for the Republic voted it a $5,000 award. The Right reacted angrily. Two committees of Congress again quizzed the librarian, and again she balked. In 1956 she was cited for contempt of Congress. She was fined and sentenced to 120 days in jail in 1957, but the verdict was overturned on appeal in 1960.

Increasingly subject to attacks in 1955 and after, the Fund for the Republic had drawn a bead on "McCarthyism," and friends of that phenomenon struck back. McCarthy rightly suspected that the Fund's inquiries into the loyalty-security program aimed to criticize it. In 1956, when Hoffman was named to the nation's U.N. delegation, McCarthy exclaimed that Congress should address Hoffman's "activities as Chairman of the Ford Foundation Fund 'To Destroy the Republic.'" Other lawmakers lambasted the Fund; J. Edgar Hoover had tart words for it; the IRS scrutinized its tax exemption as a nonprofit organization; and rightist commentators and journalists led by Fulton Lewis, Jr. offered shrill criticism.

In June 1956, HUAC slated hearings on the Fund, then backed off. Soon after, however, the Fund-sponsored study *Report on Blacklisting* was published, and HUAC interrogated the author John Cogley, albeit ineptly. Then, for good measure, HUAC took another look at the grant to the Plymouth Monthly Meeting. It managed further to divide the community and antagonize local residents; the library board reaffirmed its faith in Mrs. Knowles.

For the Fund, timing was all. Most of its major programs came to fruition after McCarthyism had hit the downswell, after the courts began to limit the second Red Scare, and while criticism of the loyalty-security mania was growing. Thus the 1956 HUAC hearings came as an ineffectual rearguard reaction to trends that were sapping the force of anti-communism.

How deeply did anti-communism gouge the social and political terrain of the 1950s? With dissent defined as dangerous, the range of political debate obviously was crimped. The number of times that books were labeled dangerous, thoughts were scourged as harmful, and speakers and performers were rejected as outside the pale multiplied. Anti-Communist extremism and accompanying pressures toward conformity had impact in such areas as artistic expression, the labor movement, the cause of civil rights, and the status of minorities in American life.

For some denizens of the Right, threats of Communist influence materialized almost anywhere. For instance, Illinois American Legionnaires warned that the Girl Scouts were being spoonfed subversive doctrines. Jack Lait and Lee Mortimer's yellow-journalistic *U.S.A. Confidential* warned parents against the emerging threat of rock and roll. It bred dope use, interracialism, and sex orgies. "We know that many platter-spinners are hopheads. Many others are Reds, left-wingers, or hecklers of social convention." Not every absurdity owed life to the vigilantes, however. A jittery Hollywood studio cancelled a movie based on Longfellow's "Hiawatha" for fear it would be viewed as "Communist peace propaganda."

Books and ideas remained vulnerable. It is true that the militant Indiana woman who abhorred *Robin Hood's* subversive rob-from-the-rich-and-give-to-the-poor message failed to get it banned from school libraries. Other locales were less lucky. A committee of women appointed by the school board of Sapulpa, Oklahoma, had more success. The board burned those books that it classified as dealing improperly with socialism or sex. A spokesman claimed that only five or six "volumes of no consequence" were destroyed. A librarian in Bartlesville, Oklahoma, was fired for subscribing to the *New Republic, Nation,* and *Negro Digest.* The use of UNESCO materials in the Los Angeles schools became a hot issue in 1952. A new school board and superintendent were elected with a mandate to remove such books from school libraries.

Local sanctions against unpopular artists and speakers often were effective. In August 1950, a New Hampshire resort hotel banned a talk by Owen Lattimore after guests, apparently riled by protests of the Daughters of the American Revolution and others, remonstrated. Often local veterans—the American Legion and Catholic War Veterans—initiated pressures. The commander of an American Legion Post in Omaha protested a local production of a play whose author, Garson Kanin, was listed in *Red Channels.* A founder of *Red Channels* warned an American Legion anti-subversive seminar in Peoria, Illinois, that Arthur Miller's *Death of a Salesman,* soon to appear locally, was "a Communist-dominated play." Jaycees and Legionnaires failed to get the theatre to cancel the play, but the boycott they mounted sharply curbed the size of the audience.

Libraries often became focal points of cultural anxieties. Not every confrontation ended like those in Los Angeles or Sapulpa, but librarians felt they were under the gun. "I just put a book that is complained about away for a while," said one public librarian. Occasionally, books were burned. "Did you ever try to burn a book?" asked another librarian. "It's *very* difficult." One-third of a group of librarians sampled in the late 1950s reported having removed "controversial" items from their shelves. One-fifth said they habitually avoided buying such books.

Academics, too, were scared. Many college and university social scientists polled in 1955 confessed to reining in their political views and activities. Twenty-seven percent had "wondered" whether a political opinion they had expressed might affect their job security or promotion; 40 percent had worried that a student might pass on "a warped version of what you have said and lead to false ideas about your political views." Twenty-two percent had at times "refrained from expressing an opinion or participating in some activity in order not to embarrass" their institution. Nine percent had "toned down" recent writing to avoid controversy. One teacher said he never expressed his own opinion in class. "I express the recognized and acknowledged point of view." Some instructors no longer assigned *The Communist Manifesto*.

About a hundred professors actually lost jobs, but an even greater number of frightened faculty trimmed their sails against the storm. Episodes far short of dismissal could also have a chilling effect. An economist at a Southern school addressed a business group, his talk, titled "Know Your Enemy," assessed Soviet resources and strengths. He was denounced to his president as a Communist. Another professor was assailed for advocating a lower tariff on oranges. "If I'd said potatoes, I wouldn't have been accused unless I had said it in Idaho." Some teachers got in mild trouble for such acts as assigning Robert and Helen Lynds' classic sociological study, *Middletown*, in class or listing the Kinsey reports on human sexuality as recommended reading. A professor once sent students to a public library to read works by Marx because his college's library had too few copies. Librarians logged the students' names.

The precise effect of all this professed anxiety was fuzzy. Many liberals claimed that Americans had been cowed into silence, that even honest anti-Communist dissent had been stilled, and that basic freedoms of thought, expression, and association had languished. The worriers trotted out appropriate comparisons: the witch trials in Salem, the Reign of Terror in France, the Alien and Sedition Acts, Know-Nothingism, and the Palmer raids. Justice William O. Douglas warned of "The Black Silence of Fear." Prominent foreigners like Bertrand Russell and Graham Greene decried the pall of fear they observed in America. On July 4, 1951, a *Madison Capital-Times* reporter asked passersby to sign a paper containing the Bill of Rights and parts of the Declaration of Independence. Out of 112, only one would do so. President Truman cited the episode to show McCarthyism's dire effects. McCarthy retorted that Truman owed an apology to the people of Wisconsin in view of that paper's Communist-line policies. Some McCarthy allies upheld the wisdom of refusing to sign any statement promiscuously offered.

McCarthy's defenders ridiculed the more outlandish laments for vanished liberties. A New York rabbi who blamed "McCarthyism" for the current spree of college "panty raids" offered a case in point. Conservative journalist Eugene Lyons was amused by an ACLU spokesman, his tonsils flaring in close-up on television, arguing "that in America no one any longer dares open his mouth." Such talk, said Lyons, led to "hysteria over hysteria." In their apologies for McCarthy, William F. Buckley and L. Brent Bozell snickered at such silliness. They found it odd that, in a time when left-of-center ideas were supposedly being crushed, liberals seemed to monopolize symposia sponsored by the major universities, even in McCarthy's home state, and that Archibald MacLeish and Bernard De Voto, two of those who condemned the enervating climate of fear, had still managed to garner two National Book Awards and a Pulitzer Prize. To Buckley and Bozell, the only conformity present was a proper one—a consensus that communism was evil and must be fought wholeheartedly.

But did such an argument miss the point? The successes enjoyed by prominent, secure liberals were one thing; far more numerous were the cases of those less visible and secure who lost entertainment and lecture bookings, chances to review books, teaching posts, even assembly-line jobs. The fight over the Communist menace had gone far beyond roistering debate or asserting the right of those who disagree with a set of views not to patronize them. People, a great number of whom had committed no crime, were made to suffer.

America in Our Time

GODFREY HODGSON

Godfrey Hodgson is a British journalist and the author of a number of insightful books about American politics. In the excerpt that follow, adapted from *America In Our Time*, Hodgson critiques the Vital Center liberalism. Hodgson believes that by discrediting the Left in America, liberals limited the debate over important public policy issues. The liberal consensus, Hodgson argues, was actually very conservative. What were the basic tenets of this consensus and why does Hodgson believe they are flawed? Does he suggest an alternative?

Confident to the verge of complacency about the perfectibility of American society, anxious to the point of paranoia about the threat of communism—those were the two faces of the consensus mood. Each grew from one aspect of the experience of the 1940s: confidence from economic success, anxiety from the fear of [Joseph Stalin] and the frustrations of power.

Historical logic made some form of consensus likely. It was natural that the new prosperity should calm the class antipathies of the depression years. It was normal that the sense of an enemy at the gate should strengthen national unity. And a reaction was predictable after the lacerating politics of the McCarthy period. But the basis for the consensus was something more than a vague mood or a reaction to passing events. The assumptions on which it was built had an intellectual life and coherence of their own. In barest outline, they can be summarized in the following set of interrelated maxims:

1. The American free-enterprise system is different from the old capitalism. It is democratic. It creates abundance. It has a revolutionary potential for social justice.
2. The key to this potential is production: specifically, increased production, or economic growth. This makes it possible to meet people's needs out of incremental resources. Social conflict over resources between classes (which [Karl] Marx called "the locomotive of history") therefore becomes obsolete and unnecessary.
3. Thus there is a natural harmony of interests in society. American society is getting more equal. It is in process of abolishing, may even have abolished, social class. Capitalists are being superseded by managers. The workers are becoming members of the middle class.
4. Social problems can be solved like industrial problems: The problem is first identified; programs are designed to solve it, by government enlightened by social science; money and other resources—such as trained people—are then applied to the problem as "inputs"; the outputs are predictable: the problems will be solved.
5. The main threat to this beneficent system comes from the deluded adherents of Marxism. The United States and its allies, the Free World, must therefore expect a prolonged struggle against communism.
6. Quite apart from the threat of communism, it is the duty and destiny of the United States to bring the good tidings of the free-enterprise system to the rest of the world.

The germ of this intellectual system, which by about 1960 had emerged as the dominant American ideology, was a simple yet startling empirical discovery. Capitalism, after all, seemed to work.

In the early 1940s, the economist Joseph Schumpeter, at work on his last book, *Capitalism, Socialism and Democracy*, reluctantly came to the conclusion that socialism—a system about which he cherished so few illusions that he expected it to resemble fascism when it came—was inevitable. Capitalism was doomed, he feared. Schumpeter was a conservative, though a highly original one, and he had arrived at this conclusion by his own line of argument. The modern corporation would "socialize the bourgeois mind," destroy the entrepreneurial motivation that was the driving force of capitalism, and thus "eventually kill its own roots." He was at pains to distinguish this position from what he saw as the almost universal vulgar anticapitalism of his time. "Every writer or speaker hastens to emphasize . . . his aversion to capitalist and his sympathy with anticapitalist interests."

Well under ten years later, the exact opposite would have been closer to the truth. In the United States (though nowhere else in the world), socialism was utterly discredited. The same transformation could be observed in popular attitudes and in intellectual fashion. In 1942 (the year that Schumpeter's book was published), a poll by Elmo Roper for *Fortune* found that only 40 per cent of respondents opposed socialism, 25 per cent said they were in favor of it, and as many as 35 per cent had an open mind. By 1949, a Gallup poll found that only 15 per cent wanted "to move more in the direction of socialism"; 61 per cent wanted to move in the opposite direction. Making all due allowance for the respondents' possibly vague notion of what socialism means, it was a startling shift, yet not more startling than that of the intellectuals.

As late as the war years, most American economists, led by Alvin Hansen, predicted that capitalism was entering a phase of chronic stagnation. Most other intellectuals took the economists at their word and assumed that the task was to replace capitalism with some more promising system.

Suddenly, in the late 1940s, the moribund system was declared not only alive but healthy. The economic *ancien régime* was acclaimed as the revolutionary harbinger of a brave new world.

In 1949 Daniel Bell wrote an article called "America's Un-Marxist Revolution."

"Keynes, not Marx," wrote Arthur Schlesinger in the same year, "is the prophet of the new radicalism."

"The world revolution of our time is 'made in U.S.A.,'" wrote Peter Drucker, the champion of management, also in 1949. "The true revolutionary principle is the idea of mass production."

And in 1951 the editors of *Fortune* magazine gave to an ambitious, much noticed synthesis of the American Way of Life a title borrowed from Marx and given currency by Trotsky. They called it *U.S.A., the Permanent Revolution:*

> There has occurred a great transformation, of which the world as a whole is yet unaware . . . No important progress whatever can be made in the understanding of America unless the nature of this transformation is grasped . . . There has been a vast dispersal of ownership and initiative, so that the

capitalist system has become intimately bound in with the political system and takes nourishment from its democratic roots. . . .U.S. capitalism is popular capitalism.

At the root of this optimistic new political philosophy, there lay an appropriately optimistic new economic doctrine. It came to be known as the New Economics, though by the time of its triumph, in the 1960s, when its licensed practitioners monopolized the President's Council of Economic Advisers, many of its leading ideas were going on thirty years old.

There were many strands to the New Economics. But the essence of it was the acceptance in the United States of the ideas of John Maynard Keynes, *not* as first received in the 1930s but as modified by American economists in the light of the success of the American economy in the 1940s.

The nub of Keynes's teaching was that, contrary to the tenets of classical economics, savings did not necessarily become investment. This was the cause of cyclical depression and of unemployment: left to itself, the capitalist system contained forces that would tend to produce stagnation. To that extent his position was pessimistic. But Keynes was a political economist. He did not think that things should be left to themselves. He believed that governments could cure the kind of deflation that had caused the great Depression by spending, and if necessary by deficit spending. He actually wrote a long letter to FDR, in early 1938, pleading with him to spend his way out of the recession. The letter was ignored. But after 1945 the university economists succeeded in persuading the more enlightened businessmen, and some politicians, that Keynes was right. Capitalism could be *made* to work. Depression and unemployment were avoidable, and it was up to government to avoid them.

From a conservative standpoint, Schumpeter introduced ideas that matched the new Keynesian orthodoxy better than he would have liked. He stressed the unique character of American capitalism. He emphasized productivity and technological change. He argued that concentration and oligopoly, which most economists had wanted government to destroy by trust busting, actually favored invention and innovation.

Unlike Schumpeter, John Kenneth Galbraith was Keynesian, and it was he who attempted the inevitable synthesis in *American Capitalism*, published in 1952. Galbraith also started from the observed fact that competition in American corporate capitalism was imperfect. He propounded the theory of what he called "countervailing power." Competition had been supposed to limit private economic power. Well, it didn't. But private power was held in check "by the countervailing power of those who are subject to it." The concentration of industry had brought into existence strong buyers—Sears Roebuck, A & P—to match strong sellers. It had also brought strong unions into existence to match strong employers.

Galbraith and Schumpeter had many disagreements. Their analyses were drawn from different premises and tended toward different conclusions. Yet they shared one common perception: the empirical observation that American capitalism was a success. "It works," said Galbraith shortly on his first page, "and in the years since World War II, quite brilliantly."

> There is another fact about the social situation in the United States that has no analogue anywhere else in the world, said Schumpeter in his second edition, published in 1946, . . . namely the colossal industrial success we are witnessing.

And a few pages later, he italicized a passage that condensed the gist of the new hope and the new pride:

> In the United States alone there need not lurk, behind modern programs of social betterment, that fundamental dilemma that everywhere paralyzes the will of every responsible man, the dilemma between economic progress and immediate increase of the real income of the masses.

In practical terms, the gospel of the New Economics could be translated into exciting propositions. Government can manage the economy by using fiscal and monetary policy. The tyranny of the business cycle, which had brought economic catastrophe and the specter of political upheaval, need no longer be tolerated. Depressions could be a thing of the past.

By changing interest rates and by increasing or decreasing the money supply—technical matters that had the added advantage of being remote from the scrutiny of everyday politics—government could flatten out fluctuations in economic activity.

The economists were emboldened to maintain that these fiscal and monetary controls could be manipulated with such precision—"fine tuning" was the phrase used—that in effect they would be able to fly the economy like an airplane, trimming its speed, course and altitude with tiny movements of the flaps and rudder. That was a later claim. The essential promise of the Keynesian system was that it would allow government to guarantee low and diminishing unemployment without inflation. It could thus banish at a stroke the worst terrors of both liberals and conservatives. At the same time, thus managed, the economy would also be able to deliver growth.

Growth was the second key concept of the new intellectual system, and the link between its strictly economic and its social and political ideas.

We are so accustomed to the idea of economic growth that it comes as a surprise to learn that it was a newer idea than Keynes's discovery of the way to beat the business cycle. Just as modern biology had to wait for the invention of the microscope and modern astronomy for the perfection of the telescope, the idea of economic growth developed only after precise techniques for measuring the gross national product became available. These were perfected only in the late 1930s, by Professor Simon Kuznets, of the University of Pennsylvania.

It is hardly possible to exaggerate the importance that the new concept assumed in the intellectual system of American liberals in the 1950s. It became the test, the aim, even the justification of free enterprise—the race, the runner and the prize.

The economic historian W.W. Rostow offered an interpretation of modern history as a contest in terms of economic growth—and called it an "anti-Communist manifesto."

The political scientist Seymour Martin Lipset came close to making it the chief criterion for judging a political system. "Prolonged effectiveness over a number of years," he suggested in his book *Political Man*, "may give legitimacy to a political system. In the modern world, such effectiveness means primarily constant economic development."

But perhaps the most lyrical description came from Walter Heller, chairman of the Council of Economic Advisers under Presidents Kennedy and Johnson. He called economic growth "the pot of gold and the rainbow."

The liberals did not worship economic growth merely as a golden calf. They saw in it the possibility of solving social problems with the incremental resources created by growth. That will be done, they hoped, without the social conflict that would be inevitable if those resources had to be found by redistributing existing wealth.

This was the hope that both Schumpeter and Galbraith had seen. Brushing aside the pessimists, Schumpeter had dared to predict in 1942 that GNP would reach $200 billion by 1950. (In the event, he was a pessimist himself: GNP in current dollars reached $284 billion by 1950.) "The huge mass of available commodities and services that this figure . . . represents," he wrote, "promises a level of satisfaction of economic needs even of the poorest members of society . . . that would eliminate anything that could possibly be described as suffering or want." And of course Schumpeter was fully aware of the ideological implications. Such a massive creation of new resources could be the key to his central dilemma. It might "annihilate the whole case for socialism so far as it is of a purely economic nature."

What Schumpeter had described as a theoretical possibility in the 1940s had become by the end of the 1950s the "conventional wisdom," and in the 1960s it was to be the foundation of public economic policy.

"Production has eliminated the more acute tensions associated with inequality," Galbraith wrote in *The Affluent Society*, a book whose title was to become a cliché to an extent that did little credit to the subtlety of its argument. "Increasing aggregate output is an alternative to redistribution."

The same idea was spelled out in the stonecutter's prose of the Rockefeller Brothers Fund's drafting committee:

> A healthy and expanding private economy means far more in terms of individual and family well-being than any reasonable expansion of government service and social programs.

"Far greater gains were to be made by fighting to enlarge the size of the economic pie," one of President Johnson's economic advisers wrote, "than by pressing proposals to increase equity and efficiency in sharing the pie." "When firing on all eight cylinders," said another, to an approving audience of bankers, "our economy is a mighty engine of social progress."

In theory, there could be little arguing with that proposition. Its truth in practice would depend on a number of questions: one's definition of social progress, the extent to which social progress could be guaranteed to follow from the application of resources, and the propensity of government to devote incremental resources to other purposes, such as fighting wars. But the relevant point here is that it was a proposition ideally suited to be one of the main props of an ideology of liberal conservatism. It offered to the liberals the hope of progress and a feeling of benevolence, and to the conservatives a vista of business prosperity and an unthreatened *status quo.*

Looking back on the decade, Paul Samuelson touched in a single paragraph all the essential elements of his generation's ideology: the optimism, the confidence that more means better, the faith in the harmony of interests between capitalism and social progress, the cankerous sense that all this must be related to the competition with communism:

"The New Economics really does work," he wrote in November 1968 on the eve of the Democrats' fall from power and of the sharpest fall in the stock market and the severest economic problems for a generation:

> Wall Street knows it. Main Street, which has been enjoying 92 months of advancing sales, knows it. The accountants who have been chalking up record profits know it . . . and so do the school nurses who measure the heights and weights of this generation . . . You can bet that the statisticians of the Kremlin know it.

No tenet of the consensus was more widely held than the idea that revolutionary American capitalism had abolished the working class, or—as approximately the same thought was sometimes expressed . . . that everybody in America was middle class now or that American society was rapidly approaching economic equality.

A small encyclopedia of statements to this effect can be garnered from the historians, the social scientists and the journalists of the time.

"The organizing concept of American society," wrote Peter Drucker, "has been that of social mobility . . . which denies the existence of classes."

"The union," said the editors of *Fortune,* "has made the worker, to an amazing degree, a middle class member of a middle class society."

"New Dealism," said historian Eric Goldman, ". . . found that it had created a nation of the middle class."

Yet another historian, Samuel Eliot Morison, boldly dated the abolition of the proletariat rather earlier than some would say the proletariat came into existence. He cited the observations of a Polish Communist visitor to confirm "a fact that has puzzled socialists and communists for a century: the American workman is an expectant capitalist, not a class-conscious proletarian."

Frederick L. Allen, on the other hand, wrote a best seller to prove that "the big change" in American life between 1900 and 1950 was the "democratization of our economic system."

One's first reaction is to yield to the cumulative weight of so many impassioned opinions and to conclude . . . what? For even the most cursory reading of such a miscellany raises questions. Had class stratification never existed in the United States, as Drucker seemed to think? But, then, can one imagine social mobility without class? Mobility between what? Had there never been an American proletariat, as Professor Morison seemed to believe? Or had there been a "big change"? Perhaps the proletariat had ceased to exist. But, then, which agency had earned the credit for this transformation? "Industrial enterprise," as some claimed? *Fortune's* unions? Or Goldman's "New Dealism"? Corporate business, labor and government may work in harmony. But they are hardly synonyms.

A second reading of this miscellany of texts and of the other evidence suggests two more modest conclusions:

1) A great many Americans, moved by the ideal of equality but perhaps also by reluctance to admit what was seen as a Marxist analysis of their own society, passionately wanted to believe that the concept of class was alien to the United States.

It suited business to believe this. It suited labor. It suited intellectuals, and it suited the press. It suited liberals, and it suited conservatives. Who was left to argue otherwise?

2) Nevertheless, something *had* happened. In the profound transformations of the 1940s the class structure of American society and its implications for politics had changed in complex and confusing ways—though not to the point of making "everybody middle class," still less of invalidating class analysis.

The abolition of the working class, in fact, was a myth. Like most myths, it did have a certain basis in fact. But it oversimplified and distorted what had really happened. It transformed a modest and temporary decline in inequality into a social revolution. At the same time, it confused the idea that many Americans were far better off than they had been, which was true, with the claim that poorer Americans had made dramatic gains at the expense of the better off, which was at best dubious.

Two developments probably explain the strength of this myth. The real performance of the economy during and after World War II made it possible to believe it. And the triumph of the liberals over the Left made a lot of people want to believe it.

The prosperity of the 1940s really was widespread. Mass unemployment ended, after twelve years. Dollar wages, especially for workers in such strongly unionized (and highly visible) industries as steel, automobiles, and rubber, rose dramatically. But real wages for most workers rose too.

There was also a highly obvious equalization of *consumption*, which looked like an equalization of wealth, all the more so because it was concentrated in the most visible forms of consumption: clothes, for example, and cars. Nylon stockings were a favorite example with economists and journalists alike. They were introduced in September 1939, the month Europe went to war. Ten years later, they were still a luxury in Europe. But in the United States, production in 1949 was 543 million pairs: every typist could afford to be dressed like a film star from ankle to thigh. The parking lots full of shiny, late-model automobiles outside factories were much commented upon; and "everybody" could afford the new electrical household gadgets.

In other ways, too, it really did look as though the rich were getting poorer and the poor richer. The rich complained bitterly about the income tax, and in fact the maximum rate rose from 54 per cent in 1932 to 91 per cent in the 1950s. Meanwhile, the after-taxes income of families in the lower income brackets was rising faster than that of the better-off families, and the income of the wealthiest 5 per cent actually dropped. John Kenneth Galbraith quoted the tax table in *The Affluent Society*, and it certainly conveyed an impression of affluence that was not only growing but also being more equally distributed.

Between 1941 and 1950, measuring in dollars of 1950 purchasing power, the income of the highest 5 per cent of all families, after income taxes, actually fell. Thereafter, the lower you descended on the income scale, the higher the gains.

Highest fifth:	up 8%
Second fifth:	up 16%
Third fifth:	up 24%
Fourth fifth:	up 37%
Lowest fifth:	up 42%

There is a pleasing regularity about that series that would seem to clinch the argument. But, unfortunately, there are several ways of looking at the distribution of income. The whole study of income and wealth, in fact, bristles with treacherous problems for the statistician. He must make up his mind whether different figures from different sources, the only ones available for different periods, are really comparable or not; whether to measure income before or after taxes; what allowance, if any, to make for tax evasion by the rich and for "transfer payments" out of taxes made by government to the poor. And unless he is most unusually naive, he will be uncomfortably aware that these are not only technical but political decisions.

The best way to measure the distribution of income is to measure what proportion of the total national income has gone at different times to different fractions of the population, ranged in order from the richest to the poorest.

When the historian Gabriel Kolko did this, he came up with a result that shattered the liberal assumption that income had been redistributed to the poor. Here is how he summarized his findings in his book *Wealth and Power in America*:

> Despite the obvious increase in prosperity since the abysmal years of the Great Depression, the basic distribution of income and wealth is essentially the same now as it was in 1939, or even 1910. Most low-income groups live substantially better today, but even though their real wages have mounted, their percentage of the national income has not changed.

Kolko computed the percentage of national personal income received, before taxes, by each tenth of the population by income, over the whole period from 1910 to 1959. He found that while the share of the highest tenth had dropped, it had dropped only from 33.9 per cent in 1910 to 28.9 per cent in 1959. And over the same period, the share of the national income that went to the whole lower half of the population dropped from 27 per cent to 23 per cent. It is certainly hard to talk about the abolition of the proletariat, or even of economic democratization, in reference to a society in which the whole poorer half of the population has been getting relatively poorer.

The same distribution tables also suggest what has actually occurred to give the illusion of social progress. The pattern is best described by comparing the proportions of the national income that went at five different dates to three fractions of the population: the rich, represented by the top tenth of all incomes; the middle class, represented by the next four tenths, taken together; the poor, represented by the lower half. (I should perhaps say that I am not suggesting that the terms "the rich," "the poor" and the "middle class" correspond to those fractions; I am merely using a convenient shorthand for three groups.)

In 1929, before the Depression and the New Deal, the top tenth received 39 per cent of the national income. The middle class got exactly the same share. And the poor got the rest: 22 per cent.

In 1941, after twelve years of massive unemployment, the poor's share had fallen still further, to 19 per cent. The share of the rich had also fallen, by five percentage points, to 34 per cent. The whole gain, at the expense of both rich and poor, had gone to the "middle class."

In 1945, after four decisive years of war, boom and full employment, the poor had . . . recovered to exactly the point where they stood before the Depression: 22 per cent. The rich had lost another five percentage points, to 29 per cent. The middle class took just short of half the national income: 49 per cent.

And in 1949 and 1959, the years of the Permanent Revolution and the Affluent Society? Nothing had changed. That was the remarkable thing. To be precise, the top tenth gained one percentage point in 1949 and had lost it again by 1959. The middle four tenths together dropped a point in 1949, and stayed on 48 per cent in 1959. The poor gained one point, moving to 23 per cent by 1959. That was all.

The fact that the distribution of income in America is not equal, and is not noticeably getting any more equal, is now generally accepted. In a study for the Joint Economic Committee of Congress published in 1972, Lester C. Thurow and Robert E. B. Lucas of M.I.T. showed that the distribution of income from 1947 to 1969 had remained approximately constant: "Everybody's income (male, female, majority, minority, rich and poor) had been rising at approximately the same rate, leaving their ratios unaffected." An analysis of the 1970 census data by Peter Henle, a Library of Congress statistician, reported what he called "a continuing slow trend towards inequality." The commonsense conclusion would seem to be that there has been essentially no change in the distribution of income in the United States since World War II.

There has been only one rather sharp change in the twentieth century. This was the gain made between 1929 and 1945 by the second and third tenths of the population at the expense of the first. Their combined share went up from 22.1 per cent in 1929 to 29 per cent in 1945 and has since remained roughly constant. The redistribution of wealth, then, such as it was, seems to have been over by 1945. And it was a redistribution not from the rich to the poor, but from the very best off to the next best off. The second and third tenths of the income scales at that time would have included some executives, managers, professionals, some higher-paid clerical workers, and the very best-paid craft and industrial workers in the strongest unions. A shift of 10 per cent of the national income in their direction scarcely constituted either the abolition of the proletariat or the coming of the middle class. Yet, by a kind of intellectual parallax error, that was how it was seen.

3

MARTIN LUTHER KING, JR. AND THE STRUGGLE FOR CIVIL RIGHTS

Perhaps no other figure was more closely identified with the civil rights movement in America than Martin Luther King, Jr. Most scholars argue that King, a charismatic leader and a spellbinding speaker, provided the movement with leadership and inspiration. His strategy of passive nonresistance created a vivid contrast between African-Americans demanding basic rights of citizenship and a repressive southern establishment employing high pressure hoses and snarling police dogs to retain their hold on power.

King emerged as a leader in the struggle for civil rights in December 1955 when he helped organize the Montgomery Bus Boycott. Over the next few years, as head of the Southern Christian Leadership Conference (SCLC), King brought his message of Christian love and nonviolence to many of the country's most racially divided cities. In 1963, his efforts in Birmingham, Alabama, nudged the Kennedy Administration into proposing legislation that resulted in the Civil Rights Act of 1964. Later that same year, King moved the nation with a stirring address before a quarter of a million people gathered near the Lincoln Memorial. "I have a dream that one day," he thundered, "the sons of former slaves and the sons of former slaveowners will . . . sit down together at the table of brotherhood. . . . I have a dream that one day . . .

little black boys and black girls will be able to join with little white boys and white girls as sisters and brothers."[1] The following year, he organized, but did not participate in, a march from Selma to Montgomery to present a petition of grievances to Alabama governor George Wallace. The ensuing violence aroused public support for passage of the Voting Right Act.

The brief selection from Taylor Branch's Pulitzer Prize winning book, *Parting the Waters*, conveys the power of King's rhetoric and captures his ability to sway an audience. Branch describes King's address in December 1955 to a gathering at the Dexter Baptist Church. The meeting, held days after Rosa Parks refused to offer her seat on a bus to a white man, set in motion the Montgomery Bus Boycott, a pivotal event in the development of the civil rights movement. Under King's leadership, Montgomery's African-Americans organized a massive and successful boycott of the city's segregated bus system.

Like Branch, the historian John Patrick Diggins contends that King was "the spiritual catalyst" of the civil rights movement. Diggins traces the influence of philosophy, the Christian gospel of social justice, and Gandhi's theory of civil disobedience on King's intellectual development. The result was an articulate and persuasive voice for African-Americans' freedom. King earned the respect of the African-American community and the admiration, and attention, of the international press.

Clayborne Carson suggests a much different interpretation. The emphasis on King's charisma and leadership, Carson contends, "conveys the misleading notion of a movement held together by spellbinding speeches and blind faith rather than by a complex blend of rational and emotional bonds." He suggests that the fight for civil rights was a mass movement where talented local leaders other than King played an important role. "If King had never lived, the black struggle would have followed a course of development similar to the one it did,"[2] he concluded.

[1]John Morton Blum, *Years of Discord: American Politics and Society, 1961–1974.* (New York: Norton, 1991), 118–19.

[2]Clayborne Carson, "Martin Luther King, Jr.: Charismatic Leadership in a Mass Struggle." *Journal of American History* 74. (September 1987), 449, 451.

Parting the Waters

TAYLOR BRANCH

Taylor Branch is a journalist and former staff member of the *Washing-ton Monthly*, *Harper's* and *Esquire*. His highly acclaimed book, which examined the civil rights movement from 1954 to '63, was awarded a Pulitzer Prize for history. What was it about King's style and rhetoric that made him such an effective speaker?

King stood silently for a moment. When he greeted the enormous crowd of strangers, who were packed in the balconies and aisles, peering in through the windows and upward from seats on the floor, he spoke in a deep voice, stressing his diction in a slow introductory cadence. "We are here this evening—for serious business," he said, in even pulses, rising and then falling in pitch. When he paused, only one or two "yes" responses came up from the crowd, and they were quiet ones. It was a throng of shouters, he could see, but they were waiting to see where he would take them. "We are here in a general sense, because first and foremost—we are American citizens—and we are determined to apply our citizenship—to the fullness of its means," he said. "But we are here in a specific sense—because of the bus situation in Montgomery." A general murmur of assent came back to him, and the pitch of King's voice rose gradually through short, quickened sentences. "The situation is not at all new. The problem has existed over endless years. Just the other day—just last Thursday to be exact—one of the finest citizens in Montgomery—not one of the finest Negro citizens—but one of the finest citizens in Montgomery—was taken from a bus—and carried to jail and arrested—because she refused to give up—to give her seat to a white person."

The crowd punctuated each pause with scattered "Yeses" and "Amens." They were with him in rhythm, but lagged slightly behind in enthusiasm. Then King spoke of the law, saying that the arrest was doubtful even under the segregation ordinances, because reserved Negro and white bus sections were not specified in them. "The law has never been clarified at that point," he said, drawing an emphatic "Hell, no" from one man in his audience. "And I think I speak with—with legal authority—not that I have any legal authority—but I think I speak with legal authority behind me—that the law—the ordinance— the city ordinance has never been totally clarified." This sentence marked King as a speaker who took care with distinctions, but it took the crowd nowhere. King returned to the special nature of Rosa Parks. "And since it had to happen, I'm happy it happened to a person like Mrs. Parks," he said, "for nobody can doubt the boundless outreach of her integrity. Nobody can doubt the height of her character, nobody can doubt the depth of her Christian commitment." That's right, a soft chorus answered. "And just because she refused to get up, she was arrested," King repeated. The crowd was stirring now, following King at the speed of a medium walk.

He paused slightly longer. "And you know, my friends, there comes a time," he cried, "when people get tired of being trampled over by the iron feet of oppression." A flock of "Yeses" was coming back at him when suddenly the individual responses dissolved into a rising cheer and applause exploded beneath the cheer—all within the space of a second. The startling noise rolled on and on, like a wave that refused to break, and just when it seemed that the roar must finally weaken, a wall of sound came in from the enormous crowd outdoors to push the volume still higher. Thunder seemed to be added to the lower register—the sound of feet stomping on the wooden floor—until the loudness became something that was not so much heard as it was sensed by vibrations in the lungs. The giant cloud of noise shook the building and refused to go away. One sentence had set it loose somehow, pushing the call-and-response of the Negro church service past the din of a political rally and on to something else that King had never known before. There was a rabbit of awesome proportions in those bushes. As the noise finally fell back, King's voice rose above it to fire again. "There comes a time, my friends, when people get tired of being thrown across the abyss of humiliation, where they experience the bleakness of nagging despair," he declared. "There comes a time when people get tired of being pushed out of the glittering sunlight of life's July, and left standing amidst the piercing chill of an Alpine November. There . . ." King was making a new run, but the crowd drowned him out. No one could tell whether the roar came in response to the nerve he had touched, or simply out of pride in a speaker from whose tongue such rhetoric rolled so easily. "We are here—we are here because we are tired now," King repeated.

Perhaps daunted by the power that was bursting forth from the crowd, King moved quickly to address the pitfalls of a boycott. "Now let us say that we are not here advocating violence," he said. "We have overcome that." A man in the crowd shouted, "Repeat that! Repeat that!" "I want it to be known throughout Montgomery and throughout this nation that we are Christian people," said King, putting three distinct syllables in "Christian." "The only weapon that we have in our hands this evening is the weapon of protest." There was a crisp shout of approval right on the beat of King's pause. He and the audience moved into a slow trot. "If we were incarcerated behind the iron curtains of a communistic nation—we couldn't do this. If we were trapped in the dungeon of a totalitarian regime—we couldn't do this. But the great glory of American democracy is the right to protest for right." When the shouts of approval died down, King rose up with his final reason to avoid violence, which was to distinguish themselves from their opponents in the Klan and the White Citizens Council. "There will be no crosses burned at any bus stops in Montgomery," he said. "There will be no white persons pulled out of their homes and taken out on some distant road and murdered. There will be nobody among us who will stand up and defy the Constitution of this nation."

King paused. The church was quiet but it was humming. "My friends," he said slowly, "I want it to be known—that we're going to work with grim and bold determination—to gain justice on the buses in this city. And we are not wrong. We are not wrong in what we are doing." There was a muffled shout of anticipation, as the crowd sensed that King was moving closer to the heart of his cause. "If we are wrong—the Supreme Court of this nation is wrong," King sang out. He was rocking now, his voice seeming to be at once deep and high-pitched. "If we are wrong—God Almighty is wrong!" he shouted, and the crowd seemed to explode a second time, as it had done when he said they were tired. Wave after wave of noise broke over them, cresting into the farthest reaches of the ceiling. They were far beyond Rosa Parks or the bus laws. King's last cry had fused blasphemy to the edge of his faith and the heart of theirs. The noise swelled until King cut through it to move past a point of unbearable tension. "If we are wrong—Jesus of Nazareth was merely a utopian dreamer and never came down to earth! If we are wrong—justice is a lie." This was too much. He had to wait some time before delivering his soaring conclusion, in a flight of anger mixed with rapture: "And we are determined here in Montgomery—to work and fight until justice runs down like water, and righteousness like a mighty stream!" The audience all but smothered this passage from Amos, the lowly herdsman prophet of Israel who, along with the priestly Isaiah, was King's favorite biblical authority on justice.

He backed off the emotion to speak of the need for unity, the dignity of protest, the historical precedent of the labor movement. Comparatively speaking, his subject matter was mundane, but the crowd stayed with him even through paraphrases of abstruse points from Niebuhr. "And I want to tell you this evening that it is not enough for us to talk about love," he said. "Love is one of the pinnacle parts of the Christian faith. There is another side called justice. And justice is really love in calculation. Justice is love correcting that which would work against love." He said that God was not just the God of love: "He's also the God that standeth before the nations and says, 'Be still and know that I am God—and if you don't obey Me I'm gonna break the backbone of your power—and cast you out of the arms of your international and national relationships.'" Shouts and claps continued at a steady rhythm as King's audacity overflowed. "Standing beside love is always justice," he said. "Not only are we using the tools of persuasion—but we've got to use the tools of coercion." He called again for unity. For working together. He appealed to history, summoning his listeners to behave so that sages of the future would look back at the Negroes of Montgomery and say they were "a people who had the moral courage to stand up for their rights." He said they could do that. "God grant that we will do it before it's too late." Someone said, "Oh, yes." And King said, "As we proceed with our program—let us think on these things."

The crowd retreated into stunned silence as he stepped away from the pulpit. The ending was so abrupt, so anticlimactic. The crowd had been waiting for him to reach for the heights a third time at his conclusion, following the rules of oratory. A few seconds passed before memory and spirit overtook disappointment. The applause continued as King made his way out of the church, with people reaching to touch him. Dexter members marveled, having never seen King let loose like that. Abernathy remained behind, reading negotiating demands from the pulpit. The boycott was on. King would work on his timing, but his oratory had just made him forever a public person. In the few short minutes of his first political address, a power of communion emerged from him that would speak inexorably to strangers who would both love and revile him, like all prophets. He was twenty-six, and had not quite twelve years and four months to live.

The Philosopher King

JOHN PATRICK DIGGINS

John Patrick Diggins is professor of history at the City University of New York Graduate Center and the author of a number of books about American intellectual and political history. He views King as a formidable intellectual figure who was influenced by a wide range of thinkers, including progressive intellectuals such as Walter Rauschen-busch, the Protestant theologian Reinhold Niebuhr, and the Indian leader Mahatma Gandhi. What were the central tenets of King's philosophy? Why was his strategy appropriate for the early phase of the civil rights struggle?

Most revolutions begin in mass protest and passion; the civil rights movement of the fifties began with a single gesture of exhaustion. On the evening of December 1, 1955, Mrs. Rosa Parks, a neatly dressed, middle-aged black woman, was riding home on a Montgomery, Alabama bus, seated behind the section for "Whites Only." She held a shopping-bag full of groceries on her lap. When two white passengers got on and saw all the seats in the white section occupied, the driver announced, "Niggers move back," ordering the blacks to give up their seats as prescribed by law. Three black passengers got up and and stood at the back of the crowded bus. Rosa Parks stayed in her seat. The driver, grumbling under his breath, pulled over to the curb, set the brakes, rose from his seat, and with a few steps stood above her. "I said to move back, you hear?" Everyone on the packed bus fell into complete silence; no one moved, especially Mrs. Parks, who continued to look out the window, refusing to even acknowl-edge the driver's presence. He waited; the passengers listened and watched for even a gesture of a reply. He repeated his order; she continued to stare into the darkness of the night. No one in the bus that evening realized they were witnessing a historic moment that would change the course of modern American history. Not even Mrs. Parks, who later stated that she was simply too tired and "bone weary" to move to the back.

But Mrs. Parks had been working with E. D. Nixon, president of the Alabama NAACP [National Association for the Advancement of Colored People] and who had earlier worked with A. Philip Randolph planning the March-on-Washington during the war. When she called him from jail that evening, he phoned Clifford Durr about bail and legal advice. Clifford and Virginia Durr were members of a small group of southern white liberals who worked with black leaders on the Alabama Council on Human Relations to find ways to improve the South's racial situation. Durr was a distinguished lawyer who had once worked in New Deal agencies and left government in protest of Truman's loyalty program. He suggested challenging the constitutionality of Alabama's segregated public transportation services. Nixon realized such an effort would require the full backing of Montgomery's black community. He then approached the Reverend Ralph Abernathy, a young, militant Baptist minister, and together they planned a bus boycott on the day that Mrs. Parks had to appear in court. It was a risky tactic, for almost all black workers in the city had to use public transportation to get to their jobs. To reach as many neighborhoods as possible and assure the full cooperation of all blacks, Abernathy called Rev. Martin Luther King, Jr., the young new pastor of the Dexter Avenue Baptist Church. On the day of the boycott King and his wife Coretta were up before dawn to check bus stops to see how many blacks were aboard. They felt they could expect no more than 60 percent to honor the boycott, but that would be a sufficient threat to Montgomery's transportation revenue. On a regular day the early buses would be jammed with black domestic workers on their way to wealthy white residential districts. The day of the boycott, the first bus arrived empty; so, too, the second; the third had two passengers, both white. As the morning wore on, those on the boycott planning commission saw a sight that surpassed all expectations: young black students thumbing rides, cars overloaded with hitchhikers, older black students cheerfully walking, a few using horse-drawn buggies, and at least one seen riding a mule. Even those who had to trek six miles to work sang as they walked along. "A miracle had taken place," King later wrote in *Stride Toward Freedom*. "The once dormant and quiescent Negro community was now fully awake."

That evening a mass meeting took place at the Holt Street Baptist Church. It was here that King, then only twenty-seven and unknown to the community and America at large, entered the pages of history. Montgomery's black leaders had sensed King's genius for pulpit oratory and late in the day they asked him to deliver the evening's sermon. Although unprepared, King rose to the occasion. He aroused the audience by shouting: "We are tired! Tired of being segregated and humiliated!" Then he led them back to reflection by calmly reminding them: "Once again we must hear the words of Jesus: 'Love your enemies. Bless them that curse you. Pray for them that despitefully use you.' If we fail to do this, our protest will end up as a meaningless drama on the stage of history." The conclusion was a perforation of duty and destiny:

> If you protest courageously, and yet with dignity and Christian love, future historians will say, 'There lived a great people—a black people—who injected new meaning and dignity into the veins of civilization.' This is our challenge and our overwhelming responsibility.

The audience rose, applauding, cheering, with hosannas of "Amen, Brother, Amen." Everyone understood why the boycott must be continued; no one present could forget the impact King had made upon their lives. One elderly woman later recalled that she "saw angels standing all around him when he finished, and they were lifting him up on their wings."

The young man who would go on to become the spiritual catalyst of the civil rights movement, a Nobel Prize winner, a symbol of courage to the sixties generation, and ultimately, the victim of an assassin's bullet, was born in Atlanta, Georgia, in 1929. His father, Martin Luther King, Sr., was the respected pastor of the prestigious and well-endowed Ebenezer Baptist Church. Although raised in a comfortable middle-class neighborhood, young Martin knew the meaning of racism. A friend on the block was told not to play with him because he was black and once a woman in the department store suddenly slapped his face. "The little nigger stepped on my foot," she complained. He was a precocious, gifted student, always reading and distracting his parents with a battery of questions. The sight of black unemployed workers standing in line in tattered clothes during the depression saddened him. Assured of his own meals, he wondered if there were children who would have enough to eat. The sight of racial cruelty was worse. When he saw police brutalizing black children or witnessed night-riding Klansmen clubbing his people in the streets, he struggled to control his rage and obey the commandments. "How can I love a race of people who hate me?" he asked. Even as a youth King took it upon himself to bear the crushing weight of guilt for both the white man's deeds and the black man's thoughts.

When he was fifteen, King attended Morehouse College, a segregated liberal arts school affiliated with Atlanta University. Upon graduation he chose not to follow his father's advice and go directly into the ministry. Instead he went to Crozer Theological Seminary in Pennsylvania and received a Bachelor of Divinity degree, graduating first in his class. In 1955 he earned a Ph.D. at Boston University, where he also met his future wife Coretta Scott, a beautiful, talented singer who had been training at the New England Conservatory of Music. Coretta originally wanted to remain in Boston, but she did not hesitate to support her husband's sense of moral duty at the expense of her own career so he could return to the racially tense South.

School for King was not simply an accumulation of degrees and credentials but a voyage of discovery into two fields that became his daily passion: religion and philosophy. He undertook an omnivorous, systematic inquiry into Plato, Rousseau, Hobbes, Locke, Nietzsche, and Kierkegaard. He attended seminars on personalism and existential philosophy and took survey courses on Hinduism and Islam. He wrote his doctoral dissertation on the contrasting theisms of Paul Tillich and Henry Nelson Wieman. Tillich was a monist who claimed God remained transcendent and beyond the things of the world; Wieman, a pluralist who believed in God's immanence and direct involvement in all worldly things. King thoughtfully sought to synthesize both. He wanted to preserve the need for unity from the relativistic threat of pluralism and the value of individuality from the all-absorbing oneness of monism. His professors were impressed with his probing, restless mind and looked forward to his career as a prominent scholar.

As much as King valued the life of the mind, the Christian gospel of social justice was a higher imperative. In developing his own intellectual vision of politics, he drew on three distinct sources and managed to assimilate them into a coherent theory of action. The first was a book that had also influenced Progressive intellectuals after the turn of the century, *Christianity and the Social Crisis* by Walter Rauschenbusch. It called upon Christians to build a new social order by replacing capitalism and the laws of Darwin with the example of Christ and the laws of love, cooperation, and solidarity. But King's anticapitalism never drove him to be tempted by the ideas of Marx, although the FBI suspected he was a communist and kept close surveillance of his personal life. His reading of Tillich's existential theology led him to conclude that communism was a "grand illusion," a false doctrine that denied man's spiritual nature, substituted for God the self-propelled movement of matter, and endowed history with its own redemptive power. King was equally skeptical of pacifism. Rauschenbusch had rejected the notion that man was the source of evil, and Christian pacifists like A.J. Muste carried the conviction of human innocence to the point of renouncing all uses of power to resolve problems. More and more King doubted that Christian love itself could effect social change or prevent human suffering. Slavery and the Holocaust were tragic reminders of the impotence of brotherly love. To overcome the dilemmas of Protestant liberalism King turned to a second source, Reinhold Niebuhr's *Moral Man and Immoral Society*, *The Irony of American History*, and *The Nature and Destiny of Man*. Niebuhr reminded King that Christian pacifists themselves were responsible for Nazism for refusing to take up arms against it. King also came to understand how man's sinful nature caused him to rationalize his own sinful deeds, the most conspicuous example being the American Founders' validation of slavery. Above all, King obtained from Niebuhr a vision of "the glaring reality of collective evil," the tendency of otherwise decent individuals to join groups and remain unaware of how their own egoistic and aggressive nature becomes magnified in group behavior. Through Niebuhr's writings King transformed himself from a Protestant moralist to a Christian "realist."

While making King aware of the reality of evil and the duty of using force to oppose it, Niebuhr's writings nevertheless were insufficient to meet the needs of black America. King knew from reading about Nat Turner's insurrection in 1831 that force and violence would be suicidal for blacks. He was far more impressed with Henry David Thoreau's dictum that small minorities, even "one honest man," could regenerate an entire society. But Thoreau's tactic of trying to change society by denouncing it and "washing" his hands of it did not make a difference, at least not politically. What was needed was not the pose of the alienated poet but an effective theory of civil disobedience. For this third source of inspiration King went outside America to learn from the life and writings of Mahatma Gandhi.

In the postwar years the dramatic Indian independence movement was led by a saintly person who challenged the moral imagination in an age of power politics. Trained as a lawyer, Gandhi chose to wear native loincloth, shawl, and sandals, fitting symbols of his belief in gentleness, persuasion, and the utmost simplicity of needs. Gandhi had learned from Thoreau the tactic of individual passive resistance to change the wrongs of society, but he transformed the lesson into an epic mass movement to purge British colonial power from India. When King first heard a lecturer explain Gandhi's idea of *satyagraha*—the "truth force" that reconciles love and power—he was spellbound. Through nonviolent strikes, boycotts, and protest marches Gandhi and his followers succeeded in winning their freedom from their oppressors. What moved King was not so much that Gandhi had won but how he had won. For Gandhi represented the first example in modern history of realizing political ends through spiritual means. King absorbed Gandhi's conviction that nonviolence implies the willingness to endure suffering without retaliation. He also shared Gandhi's conviction that the aim of nonviolence should not simply be to win victory or humiliate the opponent; instead, every effort must be made to reach the opponent's conscience and ultimately to try to achieve a reconciliation based on a new level of moral understanding. Thus Gandhi's Hindu idea of satyagraha reinforced King's interpretation of the Christian idea of agape—the love of all humanity as a single chain of brothers and sisters, the only chain that could withstand the ever-recurring forces of hatred.

During the bus boycott King preached his Gandhian inspired theory of civil disobedience to the Montgomery Improvement Association, which then set up workshops throughout the city on non-violence and direct action. Out of such efforts evolved the Southern Christian Leadership Conference (SCLC), organized in 1957 to work for black voting rights and school desegregation. Three other organizations promoted the civil rights movement in the fifties. The National Urban League, started decades earlier during the Progressive era, concentrated mainly on northern industrial cities and was of little help to southern blacks. The Congress of Racial Equality (CORE), which grew out of the prewar Fellowship of Reconciliation, combined Christian pacifism with Gandhian tactics but it, too, failed to penetrate into the deep South after the war. Meanwhile the NAACP had been fighting the cause through the courts, but when it won a legal victory, as in the *Brown* case [the landmark 1954 Supreme Court decision which outlawed the "separate but equal" doctrine], black America could not count on the president to implement it. Moral confrontation would have to supplant litigation. King and SCLC officials realized this when they finally obtained a meeting with President Eisenhower in June 1958. He was "surprised" to hear that respected black leaders had become impatient with the federal government. As the meeting broke up, Eisenhower passed by King and with the shrug of his shoulders sighed, "Reverend, there are so many problems . . . Lebanon, Algeria . . ."

Although King would become disgusted with the Eisenhower administration, his own movement had been picking up support since the Montgomery bus boycott, when he was indicted the following year for having hindered business without "just cause or legal excuse." King's arrest and trial had made the boycott front-page news and brought journalists from Europe and as far away as Taiwan, Japan, and the Phillipines. Reporters were delighted when King responded to the charge that he was a communist by giving an erudite lecture on Marx, Engels, Hegel, and Feuerbach and then explained why he preferred theological existentialism to dialectical materialism. Busily taking notes, reporters were impressed listening to an activist who could be as profound as he was persuasive. An intellectual's intellectual, he knew more about communism than most members of the Communist party.

The Montgomery boycott succeeded in integrating the bus service, but all other public institutions, including schools, remained segregated. The same resistance prevailed throughout the deep South. Autherine Lucy, a black coed, tried to enter the University of Alabama and was almost murdered by white students. In Birmingham, Alabama, Nat King Cole, the famous black singer, was attacked and beaten while singing from the stage of the city auditorium. Afterwards, the same gang of whites jumped a black youth on the street and mutilated his genitals. The mob lynching of fourteen-year-old Emmet Till in Mississippi in 1955 shocked the nation. King himself received threatening phone calls, hate mail from the KKK, was stabbed in the chest by a deranged woman, and had his house bombed. Yet like Gandhi King never lost faith in nonviolence, and like Abraham Lincoln he sensed that his political mission might result in his own fatality. "Lord, I hope no one will have to die as a result of our struggle for freedom here in Montgomery," he said. "But if anyone has to die, let it be me." After his house was bombed, he assured his followers on the street outside that his wife and children were safe. He then stated: "If I had to die tomorrow morning, I would die happy—because I've been to the mountaintop, and I've seen the Promised Land."

The civil rights movement that Martin Luther King, Jr., inspired in the fifties would realize many of its goals the following decade and after his assassination, on April 4, 1968, America would celebrate his birthday along with Washington's and Lincoln's. King always felt uncomfortable when some of his followers referred to him as a savior or the Messiah. Yet he was a spiritual force who changed the hearts and minds of black and white Americans alike, if only by making the latter feel guilty and the former proud. "We got our heads up now," said a black janitor in Montgomery, "and we won't ever bow down again—no, sir—except before God."

The Limits of Charisma

CLAYBORNE CARSON

Clayborne Carson is associate professor of history at Stanford University, senior editor, and director of the Martin Luther King, Jr., Papers Project. Why does Carson believe that scholars have given King too much credit for his leadership in the civil rights struggle? Does he suggest an alternative view?

The legislation to establish Martin Luther King, Jr.'s birthday as a federal holiday provided official recognition of King's greatness, but it remains the responsibility of those of us who study and carry on King's work to define his historical significance. Rather than engaging in officially approved nostalgia, our rememberance of King should reflect the reality of his complex and multifaceted life. Biographers, theologians, political scientists, sociologists, social psychologists, and historians have given us a sizable literature of King's place in the Afro-American protest tradition, his role in the modern black freedom struggle, and his eclectic ideas regarding nonviolent activism. Although King scholars may benefit from and may stimulate the popular interest in King generated by the national holiday, many will find themselves uneasy participants in annual observances to honor an innocuous, carefully cultivated image of King as a black heroic figure.

The King depicted in serious scholarly works is far too interesting to be encased in such a didactic legend. King was a controversial leader who challenged authority and who once applauded what he called "creative maladjusted nonconformity."[1] He should not be transformed into a simplistic image designed to offend no one—a black counterpart to the static, heroic myths that have embalmed George Washington as the Father of His Country and Abraham Lincoln as the Great Emancipator.

One aspect of the emerging King myth has been the depiction of him in the mass media, not only as the preeminent leader of the civil rights movement, but also as the initiator and sole indispensible element in the southern black struggles of the 1950s and 1960s. As in other historical myths, a Great Man is seen as the decisive factor in the process of social change, and the unique qualities of a leader are used to explain major historical events. The King myth departs from historical reality because it attributes too much to King's exceptional qualities as a leader and too little to the impersonal, large-scale social factors that made it possible for King to display his singular abilities on a national stage. Because the myth emphasizes the individual at the expense of the black movement, it not only exaggerates King's historical importance but also distorts his actual, considerable contribution to the movement.

A major example of this distortion has been the tendency to see King as a charismatic figure who single-handedly directed the course of the civil rights movement through the force of his oratory. The charismatic label, however, does not adequately define King's role in the southern black struggle. The term *charisma* has traditionally been used to describe the godlike, magical qualities possessed by certain leaders. Connotations of the term have changed, of course, over the years. In our more secular age, it has lost many of its religious connotations and now refers to a wide range of leadership styles that involve the capacity to inspire—usually through oratory—emotional bonds between leaders and followers. Arguing that King was not a charismatic leader, in the broadest sense of the term, becomes somewhat akin to arguing that he was not a Christian, but emphasis on King's charisma obscures other important aspects of his role in the black movement. To be sure, King's oratory was exceptional and many people saw King as a divinely inspired leader, but King did not receive and did not want the kind of unquestioning support that is often associated with charismatic leaders.

---

[1] Martin Luther King, Jr., speech at the University of California, Berkeley, tape recording, May 17, 1967, Martin Luther King, Jr., Papers Project (Stanford University, Stanford, Calif.)

Movement activists instead saw him as the most prominent among many outstanding movement strategists, tacticians, ideologues, and institutional leaders.

King undoubtedly recognized that charisma was one of many leadership qualities at his disposal, but he also recognized that charisma was not a sufficient basis for leadership in a modern political movement enlisting numerous self-reliant leaders. Moreover, he rejected aspects of the charismatic model that conflicted with his sense of his own limitations. Rather than exhibiting unwavering confidence in his power and wisdom, King was a leader full of self-doubts, keenly aware of his own limitations and human weaknesses. He was at times reluctant to take on the responsibilities suddenly and unexpectedly thrust upon him. During the Montgomery bus boycott, for example, when he worried about threats to his life and to the lives of his wife and child, he was overcome with fear rather than confident and secure in his leadership role. He was able to carry on only after acquiring an enduring understanding of his dependence on a personal God who promised never to leave him alone.[2]

Moreover, emphasis on King's charisma conveys the misleading notion of a movement held together by spellbinding speeches and blind faith rather than by a complex blend of rational and emotional bonds. King's charisma did not place him above criticism. Indeed, he was never able to gain mass support for his notion of nonviolent struggle as a way of life, rather than simply a tactic. Instead of viewing himself as the embodiment of widely held Afro-American racial values, he willingly risked his popularity among blacks through his steadfast advocacy of nonviolent strategies to achieve radical social change.

He was a profound and provocative public speaker as well as an emotionally powerful one. Only those unfamiliar with the Afro-American clergy would assume that his oratorical skills were unique, but King set himself apart from other black preachers through his use of traditional black Christian idiom to advocate unconventional political ideas. Early in his life King became disillusioned with the unbridled emotionalism associated with his father's religious fundamentalism, and, as a thirteen year old, he questioned the bodily resurrection of Jesus in his Sunday

---

[2]Martin Luther King, Jr. described this episode, which occurred on the evening of January 27, 1956, in a remarkable speech delivered in September 1966. It is available on a phonograph record: "Dr. King's Entrance into the Civil Rights Movement," *Martin Luther King, Jr.: In Search of Freedom* (Mercury SR 61170).

school class.[3] His subsequent search for an intellectually satisfying religious faith conflicted with the emphasis on emotional expressiveness that pervades evangelical religion. His preaching manner was rooted in the traditions of the black church, while his subject matter, which often reflected his wide-ranging philosophical interests, distinguished him from other preachers who relied on rhetorical devices that manipulated the emotions of listeners. King used charisma as a tool for mobilizing black communities, but he always used it in the context of other forms of intellectual and political leadership suited to a movement containing many strong leaders.

Recently, scholars have begun to examine the black struggle as a locally based mass movement, rather than simply a reform movement led by national civil rights leaders.[4] The new orientation in scholarship indicates that King's role was different from that suggested in King-centered biographies and journalistic accounts.[5] King was certainly not the only significant leader of the civil rights movement, for sustained protest movements arose in many southern communities in which King had little or no direct involvement.

In Montgomery, for example, local black leaders such as E. D. Nixon, Rosa Parks, and Jo Ann Robinson started the bus boycott before King became the leader of the Montgomery Improvement Association. Thus, although King inspired blacks in Montgomery and black residents recognized that they were fortunate to have such a spokesperson, talented local leaders other than King played decisive roles in initiating and sustaining the boycott movement.

---

[3]Martin Luther King, Jr. "An Autobiography of Religious Development," [c. 1950], Martin Luther King, Jr., Papers (Mugar Library, Boston University). In this paper, written for a college class, King commented: "I guess I accepted Biblical studies uncritically until I was about twelve years old. But this uncritical attitude could not last long, for it was contrary to the very nature of my being."

[4]The new orientation is evident in William H. Chafe, *Civilities and Civil Rights: Greensboro, North Carolina and the Black Struggle for Equality* (New York, 1980); David R. Colburn, *Racial Change and Community Crisis St. Augustine, Florida, 1877–1980* (New York, 1985); Robert J. Norrell, *Reaping the Whirlwind: The Civil Rights Movement in Tuskegee* (New York, 1985); and John R. Salter, *Jackson, Mississippi: An American Chronicle of Struggle and Schism* (Hicksville, N.Y. 1979).

[5]The tendency to view the struggle from King's perspective is evident in the most thoroughly researched of the King biographies, despite the fact that the book concludes with Ella Baker's assessment: "The movement made Martin rather than Martin making the movement." See David J. Garrow, *Bearing the Cross: Martin Luther King, Jr. and the Southern Christian Leadership Conference* (New York, 1986), esp. 625. See also David L. Lewis, *King A Biography* (Urbana, 1978); Stephen B. Oates, *Let the Trumpet Sound* (New York, 1982); and Adam Fairclough, *To Redeem the Soul of America: The Southern Christian Leadership Conference and Martin Luther King, Jr.* (Athens, 1987).

Similarly, the black students who initiated the 1960 lunch counter sit-ins admired King, but they did not wait for him to act before launching their own movement. The sit-in leaders who founded the Student Nonviolent Coordinating Committee (SNCC) became increasingly critical of King's leadership style, linking it to the feelings of dependency that often characterize the followers of charismatic leaders.[6] The essense of SNCC's approach to community organizing was to instill in local residents the confidence that they could lead their own struggles. A SNCC organizer failed if local residents became dependent on his or her presence; as the organizers put it, their job was to work themselves out of a job. Though King influenced the struggles that took place in the Black Belt regions of Mississippi, Alabama, and Georgia, those movements were also guided by self-reliant local leaders who occasionally called on King's oratorical skills to galvanize black protestors at mass meetings while refusing to depend on his presence.

If King had never lived, the black struggle would have followed a course of development similar to the one it did. The Montgomery bus boycott would have occurred, because King did not initiate it. Black students probably would have rebelled—even without King as a role model—for they had sources of tactical and ideological inspiration besides King. Mass activism in southern cities and voting rights efforts in the deep South were outgrowths of large-scale social and political forces, rather than simply consequences of the actions of a single leader. Though perhaps not as quickly and certainly not as peacefully nor with as universal a significance, the black movement would probably have achieved its major legislative victories without King's leadership, for the southern Jim Crow system was a regional anachronism, and the forces that undermined it were inexorable.

To what extent, then, did King's presence affect the movement? Answering that question requires us to look beyond the usual portrayal of the black struggle. Rather than seeing an amorphous mass of discontented blacks acting out strategies determined by a small group of leaders, we would recognize King as a major example of the local black leadership that emerged as black communities mobilized for sustained struggles. If not as dominant a figure as sometimes portrayed, the historical King was nevertheless a remarkable leader who acquired the respect and support of self-confident, grass-roots leaders, some of whom possessed charismatic

[6]See Clayborne Carson, *In Struggle: SNCC and the Black Awakening of the 1960s* (Cambridge, Mass., 1981); and Howard Zinn, *SNCC: The New Abolitionists* (Boston, 1965).

qualities of their own. Directing attention to the other leaders who initiated and emerged from those struggles should not detract from our conception of King's historical significance; such movement-oriented research reveals King as a leader who stood out in a forest of tall trees.

King's major public speeches—particularly the "I Have a Dream" speech—have received much attention, but his exemplary qualities were also displayed in countless strategy sessions with other activists and in meetings with government officials. King's success as a leader was based on his intellectual and moral cogency and his skill as a conciliator among movement activists who refused to be simply King's "followers" or "lieutenants."

The success of the black movement required the mobilization of black communities as well as the transformation of attitudes in the surrounding society, and King's wide range of skills and attributes prepared him to meet the internal as well as the external demands of the movement. King understood the black world from a privileged position, having grown up in a stable family within a major black urban community; yet he also learned how to speak persuasively to the surrounding white world. Alone among the major civil rights leaders of his time, King could not only articulate black concerns to white audiences, but could also mobilize blacks through his day-to-day involvement in black community institutions and through his access to the regional institutional network of the black church. His advocacy of nonviolent activism gave the black movement invaluable positive press coverage, but his effectiveness as a protest leader derived mainly from his ability to mobilize black community resources.

Analyses of the southern movement that emphasize its nonrational aspects and expressive functions over its political character explain the black struggle as an emotional outburst by discontented blacks, rather than recognizing that the movement's strength and durability came from its mobilization of black community institutions, financial resources, and grass-roots leaders.[7] The values of southern blacks were profoundly and permanently transformed not only by King, but also by involvement in sustained protest activity and community-organizing efforts, through thousands of mass meetings, workshops, citizenship classes, freedom schools, and informal discussions. Rather than merely

---

[7]For incisive critiques of traditional psychological and sociological analyses of the modern black struggle, see Doug McAdam, *Political Process and the Development of Black Insurgency, 1930–1970* (Chicago, 1982); and Aldon D. Morris, *Origins of the Civil Rights Movement: Black Communities Organizing for Change* (New York, 1984).

accepting guidance from above, southern blacks were resocialized as a result of their movement experiences.

Although the literature of the black struggle has traditionally paid little attention to the intellectual content of black politics, movement activists of the 1960s made a profound, though often ignored, contribution to political thinking. King may have been born with rare potential, but his most significant leadership attributes were related to his immersion in, and contribution to, the intellectual ferment that has always been an essential part of Afro-American freedom struggles. Those who have written about King have too often assumed that his most important ideas were derived from outside the black struggle—from his academic training, his philosophical readings, or his acquaintance with Gandhian ideas. Scholars are only beginning to recognize the extent to which his attitudes and those of many other activists, white and black, were transformed through their involvement in a movement in which ideas disseminated from the bottom up as well as from the top down.

Although my assessment of King's role in the black struggles of his time reduces him to human scale, it also increases the possibility that others may recognize his qualities in themselves. Idolizing King lessens one's ability to exhibit some of his best attributes or, worse, encourages one to become a debunker, emphasizing King's flaws in order to lessen the inclination to exhibit his virtues. King himself undoubtedly feared that some who admired him would place too much faith in his ability to offer guidance and to overcome resistance, for he often publicly acknowledged his own limitations and mortality. Near the end of his life, King expressed his certainty that black people would reach the Promised Land whether or not he was with them. His faith was based on an awareness of the qualities that he knew he shared with all people. When he suggested his own epitaph, he asked not to be remembered for his exceptional achievements—his Nobel Prize and other awards, his academic accomplishments; instead, he wanted to be remembered for giving his life to serve others, for trying to be right on the war question, for trying to feed the hungry and clothe the naked, for trying to love and serve humanity. "I want you to say that I tried to love and serve humanity."[8] Those aspects of King's life did not require charisma or other superhuman abilities.

If King were alive today, he would doubtless encourage those who celebrate his life to recognize their responsibility to struggle as he did

---

[8]James M. Washington, ed., *A Testament of Hope: The Essential Writings of Martin Luther King, Jr.* (San Francisco, 1986), 267.

for a more just and peaceful world. He would prefer that the black movement be remembered not only as the scene of his own achievements, but also as a setting that brought out extraordinary qualities in many people. If he were to return, his oratory would be unsettling and intellectually challenging rather than remembered diction and cadences. He would probably be the unpopular social critic he was on the eve of the Poor People's Campaign rather than the object of national homage he became after his death. His basic message would be the same as it was when he was alive, for he did not bend with the changing political winds. He would talk of ending poverty and war and of building a just social order that would avoid the pitfalls of competitive capitalism and repressive communism. He would give scant comfort to those who condition their activism upon the appearance of another King, for he recognized the extent to which he was a product of the movement that called him to leadership.

The notion that appearances by Great Men (or Great Women) are necessary preconditions for the emergence of major movements for social changes reflects not only a poor understanding of history, but also a pessimistic view of the possibilities for future social change. Waiting for the Messiah is a human weakness that is unlikely to be rewarded more than once in a millenium. Studies of King's life offer support for an alternative optimistic belief that ordinary people can collectively improve their lives. Such studies demonstrate the capacity of social movements to transform participants for the better and to create leaders worthy of their followers.

4

THE WOMEN'S MOVEMENT

Women have been protesting their second-class status since the beginning of the American republic. The 1920 ratification of the Nineteenth Amendment to the Constitution, giving women the right to vote, seemed to guarantee an early end to the struggle for equal rights for women. Yet events of the next twenty-five years betrayed the promise of the first two decades of the twentieth century. Although World War II saw new job opportunities for Rosie the Riveter and her sisters in work, the return of millions of soldiers after 1945 together with a society-wide longing for domestic peace and prosperity eroded most of the gains made by women during the preceding decade. When the pioneering working women of the twenties and thirties retired, they found themselves without successors as capable women dropped out of college to become full-time homemakers. With a Mrs. carrying more prestige than a MS, it is little wonder that few women with alternatives bucked the tide.

By 1960 when Betty Friedan began writing, fifteen years of enforced domesticity had taken its toll on American women. As much a clarion call as a heartfelt journal, Friedan's book helped begin a movement whose ramifications are still unsettled. While mothers responded to Friedan's words, their daughters, involved in the civil rights and anti-war movements, became radicalized by deeds. Treated as second-class citizens in other peoples' struggles, women began to realize the need for a specifically women's movement to attain equal pay for equal work and to end all other forms of discrimination.

The struggles of the women's movement achieved success in the Civil Rights Act of 1964 which forbade sexual discrimination. Laws like Title IX of the 1972 Education Amendments Act provided incentives for women's sports and affirmative action regulations insured that most institutions and organizations would have at least token female representation. Yet such victories came at a high price. Increasingly, as Carl Degler points out, gains made by women seemed to threaten the well-being of the family and raise the ire of those espousing "traditional" values. The failure of the Equal Rights Amendment to win ratification by the requisite number of state legislatures and the continued furor over abortion are two examples of the national turmoil both triggered and reflected by the women's movement.

The Problem That Has No Name

BETTY FRIEDAN

Very rarely does one book help ignite a movement. Just as *Uncle Tom's Cabin* both reflected and released emotions behind the abolitionist movement, Betty Friedan's *The Feminine Mystique* both mirrored and catalyzed the early women's movement. In this introductory chapter, she lays out the visceral feelings that led her to take up the pen. What factors influenced the intensive domesticity of the nineteen fifties? Why did women seem reluctant to challenge the status quo in that decade?

The problem lay buried, unspoken, for many years in the minds of American women. It was a strange stirring, a sense of dissatisfaction, a yearning that women suffered in the middle of the twentieth century in the United States. Each suburban wife struggled with it alone. As she made the beds, shopped for groceries, matched slipcover material, ate peanut butter sandwiches with her children, chauffeured Cub Scouts and Brownies, lay beside her husband at night—she was afraid to ask even of herself the silent question—"Is this all?"

For over fifteen years there was no word of this yearning in the millions of words written about women, for women, in all the columns, books and articles by experts telling women their role was to seek fulfillment as wives and mothers. Over and over women heard in voices of tradition and of Freudian sophistication that they could desire no greater destiny than to glory in their own femininity. Experts told them how to catch a man and keep him, how to breastfeed children and handle their toilet training, how to cope with sibling rivalry and adolescent rebellion; how to buy a dishwasher, bake bread, cook gourmet snails, and build a swimming pool with their own hands; how to dress, look, and act more feminine and make marriage more exciting; how to keep their husbands from dying young and their sons from growing into delinquents. They were taught to pity the neurotic, unfeminine, unhappy women who wanted to be poets or physicists or presidents. They learned that truly feminine women do not want careers, higher education, political rights—the independence and the opportunities that the old-fashioned feminists fought for. Some women, in their forties and fifties, still remembered painfully giving up those dreams, but most of the younger women no longer even thought about them. A thousand expert voices applauded their femininity, their adjustment, their new maturity. All they had to do was devote their lives from earliest girlhood to finding a husband and bearing children.

By the end of the nineteen-fifties, the average marriage age of women in America dropped to 20, and was still dropping, into the teens. Fourteen million girls were engaged by 17. The proportion of women attending college in comparison with men dropped from 47 per cent in 1920 to 35 per cent in 1958. A century earlier, women had fought for higher education; now girls went to college to get a husband. By the mid-fifties, 60 per cent dropped out of college to marry, or because they were afraid too much education would be a marriage bar. Colleges built dormitories for "married students," but the students were almost always the husbands. A new degree was instituted for the wives—"Ph.T." (Putting Husband Through).

Then American girls began getting married in high school. And the women's magazines, deploring the unhappy statistics about these young marriages, urged that courses on marriage, and marriage counselors, be installed in the high schools. Girls started going steady at twelve and thirteen, in junior high. Manufacturers put out brassieres with false bosoms of foam rubber for little girls of ten. And an advertisement for a child's dress, sizes 3–6x, in the *New York Times* in the fall of 1960, said: "She Too Can Join the Man-Trap Set."

By the end of the fifties, the United States birthrate was overtaking India's. The birth-control movement, renamed Planned Parenthood, was asked to find a method whereby women who had been advised that a third or fourth baby would be born dead or defective might have it anyhow. Statisticians were especially astounded at the fantastic increase in the number of babies among college women. Where once they had two children, now they had four, five, six. Women who had once wanted careers were now making careers out of having babies. So rejoiced *Life* magazine in a 1956 paean to the movement of American women back to the home.

In a New York hospital, a woman had a nervous breakdown when she found she could not breastfeed her baby. In other hospitals, women dying of cancer refused a drug which research had proved might save their lives: its side effects were said to be unfeminine. "If I have only one life, let me live it as a blonde," a larger-than-life-sized picture of a pretty, vacuous woman proclaimed from newspaper, magazine, and drugstore ads. And across America, three out of every ten women dyed their hair blonde. They ate a chalk called Metrecal, instead of food, to shrink to the size of the thin young models. Department-store buyers reported that American women, since 1939, had become three and four sizes smaller. "Women are out to fit the clothes, instead of vice-versa," one buyer said.

Interior decorators were designing kitchens with mosaic murals and original paintings, for kitchens were once again the center of women's lives. Home sewing became a million-dollar industry. Many women no longer left their homes, except to shop, chauffeur their children, or attend a social engagement with their husbands. Girls were growing up in America without ever having jobs outside the home. In the late fifties, a sociological phenomenon was suddenly remarked: a third of American women now worked, but most were no longer young and very few were pursuing careers. They were married women who held part-time jobs, selling or secretarial, to put their husbands through school, their sons through college, or to help pay the mortgage. Or they were widows supporting families. Fewer and fewer women were entering professional work. The shortages in the nursing, social work, and teaching professions caused crises in almost every American city. Concerned over the Soviet Union's lead in the space race, scientists noted that America's greatest source of unused brainpower was women. But girls would not study physics: it was "unfeminine." A girl refused a science fellowship at Johns Hopkins to take a job in a real-estate office. All she wanted, she said, was what every other American girl wanted—to get married, have four children and live in a nice house in a nice suburb.

The suburban housewife—she was the dream image of the young American women and the envy, it was said, of women all over the world. The American housewife—freed by science and labor-saving appliances from the drudgery, the dangers of childbirth and illnesses of her grandmother. She was healthy, beautiful, educated, concerned only about her husband, her children, her home. She had found true feminine fulfillment. As a housewife and mother, she was respected as a full and equal partner to man in his world. She was free to choose automobiles, clothes, appliances, supermarkets; she had everything that women ever dreamed of.

In the fifteen years after World War II, this mystique of feminine fulfillment became the cherished and self-perpetuating core of contemporary American culture. Millions of women lived their lives in the image of those pretty pictures of the American suburban housewife, kissing their husbands goodbye in front of the picture window, depositing their stationwagonsful of children at school, and smiling as they ran the new electric waxer over the spotless kitchen floor. They baked their own bread, sewed their own and their children's clothes, kept their new washing machines and dryers running all day. They changed the sheets on the beds twice a week instead of once, took the rug-hooking class in adult education, and pitied their poor frustrated mothers, who had dreamed of having a career. Their only dream was to be perfect wives and mothers; their highest ambition to have five children and a beautiful house, their only fight to get and keep their husbands. They had no thought for the unfeminine problems of the world outside the home; they wanted the men to make the major decisions. They gloried in their role as women, and wrote proudly on the census blank: "Occupation: housewife."

For over fifteen years, the words written for women, and the words women used when they talked to each other, while their husbands sat on the other side of the room and talked shop or politics or septic tanks, were about problems with their children, or how to keep their husbands happy, or improve their children's school, or cook chicken or make slipcovers. Nobody argued whether women were inferior or superior to men; they were simply different. Words like "emancipation" and "career" sounded strange and embarrassing; no one had used them for years. When a Frenchwoman named Simone de Beauvoir wrote a book called *The Second Sex*, an American critic commented that she obviously "didn't know what life was all about," and besides, she was talking about French women. The "woman problem" in America no longer existed.

If a woman had a problem in the 1950's and 1960's, she knew that something must be wrong with her marriage, or with herself. Other women were satisfied with their lives, she thought. What kind of a woman was she if she did not feel this mysterious fulfillment waxing the kitchen floor? She was so ashamed to admit her dissatisfaction that she never knew how many other women shared it. If she tried to tell her husband, he didn't understand what she was talking about. She did not really understand it herself. For over fifteen years women in America found it harder to talk about this problem than about sex. Even the psychoanalysts had no name for it. When a woman went to a psychiatrist for help, as many women did, she would say, "I'm so ashamed," or "I must be hopelessly neurotic." "I don't know what's wrong with women today," a suburban psychiatrist said uneasily. "I only know something is wrong because most of my patients happen to be women. And their problem isn't sexual." Most women with this problem did not go to see a psychoanalyst, however. "There's nothing wrong really," they kept telling themselves. "There isn't any problem."

But on an April morning in 1959, I heard a mother of four, having coffee with four other mothers in a suburban development fifteen miles from New York, say in a tone of quiet desperation, "the problem." And the others knew, without words, that she was not talking about a problem with her husband, or her children, or her home. Suddenly they realized they all shared the same problem, the problem that has no name. They began, hesitantly, to talk about it. Later, after they had picked up their children at nursery school and taken them home to nap, two of the women cried, in sheer relief, just to know they were not alone.

Gradually I came to realize that the problem that has no name was shared by countless women in America. As a magazine writer I often interviewed women about problems with their children, or their marriages, or their houses, or their communities. But after a while I began to recognize the telltale signs of this other problem. I saw the same signs in suburban ranch houses and split-levels on Long Island and in New Jersey and Westchester County; in colonial houses in a small Massachusetts town; on patios in Memphis, in suburban and city apartments; in living rooms in the Midwest. Sometimes I sensed the problem, not as a reporter, but as a suburban housewife, for during this time I was also bringing up my own three children in Rockland County, New York. I heard echoes of the problem in college dormitories and semiprivate maternity wards, at PTA meetings and luncheons of the League of Women Voters, at suburban cocktail parties, in station wagons waiting for trains, and in snatches of conversation overheard at Schrafft's. The groping words I heard from other women, on quiet afternoons when children were at school or on quiet evenings when husbands worked late, I think I understood first as a woman long before I understood their larger social and psychological implications.

Just what was this problem that has no name? What were the words women used when they tried to express it? Sometimes a woman would say "I feel empty somehow . . . incomplete." Or she would say, "I feel as if I don't exist." Sometimes she blotted out the feeling with a tranquilizer. Sometimes she thought the problem was with her husband, or her children, or that what she really needed was to redecorate her house, or move to a better neighborhood, or have an affair, or another baby. Sometimes, she went to a doctor with symptoms she could hardly describe: "A tired feeling . . . I get so angry with the children it scares me . . . I feel like crying without any reason." (A Cleveland doctor called it "the housewife's syndrome.") A number of women told me about great bleeding blisters that break out on their hands and arms. "I call it the housewife's blight," said a family doctor in Pennsylvania. "I see it so often lately in these young women with four, five and six children who bury themselves in their dishpans. But is isn't caused by detergent and it isn't cured by cortisone."

Sometimes a woman would tell me that the feeling gets so strong she runs out of the house and walks through the streets. Or she stays inside her house and cries. Or her children tell her a joke, and she doesn't laugh because she doesn't hear it. I talked to women who had spent years on the analyst's couch, working out their "adjustment to the feminine role," their blocks to "fulfillment as a wife and mother." But the desperate tone in these women's voices, and the look in their eyes, was the same as the tone and the look of other women, who were sure they had no problem, even though they did have a strange feeling of desperation.

A mother of four who left college at nineteen to get married told me:

> I've tried everything women are supposed to do—hobbies, gardening, pickling, canning, being very social with my neighbors, joining committees, running PTA teas. I can do it all, and I like it, but it doesn't leave you anything to think about—any feeling of who you are. I never had any career ambitions. All I wanted was to get married and have four children. I

love the kids and Bob and my home. There's no problem you can even put a name to. But I'm desperate. I begin to feel I have no personality. I'm a server of food and a putter-on of pants and a bedmaker, somebody who can be called on when you want something. But who am I?

A twenty-three-year-old mother in blue jeans said:

I ask myself why I'm so dissatisfied. I've got my health, fine children, a lovely new home, enough money. My husband has a real future as an electronics engineer. He doesn't have any of these feelings. He says maybe I need a vacation, let's go to New York for a weekend. But that isn't it. I always had this idea we should do everything together. I can't sit down and read a book alone. If the children are napping and I have one hour to myself I just walk through the house waiting for them to wake up. I don't make a move until I know where the rest of the crowd is going. It's as if ever since you were a little girl, there's always been somebody or something that will take care of your life: your parents, or college, or falling in love, or having a child, or moving to a new house. Then you wake up one morning and there's nothing to look forward to.

A young wife in a Long Island development said:

I seem to sleep so much. I don't know why I should be so tired. This house isn't nearly so hard to clean as the cold-water flat we had when I was working. The children are at school all day. It's not the work. I just don't feel alive.

In 1960, the problem that has no name burst like a boil through the image of the happy American housewife. In the television commercials the pretty housewives still beamed over their foaming dishpans and *Time's* cover story on "The Suburban Wife, an American Phenomenon" protested: "Having too good a time . . . to believe that they should be unhappy." But the actual unhappiness of the American housewife was suddenly being reported—from the *New York Times* and *Newsweek* to *Good Housekeeping* and CBS Television ("The Trapped Housewife"), although almost everybody who talked about it found some superficial reason to dismiss it. It was attributed to incompetent appliance repairmen (*New York Times*), or the distances children must be chauffeured in the suburbs (*Time*), or too much PTA (*Redbook*). Some said it was the old problem—education: more and more women had education, which naturally made them unhappy in their role as housewives. "The road from Freud to Frigidaire, from Sophocles to

Spock, has turned out to be a bumpy one," reported the *New York Times* (June 28, 1960). "Many young women—certainly not all—whose education plunged them into a world of ideas feel stifled in their homes. They find their routine lives out of joint with their training. Like shut-ins, they feel left out. In the last year, the problem of the educated housewife has provided the meat of dozens of speeches made by troubled presidents of women's colleges who maintain, in the face of complaints, that sixteen years of academic training is realistic preparation for wifehood and motherhood."

There was much sympathy for the educated housewife. ("Like a two-headed schizophrenic . . . once she wrote a paper on the Graveyard poets; now she writes notes to the milkman. Once she determined the boiling point of sulphuric acid; now she determines her boiling point with the overdue repairman. . . . The housewife often is reduced to screams and tears. . . . No one, it seems, is appreciative, least of all herself, of the kind of person she becomes in the process of turning from poetess into shrew.")

Home economists suggested more realistic preparation for housewives, such as high-school workshops in home appliances. College educators suggested more discussion groups on home management and the family, to prepare women for the adjustment to domestic life. A spate of articles appeared in the mass magazines offering "Fifty-eight Ways to Make Your Marriage More Exciting." No month went by without a new book by a psychiatrist or sexologist offering technical advice on finding greater fulfillment through sex.

A male humorist joked in *Harper's Bazaar* (July, 1960) that the problem could be solved by taking away woman's right to vote. ("In the pre-19th Amendment era, the American woman was placid, sheltered and sure of her role in American society. She left all the political decisions to her husband and he, in turn left all the family decisions to her. Today a woman has to make both the family *and* the political decisions, and it's too much for her.")

A number of educators suggested seriously that women no longer be admitted to the four-year colleges and universities; in the growing college crisis, the education which girls could not use as housewives was more urgently needed than ever by boys to do the work of the atomic age.

The problem was also dismissed with drastic solutions no one could take seriously. (A woman writer proposed in *Harper's* that women be drafted for compulsory service as nurses' aides and baby-sitters.) And it was smoothed over with the age-old panaceas: "love is their answer," "the only answer is inner help," "the secret of completeness—children," "a private means of intellectual fulfillment," "to cure this toothache of the spirit—the simple formula of handing one's self and one's will over to God."

The problem was dismissed by telling the housewife she doesn't realize how lucky she is—her own boss, no time clock, no junior executive gunning for her job. What if she isn't happy—does she think men are happy in this world? Does she really, secretly, still want to be a man? Doesn't she know yet how lucky she is to be a woman?

The problem was also, and finally, dismissed by shrugging that there are no solutions: this is what being a woman means, and what is wrong with American women that they can't accept their role gracefully? As *Newsweek* put it (March 7, 1960):

> She is dissatisfied with a lot that women of other lands can only dream of. Her discontent is deep, pervasive, and impervious to the superficial remedies which are offered at every hand. . . . An army of professional explorers have already charted the major sources of trouble. . . . From the beginning of time, the female cycle has defined and confined woman's role. As Freud was credited with saying: "Anatomy is destiny." Though no group of women has ever pushed these natural restrictions as far as the American wife, it seems that she still cannot accept them with good grace. . . . A young mother with a beautiful family, charm, talent and brains is apt to dismiss her role apologetically. "What do I do?" you hear her say. "Why nothing. I'm just a housewife." A good education, it seems, has given this paragon among women an understanding of the value of everything except her own worth . . .

And so she must accept the fact that "American women's unhappiness is merely the most recently won of women's rights," and adjust and say with the happy housewife found by *Newsweek:* "We ought to salute the wonderful freedom we all have and be proud of our lives today. I have had college and I've worked, but being a housewife is the most rewarding and satisfying role. . . . My mother was never included in my father's business affairs . . . she couldn't get out of the house and away from us children. But I am an equal to my husband; I can go along with him on business trips and to social business affairs."

The alternative offered was a choice that few women would contemplate. In the sympathetic words of the *New York Times:* "All admit to being deeply frustrated at times by the lack of privacy, the physical burden, the routine of family life, the confinement of it. However, none would give up her home and family if she had the choice to make again." *Redbook* commented: "Few women would want to thumb their noses at husbands, children and community and go off on their own. Those who do may be talented individuals, but they rarely are successful women."

The year American women's discontent boiled over, it was also reported (*Look*) that the more than 21,000,000 American women who are single, widowed, or divorced do not cease even after fifty their frenzied, desperate search for a man. And the search begins early—for seventy per cent of all American women now marry before they are twenty-four. A pretty twenty-five-year-old secretary took thirty-five different jobs in six months in the futile hope of finding a husband. Women were moving from one political club to another, taking evening courses in accounting or sailing, learning to play golf or ski, joining a number of churches in succession, going to bars alone, in their ceaseless search for a man.

Of the growing thousands of women currently getting private psychiatric help in the United States, the married ones were reported dissatisfied with their marriages, the unmarried ones suffering from anxiety and, finally, depression. Strangely, a number of psychiatrists stated that, in their experience, unmarried women patients were happier than married ones. So the door of all those pretty suburban houses opened a crack to permit a glimpse of uncounted thousands of American housewives who suffered alone from a problem that suddenly everyone was talking about, and beginning to take for granted, as one of those unreal problems in American life that can never be solved—like the hydrogen bomb. By 1962 the plight of the trapped American housewife had become a national parlor game. Whole issues of magazines, newspaper columns, books learned and frivolous, educational conferences and television panels were devoted to the problem.

Even so, most men, and some women, still did not know that this problem was real. But those who had faced it honestly knew that all the superficial remedies, the sympathetic advice, the scolding words and the cheering words were somehow drowning the problem in unreality. A bitter laugh was beginning to be heard from American women. They were admired, envied, pitied, theorized over until they were sick of it, offered drastic solutions or silly choices that no one could take seriously. They got all kinds of advice from the growing armies of marriage and child-guidance counselors, psychotherapists, and armchair psychologists, on how to adjust to their role as housewives. No other road to fulfillment was offered to American women in the middle of the twentieth century. Most adjusted to their role and suffered or ignored the problem that has no name. It can be less painful, for a woman, not to hear the strange, dissatisfied voice stirring within her.

The Promise of Education

BARBARA MILLER SOLOMON

Barbara Solomon, who taught at Harvard University until her retirement, has written the most comprehensive treatment of women and higher education in America. In this chapter, she summarizes the challenges faced by women seeking college and post-graduate education in the post-war period. What did writers in the immediate post-war era period think was the purpose of higher education for women? To what extent did such higher education necessarily undermine the nineteen fifties status quo?

In this chapter we will examine women's paths in higher education from World War II to the present. During this period women dealt with an array of conflicting demands that affected their aspirations in an accelerating, shifting sequence of events that finally produced an explosion and revitalized feminism. Thus, in the 1970s women of several generations initiated demands for female equality and challenged educational institutions to fulfill the promises of liberal education.

At the outset of this forty-year period sweeping changes in opportunities during World War II fed the educated woman's sense of new choices within her grasp, waiting to be seized. As earlier, women, when needed in the public sphere, received encouragement to enter "male" fields of training for future employment. For the short time of national emergency the curriculum provided women with opportunities that seemed to belie sex labels. Whereas women students in the 1930s rarely entered fields like engineering and the hard sciences, the war overturned this educational block at the training level. With coeducational schools lacking male students, professors paid more attention to talented women at the undergraduate and graduate levels in all fields. At women's colleges like Vassar the proportion of students majoring in the sciences peaked at 26 percent in the early 1940s; at Barnard women began to receive training in meteorology and electronics.

Even Harvard University started to open its doors to undergraduate women in 1943 through the new Harvard/Radcliffe agreement. In addition, two years later twelve women were admitted to the Medical School, and in the fall of 1950 a handful entered the Law School. Clearly the war-time crisis, in stimulating plans for future admission of women, also affirmed confidence in their abilities. Appropriately in these years of relative openness the United States Armed Services had offered women places in eight branches, although women had to meet somewhat higher admission standards than men.

All the advances enacted in World War II were real; but predictably at war's end both women's opportunities and interests diminished. Mabel Newcomer's evidence shows that the percentage of physics and chemistry majors at Vassar dropped by more than 50 percent in the decade following the war. Similarly across the nation fewer women received doctorates in physics. It was more common for the Vassar graduate to give up the possibility of a good research job or the pursuit of a Ph.D. if it appeared to threaten her chances of marrying. The rapid decline in numbers of candidates in the medical profession was striking: in 1949 women comprised 12 percent of medical school graduates; but by the mid-fifties the proportion had slid to 5 percent, even lower than that in 1941. Although the early 1940s were peak years for women's representation among academic personnel, the next twenty saw their decline, from 27.7 percent in 1940 to 24.5 percent in 1950, dropping even more—to 22 percent—by 1960. The postwar years thus became a time of reduced options and expectations; yet individuals who had been able to exploit the opportunities of the early forties had distinct advantages in sustaining or developing careers further. Some college graduates who got jobs during the war in banks or filled vacancies on newspapers managed to hold on to them afterward, even if they did not advance as swiftly as men. Professional women who had responsible positions in the armed forces continued in government, academia, or business.

Whatever impediments professional women—Ph.D.s, M.D.s, or L.L.D.s—experienced after the war, their situation was better than that of the most talented women in industry, where union rules and lower rates of peacetime production ousted almost all skilled workers. Yet Rosie the riveter, the doctor of philosophy, the lawyer, and the physician still had something fundamental in common: in peacetime American women lacked clout at the highest levels everywhere—in the industrial labor force, in academia, and in the professions. Only the fortunate were employed; many more found that returning veterans, who had priorities by law, regained old positions. Women did not begrudge the former soldiers, now mature men, their ambitions and special opportunities; few young women realized that their own access to undergraduate education and professional schools lessened as a result of the expanding opportunities for veterans. Due to a general acceptance of male priority, the memory of the versatilely employed woman soon faded as it had after World War I.

Women suffered a large setback when the operation of the GI bill reduced female access to higher education. Under the federal program the millions of veterans had an opportunity for further education. Governmental subsidies to the colleges ensured a warm welcome to the returning soldiers; even women's colleges, including Vassar, Finch, and Sarah Lawrence, admitted males. Men flooded campuses to take all kinds of degrees, especially at the well-known public and private schools. In 1947 veterans comprised 49 percent of the total college enrollment and 69 percent of college men. As a result of veterans' benefits black colleges found males temporarily outpacing females in enrollments by several thousands; at the end of the decade the 6,467 bachelor's degrees earned by men constituted almost half of the 13,198 conferred. Women as veterans were among the eligible everywhere, but they represented less than 3 percent of those in the armed services. By 1956, 2,232,000 veterans had been educated under the GI bill, of whom 64,728 were women.

During their takeover veterans changed the character of higher education and enhanced the larger public's respect for schooling. Intellectual excitement and the professional (or vocational) purpose of mature young men electrified the campuses. At least 20 percent of the veterans, among them some who were black, would not have attended college without this federal support. The development then of various educational institutions, including community colleges and adult education programs, would ultimately attract many more women; but in this critical period between 1945 and 1956, women as a group were handicapped by the male influx into academia.

Just as GIs transmitted their seriousness about the business of education, so they also established new patterns of collegiate domesticity; almost half the veterans returning to school were married. The presence of domestic couples on campuses was contagious, with female undergraduates seeking to "catch" a husband. To some the immediate goal of matrimony outstripped the value of a college degree. Although colleges increasingly permitted wives to enroll as undergraduates, those who were married (often to veterans) tended to leave school.

This pattern started during the war, when students took defense jobs instead of finishing college, with a resulting decline in female enrollments of 25,000 between 1940 and 1944. The trend accelerated in 1946 when increasing numbers of the undergraduate female student body dropped out to marry. If more young females seemed indifferent to higher aspirations then, their mood matched society's eroding expectations for them quite well.

Those who pursued serious academic studies, especially in relation to careers in the prestigious "male" fields of medicine, law, the ministry, or academia, took lonely paths. Graduate education became more competitive, due to the vast numbers of men entering and the priority given to veterans. Graduate women had to be far better qualified than men to gain admission; and married women desiring to enroll part-time found it very difficult. Women as potential graduate students and professional trainees often found themselves rejected, due in part to the discriminatory quotas favoring veterans. Although later studies blamed women for not pursuing professional goals, manifestly they had severely limited access to institutions in this period.

Nonetheless, the smaller percentages of women who obtained Ph.D.s in 1950 and 1960 (10–12 percent), as compared to 1930 (16-18 percent) need careful interpretation. Percentages declined, but absolute numbers increased. Similarly, at the undergraduate level, women students lost ground relative to men; the proportion of women among college students decreased from 47.3 percent in 1920 to 35.2 percent in 1958. Once again, however, in actual numbers women advanced. They received 55,000 of the B. A.s in 1930, and 139,000 in 1960; the number of M. A.s quadrupled, from less than 6,000 in 1930 to 24,000 in 1960; and the number of Ph.D.s tripled, from 350 in 1930 to 1,030 in 1960.

The postwar generations of college-educated women also became more diverse in religious and ethnic representation. By 1960 the enrollment included larger numbers of Catholics, Jews, and the smaller

Protestant sects. Nonetheless, this greater religious representation did not signify greater class diversity. Christopher Jencks and David Riesman, in generalizing on the post-college enrollments of both men and women, noted that, contrary to the authors' expectations, the increase among the upper-middle classes "seems to have been greater" than the increase in lower-middle and working-class enrollments. In applying this observation to women students it is assumed that female representation from poorer families remained even less; most parents were more disposed to make an educational investment in a son rather than a daughter, with the exception of black families.

Irrespective of social class, marital status, and economic need, the college woman made a swift transition from student to paid worker in the expanding economy of the 1950s and 1960s. Women had a substantial place in the labor force because there were more jobs than men could fill. By the mid-twentieth century women's participation belied or contradicted the stereotyped view of their functioning exclusively as wives and mothers. That educated women with or without children worked for most or a good part of their adult lives became increasingly the norm and not the exception, despite expectations to the contrary. Still the common belief held that collegiate instruction should somehow prepare women for female roles and foster their aspirations strictly within bounds. Wherever the potential diversity of women's lives became fulfilled, the liberal education of women became the main target of attack.

Women's liberal education in the late forties became the focus of a backlash in which the old disagreement over the purposes of educating women was rekindled. Fearful of the continuing changes in work patterns and in expectations of women trained during and after the war, educators, relying on studies in psychology from a Freudian perspective, again succumbed to curricular arguments for a feminine education. The proponents cited wartime and postwar surveys of college women to justify making liberal education for women different from that for men. Such studies reported confusion and discontent among many graduates; they felt unprepared for the overwhelming domesticity that they confronted after marriage. A 1942 study by Robert Foster and Pauline Park Wilson claimed to document attitudes of 1930s graduates regretting their lack of preparation for domestic roles. Such surveys gave further evidence that women in a wide spectrum of colleges wanted courses on family life. Both Willa Player's report (1948) on students of Bennett

College in 1947 and Jeanne Noble's study of black sorority women in 1953 showed that "preparation for marriage and family life was important." Although students when queried expressed interest in domestic courses, often their intention was to supplement, not to replace, regular academic subjects. In view of anticipated early matrimony it was reasonable for women to seek more information about marriage, birth control, and psychology; interestingly, their male classmates often joined them.

Overreacting educators interpreted these responses to mean that women wanted solely a domesticity for which higher education unfitted them. Lynn White, Mills's president, shrewdly exploited the results of the surveys to call for a "feminine" liberal education to counteract "our present peculiar habit" of educating our daughters "as if they were men." With a view reminiscent of nineteenth-century educator Catharine Beecher, White recommended enlarging the female professoriat for the education of women in their primary role, that of enriching home and community. Although he admitted that females needed to be prepared to hold jobs before marriage, he opposed their taking advanced degrees. White pontificated that feminine studies would include "the theory and preparation of a Basque paella, or a well-marinated shish kabob." Even anthropologist Margaret Mead, herself a professional and wife and mother, seemed to give support to White's views by asking: "Have we cut women off from their natural closeness to their children, taught them to look for a job instead of the touch of a child's hand, for status in a competitive world rather than a unique place by a glowing hearth?" Notions of domesticity with some variation intruded wherever women were educated. Even at Radcliffe, identified as a Bluestocking haven, the president, W. K. Jordan, informed entering freshmen throughout the fifties that their education would prepare them to be splendid wives and mothers, and their reward might be to marry Harvard men.

Though few educators, if asked directly, would have moved to the curricular extremes advocated by White, most felt obliged to review their own thinking on the purposes of educating women. The campaign for "feminine" education put the proponents of rigorous study in the arts and sciences on the defensive. Rarely did they examine the potentially radical implications of liberal education for women. An exception, Harold Taylor, president of Sarah Lawrence, stood out in declaring that education should help women "find their own fulfillment" without making their needs subservient to the "needs of men."

Renaissance scholar Rosemond Tuve, a professor at Connecticut College for Women, went further, stating that women were "never taught by this society to see that being a success as a woman is inextricably connected with being a success as a human being." Tuve knew the enemy: Lynn White's "feminine" curriculum and the early marriages that accompanied the education. She posed an essential question: Why should women be told that "they had to choose between marrying and caring intensely about scholarship?"

Too often educators made accommodations to the advocates of domesticity. Even those who objected to the closing off of careers for women expressed themselves with such restraint that real encouragement seemed wanting. Barnard's president Millicent McIntosh, for example, asserted that "a girl does not need courses in baby tending to prepare her for motherhood, but she does need a philosophy which does not belittle the home as a place unworthy of her best, and does not glorify the job as important beyond everything else." This answer, while upholding the liberal values in education, also upheld the domestic ones. McIntosh was not alone in giving ambiguous signals to students. Bryn Mawr's president Katharine McBride, a trained psychologist, believed in fundamental role differences for men and women but was also impressed with the range in abilities among women. This range, she wrote, should influence their training: "If women are to go beyond their function as wife and mother, then this fact of wide diversity has great significance for education." Who knew what McBride meant?

Barnard professor of sociology Mirra Komarovsky wrote more discerningly about the conflicts of undergraduate women dealing with two roles: first, the feminine, whatever the variants—whether the "good sport," the "glamour girl," the "young lady," or the "domestic home girl"—which were always described with reference to differences between men and women; and second, the so-called modern, which "demands of the woman much of the same virtues, patterns of behavior, and attitudes that it does of the men of a corresponding age." Neither role could be overlooked, and therein lay the dilemmas of the young, which Komarovsky analyzed very clearly.

It took intellectual courage to question the premises of "feminine" education. Its exponents were anti-feminists who rested their claims not only on the old religious beliefs about woman's place and her duties but also on the Freudian gospel that decreed anatomy as destiny for women. This so-called "scientific" rationale rendered public judgments against careers for women all the more powerful: An influential Freudian, Helene Deutsch, in her *The Psychology of Women* (1944) condemned "the more masculine women's interests which turned toward aims in the pursuit of which femininity is felt as troublesome and is rejected." Psychoanalyst Deutsch, in fact a devoted wife and mother, described the overwhelming conflicts of the professional mother: "After each success she achieves in her professional activity, instead of feeling satisfaction she is tormented by guilt feelings with regard to her children." In *Modern Woman: The Lost Sex* (1947), Ferdinand Lundberg and Maryna Farnham concluded that "contemporary women in large numbers are psychologically disordered" by the strivings to be both wife and mother and professional.

A working mother who escaped the guilt implicit in such analyses had still to answer to the popular child guidance expert Dr. Benjamin Spock, who in the fifties made child-centeredness basic to good family life. Mothers who adhered to his viewpoint took full responsibility for the successes and failures of children. At a time when motherhood might have been considered a part-time occupation—though a lifetime commitment—these combined influences demanded from women more than full-time attention to the young. Motherhood was the primary function that no real woman would deny; and in the fifties women felt the burden of demonstrating their fitness for the maternal role.

How were students to make choices given the array of advice? One student editor commented on the difficult choices: "The future of the Barnard graduate may be a professional or more routine career, marriage or a combination. We don't come to college to learn the finer points of motherhood, but our education should be sufficiently broad and faceted to give sure preparation for all the possibilities we face." This student understood the essence of the liberal education: that with it one could go on into any of the roles of an educated woman—wife, mother, careerist. What uses she made of her liberal education were still up to the individual. Nonetheless, for most female undergraduates in these postwar decades, it was not easy to admit personal ambition privately, let alone express it openly. The idea of stating that one would become a writer, a doctor, or a professor would have sounded absurd. What even the most brilliant heard, as Sylvia Plath showed in *The Bell Jar*, was that they must want, above all, to be married. From all sides came pressure for the American college girl to prove herself as a wife and mother.

After World War II women who continued professional and academic training despite lack of encouragement did not have the support of large numbers of peers or of a public women's movement, and in time visible and invisible barriers became increasingly oppressive. Although the breaking point came only during a convergence of public crises, the seeds of the new feminism were being planted throughout the postwar era. The women's movement was reborn at the end of the 1960s.

Many educated women graduating during and after World War II were more or less happily absorbed in their private lives, and some studies in the fifties emphasized women's contentment with their domestic roles. It was not then recognized that unfulfilled aspirations haunted others. In an informal analysis of her 1942 Smith College classmates, Betty Friedan in 1957 uncovered the dissatisfaction of well over one-half of her respondents, who reported that the role of wife and mother did not "sufficiently" utilize their "creative abilities." Her publication of *The Feminine Mystique* in 1963 brought responses from around the world; individual women experiencing shocks of recognition learned that they were not alone. Friedan's exposure of the pervasive cult of femininity, "the problem that had no name," did not create the new wave of the women's movement but provided one leader for it. At the same time that Friedan wrote, sociologist Alice Rossi illuminated professional women's dilemmas in her memorable address entitled "The Equality of the Sexes: An Immodest Proposal," presented in 1963 at a *Daedalus* conference in Cambridge, Massachusetts.

Even while living out the "feminine mystique," more women questioned their life patterns; Friedan's analysis pointed to the negative role models that one generation of college-educated women may have provided for their daughters, who reclaimed from their mothers' disappointments a new set of feminist aspirations. Expectations of several generations laid the groundwork for the new explosion in the late 1960s, with consequences for educated and uneducated alike.

Although the resurgence of the women's movement did not begin on college campuses, within a few years colleges were transformed by it, as well as by other aspects of social awakening that escalated in the 1960s. Of critical importance was the forging of a new civil rights movement by black Americans. Moreover, a young president of the United States at the start of the decade symbolized heightening expectations throughout American society.

Older women graduates from the 1920s to the early 1940s welcomed the 1960 Commission on the Status of Women established by

President John F. Kennedy and chaired by Eleanor Roosevelt. These women were professional and club women, long concerned with women's economic and political rights under the law. Some believed in the equal rights amendment advocated by the National Women's Party and the National Federation of Business and Professional Women's Clubs; but more women, the constituency of the League of Women Voters, opposed the ERA. The *Report of the Commission on the Status of Women* in 1963 deliberately ignored the issue, but with the continuing pressure from women's groups the long-sought Equal Pay Act passed that year. An even greater triumph followed in 1964 with the inclusion of Title Seven in the Civil Rights Act, making sexual, racial, and religious discrimination illegal. But although an Equal Employment Opportunity Commission was established in 1965 to implement this legislation, it refused to consider cases of economic discrimination against women. The EEOC faced formidable opponents in the leadership of state commissions on the status of women, which had been started to carry on the work of the national commission. Frustrated by the EEOC's failure to respond, these leaders, including Betty Friedan, founded a female civil rights organization, the National Organization for Women (NOW). By 1968 women who earlier had not thought about the ERA now made it their political goal. Thus one branch of the modern women's movement came into being.

Women's consciousness was catapulted to a new level by black people's demands for equality. The Supreme Court decision in *Brown v. the Board of Education* in 1954 transformed the civil rights movement for black people of several generations. Rosa Parks's refusal to sit at the back of a Montgomery bus augured other actions, and before long the younger generation of the black elite reacted with new tactics. The 1960 Woolworth sit-ins in Greensboro represented undercurrents that created a tidal wave among educated young black men and women that was not feminist but racial in its purpose. These students, in creating new forces of social activism, had either direct or indirect support of their families, communities, and colleges. As the movement expanded, women of Bennett, Spelman, Fisk, and Tougaloo colleges, among others, were soon protesting, picketing, and being jailed along with men.

Quite separately southern white college women found their way into the civil rights cause, but without family or institutional support. Sara Evans has described movingly their responses to the Christian doctrines they had heard since childhood. Such women students gathered in small groups at colleges from the University of Texas to Duke and Vanderbilt universities, in local YWCAs, Methodist churches, and other voluntary religious organizations.

Student meetings and protests not only launched an interacial movement, but black and white women discovered in various activities bonds of womanhood. Not through college courses on women's needs, but out of concern with the ideals of democracy came the unexpected awakening of feminist consciousness. Black women were the first to rebel against their subordinate roles in the civil rights movement, in 1964; soon white women protested against similar treatment. Out of their group discussions and position papers came another shock of recognition concerning discrimination against women by male colleagues. In each cause of the sixties, from Free Speech and civil rights to anti-war protests, women worked with men without being allowed to share in the policy making and critical decisions. At a convention of the National Conference on New Politics in Chicago, Shulamith Firestone was told to "cool down, little girl," when she demanded a discussion of women's roles in the politics of the New Left. Black and white women alike learned what female activists had faced a century earlier in anti-slavery, temperance, and other causes; most men considered women's opinions as secondary.

The younger liberationist branch of the women's movement was born of the recognition that participation of females was not acknowledged as equal to that of males. The first black and white women activists shared the need to be valued as persons and so rediscovered what it meant to be a woman and to gain strength from a group. In their spontaneous discussions the younger women addressed the more private aspects of women's lives and formulated demands that transformed the questions women asked themselves. The various constituencies among the liberationists, in attacking the modern patriarchal society, stirred the aspirations of diverse groups of American women. It was not coincidental that the resurgence of the women's movement occurred when there were millions of women in the work force and thousands in the professions who had experienced discrimination in wages and salaries and who were all the more ready to respond to feminist demands. The outpouring of protest, anger, and questions about the place of women came from all directions—colleges, work force, professions, and voluntary organizations—and brought women of different ages and groups into the women's movement.

From the beginning the movement had different meanings for different generations and for women of diverse social backgrounds. Whatever the motive, they learned to value women's group support. Organizations like NOW identified with the liberal rights tradition to effect changes in the laws; the liberationist principles strengthened the resolve of individuals to make personal choices, whether conventional or not. Women who had attended college in the fifties and sixties became leaders in the liberationist wing. Often they had been drawn together through civil rights activism, and already they were working women—journalists, writers, and scholars. Thousands of women all over the country discovered in consciousness raising that they need not be alone in resolving conflicts of work, study, creativity, and personal relationships.

For undergraduate women in the seventies the women's movement became connected with the general student politicization of the late sixties. The demands of both sexes had a wide impact on the liberal arts colleges, in the classroom and beyond. Undergraduates gained representation on some faculty committees and made their opinions count on curricular as well as social matters. Moreover, educators at men's colleges, already concerned with rising costs and declining applicant pools, acknowledged their students' preference to have women enrolled with them. Reluctantly, in the early seventies, resistant colleges like the University of Virginia, Yale, and Princeton gave up the battle and admitted women. Wesleyan once again received females and moved to coresidential living. By 1983, when Columbia opened its door to women undergraduates, there were only a handful of all-male colleges left. Many women's colleges, notably Vassar, found it similarly expedient to admit men. Others, like Wellesley, Bryn Mawr, and Mills denied calls for coeducation but affiliated informally with nearby coeducational institutions. Thus, the women's colleges of the 1980s bore little resemblance to the nineteenth-century models, where men were hardly allowed to walk across campus. Both male and female students generally demanded an end to parietal restrictions. Rules that had been difficult to enforce crumbled everywhere. Essential to the new permissiveness on campuses were the advances in birth control technology and its availability. An important consequence of the new freedom, particularly for women, was the removal of one incentive for early marriages.

The feminist movement affected the education of women and men in all kinds of institutions, both undergraduate and professional. As a result of federal legislation and accompanying affirmative action regulations, public efforts to reduce and eliminate discrimination against women in academia, as well as in the work place, helped individuals to assert themselves, to reject age-old prejudices.

Women's collegiate athletics was one area revolutionized in the 1970s as a result of the women's movement and an inclusion in the 1972 education amendment of Title IX that prohibits sexual discrimination by schools that receive federal financial assistance. Before Title IX there were no women's collegiate championships; in 1984, there were thirty national contests. Similarly, where once there had been no athletic scholarships for women, by 1984 ten thousand were available (although men still had far more). For the decade between 1972 and 1982 the gains in female athletics were great. Yet these may be threatened by the 1984 Supreme Court decision in the *Grove City College* case that interprets Title IX narrowly. Moreover, female athletic directors caution that women still receive mixed messages about their participation in athletics: the sportswoman has yet to reconcile her femininity with her athletic prowess.

The women's movement not only invigorated extracurricular athletics, but challenged the liberal arts curriculum. All institutions were forced to address the legacy of the sixties—an awakened feminist consciousness—and one result was an enlargement of the curriculum to include courses relating to women. Many disciplines have been affected by women's interest in their roles and their past. The remarkable convergence of interested scholars and students created an extraordinary climate for productive scholarship. The new questions posed by scholars who give women a central place in their investigations enrich and alter perspectives in every field. Just as women take their identities from many roles and activities, so does the study of women lend itself to interdisciplinary approaches, what we call women's studies. Many schools offer B.A., M.A. and Ph.D. programs either in women's history or in women's studies. At other institutions that give little encouragement departmentally, individual faculty members transmit the excitement of these new approaches. Students who make even a small excursion into this terrain are rewarded by innovative viewpoints on traditional materials of study. Though women scholars predominate in this area, men are also making contributions. The interest of general readers as well remains strong in the 1980s.

Not only in the classroom, but also in the public sphere, female consciousness raising grew, with the result that more and more middle- and working-class women looked to education for training in the professions and in politics. Finally, community colleges, supported primarily by government funding, made it possible for poor women to consider the option of higher education.

In my opinion the women's movement became, indirectly, a catalyst for the enormous increase of women students at two-year colleges. Such institutions had existed earlier; what was exciting in the seventies, however, was the rising number of women of all ages entering community colleges. Not all were feminists, but in the high tide of the women's movement consciousness of the importance of education for women caught on. As in the past women studied for different reasons: the vocational motive, the desire for a better job, was paramount; many older women, who had never gone to college or who had dropped out to marry and have babies, also found that they were now ready to study in order to have something of "one's own." Of course, the reasons often overlapped.

Observers caution against too optimistic a view of the vast enrollments of women at two-year institutions. While the majority apparently do not continue to four-year schools, a proportion do enroll at liberal arts colleges. I maintain that, as in earlier times, these individuals, attending for many different, personal reasons, even with the irregularity of their course enrollment, could gain what they wanted and discover more than they had anticipated.

Three older women, one native black, one white from a rural background, one a Spanish immigrant, who attended community colleges, were asked informally to comment on their education. Each indicated that her studies meant more to her than subject matter and training. When asked what difference attending college had made, all said that they had gained self-confidence. The first who was bored in high school and did not attend college until she was in her late forties remembered that earlier in her education no one had "pushed" her. She was grateful that the community college teachers had made demands on her. Before this, she said, "I did not know that I was creative." The second woman said of her education, "It's given me the freedom that it is okay to be a woman." The third went furthest, saying, "I could not have survived without it." This woman, who has completed a B.A., and M.A., and is finishing a Ph.D while working full-time, added, "It has allowed me to become a model for my daughters." Asked about feminism, the black alumna remarked, "We're not into that. We've got it." By contrast, the third answered, "I could have gone all of my life being a feminist without knowing it." She underlined the importance of women's studies in making women aware of the potentialities offered to them by their education. By becoming students these women gained self-knowledge as well as academic knowledge. They and many others are the beneficiaries of the tradition of higher education for women.

The community college graduates were part of a trend, in which older women increasingly became students. By 1980 approximately one-third of collegians were twenty-five years of age or older, and most of these were women. Moreover, the proportion of those who were thirty-five years or older rose to 12.3 percent in 1979. We recall that a few eighteenth-century matrons, who had been denied liberal study, recognized the need for educating the younger generation. Two hundred years later the circle of history is complete; older women now seek the education that younger ones take for granted.

In retrospect the period from World War II began at a low point in women's enrollments. In the context of the whole twentieth century, however, this appears to have been an aberration: the proportion of women among college students is higher today than ever. More important, the late twentieth century sees changes in women's attitudes, expectations, and demands. Earlier, women's advancement seemed to rest entirely on individuals' achievements, but both women and the society perceived these achievements as exceptions. To move beyond exceptions, women by the 1970s increasingly realized the necessity of public recognition and governmental response to blatant and less obvious inequities. Thus, women rediscovered the importance of working together. In the 1980s the momentum of the women's movement still provides consciousness and impetus. How can women sustain this momentum? Will they?

At a Crossroads

CARL DEGLER

While during the nineteen seventies it seemed apparent that the women's movement would continue unopposed in its bid to change significantly American society, subsequent events proved otherwise. In this excerpt from his history of women and the family, Stanford University historian Carl Degler explains some of the reasons for the tensions surrounding the women's movement. Do gains for the women's movement come at the expense of the family, particularly children? Can government or individual employers take up the slack in order to bolster the family's place in American society without jeopardizing the individual woman and her family's right to choose a particular lifestyle?

By 1967, young educated women, who had not been especially attracted by Friedan's obviously middle-class organization, began to awaken to the issue of women's rights. The most dramatic example of that awakening occurred at the left-wing National Conference for a New Politics when militant blacks demanded 50 per cent of the seats as a recognition by whites of the justice of their cause. When women asked for a comparable representation in the light of their being 51 per cent of the population, they were summarily turned down. (The black Civil Rights leader Stokely Carmichael was reported to have said "the position of women in our movement should be prone.") The result of such relegating of women to subordinate places in the movement was that many young woman activists now saw the necessity for women to separate their cause from that of blacks or any political movement that was not devoted primarily to the interests of women. As one of the radical women said at the time of the Conference for a New Politics, "We intend to make our own analysis of the system, and put our interests first, whether or not it is convenient for the (male dominated) Left." Although probably few of the young women who had moved into politics because of the Civil Rights movement of the 1960s knew it, this sudden recognition of the dangers of subordinating the cause of women to that of other minorities or policies was not a new experience for feminists. A century earlier Elizabeth Cady Stanton and Susan B. Anthony confronted it at the time of the ratification of the Fourteenth and Fifteenth amendments. They were then admonished to remember that "This is the Negro's Hour" and they must not confuse the issue by seeking the ballot, too.

By the opening years of the 1970s a number of organizations dedicated to pressing for equality for women had been formed in addition to NOW. Among them were the Women's Equity Action League, established in 1968 by academic and professional women, and the Women's Political Caucus, which, under the leadership of Friedan, Bella Abzug, Gloria Steinem, and Fannie Lou Hamer of Civil Rights fame, sought to open politics to feminist women. Groups of radical feminist women, like the Red Stockings and The Feminists, carried the argument to the extreme of having as little as possible to do with men, proclaiming them the enemy. Ti Grace Atkinson, one of the leaders of The Feminists, announced that, though she would be happy to debate or act with men for public purposes in behalf of women's rights, she would have nothing to do with men in her private life. The Feminists regarded heterosexual intercourse as oppressive and permitted only a third of their members to be married to or to live with men. As the ideology of The Feminists implied, one consequence of radical feminism was a forthright recognition of lesbianism. And so attractive was this ultimate appeal to sisterhood that for a time in the middle 1970s the issue threatened to divide irrevocably the women's movement. At the end of the decade, however, it was evident that, extreme as some ideologues of the movement might be, the great majority of women active in the cause were neither lesbians nor anti-male in outlook or intention. That this was so was evident at the highly successful national conference of several thousand women of all political and ideological persuasions held in Houston, Texas, in November 1977, to write a national agenda for women's rights. Significantly, the meeting was funded by the Federal government, an unprecedented sign of the success of the women's cause.

The remarkable rapidity with which the women's movement captured the allegiance of so many women and men, as well as gaining the attention and support of the mass media, the academic community, government, and even business, was explained by several things. The increasing participation of married women in the work force was certainly a part of the explanation. And the general concern for equality which the Negro Rights Revolution sparked was certainly another. Then there was also a less easily recognized demographic fact, which was at once a consequence and a cause of the acceptance of women's rights. That was the unprecedentedly high proportion of women between the ages of 20 and 24 who were single. In 1974 the figure was 40 per cent, though in 1960 it had been only 28 per cent. Yet even the 1960 figure was the highest in the 20th century. Although the trend ran through all educational levels, it was especially noticeable among college-trained women. Later we will look again at this figure, since it also says something about women's attitudes toward marriage. But here its relevance is that it helps to account for women's interest in feminism, just as feminism may help to explain why young women were not marrying as young as they once had. So striking was the success of the women's movement that in 1978 veteran social-commentator David Riesman, in reviewing the great social upheavals of the late 1960s, told a British audience that the women's movement was "possibly the most lasting legacy of the . . . period of protests."

That success, however, was not total. The most striking failure was the inability of the organized women's movement to add the Equal Rights Amendment to the Constitution. The amendment had been around for half a century before most women's organizations took an interest in it, as we have seen. So hostile were most women leaders and groups like organized labor to the ERA that it was plausibly alleged that one of the reasons President John F. Kennedy appointed his Commission on the Status of Women in 1961 was to head off the rising support for ERA in Congress. Both major parties had supported ERA in their platforms as early as 1944, and only the resistance of organized labor and most women leaders prevented it from being in the platforms of 1964 and 1968. To many women leaders, as Esther Peterson, the head of the President's Commission on Women, later remarked, the ERA was "a headache." By endangering protective legislation for women it seemed only harmful to working women and of little use to professional women. It was for such reasons, too, that the Women's Bureau opposed the ERA throughout the 1960s. Then, under the leadership of Elizabeth B. Koontz, the first black woman to head the Bureau, a new turn was made. At Koontz's initiative, the Bureau in 1970 sponsored a conference on women which concluded with an endorsement of the ERA. That same year the Department of Labor itself reversed its long-standing opposition to the amendment. By 1972 the two houses of Congress had passed the amendment and sent it to the states. At that point ratification seemed relatively easy to accomplish, especially as the legislatures of several dozen states almost immediately voted for it. By the middle 1970s, however, one state legislature after another began to reject it, even though ratification lacked only a handful of states. By the summer of 1978 it became evident that the seven-year limit which had been placed upon the ratification period would expire before any of the remaining states would meet to act on the amendment. A quick campaign in behalf of extension of the time of ratification was successful, though not without acrimonious debate between proponents and opponents of the amendment. The opposition was measured in the limiting of the extension to only another three and one-half years.

The cause for the delay in ratification was complex and yet familiar. Part of the reason undoubtedly was that the amendment seemed to threaten some women as well as men. The remarks of Senator Sam Ervin, from North Carolina, who urged the Senate not to pass the amendment, probably reflected the view of many male opponents. "Keep the law responsible where the good Lord put it," he pleaded, "on the man to bear the burdens of support and the woman to bear the children." It was significant that only Tennessee and Texas of all the states of the former Confederacy ratified the amendment; Tennessee had been the single exception in the South's resistance to the Nineteenth Amendment sixty years before. The conservative South was still doubtful about the emancipation of women.

This time, too, women were active against the amendment, just as they had been in opposition to the suffrage. Phyllis Schlafly, a conservative Republican, had stumped the country for years telling women and legislators that the amendment would deprive them of their rights as wives and mothers and that it would, among other things, compel women to serve in the armed services in time of war. In some legislatures women members actually voted against ratification. A Gallup poll as late as July 1978 reported that a majority of the people in the country favored the ERA, including substantial proportions of men. But it was not without significance that more men than women supported the ERA. Forty-five per cent of women said that they either opposed the ratification or had no opinion. The women's movement, in short, was not able to overcome the fears of many women that the amendment would disturb or threaten their traditional place in the family, just as many women during the suffrage fight earlier in the century had feared its impact on the relation between husband and wife. Despite the contentions of Schlafly and other opponents, however, nothing in the ERA, any more than in the suffrage, would require individual women or men to alter their relations within marriage, though it would certainly facilitate changes in the direction of a wife's equality within marriage if that was what she wanted.

In a sense, the very success of the women's movement made it possible for opponents of the ERA to contend that the amendment was unnecessary. For, thanks to the Civil Rights Act of 1964, the various executive orders, and a series of judicial interpretations in favor of women's equality, all of the major barriers to equality of opportunity for women had already been removed without an ERA. The truth was that, despite the assertions from both sides, ratification of the amendment would not change much, so complete had been the legal and constitutional transformation brought about by the feminist revival. It was true, though, that passage of the ERA would imbed in the Constitution the legal basis for the feminist gains of the preceding decade and thus make their repeal difficult in the future. It would also hasten the removal of the few remaining legal obstacles to full equality of opportunity between the sexes.

Although the mass of women may not have been enthusiastic about the ERA, that fact ought not to leave the impression that the women's movement had not had a profound impact on large numbers of women. A poll by *Redbook* magazine in 1973 showed that 66 per cent of its readers favored the movement and 45 per cent admitted that it had raised their consciousness about women's opportunities. Less than 2 per cent of the women queried believed that women could realize their full potentialities by being a wife and mother only. Here was as good a sign as any of the interaction between the movement of married women into the work force and the rise of the women's movement.

Readers of *Redbook*, however, were generally members of the middle class, and the prominence of that class in the new women's cause was one of its limitations. The women's movement was not able to transcend class or racial divisions among women. Throughout the history of feminism the problem of class divisions had always been present. During the earlier years of the 20th century there had been some efforts to link women of the working and middle classes. But not even those linkages now existed; in 1947, for example, the Women's Trade Union League had been disbanded at the suggestion of organized labor. The National Organization for Women, it is true, sought to attract ethnic and racial minority women into its ranks, but largely without success. And it probably was visionary to expect that women would be able to transcend class or race when men certainly had not succeeded in doing so. But, then, men did not have the common gender oppression that was believed to unite all women.

The heart of the matter was that feminism had always been a middle-class cause, so the new feminism, as represented by an organization like NOW was no exception. The interests of middle-class, college-educated women, who were at once the target of Betty Friedan's arguments and the source of her organization's membership, had concerns quite different from those of most working-class women. The sense of personal frustration that the *Feminine Mystique* spoke out against, and the appeal of careers that attracted many college-educated middle-class women to the women's movement, left working-class women largely untouched. A job to such women was considerably less attractive, however useful and even necessary it might be as a temporary or occasional source of family income. Sociologist Mirra Komarovsky reported in a study of working-class wives made at the end of the 1950s that "we find little evidence of status frustration among working-class wives. They accept housewifery," she concluded. She discovered no signs of that sense of frustration in the home that had been so prominent among middle-class wives she had studied earlier. A more recent, though impressionistic study of lower-middle-class women conducted by Louise Howe quoted a homemaker in the 1970s as asserting "that a lot of women are much better off married and at home than they would be at some low-paying job and they know this; they've usually worked before, after all. So when they hear some feminist writers or lawyers or something like that say that jobs are so terrific, they know that for the average woman that's a lot of baloney." Lillian Rubin in her recent study of working-class families in northern California pointed out that though the marriages which many young women of this class witnessed among their elders were hardly ideal, matrimony nevertheless often seemed better than the alternatives: "a job they hate, more years under the oppressive parental roof." Even when they continued to work after marriage—they considered it temporary. They simply did not see work outside the home as part of their role as they certainly considered it a part of men's lives.

Demographer Judith Blake has pointed out that a very high proportion of women who work in the United States, regardless of their class, see work as temporary or hope to escape from it at some time. Her figures show that half or more of working women do not want to work, or desire part-time jobs. She cited a Harris poll of 1972 in which a national sample of women was asked how often they felt that "having a loving husband who is able to take care of me is much more important to me than making it on my own." Even among women under thirty, Blake reported, at least half said "frequently," while another 20 per cent said they felt that way occasionally. A fourth said "hardly ever." These data are also related to studies which show that a substantial proportion of husbands, even in the 1970s, tend to be less happy when their wives work. (Since a wife who does not work can usually be expected to devote more time to her husband's comfort, that reaction is not unexpected.) A 1973 survey of families in general found that when a wife worked full-time—that is, as a kind of career—38 per cent of husbands said they were "very happy in their marriage"; when the wives worked part-time the proportion rose to 45 per cent, and when the wives were at home the figure went up to 50 per cent. In short, for many nonprofessional women, whether from the working or middle classes, work outside the home might well seem to threaten their relation with their husbands. Moreover, the individualistic goals behind the women's movement did not have much appeal to them, since the jobs they would hold were rarely intrinsically interesting or fulfilling. And, as Helena Lopata has shown in her study of modern housewives, many middle-class women found deep satisfaction in their families and volunteer work. And despite the increased activity of women outside the home, the great majority of housewives she studied listed home and family activities ahead of any outside work, including church and community endeavors. Thus for many women, perhaps a majority, equality of opportunity in employment was not a real issue, especially if it seemed to compete with or threaten family relations.

If a large proportion of women do not pursue their individuality as far as the modern women's movement counsels, that does not mean that the internal relationships within the family are not changing. Indeed, it is the thesis of this book that the modern family ever since its emergence at the beginning of the 19th century has been changing, often, as we have seen, under the influence of women's push for autonomy and individuality. In fact, over the last two centuries the changes within the family have frequently aroused alarm and comment. During the late 19th century the source of anxiety was the fall in the birth rate of the native, white middle class as compared with that of immigrants. And then at the opening of the 20th century the upsurge in divorce sparked a spirited national debate on the imminent demise of the family. In the 1920s and 1930s sociologists fretted over the fact that the family no longer seemed to have any economic function, such as it presumably had in pre-industrial days. "Even if the family doesn't produce thread and cloth and soap and medicine and food," sociologist William Ogburn rather defensively wrote in 1928, "it can still produce happiness." In our own time, despair over the future of the family has spawned such a mass of lugubrious studies that in 1977 the president of the Carnegie Corporation asked in the introduction to a new study on the family, "What happened and is happening to the American family? Is it still viable?" During the early 1970s, radical psychologists like R. D. Laing and David Cooper proudly planned for *The Death of the Family*, as Cooper phrased it in a book with that title. They traced all that was wrong with children or society to the allegedly oppressive character of the nuclear, overly protective bourgeois family of industrial societies. At the same time, conservative psychologists like Urie Bronfenbrenner blamed the family for what was wrong with children and with society, but for just the opposite reasons: the family was too permissive, too uninvolved with child-rearing and mothering. "America's families and their children are in trouble," warned Bronfenbrenner in 1972. "Trouble so deep and pervasive as to threaten the future of our nation. The source of the trouble is nothing less than a national neglect of children and of those primarily engaged in their care: America's parents." In another article Bronfenbrenner ascribed the alienation of the young and the rise of juvenile crime to the increase in divorce, working mothers, and the single-parent household. A mother's continual presence in the household during a child's growing up, Bronfenbrenner insisted, was essential. He deplored the increasing tendency of women to be employed away from home even if they had small children. And it will be recalled that in 1975 about a third of women with children under three years of age were in fact in the work force.

Radical social critics also found the American family defective. Historian Christopher Lasch reviewed the 20th-century literature on family sociology and psychology and found it, at the very least, conceptually confused. The argument of some sociologists that the family could divest itself of productive functions and still be a significant force in the lives of children Lasch thought wrong. "The so-called functions of the family form an integrated system," Lasch contended. Some functions cannot be abandoned without affecting all the others detrimentally. "The only function of the family that matters is socialization; and when protection, work, and instruction in work have all been removed from the home," he insisted, "the child no longer identifies with his parents and internalizes their authority in the same way as before, if indeed he internalizes their authority at all."

There is no question that over the last two hundred years the family has been shedding, one by one, virtually all the functions it fulfilled in previous centuries. No longer is the family the principal place of learning for the child; it has long since ceased to provide either medical or psychological care, except of the most trivial kinds. Members of the family who need such help usually seek it elsewhere. It has been a century or more at least since religious life was centered at the family hearth or dinner table. Almost as many years have passed since the family ceased to be an economic unit in which members worked together to earn a collective living. The principal function of the modern family, at least over the last century and a half, has been to rear children and provide a haven, a place of rest, refreshment, and spiritual replenishment for its members. A sociologist put it well in the 1920s when he wrote that the function of the family was to "provide the best care for children, furnish a humanely satisfying affectional relationship and contribute to the personality development of parents and offspring."

Modern critics of the family often deplore this loss of functions, but it is not at all clear that the loss has been severe or even important. It is quite possible that divestiture of functions has been a gain in that it has permitted a concentration upon the primary functions of the family without the distractions that must have occurred when the family was expected to be doctor, farmer, manufacturer, food preserver, tailor, baker, and carpenter as well as source of affection, spiritual comfort, and teacher of values. To be everything may come close to being nothing. Once it is assumed that the primary function of the family is to provide love, support to children, and affection between spouses, it might be said that the modern family, unlike those of earlier ages, is for the first time free to perform its primary purposes without internal distraction. It is possible, in short, that not much of value has been lost at all.

In any event, at least one of the so-called lost functions seems to be returning. It is true that family members in industrial America have not worked in a common economic enterprise as most persons did when the typical family lived on a farm. Yet today, after the Second Transformation in women's work, it is hardly accurate to consider most wives as nonproducers. After all, almost half of American married women are now employed at some job outside the home. And in 1975 only about a third of families in which both spouses were present was the husband the sole breadwinner. (As recently as 1950, 56 per cent of such families counted the husband as the only earner.) Moreover, as productive workers outside the home, married women are no less than in earlier times earners for the family. They work to contribute to the family, not to increase their individuality. In that way, at least, it is possible to view the new pattern of work for married women as a return to the pre-industrial one. In fact, English sociologists Michael Young and Peter Willmott have been so impressed with the similarity between the old, pre-industrial family and the new pattern of work for married women that they have coined a term to differentiate the two. Because they see the modern family as more egalitarian in the internal relationship between husband and wife they call it "the symmetrical family" to distinguish it from the male-dominated (patriarchal) family of previous centuries. They recognize what is true for the American equivalent of the symmetrical family—namely, that, though husband and wife may still not be fully equal, they are more so than ever before, in part at least because the wife is employed. Most women, in short, are clearly productive members of the family today, even though they may not be independent. But then in the pre-industrial patriarchal family women were not independent, either. Finally, although the family of the 20th century may have changed in this respect from that of the 19th, its essential nature, which first became apparent in the early 19th century, has not altered. Women are still the primary child-rearers, even when they work, and the purpose of their work, in the main, is to support and advance the family, not to realize themselves as individuals.

There is another way in which the family today has changed while still retaining the essential features that emerged in the early 19th century. Affection between spouses and the love and care of children are still at the center of the modern family in America. But by the second half of the 20th century the center of gravity of the family has shifted from children to spouses. The cause for the change is at least twofold. One is that people of both sexes now live longer than ever before, and the other is that women now bear fewer children and have them closer together. A century ago, for instance, the average woman spent about twenty years in child-bearing and child-rearing—that is, until age 42, when her last child went off to school. Those years constituted about 51 per cent of her married life because the average husband died at age 56. By the middle of the 20th century, however, with fewer children and greater longevity for herself and her husband, a woman spent less than 20 per cent of her married life in such activities. Moreover, a century ago the average husband died two years before the average age of marriage of the family's youngest child. Thus, for most husbands and wives, there were at most only a few years together after family responsibilities had been met. During the second half of the 20th century, however, a husband's death, on the average, does not occur until he is almost 68, which, again on the average, is twenty years after the marriage of the couple's last child. Modern parents, in short, can expect a quarter of a century of life together without children at all—not to mention some forty years without small children. Surely this is quite a different intrafamilial experience than Americans have known during most of the nation's history. (Women today can also expect some ten years of widowhood, on the average, as against a mere four years a century ago.)

This long period during which couples live by themselves without children is so recent a social development that its meaning for the family has barely been studied at all. Some jaundiced observers have implied that an upsurge in marital disruptions will occur once the prop of children has fallen away. But figures as late as 1969 still show that the highest divorce rates are among ages 20 to 24, and there is no sign as yet of a rise among the so-called "empty nest" age groups. In fact, studies of marital happiness by age report that couples identify their period of greatest happiness as that after the children have left home for good. The years of child-rearing, on the other hand, are usually reported by parents as a time of tension and dissatisfaction, rather than of greatest happiness.

If one side of the modern family was that it provided an intense emotional ambience and support for its members, that gain carried a price: it could be lost. For if marriage was the ideal relationship and the home the ideal sanctuary, as so much of 19th-century advice literature insisted, then when marriage and family were disrupted the pain inflicted was that much greater. And for over a century now Americans have been aware of and worried about their rising divorce rate, which indeed has long been among the world's highest. Paradoxically, one reason divorces have become increasingly common is just that Americans have invested so heavily in marriage and family: when expectations are so high, it is inevitable that they will not be fully achieved. Even more important as a source of marital disruption is that modern marriage—that is, the kind which emerged at the end of the 18th century—has placed an increasingly heavy emphasis upon affection between spouses. When the family provided education, medical care, subsistence, and work, as well as love and companionship, divorce or separation was hardly the first thing one thought of when disagreements broke out between spouses. But when love is the purpose as well as the cement of marriage, a diminution of affection naturally leads to thoughts of dissolution. For what can be the justification of a modern marriage when love and companionship have fled? Moreover, as the opportunities for work for women increased, the practicality of escaping from an unsatisfactory marriage improved for women. And insofar as husbands objected to their wives' working, that, too, has increased the likelihood of divorce. At least one modern study has reported that as a wife's earnings increase so do the probabilities of marital break-up. The marriage least likely to disrupt is one in which a husband is clearly the sole breadwinner.

5

VIETNAM

The American involvement in Indochina in general and Vietnam in particular began by accident. The French government, which had seized Indochina in the last century, had reclaimed its colonies in 1945 determined to retain possession. Although the United States had continually proclaimed its opposition to imperialism, during the Korean War, in order to aid France and thereby cement the security of Western Europe, the American government agreed to give military aid to the French government which was now fighting Vietnamese forces pledged to ending French subjugation.

By 1954 the French government, defeated in the epic battle of Dien Bien Phu, decided to end the struggle. At a conference in Geneva the French and Viet Minh delegations, together with representatives from Britain and the Soviet Union, agreed to divide Vietnam temporarily at the seventeenth parallel. Free elections were scheduled for 1956. In the interim, the Viet Minh forces, led by Ho Chi Minh, would control the north while the pro-western government of Ngo Dinh Diem would govern the south.

The United States never signed the Geneva accords and gave tacit approval when in 1955 Diem refused to abide by their terms. While the American government, now led by President Dwight D. Eisenhower, refused to send American troops to Vietnam, it displayed no hesitation in providing the Diem government with ever-increasing aid to fight the Viet Cong insurgency which had begun in 1958.

When John F. Kennedy took office in 1961, he faced a crisis in neighboring Laos. Kennedy shared the bi-partisan consensus which saw the Communist world as monolithic. Virtually all American policy makers maintained that a victory for Communist forces in Indochina was equally a victory for the Soviet Union. Furthermore, Communism seemed on the move during the early sixties. The Kennedy administration believed that the "free world" was under attack in Berlin, in Cuba and in Indochina. Pledged to fight any fight, bear any burden, the Kennedy administration reached a negotiated settlement in Laos while steadily increasing the number of American military advisors in Vietnam. The road proved ever more slippery. First, the American embassy reported increasing Communist control over the countryside. Exacerbating the situation was the South Vietnamese population's resentment of the Diem government's corruption and fervent Catholicism. Violent Buddhist demonstrations combined with Communist victories in the countryside convinced the American government in November 1963 to acquiesce in a coup which overthrew the Diem government and initiated a succession of increasingly weak military governments.

Lyndon Johnson immediately learned of the problematic situation in Vietnam when he took office after Kennedy's assassination on November 22, 1963. Yet the American government continued to believe that increased United States military involvement could make the difference. In August 1964, Johnson used an incident in the Tonkin Gulf to get from Congress a resolution giving the executive branch carte blanche to expand the war. Having pledged during the 1964 presidential campaign not to allow American boys to fight the battle of Asian boys, Johnson proceeded to do the opposite. As Stanley Karnow relates, in early 1965 the Johnson administration agreed to allow relentless bombing of North Vietnam.

Although attractive to American leaders because of its cheap cost to American lives, bombing proved insufficient to do the job required of it. Now began the unceasing escalation of American fighting strength in Vietnam: 75,000 troops in the summer of 1965, 160,000 in December 1965, 450,000 in mid-1967 and 543,000 at the end of 1968. Always promised a light at the end of the tunnel, the American public only saw more darkness. By 1967 the war had come home. Student protests against the war, motivated by idealist and pragmatic reasons, disrupted campuses and campaigns. Credibility was also defeated—Americans found themselves questioning their government's position on Vietnam and then beginning to question Washington's position on other issues.

When the Tet offensive occurred in February 1968, the American public's patience abruptly snapped. Notwithstanding American commander William Westmoreland's oft-repeated opinion that Tet was a defeat for the enemy, the bombardment of the American embassy in Saigon and the Communist takeover, albeit short-lived, of the city of Hue, convinced the American public that the Vietnam war could not be won. His popularity and credibility destroyed, Johnson, on March 31, declared he would neither seek nor serve another term as President but would devote himself to finding a peaceful solution to the Vietnam war. It would take seven more years before the final ignominious withdrawal of all Americans from Vietnam. The scars from that conflict are still with us.

The Slippery Slope

STANLEY KARNOW

In his massive tome and by virtue of the public television series it accompanied, Stanley Karnow helped define the post-1980 debate on the Vietnam war. In this excerpt Karnow describes how President Johnson and his advisors made the crucial decisions that led to full American involvement in the Vietnam ground war. Does the modern president have too much authority in foreign policy decision making? Is it possible or even desirable for dissident voices to be heard during the formation of American foreign policy?

In pressing the president to make a decision, [General Maxwell] Taylor [American Ambassador to South Vietnam] had recommended that Mac [McGeorge] Bundy [National Security Advisor] visit Vietnam to appraise the situation. Bundy had never been there and was "physically detached from the local scene," and he might assure Johnson that "we are missing no real bets in the political field." So Bundy scheduled a trip for the beginning of February 1965. But he was scarcely going with an open mind.

Late in January, after conferring with [Robert] McNamara [Secretary of Defense] he addressed a memorandum to Johnson stressing that "both of us are now pretty well convinced that our present policy can lead only to disastrous defeat." To expect the emergence of a stable regime in Saigon was futile. The Vietcong, encouraged by America's "unwillingness to take serious risks," was "gaining in the countryside." The worst course was to continue "this essentially passive role." The United States could either negotiate and "salvage what little can be preserved," or resort to armed power to "force a change" of Communist strategy. They favored the military alternative, though, they added, other plans ought to be "carefully studied." Either way, "the time has come for hard choices."

Mac Bundy departed for Saigon, coincidentally, just as the new Soviet prime minister, Aleksei Kosygin, left Moscow for Hanoi. Kosygin had embarked on his journey at the invitation of the North Vietnamese leaders, who were then angling for more Soviet military aid. He was prepared to fulfill their request—but on condition that they follow Soviet rather than Chinese guidance. Fearing that a wider war might jeopardize the Soviet policy of "peaceful coexistence" with the United States, he also tried to persuade them to consider a compromise solution. His talks in Hanoi, ironically, were as stormy as Taylor's wrangles in Saigon. One Soviet participant later described the North Vietnamese to me as a "bunch of stubborn bastards."

A Vietcong attack against a U.S. base near Pleiku, in the central highlands of South Vietnam, was to have a shattering impact on both Kosygin's and Bundy's journeys—and propel the conflict into a fresh phase.

Pleiku, traditionally a market town for the region's mountain tribes, had become the site of a South Vietnamese army headquarters that directed patrols against Communist infiltration routes threading through the jungles from Laos and Cambodia. A detachment of American special forces and other military advisers was billeted three miles away at Camp Holloway, whose perimeter was heavily protected by barbed wire and sandbag bunkers. A fleet of U.S. transport and observation aircraft and helicopters was parked at a nearby strip, and both South Vietnamese and American soldiers guarded the area.

Specialist Fourth Class Jesse Pyle of Morina, California, on sentry duty, sat shivering in a trench during the cold night of February 6–7. A nearby noise jarred him at about 2:00 A.M. Clambering out to investigate, he spotted shadows crossing the compound. He shouted, then started shooting. At that instant, a hail of mortar shells exploded, and the rattle of automatic fire could also be heard. An American screamed in the darkness: "We're going to die. We're all going to die."

Eight Americans died and more than a hundred others were wounded, and ten U.S. aircraft were destroyed. Nearly all the Vietcong assailants escaped. The body of one, found inside the enclosure, contained a detailed map of the camp—testimony to a meticulous job of espionage.

Mac Bundy, his mission completed, was packing to leave Vietnam that February morning when news of the Pleiku attack reached him. Joining Taylor and Westmoreland at U.S. military headquarters in Saigon, he was tense and abrupt—behaving, as Westmoreland afterward recalled, like many civilians in authority who display a "field marshal psychosis" once they have "smelled a little gunpowder." They quickly agreed that the "streetcar" had arrived. Bundy telephoned the White House to urge that American air raids against North Vietnam begin promptly, in accordance with the long-standing Pentagon plan quaintly entitled "Punitive and Crippling Reprisal Actions on Targets in North Vietnam." Contrary to most accounts, Bundy did not make his proposal under emotional stress on the spur of the moment. "That's nonsense," he explained to me years later. "I had already recommended retaliation beforehand."

Bundy also cabled President Johnson to make clear his conviction that a tough U.S. move was imperative. His message confirmed what he had told Johnson before going to Vietnam: the prospects there were "grim," the Vietcong's "energy and persistence are astonishing," and both the Vietnamese and Americans he saw were uncertain "whether a Communist victory can be prevented." The "one grave weakness" in the U.S. posture was "a widespread belief that we do not have the will and force and patience and determination to take the necessary action and stay the course." To negotiate an American withdrawal "would mean surrender on the installment plan." So the only alternative was "continuous" bombing of North Vietnam—not merely "episodic responses geared on a one-for-one basis to 'spectacular' outrages," which would "lack the persuasive force of sustained pressure." The United States could anticipate "significant" losses, yet the program "seems cheap . . . measured against the costs of defeat." The Pleiku attack, Bundy concluded, had "produced a practicable point of departure."

Johnson convened his national security advisers, expanding the group to include Mike Mansfield, Senate majority leader, and John McCormack, speaker of the House of Representatives. Johnson plainly announced at the outset his intention to punish the North Vietnamese—as if they had struck him personally. "I've gone far enough," he barked. "I've had enough of this." Most of those present concurred, among them George Ball, who felt that at this juncture discretion was the better part of valor. But Mansfield and Vice-President Hubert Humphrey dissented. Johnson banished Humphrey from Vietnam deliberations for the next year, and quietly rehabilitated him only after Humphrey pledged to subscribe to the official administration line. Humphrey, the prototype of the unalloyed liberal, was tormented by Vietnam for the rest of his life.

Within hours, Operation Flaming Dart was under way, as the carrier *Ranger* launched its jets to bomb a North Vietnamese army camp near Dong Hoi, a coastal town sixty miles above the seventeenth parallel dividing North and South Vietnam. The South Vietnamese were brought into the first mission to boost their morale, and Air Vice Marshal Nguyen Cao Ky interrupted his political maneuverings in Saigon to lead their aircraft. But the initial raid fizzled because of foul weather.

A major casualty of the attack was Kosygin's initiative to persuade the North Vietnamese leaders to consider negotiations. Now they could claim to be victims of U.S. "aggression," worthy of total support from the Communist powers. And Kosygin, compelled to defend the Soviet Union's "anti-imperialist" image, had no choice but to fulfill their requests for unconditional military aid. They may have planned the Pleiku assault to incite an American reaction that would put him on the spot. In any case, new shipments of sophisticated Soviet surface-to-air missiles began to arrive at the port of Haiphong ten days after Kosygin's return to Moscow.

Mac Bundy had cautioned Johnson to alert the American people to the "fundamental fact" that "the struggle in Vietnam will be long" and that "there is no shortcut to success." Johnson disregarded the advice. He shrouded himself in silence—or, on occasion, privately told visitors to ignore the histrionic newspaper headlines and television broadcasts that, as usual, exaggerated events. Unwittingly, he was broadening the "credibility gap" that had dogged his White House years and would eventually prove politically fatal. By the middle of February, for example, James Reston of *The New York Times* was already denouncing his duplicity: "The time has come to call a spade a bloody shovel. This country is in an undeclared and unexplained war in Vietnam. Our masters have a lot of long and fancy names for it, like escalation and retaliation, but it is a war just the same."

But Johnson knew better than Reston that Americans placed their faith in the president in difficult moments, and the opinion surveys bore him out. Almost 70 percent of the nation gave him a "positive" rating, with the same proportion supporting a bombing strategy as the "only way" to "save" Vietnam. Nearly 80 percent believed that an

American withdrawal would open Southeast Asia to Communist domination, and an equal proportion favored a U.S. combat troop commitment to block that possibility. So Johnson, whose pockets always bulged with the latest polls, felt confident that the public would uphold him whatever the journalists said.

As he intensified the war in early 1965, Johnson tried to manage the nation's perception of his policies—and his aides devoted as much attention to vocabulary as they did to strategy. To mute anxieties, his spokesmen withheld the real dimensions of the conflict from the American people, pursuing what one of them termed "a policy of minimum candor": a deliberate tactic to disclose only the barest essentials without blatantly lying. The president also wanted to warn the North Vietnamese that worse lay ahead unless they met his demands, but he was wary of resorting to belligerent rhetoric that might provoke drastic Soviet or Chinese intervention. So as the war grew, so did a lexicon of special phrases contrived to convey particular signals to the enemy.

American officials said that the bombing of North Vietnam after the Pleiku attack was "appropriate and fitting," which is how they had described the raid after the Tonkin Gulf incident six months earlier. On February 11, describing the next strike against the north, they referred to "air operations" designed to stop the "pattern of aggression"— thereby suggesting that a prolonged offensive was about to supersede individual reprisals. The labels changed as Johnson retired Flaming Dart, which had been retaliatory, and authorized Rolling Thunder, a continuous bombing program that would go on for three years, its name borrowed from the words of a hymn.

Started on March 2, as more than a hundred U.S. aircraft raided a North Vietnamese ammunition dump, Rolling Thunder was originally scheduled to last eight weeks. Johnson himself closely supervised it, boasting that "they can't even bomb an outhouse without my approval." But by April, as General Wheeler told McNamara, the strikes had "not reduced in any major way" North Vietnam's military capabilities or seriously damaged its economy, and the Hanoi regime "continues to maintain, at least publicly, stoical determination." The air offensive had failed.

The answer was typically American: more and bigger. Soon the operation became "sustained pressure," and B-52s armed with napalm and cluster bombs joined the action. By the time the Nixon administration signed a cease-fire agreement in January 1973, the United States had dropped on North Vietnam, an area the size of Texas, triple the bomb tonnage dropped on Europe, Asia, and Africa during World War II. Yet Vietnam was different. The dikes along the Red River, whose destruction would have flooded the valley and killed hundreds of thousands of people, were never targeted. Nor were North Vietnam's cities subjected to the kind of "carpet bombing" that obliterated Dresden and Tokyo. Bombs devastated parts of North Vietnam, particularly the area above the seventeenth parallel, where troops and supplies were massed to move south, but Hanoi and Haiphong were hardly bruised.

For Johnson, the choices were simple: either the United States plunged into war or faced defeat. Once again, he canvassed opinions and got a predictable range of views. No outsider, unfamiliar with the governmental process, could even faintly imagine the mountains of memorandums and hours of dialogue consumed in the tortured deliberations.

Senator [J.William] Fulbright went to the White House at Johnson's invitation. He sat silently, trying to stay attentive as Johnson droned on, explaining how he had offered peace to the Communists but had been spurned, had been spit in the eye. Now, with the Vietcong attacking and the South Vietnamese about to cave in, his only choice was to send American boys out there. He hoped that Bill Fulbright would stand up and tell the Senate how patient he had been. Fulbright's eventual Senate speech disappointed Johnson. Though he opposed America's "unconditional" withdrawal from Vietnam, he also opposed "further escalation" that threatened to drag the nation into "a bloody and protracted jungle war in which the strategic advantages would be with the other side." The Communists should be offered a "reasonable and attractive alternative to military victory" through negotiations. Johnson never forgot or forgave this "betrayal," and the two southern Democrats, Senate colleagues for years, ceased to speak to each other.

George Ball, keeping his misgivings private, handed Johnson another set of dire premonitions. An "investment trap" loomed: American soldiers would "begin to take heavy casualties in a war they are ill-equipped to fight in a noncooperative if not downright hostile countryside"; to compensate for the losses, more troops would be sent out, and eventually the involvement would be "so great that we cannot—without national humiliation—stop." Still, Ball predicted, "humiliation would be more likely than the achievement of our objectives—even after we have paid terrible costs." So, he urged, maintain the U.S. force pledged at its current level, but start an active search for a "compromise settlement."

Other Johnson aides were also uncertain. Rusk, always sensitive to global consequences, linked America's presence in Vietnam to "the integrity of the U.S. commitment" throughout the world, yet he wondered whether Westmoreland was not exaggerating the danger. Taylor continued to vacillate—a hint, perhaps, that a year in Saigon was unhinging him. In early June, he conceded that American combat troops "will probably be necessary," but now, at the end of the month, he questioned the need for them, saying that the best they could do was to hold a few enclaves. The CIA echoed his sentiment; their latest study concluded that a large U.S. force would fail to halt the Communists, who clung to the conviction that "their staying power is inherently superior" to that of the Americans and South Vietnamese. The Communists would thus intensify "their present strategy of attrition and subversion," aiming to undermine the Saigon government "through exhaustion and internal collapse."

[William] Bill Bundy [Assistant Secretary of Defense, later Assistant Secretary of State for Far East] proposed a "middle way." He ruled out withdrawal, but he also doubted that an American buildup would work. Unless the South Vietnamese army performed better, "our own intervention would appear to be turning the conflict into a white man's war, with the United States in the shoes of the French." He recommended that no more than a hundred thousand American troops be committed, both to hold the line and to be tested in the coming months. And after that? Perhaps the "Vietcong tide could be stemmed." The North Vietnamese, facing a "stalemate," might compromise. Or maybe the Saigon regime would "throw in the sponge and make a deal" with the Communists. His "middle way," at least in the short term, avoided the "clear pitfalls" of either quitting or brutal escalation. He, too, was unsure.

Not so McNamara and the Pentagon brass. They pleaded with Johnson to grant Westmoreland's troop request, and McNamara went even further. He stressed that Johnson had to call up the reserves—the force of former servicemen—a politically explosive step tantamount to an announcement of full-scale war. He also proposed a massive offensive against North Vietnam—mining its harbors, destroying its airfields, obliterating its rail and road bridges, and wiping out every installation of military value, from ammunition dumps and oil storage facilities to power plants and barracks. He suggested a few token diplomatic gestures, like enlisting Soviet help in the quest for accommodation, but only to sanctify an armed approach designed to dramatize to the Communists that "the odds are against their winning."

Mac Bundy recoiled at the program, terming it "rash to the point of folly." Not only was an extravagant campaign against North Vietnam preposterous, but putting a huge American force into Vietnam was "a slippery slope toward total U.S. responsibility and corresponding feckessness on the Vietnamese side." What, Bundy asked, was the ceiling on the American liability? Could U.S. troops wage an antiguerrilla war, the "central problem" in South Vietnam? And above all, what was "the real object of the exercise"? To get to the conference table? If so, "What results do we seek there?" Or was the investment simply intended "to cover an eventual retreat"? In that case, "Can we not do that just as well where we are?"

The younger [Mac] Bundy was not being gratuitously tough on McNamara, one of his close friends. Nor was he a cut-and-run type. He shared the assumption that Vietnam was vital to America's interests. But as chief of Johnson's national security staff, he wanted the president's cabinet—and the president himself—to ponder the crucial questions. The questions were posed, but they were never deeply examined.

After screening the assorted ideas that cluttered his desk, Mac Bundy counseled Johnson to "listen hard" to Ball but to discard his proposal—and then "move to the narrower choice" between the Bill Bundy and McNamara options. Their recommendations were to be discussed toward the end of July, the deadline for a final decision. "I was not about to send additional men without the most detailed analysis," Johnson later recalled. But he had already made up his mind—and his apparent probe of the issues was largely contrived.

Johnson ordered McNamara back to Vietnam to reassess the situation. McNamara arrived on July 16, accompanied by [General Earle] Wheeler and Henry Cabot Lodge, who had just agreed to return to Saigon for another tour as ambassador, succeeding Taylor. The group went to dinner that evening with Ky and Thieu, who had grabbed power a few weeks earlier. Ky showed up in a tight white jacket, tapered trousers, patent leather shoes, and red socks, looking like a saxophone player in a second-rate nightclub. McNamara did a double take at the sight of the new South Vietnamese leader on whom America's fate hung so precariously. One U.S. official in the party muttered, "At least no one could confuse him with Uncle Ho."

McNamara was supposed to devote several days to his "fact-finding" mission. But a day after his arrival, he received an ultrasecret cable over the CIA's "back channel" from his deputy, Cyrus Vance. President Johnson had decided to go ahead with Westmoreland's troop request, and he wanted McNamara to return to Washington immediately. As Westmoreland noted afterward, the policy debate "turned out, in a way, to be moot."

McNamara came back with a lengthy memorandum, and his confidential comments again bore little resemblance to his public remarks. He told reporters that the U.S. forces in Vietnam were inflicting "increasingly heavy losses" on the Vietcong, but he informed Johnson privately that conditions were "worse than a year ago." Communist infiltration into the south had not been daunted by the American bombing, and the Saigon government's chances for survival over the next six months were "less than even." Then he gave Johnson the bad news. By early 1966, he said, Vietnam would need not only the number of U.S. soldiers Westmoreland requested, but another hundred thousand or more. And that meant, McNamara again stressed, mobilizing the reserves and the national guard—putting the country on a war footing, in effect. Otherwise, America could not meet its global security responsibilities.

Johnson could see even farther ahead. Though he never revealed it publicly, he already sensed by July 1965 that Vietnam would require six hundred thousand American men and cost billions of dollars. But as he opened a week-long series of White House sessions on July 21, Johnson fostered the impression that he was groping for answers. "I want this discussed in full detail," he said, his narrow eyes darting around the table at [Dean] Rusk [Secretary of State], McNamara, Wheeler, Mac and Bill Bundy, and the others. He wanted to weigh all the options. What results can we expect? Do we have to defend the world? Who else can help? What are the alternatives?

Relentlessly, almost plaintively, he went through the motion of firing questions, particularly at Ball, his devil's advocate. And he continued the next day with his generals and admirals. Can American boys fight Asians in the jungle? Will the North Vietnamese pour in more men? Might they call for Chinese or Russian volunteers? How much will this cost us? Are we getting into something we cannot finish? Johnson convened other meetings with only two or three aides, and he consulted outsiders like John McCloy, the distinguished New York banker who had advised presidents since the Roosevelt era. Edging closer to the deadline, he communed with Abe Fortas.

Johnson wanted to portray himself as a model of moderation— partly to reassure the American people that he was not going to war, partly to avoid a Soviet or Chinese response. He rejected McNamara's plea to call up the reserves, and he parceled out the American troop shipments to Vietnam. He could not conceal his decision, but he could muffle it. On July 28, 1965, at midday, when the television audience is smallest, he soberly announced, "I have asked the commanding general, General Westmoreland, what more he needs to meet this mounting aggression. He has told me. And we will meet his needs. We cannot be defeated by force of arms. We will stand in Vietnam."

The Beginning of the End

GEORGE C. HERRING

George Herring, professor of history at the University of Kentucky, has written one of the best accounts of the American involvement in the Vietnam war. In this excerpt he discusses the Tet offensive. More than any other event the startling, if ephemeral, success of a North Vietnamese offensive after years of American involvement in the war turned Americans, both politicians and private citizens, against a continuation of the war at least as then being fought. How does a President build a consensus in favor of a war? Why did the administration continue to support the South Vietnamese government?

While the United States was preoccupied with Khe Sanh, the North Vietnamese and Vietcong prepared for the second phase of the operation. The offensive against the cities was timed to coincide with the beginning of Tet, the lunar new year and the most festive of Vietnamese holidays. Throughout the war, both sides had traditionally observed a cease-fire during Tet, and Hanoi correctly assumed that South Vietnam would be relaxing and celebrating, soldiers visiting their families, government officials away from their offices. While the Americans and South Vietnamese prepared for the holidays, Vietcong units readied themselves for the bloodiest battles of the war. Mingling with the heavy holiday traffic, guerrillas disguised as ARVN [South Vietnamese] soldiers or civilians moved into the cities and towns, some audaciously hitching rides on American vehicles. Weapons were smuggled in on vegetable carts and even in mock funeral processions.

Within twenty-four hours after the beginning of Tet, January 30, 1968, the Vietcong launched a series of attacks extending from the demilitarized zone to the Ca Mau Peninsula on the southern tip of Vietnam. In all, they struck thirty-six of forty-four provincial capitals, five of the six major cities, sixty-four district capitals, and fifty hamlets. In addition to the daring raid on the Embassy, Vietcong units assaulted Saigon's Tan Son Nhut Airport, the presidential palace, and the headquarters of South Vietnam's general staff. In Hue, 7,500 Vietcong and North Vietnamese troops stormed and eventually took control of the ancient Citadel, the interior town which had been the seat of the Emperors of the Kingdom of Annam.

The offensive caught the United States and South Vietnam off guard. American intelligence had picked up signs of intensive Vietcong activity in and around the cities and had even translated captured documents which, without giving dates, outlined the plan in some detail. The U.S. command was so preoccupied with Khe Sanh, however, that it viewed evidence pointing to the cities as a diversion to distract it from the main battlefield. As had happened so often before, the United States underestimated the capability of the enemy. The North Vietnamese appeared so bloodied by the campaigns of 1967 that the Americans could not conceive that they could bounce back and deliver a blow of the magnitude of Tet. "Even had I known exactly what was to take place," [General William] Westmoreland's [Commander of American forces in South Vietnam] intelligence officer later conceded, "it was so preposterous that I probably would have been unable to sell it to anybody."[1]

Although taken by surprise, the United States and South Vietnam recovered quickly. The timing of the offensive was poorly coordinated, and premature attacks in some towns sounded a warning which enabled Westmoreland to get reinforcements to vulnerable areas. In addition, the Vietcong was slow to capitalize on its initial successes, giving the United States time to mount a strong defense. In Saigon, American and ARVN forces held off the initial attacks and within several days had cleared the city, inflicting huge casualties, taking large numbers of prisoners, and forcing the remnants to melt into the countryside. Elsewhere the result was much the same. The ARVN fought better under pressure than any American would have dared predict, and the United States and South Vietnam used their superior mobility and firepower to devastating advantage. The Vietcong launched a second round of attacks on February 18, but these were confined largely to rocket and

---

[1]Quoted in William C. Westmoreland, *A Soldier Reports* (Garden City, N.Y., 1976), p. 321.

mortar barrages against U.S. and South Vietnamese military installations and steadily diminished in intensity.

Hue was the only exception to the general pattern. The liberation of that city took nearly three weeks, required heavy bombing and intensive artillery fire, and ranks among the bloodiest and most destructive battles of the war. The United States and South Vietnam lost an estimated 500 killed while enemy killed in action have been estimated as high as 5,000. The savage fighting caused huge numbers of civilian casualties and created an estimated 100,000 refugees. The bodies of 2,800 South Vietnamese were found in mass graves in and around Hue, the product of Vietcong and North Vietnamese executions, and another 2,000 citizens of Hue were unaccounted for and presumed murdered. The beautiful city, with its many architectural treasures, was left, in the words of one observer, a "shattered, stinking hulk, its streets choked with rubble and rotting bodies.[2]

It remains difficult to assess the impact of the battles of Tet. The North Vietnamese and Vietcong did not force the collapse of South Vietnam. They were unable to establish any firm positions in the urban areas, and the South Vietnamese people did not rise up to welcome them as "liberators." Vietcong and North Vietnamese battle deaths have been estimated as high as 40,000, and although this figure may be inflated, the losses were huge. The Vietcong bore the brunt of the fighting; its regular units were decimated and would never completely recover, and its political infrastructure suffered crippling losses.

If, in these terms, Tet represented a "defeat" for the enemy, it was still a costly "victory" for the United States and South Vietnam. ARVN forces had to be withdrawn from the countryside to defend the cities, and the pacification program incurred another major setback. The destruction visited upon the cities heaped formidable new problems on a government that had shown limited capacity to deal with the routine. American and South Vietnamese losses did not approach those of the enemy, but they were still high: in the first two weeks of the Tet campaigns, the United States lost 1,100 killed in action and South Vietnam 2,300. An estimated 12,500 civilians were killed, and Tet created as many as one million new refugees. As with much of the war, there was a great deal of destruction and suffering, but no clearcut winner or loser.

[2]Dave Richard Palmer, *Summons of the Trumpet* (San Rafael, Calif., 1978), p. 194.

To the extent that the North Vietnamese designed the Tet Offensive to influence the United States, they succeeded, for it sent instant shock waves across the nation. Early wire service reports exaggerated the success of the raid on the Embassy, some even indicating that the Vietcong had occupied several floors of the building. Although these initial reports were in time corrected, the reaction was still one of disbelief. "What the hell is going on?" the venerable newscaster Walter Cronkite is said to have snapped. "I thought we were winning the war!"[3] Televised accounts of the bloody fighting in Saigon and Hue made a mockery of Johnson and of Westmoreland's optimistic year-end reports, widening the credibility gap, and cynical journalists openly mocked Westmoreland's claims of victory. The humorist Art Buchwald parodied the general's statements in terms of Custer at Little Big Horn. "We have the Sioux on the run," Buchwald had Custer saying. "Of course we still have some cleaning up to do, but the Redskins are hurting badly and it will only be a matter of time before they give in."[4] The battles of Tet raised to a new level of public consciousness basic questions about the war which had long lurked just beneath the surface. The offhand remark of a U.S. Army officer who had participated in the liberation of the delta village of Ben Tre—"We had to destroy the town to save it"—seemed to epitomize the purposeless destruction of the war. Candid photographs of the police chief of Saigon holding a pistol to the head of a Vietcong captive—and then firing—starkly symbolized the way in which violence had triumphed over morality and law.[5]

The Tet Offensive left Washington in a state of "troubled confusion and uncertainty."[6] Westmoreland insisted that the attacks had been repulsed and that there was no need to fear a major setback, and administration officials publicly echoed his statements. Johnson and his advisers were shocked by the suddenness and magnitude of the offensive, however, and intelligence estimates were much more pessimistic than Westmoreland. Many officials feared that Tet was only the opening phase of a larger Communist offensive. Some felt that Khe Sanh was still the primary objective, a fear that seemed to be borne out when

[3]Quoted in Oberdorfer, *Tet!* p. 158.

[4]*Washington Post*, February 6, 1968.

[5]Oberdorfer, *Tet!* pp. 164–171, 184–185; George A. Bailey and Lawrence W. Lichty, "Rough Justice on a Saigon Street: A Gatekeeper Study of NBC's Tet Execution Film," *Journalism Quarterly*, 49 (Summer 1972), 221–229.

[6]Townsend Hoopes, *The Limits of Intervention* (New York, 1970), p. 145.

the besieging forces renewed their attack on the Marine base in early February. Others feared a major offensive in the northern provinces or a second wave of attacks on the cities. An "air of gloom" hung over White House discussions, and General [Earle] Wheeler [Chairman of Joint Chiefs of Staff] likened the mood to that following the first Battle of Bull Run.[7]

The President responded with a stubborn determination to hold the line at any cost. He insisted that Khe Sanh must be held and advised Westmoreland that he was prepared to send whatever reinforcements were needed to defend the threatened fortress or meet any other threat. "The United States is not prepared to accept a defeat in South Vietnam," Wheeler advised Saigon, ". . . if you need more troops, ask for them." When Westmoreland indicated that he would appreciate any help he could get, Johnson immediately ordered an additional 10,500 men to Vietnam. In the first few weeks after Tet, the President's main concern seemed to be to "get on with the war as quickly as possible," not only by sending reinforcements but also by stepping up the air attacks against North Vietnam.[8]

From the standpoint of the military, the new mood of urgency in Washington provided a timely opportunity to force decisions that had been deferred for too long. Wheeler and the Joint Chiefs had been pressing for mobilization of the reserves since 1965, and by February 1968 they were certain this step must be taken at once. The Tet Offensive raised the distinct possibility that significant reinforcements would have to be sent to Vietnam. North Korea's seizure of the American warship *Pueblo* in January and a new flareup in Berlin aroused fears that additional troops might have to be dispatched to these perennial Cold War trouble spots. Available forces were nearly exhausted, and Wheeler feared that unless the United States mobilized the reserves immediately it could not meet its global commitments.

Confident that he could exploit the enemy's defeat at Tet and buoyed by the President's apparent willingness to send substantial reinforcements, Westmoreland revived his 1967 proposals to expand the war. The enemy's decision to throw in "all his military chips and go for broke," the General advised Washington, provided the United States

---

[7]Earle Wheeler oral history interview, Johnson Papers.

[8]Herbert Schandler, *The Unmaking of a President: Lyndon Johnson and Vietnam* (Princeton, N.J., 1977), p. 91; "March 31 Speech," Johnson Papers, National Security File, National Security Council Histories: March 31, 1968 Speech, Box 47.

a "great opportunity." The North Vietnamese and Vietcong could not afford the heavy losses sustained in the Tet Offensive, and with large numbers of additional troops Westmoreland was certain he could gain the upper hand. His "two-fisted" strategy envisioned an "amphibious hook" against North Vietnamese bases and staging areas across the demilitarized zone, attacks on the sanctuaries in Laos and Cambodia, and an intensified bombing campaign against North Vietnam. By taking the offensive at a time when the enemy was overextended, the General was confident that he could significantly shorten the war.[9]

Wheeler and Westmoreland conferred in Saigon in late February and devised an approach to force the President's hand. Wheeler appears to have been considerably less optimistic about the immediate prospects in Vietnam than Westmoreland, but he agreed that whether Tet provided new opportunities or posed increased dangers, it justified a call for major reinforcements. The two men settled on the figure of 206,000 men, a number large enough to meet any contingency in Vietnam and to force mobilization of the reserves. Roughly half of the men would be deployed in Vietnam by the end of the year; the rest would constitute a strategic reserve. Wheeler raised no objections to Westmoreland's proposed changes in strategy, but he persuaded the field commander that it would be best to defer such recommendations until the President had approved the new troop level. He was keenly aware of Johnson's opposition to widening the war, and he apparently feared that if he presented the case for additional troops on the basis of an optimistic assessment and an offensive strategy, he would be turned down again. Troops, not strategy, offered the "stronger talking point."[10]

Wheeler's report to Washington was deeply pessimistic. Describing the Tet Offensive as a "very near thing," he warned that the initial enemy attacks had almost succeeded in numerous places and had been turned back only by the "timely reaction of the United States forces." The North Vietnamese and Vietcong had suffered heavily, but they had repeatedly demonstrated a capacity for quick recovery, and they would probably attempt to sustain the offensive with renewed attacks. Without additional troops, he concluded, the United States must be "prepared to accept some reverses," a line calculated to sway a President who had already made clear he was not willing to accept defeat.

[9]John B. Henry, "February 1968," *Foreign Policy*, 4 (Fall 1971), 17.
[10]*Ibid.* 21.

Wheeler insisted that large-scale reinforcements were necessary to protect the cities, drive the enemy from the northern provinces, and pacify
the countryside. His pessimism may have been sincere; he had never
been as confident as Westmoreland. It seems clear, however, that by
presenting a gloomy assessment he hoped to stampede the administration into providing the troops needed to rebuild a depleted strategic reserve and meet any contingency in Vietnam. His proposal reopened in
even more vigorous fashion the debate that had raged in Washington
throughout 1967.[11]

Wheeler's report shocked a government already in a state of deep
alarm. In terms of policy choices, it posed a hard dilemma. The General
suggested that denial of the request for 206,000 troops could result in a
military defeat, or at least in an indefinite continuation of the war. Acceptance of his recommendations, on the other hand, would force a
major escalation of the war and the imposition of heavy new demands
on the American people in an election year and at a time when public
anxiety about Vietnam was already pronounced. Not inclined to make
a hasty decision on a matter fraught with such grave implications, Johnson turned the problem over to Clark Clifford, who had just replaced
McNamara as Secretary of Defense, with the grim instruction: "Give
me the lesser of evils."[12]

Trusted advisers from outside the government seem to have
clinched it for Johnson. To move the President from his indecision,
Clifford suggested that he call his senior advisory group, the Wise Men,
back to Washington for another session on Vietnam. After a series of
briefings by diplomatic and military officials on March 26, the group, in
a mood of obvious gloom, reported its findings. A minority advocated
holding the line militarily and even escalating if necessary, but the majority favored immediate steps toward deescalation. After its last meeting in November, McGeorge Bundy reported, the group had expected
slow and steady progress. This appeared not to have happened, however, and the majority view, as summed up by former Secretary of State
Dean Acheson, was that the United States could "no longer do the job
we set out to do in the time we have left and we must begin to take
steps to disengage." The Wise Men disagreed among themselves on

[11]Wheeler Report, February 27, 1968, excerpted in Neil Sheehan et al., *The Pentagon Papers as Published by the New York Times* (New York, 1971), pp. 615–621.
[12]Lyndon B. Johnson, *The Vantage Point* (New York, 1971), pp. 392–393.

what needed to be done, some proposing a total and unconditional bombing halt, others a shift in the ground strategy. Most of them agreed that the goal of an independent, non-Communist South Vietnam was probably unattainable and that moves should be made toward eventual disengagement. "Unless we do something quick, the mood in this country may lead us to withdrawal," Cyrus Vance warned.[13] "The establishment bastards have bailed out," an angry and dispirited Johnson is said to have remarked after the meeting.[14]

Keeping his intentions under wraps until the very end, the President in a televised address on March 31 dramatically revealed a series of major decisions. Accepting Rusk's proposal, he announced that the bombing of North Vietnam would henceforth be limited to the area just north of the demilitarized zone. Responding to the entreaties of Clifford and the Wise Men, however, he went further. "Even this limited bombing of the North could come to an early end," he stressed, "if our restraint is matched by restraint in Hanoi." He named the veteran diplomat Averell Harriman as his personal representative should peace talks materialize, and he made clear that the United States was ready to discuss peace, any time, any place. In a bombshell announcement that caught the nation by surprise, Johnson concluded by saying firmly: "I shall not seek, and I will not accept, the nomination of my party for another term as your President." He later revealed that for some time he had considered not running for reelection. He was exhausted physically and emotionally from the strains of office. He realized that he had spent most of his political capital and that another term would be conflict-ridden and barren of accomplishment. By removing himself from candidacy, he could emphasize the sincerity of his desire for negotiations and contribute to the restoration of national unity and domestic harmony.[15]

Johnson's speech is usually cited as a major turning point in American involvement in Vietnam, and in some ways it was. No ceiling was placed on American ground forces, and the President did not obligate

[13]Summary of notes, March 26, 1968, Johnson Papers, Meeting Notes File, Box 2. The "Wise Men" were Dean Acheson, George Ball, McGeorge Bundy, Douglas Dillon, Cyrus Vance, Arthur Dean, John McCloy, Omar Bradley, Matthew Ridgway, Maxwell Taylor, Robert Murphy, Henry Cabot Lodge, Abe Fortas, and Arthur Goldberg.

[14]Quoted in Roger Morris, *An Uncertain Greatness: Henry Kissinger and American Foreign Policy* (New York, 1977), p.44. Johnson was furious with the negative tone of the March 26 briefings. The "first thing I do when you all leave is to get those briefers . . . ," he told one of the Wise Men. Notes, March 26, 1968, Johnson Papers, Diary Backup File, 95. See also Depuy oral history interview, Depuy Papers.

[15]*Public Papers of Lyndon B. Johnson, 1968–1969* (2 vols.; Washington D.C., 1970), I, 469–476. On Johnson's decision not to run, see also George Christian memorandum, March 31, 1968, Johnson Papers, Diary Backup File, Box 96.

himself to maintain the restrictions on the bombing. Indeed, in explaining the partial bombing halt to the Embassy in Saigon, the State Department indicated that Hanoi would probably "denounce" it and "thus free our hand after a short period."[16] Nevertheless, the circumstances in which the March decisions were made and the conciliatory tone of Johnson's speech made it difficult, if not impossible, for him to change course. March 31, 1968, marked an inglorious end to the policy of gradual escalation.

The President did not change his goals, however. The apparent American success in the battles of Tet reinforced the conviction of Johnson, Rusk, and Rostow that they could yet secure an independent, non-Communist South Vietnam. "My biggest worry was not Vietnam itself," the President later conceded, "it was the divisiveness and pessimism at home. . . . I looked on my approaching speech as an opportunity to help right the balance and provide better perspective. For the collapse of the home front, I knew well, was just what Hanoi was counting on."[17] By rejecting major troop reinforcements, reducing the bombing, shifting some military responsibility to the Vietnamese, and withdrawing from the presidential race, Johnson hoped to salvage his policy at least to the end of his term, and he felt certain that history would vindicate him for standing firm under intense criticism. Johnson's speech did not represent a change of policy, therefore, but a shift of tactics to salvage a policy that had come under bitter attack.

The new tactics were even more vaguely defined and contradictory than the old, however. The March decisions marked a shift from the idea of graduated pressure to the pre-1965 concept of saving South Vietnam by denying the enemy victory. Precisely how this was to be achieved was not spelled out. The debate over ground strategy was not resolved, and Westmoreland's successor, General Creighton Abrams, was given no strategic guidance. Administration officials generally agreed that ground operations should be scaled down to reduce American casualties, but it was not clear how they would contribute to the achievement of American goals. The bombing was to be concentrated

---

[16]"March 31 Speech," Johnson Papers, National Security File, National Security Council Histories: March 31, 1968 Speech, Box 47.

[17]Johnson, *Vantage Point*, p. 422

against North Vietnamese staging areas and supply lines, but it had not reduced infiltration significantly in the past and there was no reason to assume it would be more effective in the future. The exigencies of domestic politics required acceptance of the concept of Vietnamization, and the surprising response of the ARVN during Tet raised hopes that it would work. There was little in the past record of various South Vietnamese governments to suggest, however, that Thieu and his cohorts could conciliate their non-Communist opponents and pacify the countryside while effectively waging war against a weakened but still formidable enemy. Negotiations were also desirable from a domestic political standpoint, but in the absence of concessions the administration was not prepared to make, diplomacy could accomplish nothing and its failure might intensify the pressures the talks were designed to ease. In short, the tactics of 1968 perpetuated the ambiguities and inconsistencies that had marked American policy from the start.

U.S. policy in the months after Tet makes clear that, although the Johnson administration spoke a more conciliatory language and altered its tactics, it had not retreated from its original goals. The President made good on his pledge to negotiate, accepting, after numerous delays. Hanoi's proposal to send representatives to Paris for direct talks. From the outset, however, he refused to compromise on the fundamental issues. In the meantime, the United States sought to keep maximum pressure on enemy forces in South Vietnam and assisted the South Vietnamese in a frantic drive to gain control of the countryside, while making plans for a gradual shift of the military burden to the ARVN. The result was to harden the stalemate, leaving resolution of the problem to the next administration.

Despite the accommodating tone of Johnson's March 31 speech, the administration approached the reality of negotiations with extreme caution. Hanoi's positive response caught Washington by surprise, and many U.S. officials suspected a clever North Vietnamese ploy to exploit antiwar sentiment in the United States. The administration had no choice but to accept the enemy's proposal for direct talks, but it was determined not to rush into negotiations. Although Johnson had vowed to send representatives "to any forum, at any time," he rejected Hanoi's proposed sites of Phnom Penh, Cambodia, and Warsaw, where, he said, the "deck would be stacked against us."[18]

---

[18]*Ibid.*, pp. 505–506.

The two nations finally agreed to meet in Paris, and the administration took a hard line from the outset. Harriman and Clifford advocated a generous initial offer to get negotiations moving and extricate the United States from Vietnam as quickly as possible. Johnson's other advisers were not persuaded, however. Westmoreland and Bunker claimed that the U.S. position in South Vietnam had improved significantly and that the administration would be negotiating from strength in Paris. Johnson and his advisers expressed grave doubts that the talks would lead to anything. They were certainly sincere in their desire for peace, but the terms for which they were prepared to hold out made virtually certain that nothing would be accomplished. Rusk insisted that the United States should get North Vietnam "to make concessions" or "take responsibility for breaking off the talks." In return for a complete bombing halt, administration officials seemed inclined to back off from the San Antonio formula. Rusk even talked about holding out for North Vietnamese observance of the 1962 Geneva Accords on Laos and reestablishment of the demilitarized zone. The United States was opposed to a cease-fire that would tie its hands militarily in the south, and in terms of a political settlement Rusk spoke hopefully of restoration of the status quo antebellum.[19]

Formal talks opened in Paris on May 13 and immediately deadlocked. North Vietnam had agreed to talks as part of its broader strategy of fighting while negotiating. It probably had no interest in substantive negotiations while the military balance of forces was unfavorable, and it may have viewed the Paris talks primarily as a means of getting the bombing stopped, exacerbating differences between the United States and South Vietnam, and intensifying antiwar pressures in the United States. The North Vietnamese made clear that they were establishing contact with the United States to secure the "unconditional cessation of U.S. bombing raids and all other acts of war so that talks may start." The Johnson administration was willing to stop the bombing, but, as in the past, it insisted on reciprocal steps of deescalation. Hanoi continued to reject the American demand for reciprocity and refused any terms which limited its ability to support the war in the south while leaving the United States a free hand there.

[19]Notes on meeting, May 6, 1968, Johnson Papers, Meeting Notes File, Box 3; Harold Johnson notes on meetings, May 6, 8, 1968, Harold Johnson Papers, Box 127; Andrew Goodpaster oral history interview, U.S. Army Military History Institute, Carlisle Barracks, Pa.

The American delegation subsequently introduced a new proposal, actually a variant of the old two-track plan, in an attempt to break the impasse. The United States would stop the bombing "on the assumption that" North Vietnam would respect the demilitarized zone and refrain from further rocket attacks on Saigon and other cities, and that "prompt and serious talks" would follow. The offer brought no formal response or any indication that one might be forthcoming. American officials complained that the North Vietnamese seemed prepared to sit in Paris "and even read the telephone directory if necessary to keep non-productive talks going," and the Joint Chiefs pressed relentlessly for reescalation, including B-52 strikes against North Vietnamese sanctuaries in Cambodia.[20]

Fearful that the talks might drag on inconclusively, perpetuating the war and exacerbating domestic divisions, the chief American negotiator, W. Averell Harriman, urged the President to compromise. Although North Vietnam had not responded formally to the American proposal, Vietcong rocket attacks had subsided and there were indications that significant numbers of North Vietnamese troops had been withdrawn from the south. Harriman argued that the military lull could be interpreted as the sign of deescalation the United States had sought, and he pressed Johnson to stop the bombing and reduce the level of American military activity while making clear the next move he expected from Hanoi. Clifford supported Harriman's proposal, but the military argued that the lull was simply a regroupment for the next offensive and warned that stopping the bombing would endanger American troops. Johnson flatly rejected Harriman's proposal. Indeed, at a press conference on July 31, he threatened that if there were no breakthrough in Paris, he might be compelled to undertake additional military measures. "Our most difficult negotiations were with Washington and not Hanoi . . . ," one U.S. diplomat later lamented, "we just couldn't convince the President that summer."[21]

While standing firm in Paris, the administration used every available means to strengthen its position in South Vietnam. The United States stepped up the pace of military operations in the spring of 1968.

---

[20]Notes on National Security Council meeting, May 22, 1968, Johnson Papers, National Security File, NSC Meetings, Box 3; notes on meetings, May 25, 28, Johnson Papers, Meeting Notes File, Box 3.
[21]Quoted in Allan E. Goodman, *The Lost Peace: America's Search for a Negotiated Settlement of the Vietnam War* (Stanford, Calif., 1978), p. 69.

The air war in the south reached a new peak of intensity, as B-52s and fighter-bombers relentlessly attacked infiltration routes, lines of communication, and suspected enemy base camps. The number of B-52 missions tripled in 1968, and the bombs dropped on South Vietnam exceeded one million tons. In March and April, the United States and South Vietnam conducted the largest search-and-destroy mission of the war, sending more than 100,000 troops against enemy forces in the provinces around Saigon. "Charlie [the Vietcong] is being relentlessly pursued night and day and pounded to shreds whenever and wherever we catch him," one U.S. officer exclaimed.[22] The scale of American military operations diminished somewhat in the summer and fall as Abrams shifted to small-unit patrols and mobile spoiling attacks, but throughout the remainder of the year the United States kept intense pressure on enemy forces in South Vietnam.

The United States and South Vietnam also launched an Accelerated Pacification campaign to secure as much of the countryside as possible in the event serious negotiations should begin. Abrams committed a major proportion of American and ARVN manpower to the program, and local defense forces were enlarged and given modern military equipment. To use their resources more effectively, the United States and South Vietnam focused their pacification efforts in certain key areas. U.S. and South Vietnamese officials energetically applied both carrot and stick to cripple an already weakened Vietcong. The Chieu Hoi Program, which offered amnesty and "rehabilitation" to defectors, was intensified, as was the Phoenix Program, a direct attack on the Vietcong infrastructure through mass arrests. By late 1968, for the first time, the United States and South Vietnam had committed a major portion of their resources and manpower to the task of controlling the countryside.[23]

The United States also pressed forward with Vietnamization. American officials candidly admitted that the South Vietnamese were nowhere near ready to assume the burden of their own defense. "If you took out all the United States . . . forces now," Abrams conceded, "the Government would have to settle for a piece of Vietnam."[24] New plans

[22]Frank Clay to Mr. and Mrs. Lucius Clay, May 15, 1968, Frank Clay Papers, U.S. Army Military History Institute, Carlisle Barracks, Pa.

[23]Douglas S. Blaufarb, *The Counterinsurgency Era: U.S. Doctrines and Performance* (New York, 1977), pp. 264–265.

[24]A. J. Langguth, "General Abrams Listens to a Different Drummer," *New York Times Magazine* (May 5, 1968), 28.

were nevertheless drawn up to expand and upgrade the South Vietnamese armed forces and to shift to them gradually the primary responsibility for military operations. The force level was increased from 685,000 to 850,000, training programs were drastically expanded, and ARVN units were given the newest equipment. To increase the combat-readiness of Vietnamese troops and to smooth the transition, Abrams employed ARVN and American units in combined operations.[25]

Pacification and Vietnamization were both long-range undertakings, however, and the frenzied efforts of 1968 could not make up for years of neglect. It was the end of the year before the pacification program got back to where it had been before Tet. The establishment of a presence in the villages was not tantamount to gaining the active support of the people, something that could not be accomplished overnight. The ARVN was larger and better equipped, but its basic problems remained uncorrected. Desertions reached an all-time high in 1968; an acute shortage of qualified officers persisted. At the end of the year, American advisers rated two ARVN divisions "outright poor," eight no better than "improving," and only one "excellent."[26] Americans detected among the Vietnamese a stubborn, if quiet, resistance to the whole notion of Vietnamization. Clifford returned from a visit to Saigon "oppressed" by the "pervasive Americanization" of the war. The United States was still doing most of the fighting and paying the cost. "Worst of all," he concluded, "the South Vietnamese leaders seemed content to have it that way."[27]

---

[25]J. Lawton Collins, Jr., *The Development and Training of the South Vietnamese Army, 1950–1972* (Washington, D.C., 1975), pp. 85–88, 100–101, 104–105, 117–118.

[26]Robert Shaplen, *The Road from War: Vietnam, 1965–1970* (New York, 1970), p. 250.

[27]Clifford, "Viet Nam Reappraisal," pp. 614–615; also Clifford to Johnson, July 16, 18, 1968, Clifford Papers, Box 5.

The American Imbroglio

NEIL SHEEHAN

Journalist Neil Sheehan covered the Vietnam War since the first
American involvement. For over a decade he immersed himself in the
biography of John Paul Vann, an American army officer and advisor to
the South Vietnamese government who within himself mirrored the
contradictions of American foreign policy. In this excerpt Sheehan
describes Vann's funeral and in particular the generational rift seen in
many American families. Why was the Vietnam War so unpopular
with the "younger generation"? Why do some writers call it America's
first lower-class war?

It was a funeral to which they all came. They gathered in the red
brick chapel beside the cemetery gate. Six gray horses were hitched to a
caisson that would carry the coffin to the grave. A marching band was
ready. An honor guard from the Army's oldest regiment, the regiment
whose rolls reached back to the Revolution, was also formed in ranks
before the white Georgian portico of the chapel. The soldiers were in
full dress, dark blue trimmed with gold, the colors of the Union Army,
which had safeguarded the integrity of the nation. The uniform was un-
suited to the warmth and humidity of this Friday morning in the early
summer of Washington, but this state funeral was worthy of the discom-
fort. John Paul Vann, the soldier of the war in Vietnam, was being
buried at Arlington on June 16, 1972.

The war had already lasted longer than any other in the nation's
history and had divided America more than any conflict since the Civil
War. In this war without heroes, this man had been the one compelling
figure. The intensity and distinctiveness of his character and the courage

and drama of his life had seemed to sum up so many of the qualities Americans admired in themselves as a people. By an obsession, by an unyielding dedication to the war, he had come to personify the American endeavor in Vietnam. He had exemplified it in his illusions, in his good intentions gone awry, in his pride, in his will to win. Where others had been defeated or discouraged over the years, or had become disenchanted and had turned against the war, he had been undeterred in his crusade to find a way to redeem the unredeemable, to lay hold of victory in this doomed enterprise. At the end of a decade of struggle to prevail, he had been killed one night a week earlier when his helicopter had crashed and burned in rain and fog in the mountains of South Vietnam's Central Highlands. He had just beaten back, in a battle at a town called Kontum, an offensive by the North Vietnamese Army which had threatened to bring the Vietnam venture down in defeat.

Those who had assembled to see John Vann to his grave reflected the divisions and the wounds that the war had inflicted on American society. At the same time they had, almost every one, been touched by this man. Some had come because they had admired him and shared his cause even now; some because they had parted with him along the way, but still thought of him as a friend; some because they had been harmed by him, but cherished him for what he might have been. Although the war was to continue for nearly another three years with no dearth of dying in Vietnam, many at Arlington on that June morning in 1972 sensed that they were burying with John Vann the war and the decade of Vietnam. With Vann dead, the rest could be no more than a postscript.

He had gone to Vietnam at the beginning of the decade, in March 1962, at the age of thirty-seven, as an Army lieutenant colonel, volunteering to serve as senior advisor to a South Vietnamese infantry division in the Mekong Delta south of Saigon. The war was still an adventure then. The previous December, President John F. Kennedy had committed the arms of the United States to the task of suppressing a Communist-led rebellion and preserving South Vietnam as a separate state governed by an American-sponsored regime in Saigon.

Vann was a natural leader of men in war. He was a child of the American South in the Great Depression, a redneck born and raised in a poor white working-class district of Norfolk, Virginia. He never tanned, his friends and subordinates joked during that first assignment in Vietnam. Whenever he exposed himself to the sun by marching with the

South Vietnamese infantrymen on operations, which he did constantly, his ruddy neck and arms simply got redder.

At first glance he appeared a runty man. He stood five feet eight inches and weighed 150 pounds. An unusual physical stamina and an equally unusual assertiveness more than compensated for this shortness of stature. His constitution was extraordinary. It permitted him to turn each day into two days for an ordinary man. He required only four hours of sleep in normal times and could function effectively with two hours of sleep for extended periods. He could, and routinely did, put in two eight-hour working days in every twenty-four and still had half a working day in which to relax and amuse himself.

The assertiveness showed in the harsh, nasal tone of his voice and in the brisk, clipped way he had of enunciating his words. He always knew what he wanted to do and how he wanted to do it. He had a genius for solving the day-to-day problems that arise in the course of moving forward a complicated enterprise, particularly one as complicated as the art of making war. The genius lay in his pragmatic cast of mind and in his instinct for assessing the peculiar talents and motivations of other men and then turning those talents and motivations to his advantage. Detail fascinated him. He prized facts. He absorbed great quantities of them with ease and was always searching out more, confident that once he had discovered the facts of a problem, he could correctly analyze it and then apply the proper solution. His character and the education the Army had given him at service schools and civilian universities had combined to produce a mind that could be totally possessed by the immediate task and at the same time sufficiently detached to discern the root elements of the problem. He manifested the faith and the optimism of post-World War II America that any challenge could be overcome by will and by the disciplined application of intellect, technology, money, and, when necessary, armed force.

Vann had no physical fear. He made a habit of frequently spending the night at South Vietnamese militia outposts and survived a number of assaults against these little isolated forts of brick and sandbag blockhouses and mud walls, taking up a rifle to help the militiamen repel the attack. He drove roads that no one else would drive, to prove they could be driven, and in the process drove with slight injury through several ambushes. He landed his helicopter at district capitals and fortified camps in the midst of assaults to assist the defenders, ignoring the shelling and the antiaircraft machine guns, defying the enemy gunners to kill him. In the course of the decade he acquired a reputation for invulnerability. Time and again he took risks that killed other men and always survived. The odds, he said, did not apply to him.

A willingness to take risks in his professional life was another quality he had in great measure. He displayed it during his first year in Vietnam, from March 1962 to April 1963, and showed it often in later years. While serving as senior advisor to a South Vietnamese infantry division in the Mekong Delta that first year, Vann saw that the war was being lost. The ambassador and the commanding general in South Vietnam were telling the Kennedy administration that everything was going well and that the war was being won. Vann believed then and never ceased to believe that the war could be won if it was fought with sound tactics and strategy. When the general and his staff in Saigon did not listen to him, and his reports aroused their displeasure, he leaked his meticulously documented assessments to the American correspondents in the country. He was reassigned to the Pentagon at the end of his tour, and he conducted a campaign there to try to convince the nation's military leadership that corrective action had to be taken if the United States was not to be defeated in Vietnam. He was rebuffed. Having completed twenty years of active duty, he chose to retire from the Army on July 31, 1963. His retirement was interpreted by most of his friends and associates as an act of protest so that he could speak out publicly on the war. Vann proceeded to do precisely that in newspaper, magazine, and television interviews and in speeches to whatever groups would listen to him.

He went back to Vietnam in March 1965 as a provincial pacification representative for the Agency for International Development (AID). He was never to return to the United States, except for occasional home leaves, until his death. He distinguished himself as pacification representative in one of the most dangerous provinces in the country just west of Saigon and by the end of 1966 was made chief of the civilian pacification program for the eleven provinces in the corps region surrounding the capital. In his reports to his superiors during those years, Vann denounced as cruel and self-defeating the indiscriminate bombing and shelling of the countryside which the U.S. high command was conducting to try to deprive the Vietnamese Communists of their population base. Large sections of the peasantry were driven into slums in the cities and into refugee camps near the district capitals and larger towns. Vann never hesitated to use whatever level of force he felt was required to further his cause, but he considered it morally wrong and stupid to wreak unnecessary violence on the innocent.

In 1967 his professional boldness again put him in disfavor with those in authority. He warned that the strategy of attrition being pursued by Gen. William Westmoreland with a 475,000-man American army was not succeeding, that security in the countryside was worsening, that the Vietnamese Communists were as strong as ever. Vann was vindicated when, on January 31, 1968, the Communists took advantage of Tet, the Vietnamese Lunar New Year holiday, to launch a surprise offensive against installations in cities and towns throughout the country, penetrating even the U.S. Embassy compound in the middle of Saigon. The war-of-attrition strategy was discredited. Westmoreland was relieved as commanding general in Vietnam.

Although Vann hurt his family and others close to him in his personal life, his loyalty to friends, associates, and subordinates seemed limitless over the years. After the Tet Offensive his best Vietnamese friend, a former lieutenant colonel and province chief who had left the South Vietnamese Army to go into politics, launched a complicated scheme to negotiate a settlement to the war and started to denounce the Saigon regime. Several senior U.S. officials suspected Vann's friend of seeking to form a coalition government with the Communists in the hope of securing a prominent place for himself. Vann disapproved of his friend's negotiating scheme, but he risked his career again in a vain attempt to save his friend from jail. He was nearly dismissed and sent home. Vann also parted over the war with his best American friend, Daniel Ellsberg, who had earlier been a comrade in the struggle to make the Vietnam endeavor succeed. Ellsberg began an antiwar crusade in the United States while Vann continued his crusade to win the war in Vietnam. Their friendship remained intact. When Vann was killed, Ellsberg was preparing to go on trial in the Federal District Court in Los Angeles for copying the Pentagon Papers. Vann had told Ellsberg that he would testify in his behalf. Ellsberg wept at the loss of the man to whom he had been closest in life.

Despite his maverick behavior, Vann had gradually risen in the system. His leadership qualities and his dedication to the war had assisted his promotion, as had a realization by those in power in Saigon and Washington that his dissent over tactics or strategy was always meant to further the war effort, not to hinder it. In May 1971 he was made senior advisor for the corps region comprising the Central Highlands and the adjacent provinces on the Central Coast. He was given authority over all U.S. military forces in the area, along with control of those civilians and military officers assigned to the pacification program. The position made him, in effect, a major general in the U.S. Army. The appointment was unprecedented in the history of American wars, as Vann was technically a civilian employed by AID. In addition, he covertly shared command of the 158,000 South Vietnamese troops in the corps because of a special relationship he had developed with the South Vietnamese general who was his counterpart. The influence he wielded within the U.S. civil-military bureaucracy and the Saigon government structure made him the most important American in the country after the ambassador and the commanding general in Saigon. His accumulated expertise and aptitude for this war made him the one irreplaceable American in Vietnam.

Vann's political credo was the set of beliefs characteristic of the United States that had emerged from World War II as the greatest power on earth, the view of self and the world that had carried America to war in Vietnam in the fullness of this power. To Vann, other peoples were lesser peoples; it was the natural order of things that they accept American leadership. He was convinced that having gained the preeminence it had been destined to achieve, the United States would never relinquish the position. He did not see America as using its power for self-satisfaction. He saw the United States as a stern yet benevolent authority that enforced peace and brought prosperity to the peoples of the non-Communist nations, sharing the bounty of its enterprise and technology with those who had been denied a fruitful life by poverty and social injustice and bad government. He assumed that America's cause was always just, that while the United States might err, its intentions were always good. He was simplistic in his anti-Communism, because to him all Communists were enemies of America and thus enemies of order and progress.

He saw much that was wrong about the war in Vietnam, but he could never bring himself to conclude that the war itself was wrong and unwinnable. To admit this would have been to admit the inevitability of defeat, and at a certain point in him intellect stopped and instinct took over. He could not abide defeat, defeat for himself or for his vision of America. He believed that America had staked that vision in Vietnam and he knew that he had made his stake there. That spring, when many around him had despaired at the height of the North Vietnamese

Army offensive, he had said no, they would not retreat, they would stand and fight. He had fought and won the battle and then he had died. This was why some of those who had assembled at Arlington on June 16, 1972, wondered if they were burying with him more than the war and the decade of Vietnam. They wondered if they were also burying with him this vision and this faith in an ever-innocent America.

Jesse [Vann, John Paul Vann's 21 year old son] had been thinking about the war again since his father's death. His father's death had made him realize that the war was as alive as ever and that he and the other people had started to accept its existence. Passively accepting the war was wrong, Jesse thought, and he was not going to tolerate this complicity in himself any longer. Jesse was the son most like his father in his refusal to endure anything that denied him the freedom to live life as he wanted to live it. He stood out at the funeral, with his blond hair falling defiantly over his shoulders, unfurled from the ponytail in which he customarily wore it. He had learned how to put his hair up into a hairnet and hide it under a wig when he had to in order to find a job and earn a living. Today he flaunted its length. Jesse's beard was also unkempt. A year or two earlier his father had mailed him a blue polyester suit from Hong Kong. His elder brother, John Allen, had asked him to wear the suit to the funeral, but Jesse disliked suits, regarding them as uniforms. He was wearing only the coat of the suit, with a pair of purple knit slacks he had selected in a Denver store and his mother had paid for before they had flown to Washington. His shoes were a two-tone white-and-black pair that had been his late grandfather's golf shoes. His grandmother had supplied them as a substitute for the dirty brown canvas crepe-soled shoes that he normally wore.

Jesse decided he would give his father a parting gift, the gift of his own honesty and his willingness to take a stand for what he believed to be right. He would leave half of his draft card on the coffin with his father as a token of the gift. Then he would complete the gift by handing the other half of the card to Richard Nixon when the family drove to the White House in a little while for a ceremony at which Nixon was to honor his father with a posthumous award of the Presidential Medal of Freedom. Jesse had always refused to accept the draft, but there was no longer any need for him to go to jail because of his refusal, other than to be honest and to take a stand. He was immune now from actually being drafted. Several years earlier, he had been in danger of going to prison for draft resistance. Jesse's draft board in Colorado had classified him as delinquent then for his refusal to cooperate. Delinquent status meant that he would shortly have been faced with the choice of prison or induction into the Army. (He had ruled out fleeing to Canada.) John Allen had put on his college ROTC uniform, gone to the draft board office, and told the middle-aged woman who was the clerk that their father was serving in Vietnam in an important position. He had talked her into changing Jesse's status to 1-Y, temporarily unfit for service, because Jesse was seeing a psychiatrist. John Allen had acted without consulting either Jesse or their father. He had by then assumed the role of the man in the family because of Vann's absence. John Allen had known that Jesse would continue to resist the draft and that their father was unsympathetic to Jesse's argument that his conscience forbade him to serve in Vietnam. A few months before his father's death, Jesse had received a new draft card in the mail. The board had reclassified him as 4-F, permanently unfit for service. Jesse didn't know why the board had exempted him in this way. He had stopped seeing the psychiatrist after a few months in 1969, and he had no physical or mental disability.

Someone handed Jesse a rose to leave on the coffin. He took out his draft card, ripped it in half, put Nixon's half back into his pocket, and tucked the half he was giving his father under the rose, between the bloom and a branch of the stem, to try to conceal what he was doing. He laid both on top of the silver-gray coffin alongside the other roses his mother, his brothers, and his father's relatives had placed there. "Here, this is all I can give you now; this is all I can do," he said to his father. He turned away and went over to talk to Dan Ellsberg for a few minutes before it was time to leave for the White House. Jesse thought of what he would do when the family walked into the Oval Office for the ceremony and Nixon put out his hand to shake Jesse's. Instead of shaking hands, Jesse would silently present Nixon with his half. Half of a draft card would speak for him. It was a crime to refuse to carry one's draft card and an additional crime to mutilate one. Jesse wondered if it was a third crime to present a mutilated half to the president. He did not look forward to going to jail, but he believed his act of protest would be worth it. One of his friends had already gone to a federal prison for refusing to be drafted.

Jesse's younger brother, Tommy, eighteen, saw him tear the draft card in two and asked him what he was doing. Jesse reluctantly explained what he had in store for Nixon. Tommy could not keep Jesse's exciting plan to himself and told Peter about it on the way to the

White House. The sirens of two police motorcycles cleared the way for the limousines to run the red lights, because the ceremony was scheduled to begin at noon and the men in charge of the funeral did not want to keep the president waiting. Tommy approved of Jesse's scheme. He had a theory that Nixon was not bothered by the dying and the maiming and the other suffering of the war because none of it had ever personally touched Nixon or anyone close to him. Nixon had never experienced the war as the Vanns and other families Tommy knew had felt it, families who had lost a son or a father to death, or feared for one wounded, or grieved over a son who had made the opposite choice of resistance and jail or exile. Neither of Nixon's sons-in-law had gone to Vietnam to fight as Johnson's sons-in-law had done. He was anticipating the expression on Nixon's face when Jesse handed him half of a mutilated draft card. The war might at last come home to Richard Nixon, Tommy thought.

Peter said that Jesse's plan was stupid. Peter had been looking forward to this opportunity to meet the president.

At the White House the family was shown to the Roosevelt Room, about five paces across the hall from the Oval Office, for what was supposed to be a wait of a few minutes. Nixon was finishing a high-level discussion of welfare reform begun while the funeral was taking place at Arlington. Vann's half sister, Dorothy Lee, a housewife from Norfolk, Virginia, and his half brothers, Frank, a carpenter and construction supervisor, and Eugene, a senior master sergeant in the Air Force, had also ridden over from Arlington to witness the award of the medal.

Jesse tried to ease the strain within himself by inspecting the rust-colored wall-to-wall carpet. He was currently earning his livelihood on his knees laying carpets in Texas. He was observing that the Roosevelt Room carpet had been shoddily installed and that he could have done a better job when John Allen confronted him. Jesse's older brother had also noticed him doing something odd beside the coffin. The conversation between Tommy and Peter in the limousine, which John Allen had overheard, had given him the explanation.

"Don't do it, Jesse!" he said.

"Why not?" Jesse asked.

"This day is not for you, Jesse," his brother said, keeping his voice low and controlled to try to prevent anyone else in the room from overhearing them. "This is for Dad. This is what Dad lived for and what he died for. Don't belittle him by doing this."

The day that John Allen saw as the vindication of their father would be destroyed. The White House press corps would be covering the ceremony. The spectacle of the long-haired son of a legendary American warrior in Vietnam handing the president half of his draft card, after leaving the other half with his father on top of the coffin, would make quite a story.

Tommy guessed what they were arguing about and came over to defend Jesse. "But this is what Jesse believes in," he said. The three of them began to argue over whether Jesse's right to express his opposition to the war took precedence over the public vindication of their father's career. Jesse's uncles overheard the argument and joined in the attempt to dissuade him.

"If you're thinking of doing that, I won't go in there," his Uncle Frank, a balding, stocky man, said.

"Well, you do what you want," Jesse replied. "I have to do what I have to do."

His Uncle Eugene, the Air Force senior master sergeant with the seven stripes of his rank on the sleeves of his tunic, resembled Jesse's father in the way his face got red when he was angry. He was called Gene in the family. "Jesse," he said, "your father was my brother and I've known him a hell of a lot longer than you have. He believed so strongly in what he was fighting for that to do this to him would be a slap in his face."

"Leave me alone," Jesse said to them all. "I have my own conscience to obey."

John Allen walked over to his mother. After a trip to the powder room, Mary Jane had been chatting in another corner of the Roosevelt Room with Dorothy Lee. She had taken a small dose of Valium at the hotel before the funeral to try to control her emotions. The drug was having only a partial effect. She looked composed in a simply tailored slate-blue dress. She was wearing her glasses, however, to hide her red-rimmed eyes.

"Mom," John Allen said, "Jesse wants to give Nixon half of his draft card. We can't let this happen."

Mary Jane started sobbing again as she had in the chapel when they wheeled in the coffin. She went to Jesse and pleaded with him. "Please Jesse, please, for your father, don't do this. This is your father's day, not yours, or mine, or anybody else's. You would disgrace him." His mother's pleading troubled Jesse, but he would not relent.

The Department of the Army civilian official who was supervising the funeral and a captain assisting him rushed out of the room to find someone on the White House staff. They met Lt. Gen. Brent Scowcroft, an Air Force officer who was then a brigadier general and the president's military assistant, in the hallway. He was heading toward the Roosevelt Room to see if the family was ready, because one of his duties was to supervise such ceremonies. He had known Vann slightly and liked him. They warned Scowcroft what was happening and then one of them brought out John Allen to relate what Jesse intended.

"That's impossible," Scowcroft said.

"We really don't know how to stop him," John Allen said. "He's determined to do it."

Scowcroft walked into the Oval Office, gave the president the briefest possible explanation of what was occurring, and said there would be a slight delay while he handled the problem. A career staff officer, Scowcroft was known for his businesslike approach to crises large and small.

He went into the Roosevelt Room and drew Jesse aside from the group that was haranguing him. Scowcroft spoke to Jesse in a calm voice.

"Listen," he said, "whatever you think about the war and whatever you want to do about it, this ceremony is to honor your father. There is no way you can do this and not ruin the ceremony. Unless you promise us you won't give your draft card to the president, unless you promise us you won't do this, we'll have to cancel the ceremony."

Jesse had already begun to weaken under his mother's continued pleading and because his Uncle Frank, in contrast to the others, had quieted down and tried to reason with him in similar fashion. The calm tone of this man made a further impression on him. He decided that he might be exploiting for his own ends a situation in which he was present only because of his father. He might not have a moral right to do that. Since he couldn't act with a clean conscience, he wouldn't act at all. Anyway, he wasn't being given much choice. "Okay, okay," he said to Scowcroft, "I promise not to do it."

Scowcroft squeezed Jesse's forearm and gave him one of those "Good boy!" looks. He turned to John Allen. "Will he or won't he?" Scowcroft asked.

"If he says he won't do it, he won't do it," John Allen answered. Scowcroft returned to the Oval Office and told the president that the ceremony could go forward.

6

THE GREAT SOCIETY

In a commencement speech at the University of Michigan in 1964, President Lyndon Johnson outlined his vision of the Great Society. "We have the opportunity," he told the crowd, "to move not only toward the rich society and the powerful society, but upward to the Great Society." The President envisioned a nation where "men are more concerned with the quality of their goals than the quality of their goods." Pledging to fulfill the "ideals" of the Kennedy Administration, Johnson proposed action on civil rights, medical care, education, and welfare. Following a smashing victory over conservative Republican Barry Goldwater in the 1964 presidential election, Johnson moved swiftly to fulfill his promise.

Over the next few months, Johnson designed and the Eighty-ninth Congress approved legislation to assist the poor and guarantee civil rights, eliminate water and air pollution, aid urban areas, provide education for the young and medical care for the aged. The Great Society represented the greatest burst of reform since the New Deal. "Working in the White House during this period produced on occasion an almost eerie feeling," observed one participant. "The legislation rolled through the House and Senate in such profusion and so methodically that you seemed part of some vast, overpowering machinery, oiled to purr."

A number of problems prevented the Great Society from realizing its full potential. Johnson's personal style certainly hampered many of his reforms. "If egomania is an occupational disease of most politicians and virtually all presidents," commented one scholar, "Johnson carried the illness to its most extreme form." In his desire to surpass his idol Franklin D. Roosevelt, Johnson sometimes pushed through Congress legislation that had not been carefully developed or planned. "Hurry, boys, hurry," he told his aides. "Get that legislation up to the Hill and out. Eighteen months from now ol' Landslide Lyndon will be Lame-Duck Lyndon."

Conceptual and administrative problems plagued many Great Society initiatives. The reforms were frequently overmatched by the complexity of the problems they were trying to solve. Some programs, like welfare, required creation of a large and inefficient bureaucracy. Like other liberals of his generation, Johnson underestimated structural limitations—underemployment, low wages, discrimination—that frequently limited opportunity, and he possessed unbridled confidence in the power of the government to achieve change. As a consequence, Johnson raised expectations which his modest proposals could not fulfill.

Public attitudes toward Johnson and his reforms also shifted after 1965. African-American riots hardened white resistance to further steps to alleviate discrimination and poverty. But most of all, Vietnam shattered Johnson's fragile consensus. By late 1965, students were attending mass demonstrations, burning draft cards, and chanting slogans like, "Hey, Hey, LBJ, how many kids did you kill today." Many establishment figures, frustrated with the war's direction, raised questions about America's commitment to Southeast Asia. Liberals complained that the war drained resources needed at home. "The pursuit of widened war has narrowed domestic welfare programs making the poor—white and Negro—carry the heaviest burdens both at the front and at home," Martin Luther King charged. By 1966, Congress, reflecting voter anxiety about crime, urban unrest, and inflation, became increasingly hostile to reform.

Critics, however, often overlook the enormous gains made during these years. Enrollment in elementary and secondary schools increased from 39 million in 1962 to 46 million in 1970. The number of families living in poverty plummeted from 40 million in 1959 to 25 million in 1968. The median family income rose noticeably between 1964 and 1968. General improvement of economic conditions explains some, but not all, of the increase. Voting rights made a vast difference for millions of African-Americans. The 29,000 registered African-Americans in Mississippi in 1964 grew, by 1980, to 330,000; in Alabama, from 110,000 to 350,000; in Louisiana, from 165,000 to 456,000.

In the selections that follow, Frederick Siegel examines the evolution of the Great Society, placing emphasis on Johnson's shrewd political and legislative skills. Though recognizing his limitations, Siegel argues that Johnson "tried to redefine the structure of opportunity in America." James T. Patterson takes aim at the centerpiece of Johnson's program—the war on poverty. His account emphasizes the conceptual confusion, poor planning, stingy funding, and conservative public attitudes which denied the President a clear victory. Allen Matusow shows how America's growing involvement in Vietnam drained resources from domestic initiatives and divided Johnson's fragile reform coalition.

Troubled Journey

FREDERICK F. SIEGEL

In his book, *Troubled Journey*, the historian Frederick F. Siegel examines American society in the years after 1941. He believes that national politics since Roosevelt has consisted of "a running duel between the shifting coalitions that comprise the heirs and enemies" of the New Deal. How does Johnson and his Great Society reforms fit into this continuing debate?

On November 22, 1963, in the same plane that carried the slain chief executive's body back to Washington, Lyndon Baines Johnson was sworn in as the thirty-sixth President of the United States. Lyndon Johnson was a Rabelaisian, larger-than-life figure. A tall man from Texas, a state with a reputation for producing outsized characters, Johnson had the face of a riverboat gambler and the political skills of a master politician. He was only ten years older than Kennedy, but he came from a different generation and a different world. A product of Depression era poverty, Johnson's political views had been shaped in part by his political hero, Franklin Delano Roosevelt. Styling himself after FDR, Johnson liked to be called LBJ. If Kennedy had been born with a silver spoon in his mouth, Johnson grew up with the taste of dirt in his. He came from the desperately poor hill country of West Texas. "When I was young," Johnson told reporters, "poverty was so common that we didn't know it had a name."

A self-made man, Johnson fought his way to the top of the Texas political heap. A man of wildly conflicting impulses, he was driven on the one hand by greed and an unquenchable thirst for success and on the other by a genuine concern for the plight of those who had shared his childhood poverty. Johnson's Texas was a one-party state. The Democratic Party in Texas was a circus tent organization that included everyone from right to left, from business big and little to labor, blacks, and Mexican-Americans. The key to success in that situation was to create a consensus everyone could live with. Johnson became a master of using his extraordinary persuasive skills to engineer agreement between diverse interests. Elected to Congress in 1937, he made his mark bringing together within the Democratic Party rapacious *nouveau riche* Texas oil millionaires and conscious-stricken Northern liberals whose political divisions paralleled those of his own vast personality. He was elected to the Senate in 1948 by the narrowest of margins, leading his detractors to joke about "Landslide Lyndon." But once there, he rose, with the support of his fellow Texan and mentor, Speaker of the House Sam Rayburn, to become Majority Leader of the Senate in 1955 after serving only one term.

Johnson became one of the most powerful and effective Majority Leaders the Hill has ever known. He was an overpowering figure with the psychic energy of a natural phenomenon. When a congressman was asked why he had changed his mind on a key vote, he answered: "Well, it's this way. Lyndon got me by the lapels and put his face on top of mine and talked and talked and talked. I figured it was either getting drowned or joining." Extremely intelligent without being an intellectual, he was a reader of men, not books. Johnson, as an English reporter described it, "comes into a room slowly and warily, as if he means to smell out the allegiances of everyone in it." He combined a rare ability to look inside his fellow politicians with a near-photographic memory for details, so that, as one aide put it, "not a sparrow falls on Capitol Hill" without LBJ knowing.

The Kennedy loyalists and intellectuals were among the few who seemed totally immune to his political sway. They viewed the rough-hewn Johnson as a boor and a usurper, much as FDR's retinue looked down on the man from Missouri, Harry S. Truman. For the Kennedyites, brother Bobby was the true heir to the throne, so that the Johnson presidency was simply an unfortunate interregnum. Kennedy's intellectual camp followers were exhilarated by a President who brought taste to the White House and recognition for them. Enthralled by the magic of Camelot, "they received his words and images," said literary critic Alfred Kazin, "as children 'read' the pictures in a storybook." Johnson, on the other hand, reminded intellectuals of what the rest of the country was like. He reminded us of who we were—and some, said Richard Whalen, conceived their dislike of him in that moment.

For his part, Johnson brushed aside the snubs and moved quickly to calm the nation by proclaiming his intent to carry on Kennedy's noble mission. As powerful as he was, Johnson was somewhat in awe of his Ivy League advisers, something that worried Rayburn. After an obviously impressed Johnson recited the extraordinary academic credentials of his Cabinet, the Speaker snorted, "I just wish one of them had been elected anything, even deputy sheriff."

To prove he was worthy of the office and not just another parochial Southerner, Johnson moved quickly to push Kennedy's civil rights legislation, long blocked by his fellow Dixie politicians. As Johnson explained it: "If I didn't get out in front on this issue" the liberals "would get me . . . I had to produce a civil rights bill that was even stronger than the one they'd have gotten if Kennedy had lived." And produce he did. Defying all the writers, politicians, and analysts who spoke of the "deadlock of democracy," Johnson used his unparalleled skills to break the Southern filibuster. He pushed through Congress the most sweeping civil rights legislation since the end of the First Reconstruction. The 1964 Civil Rights Act, described by Supreme Court Justice Arthur Goldberg as the "vindication of human dignity," became the cornerstone of civil rights law. It provided legal and financial support for cities desegregating their schools, banned discrimination by businesses and unions, created an Equal Opportunities Commission to enforce that ban, and outlawed discrimination in places of public accommodation.

With the Civil Rights Act passed and his own legitimacy established, Johnson turned to putting his own stamp on the presidency. Declaring, "We are not helpless before the iron law of [traditional] economics," Johnson called for a "War on Poverty" as Kennedy had called for a war on Communism.

The "War," wrote *Time* magazine, reflected the "uniquely American belief" that "evangelism, money and organization can lick just about anything." Americans generally believed that "a rising tide lifts all boats," but a spate of books on poverty, particularly Michael Harrington's powerful *The Other America*, showed that a substantial number of Americans, black and white, silently suffered from such serious deprivation that they would be unaided by the general prosperity. The very poor, argued anthropologist Oscar Lewis, were trapped in a culture of poverty, a culture which, in the words of Harrington, meant that "the poor are not like us. . . . They are a different kind of people."

Social science promised a way to reach the culturally distant world of severe poverty. On assuming the presidency Johnson inherited an economic growth rate that had more than doubled from 2.1 percent to 4.5 percent since 1960 and which, with mild inflation, was pouring extraordinary amounts of money into federal coffers. This "social surplus," the excess of revenues over expenditures, provided nearly four billion dollars a year for new public spending. The flow of money was so great that Governor Earl Long of Louisiana whimsically suggested massive spending for two highway systems, one reserved for drunks. Johnson's economic advisers assured him that the unprecedented surpluses would continue indefinitely. Pointing to the great success of the 1964 tax cut, which seemed to demonstrate their ability to put their theories into practice, the "new" economists claimed that, through Keynesian "demand management," they had discovered the secret of constant non-inflationary growth. In short, the continuing surplus created by "demand management" meant that poverty could be abolished without undue sacrifice from the rest of the population. There would be a "maximum of reform with a minimum of social disruption."

While the economists were guiding the fiscal ship of state, their fellow experts, the sociologists, devised programs to provide the poor with nutritional aid, health and schooling benefits, job training, and even dignity and respect. The programs were institutionalized as part of Johnson's Economic Opportunity Act of 1964. The act appropriated nearly a billion dollars for projects such as the Head Start program to assist disadvantaged preschoolers, the Job Corps for high school dropouts, a domestic Peace Corps—Volunteers in Service to America (VISTA)—a Neighborhood Youth Corps, and a Community Action Program designed for the "maximum feasible participation" by the poor it was meant to aid.

Flushed by his legislative successes, LBJ headed into the 1964 presidential campaign by asking for even broader social measures as part of what he called "The Great Society." Like Kennedy's New Frontier, the Great Society was a presidential answer to the quest for national and thus in many cases individual purpose in an increasingly secular age. It was to be the fulfillment of the American creed of equal opportunity—a grand mobilization of expertise, this time to fight poverty and disease, as depression, fascism, and Communism had been fought previously. In LBJ's own inspiring words: "This nation . . . has man's first chance to create a Great Society: a society of success without squalor, beauty without barrenness, of genius without the wretchedness of poverty. We can open the doors of learning. We can open the doors of opportunity and closed community—not just to the privileged few, but, thank God, we can open doors to everyone." Rhetoric (glorious though it was) aside, Johnson's proposals for a Great Society hinged on passing a twenty-five-year backlog of liberal Democratic legislation on health, education, racial discrimination, and conservation that had been sitting on the rear burner ever since the New Deal flame was snuffed out by the Republican/Dixiecrat coalition in 1937.

The Great Society program, which vested vast new powers in the federal government, promised to rearrange the relationship between Washington and the rest of the nation. For American liberals the growth of federal power meant the chance to complete the racial reforms begun by Reconstruction and the economic reforms begun by the New Deal without a fundamental restructuring of American society. But for many others, those who "understood the American creed, not as a common set of national values, but as a justification for their particular set of local values," the Great Society proved to be deeply unsettling. Their fears, however, were never fully aired, nor was Johnson given the chance to build a national consensus for the Great Society, because Barry Goldwater, his opponent in 1964, gave LBJ the enormous advantage of running as a social reformer while still seeming to be the less radical of the two.

Johnson's Republican opposition came from a group of youth activists deeply opposed to American policies in Vietnam and bitterly hostile to what they called the "Establishment," symbolized by Nelson Rockefeller. Their movement was directed by Stephen Shadeg, who had been heavily influenced by the thought and tactics of Chairman Mao. Their candidate, described by conservative William Buckley as one of "the few genuine radicals in American life," was Barry Morris Goldwater, junior senator from Arizona.

The Goldwater movement was built on the strength of the old Taftite right, the "veterans of the thirty years' war with the New Deal." Like Taft, Goldwater would say, "Yes, I fear Washington, more than I fear Moscow." But most of all Goldwater feared what he saw as Moscow's influence in Washington, so that as a first-term senator he was one of the diehards who opposed the censure of McCarthy after almost the entire Senate had turned against the demagogue from Wisconsin. The old right had been repeatedly defeated, in its struggle to control the Republican Party, by what it called the Eastern establishment, otherwise known as the "two-bit New Dealers" or "me-too Republicans." But in 1964 the Goldwater movement defeated the Rockefeller Republicans by mobilizing two new political elements: nouveau riche anti-union oilmen and aerospace men of the Southwest, and ideologically charged conservative youth.

Like their left-wing counterparts, these young conservatives disdained the soft society of welfarism with all its compromises and government paternalism. They complained of a "sickness in our society and the lack of a common purpose" that might "restore inner meaning to every man's life in a time too often rushed, too often obsessed with petty needs and material greeds." Contemptuous of businessmen who placed profit before free market ethics, they dreamed of a world made whole by the heroic deeds of rugged individuals untrammeled by the heavy hand of the state. Their allies, the Texas oilmen and aerospace entrepreneurs, however, were beneficiaries of vast government subsidies such as the oil-depletion allowance. But both were united in their hostility to the Rockefeller wing of the Republican Party. And both subscribed to the notion that only a laissez-faire economy could create the disciplined individuals with the character and fortitude necessary to sustain democracy. Politics for the activists was not so much a matter of pursuing material interests as a national screen on which to project their deepest cultural fears. They were part of a mood, a mood of deluxe puritanism, as much as an ideology, and in the words of Richard Whalen, "Barry Goldwater was the favorite son of their state of mind."

But even with his activists and oilmen, Goldwater, like Taft before him, might have lost the nomination if it hadn't been for the first nationwide stirrings of a white backlash against the civil rights movement. Interest in Goldwater was flagging when Alabama's Governor George Wallace, a flaming segregationist, made a surprising showing in liberal Wisconsin's Democratic primary. The Wallace showing revived interest in Goldwater, who was seen as the Republican most opposed to federal intervention on behalf of Afro-Americans. When Goldwater was nominated, Wallace's candidacy collapsed, suggesting a considerable overlap in the two men's donors and constituencies. Tall, trim, and handsome, the altogether affable Goldwater was not personally a bigot. A member of the NAACP, Goldwater was the kind of terribly sincere fellow everyone likes to have for a neighbor or a fraternity brother. He came to popular attention by spearheading congressional criticism of Walter Reuther and by his outspoken calls for a holy crusade against

Communism in general and Castro in particular. But as Goldwater told reporter Joseph Alsop: "You know, I haven't really got a first-class brain." And it showed. His combination of bland and outrageous statements alienated all but the right wing of the Republican Party from his candidacy. He could in the same speech assert that "where fraternities are not allowed, Communism flourishes" and then, warming to his message, suggest that nuclear weapons be used against Cuba, China, and North Vietnam if they refused to accede to American demands. Goldwater was unafraid of voicing unpopular views. He called for the abolition of the TVA, an end to the graduated income tax, and the elimination of Social Security, while campaigning forthrightly for the elimination of the union shop. "My aim," he said, "is not to pass laws but to repeal them." Here, in the words of Phyllis Schlafly, was "a choice and not an echo."

There was really no need for Johnson to criticize Goldwater's campaign for being too radical. Goldwater did it for him, proclaiming on national TV that "extremism in the defense of liberty is no vice." When the Goldwaterites adopted the slogan "In your hearts you know he's right," Democrats responded with "In your guts you know he's nuts." Johnson replied to Goldwater's "no substitute for victory" rhetoric on Vietnam with a proclamation of restraint. "We are not," LBJ told the American people, "about to send American boys nine or ten thousand miles from home to do what Asian boys ought to be doing for themselves." It is a virtual replay of the Truman-MacArthur struggle, with the same outcome.

With the successful focusing of the campaign on Goldwater's artless "shoot from the lip" pronouncements—"The child has no right to an education; in most cases he will get along very well without it"— Johnson's own measures at home and abroad went undebated. It was a curious consequence of the 1964 campaign that the fundamental issues raised by both Johnson's social innovations and Goldwater's ideological thrust went almost unnoticed, producing a curiously empty campaign which ironically denied Johnson the opportunity to build support for the Great Society. The consensus that emerged instead was that Barry Goldwater was unfit for office. The reaction to Goldwater was so broadly negative that the party which once denounced "economic royalists" now found Wall Street and big business flocking to its banner. Johnson attracted the nation's corporate elite in creating what Oscar Gass has called a Grossblock, a coalition of upper-middle-class professionals and lower-middle-class blue-collar workers, big business and labor, Catholics and Protestants, blacks and whites outside the Deep South, in a national replication of the Texas Democratic Party's "one big tent."

LBJ swept to victory with 61 percent of the vote, only 5 points short of doubling Goldwater's total. The Democrats gained 2 seats in the Senate and 37 in the House, creating enormous Democratic majorities.

LBJ's victory was so overwhelming that commentators openly speculated about the impending death of both conservatism and the Republican Party. We are left, said one observer, with a "one and a half party system." But an analysis of local voting patterns revealed something very different. On a host of social issues, ranging from prayer in the public schools to calls for cutting federal expenditures and reducing welfare spending, the electorate was far closer to Goldwater than to Johnson. Goldwater the candidate was repudiated, but on a local level conservatism was intact and even thriving. In California, for instance, areas which went strongly for LBJ also voted to repeal the state's anti-discriminatory fair housing laws by a better than two-to-one margin. Similarly, in Maryland, areas which had supported George Wallace when he made his strong showing in the Democratic primary there went overwhelmingly for LBJ in the general election. These Maryland voters were in favor of the civil rights bill even as they feared black militancy.

Goldwater's defeat was of such proportion that ironically it served to break the hold conservative Democrats held over their own party. So many Northern liberals triumphed in congressional races against Republicans "dragged down by Barry" that for the first time the Democrats had clear majorities in both houses without having to rely on their Dixiecrat allies. On the other hand, Goldwater, by piggybacking his right-to-work rhetoric on George Wallace's states' rights racism, had carried the Deep South, breaking the Democrats' century-long hold over that region. And while the Goldwater campaign rhetoric was most noted for its fire-eating foreign policy, it was Goldwater's appeal to the white backlash against black militancy that had garnered most of his votes North and South.

Lyndon Johnson was keenly aware that the American political system's balance of powers had been designed for stalemate. As a young congressman, he had seen FDR, at the height of his power, humbled when he tried to pack the Supreme Court. Johnson realized that unless he moved quickly to take advantage of his landslide victory, the naturally parochial tendencies of the Congress would block his Great Society initiatives. Johnson moved rapidly to circumvent the established interests in Congress. Instead of asking congressmen for legislative proposals, he organized task forces composed of administration aides and social reform academics to draw up legislation which would then be presented to the sachems as a fait accompli. Or as LBJ put it to his aides, "I want to see a whole bunch of coonskins on the wall."

The programs Johnson deemed most important were Medicare to protect the elderly from catastrophic losses and aid to elementary education to upgrade the schooling for both black and white poor. Legislation for Medicare and aid to elementary education had been proposed by Democrats ever since the mid-1940s but had always met fierce opposition from the American Medical Association and proponents of states' rights. Johnson knew that if he won on these two issues, "the momentum," as historian Jim Heath has put it, "would carry over, making it relatively easy to enact the rest of his legislative program." As before, the powerful AMA put up a tenacious fight against any form of federally guaranteed health insurance for the elderly, portraying it as a step on the road to socialized medicine. But Johnson, aided by the wily Wilbur Mills, of the House Ways and Means Committee, not only got Medicare passed; in a little-noticed maneuver, Medicaid, health care for the indigent, was tacked on. LBJ flew to Independence, Missouri, to sign the bill in front of a smiling Harry S. Truman. On January 12, 1965, only five days after the Medicare legislation was approved, LBJ sent the politically explosive aid to elementary education bill to Congress. Part and parcel of the War on Poverty, the bill was opposed by Protestant fundamentalists who wanted to deny federal money to the Catholic schools and by segregationists who saw Washington's money as the beginning of federal control over local schools. Here Johnson, aided by Senator Wayne Morse, achieved what the senator called a "back-door victory," by overtly ignoring racial and religious questions in order to target money regionally on the basis of population below the poverty level in a given area.

With Medicare and aid to education passed, Johnson moved quickly to complete what critics called his "revolution from above." If the word "revolution" was overblown, the critics were right to see that LBJ made unprecedented use of the federal budget. "No previous budget had ever been so contrived to do something for every major economic interest in the nation." But LBJ offered something for almost all his supporters: tax cuts for big business; billions of dollars for Appalachian social and economic development; the first major additions to our national parks and the first comprehensive air and water pollution standards for environmentalists; truth in packaging legislation for consumers; federal aid for mass transit for city dwellers; a subsidy boost for farmers; a National Arts and Humanities Foundation for academics; and, in LBJ's own words, "the goddamnedest toughest voting rights act" and Model Cities, low-cost housing, job-training programs, and slum clearance for blacks. At the end of this spate of legislation, the Democratic leadership on the Hill spoke jubilantly of the "fabulous 89th" Congress as "the Congress of fulfillment," "the Congress of accomplished hopes," "the Congress of realized dreams."

In the words of liberal policy analyst Sar Levitan, a great deal of LBJ's agenda involved "unabashedly class legislation. . . . designating a special group in the population as eligible to receive the benefits of American law." Class legislation was nothing new in American politics—federal insurance for overseas corporate investments and the mortgage tax deduction for homeowners are examples. What was different about the Great Society was that it extended such special benefits to those who were least well off. Johnson's left-wing critics complained that in order to aid the poor, his legislation provided a windfall for a multitude of contractors and middlemen who ultimately were the greatest beneficiaries. There is a good deal of truth to this charge. The doctors who fought Medicaid so bitterly were to number among its prime beneficiaries. Building contractors often became wealthy through Model Cities renewal efforts. This said, however, it is unlikely that any of the legislation directed at alleviating poverty could have passed a Congress composed of men representing American business and middle-class interests unless they too were cut in on federal largess.

Johnson, the adventurous conservative, was denounced as a "Red" by fiscal conservatives and simply a pork-barrel New Dealer by leftists, but both charges were wide of the mark. The New Deal was designed to aid widows, orphans, and the indigent; in short, it represented help for those worst off without addressing the underlying issues of social fairness. The Great Society, without being socialist, tried to partially redefine the structure of opportunity in America. Its aim was not simply to provide handouts to the poor; rather, it attempted to make the competitive race of life a bit fairer. The Great Society had a dramatic effect in relieving poverty. From 1964 to 1968 more than 14 million Americans moved out of poverty as the proportion of the impoverished was halved from 22 to 11 percent of the nation. Just as FDR's New Deal had incorporated working-class immigrants and organized them into the mainstream of American life, LBJ's Great Society tried to do the same for blacks and the poverty-stricken.

America's Struggle Against Poverty

JAMES T. PATTERSON

James T. Patterson, Ford Foundation and University Professor of History at Brown University, is the author of a number of acclaimed books on twentieth-century American history. In the excerpt that follows, adapted from *America's Struggle Against Poverty, 1900–1985*, Patterson examines the Office of Economic Opportunity, which was designed to oversee the poverty program. Does Patterson consider the war on poverty a success or a failure? Why was Johnson so infatuated with the community action programs?

Once [Sargeant] Shriver's [Office of Economic Opportunity] Task Force had completed its work, and Johnson had endorsed its product as the "center-piece" of his legislative program, it was highly likely that Congress would approve it. That they did, on partisan votes in the summer of 1964. Shriver, named to head the OEO, charged ahead with characteristic enthusiasm. An inspirational leader, he quickly attracted what one observer called "just an awful lot of good, bright, liberal, solid people." Shriver's qualities of energy and salesmanship adapted well to a new program that aimed to bypass existing governmental bureaucracies.

But almost from the start, the OEO encountered administrative difficulties, most stemming from confusion over goals. When the bill passed in August, the economist Robert Theobald grumbled that it exposed a "lack of research. We don't know enough. We are flying blind." Shriver himself conceded later, "It's like we went down to Cape Kennedy and launched a half dozen rockets at once." Americans, he agreed, "are just plain confused about what the poverty program is all about. It's like giving an American sports page to an Englishman."

Confusion resulted from the very structure of the package. Some framers had expected OEO to coordinate programs that would actually be administered by Cabinet departments, and this did happen to an extent: Labor ran the Neighborhood Youth Corps, HEW some provisions relating to higher education and training. But OEO operated the Job Corps, VISTA, and the community action programs. Assumption of these tasks enabled OEO to evade the incessant feuding that plagued HEW and Labor. But it saddled a new agency with formidable operating functions. No government agency can easily wear two hats, and that was doubly true of OEO, which lacked experienced staff to administer action programs.

OEO's dual role intensified the ever-present bureaucratic struggles between departments in Washington. From the start Labor Secretary Willard Wirtz proved hostile to the new agency. Wilbur Cohen went so far as to call Wirtz "constantly a pain in the neck." Although it ran the Neighborhood Youth Corps, the Labor Department supplied OEO with virtually no data on its programs. Bertrand Harding, who took over as deputy administrator of OEO in 1966, recalled that the old-line departments viewed the free-wheeling Shriver as antiestablishment. Many of OEO's difficulties, he said, were with the "other established agencies. They hated our guts, most of them."

Some thought Shriver's presence exacerbated the problems. His strengths as an administrator lay in what [Daniel Patrick] Moynihan later called his "infectious energy" and in his tireless efforts to publicize the program and cultivate congressional contacts that prevented radical cuts in the OEO budget. But Johnson loyalists distrusted him, for he was a Kennedy brother-in-law. Some associates found him inattentive to orderly management and unwilling to share authority. "He runs his office like a big-business corporation," one aide complained. "Occasionally he may bestow lavish praise, more often he forgets who accomplished what." Another aide noted that Shriver "never readily agreed to delegate a damned thing." A third dismissed him as "a hundred per cent operator by temperament." These criticisms are one-sided and fail to mention the intellectual excitement that existed in OEO under Shriver's direction. Still, the poverty program suffered from considerable infighting and confusion.

But administrative problems caused only some of OEO's early difficulties. Many contemporaries had other complaints. Some liberal social workers worried about what one aptly called the "severe dangers of over-sell." None of the OEO programs, he warned, "including the so-called new efforts, are sufficiently broad and comprehensive to make a major dent in the problem of economic poverty." Within six months of passage of the program, the National Association of Social Workers issued a position paper entitled "Poverty," a classic statement of activist social work philosophy that emphasized the limits of enhancing opportunity. Antipoverty programs, it said, "should be such as to assure income as a matter of right, in amounts sufficient to maintain all persons throughout the nation at a uniformly adequate level of living."

Social workers objected especially to the bulldozing intervention of OEO bureaucrats. In March 1965, when the NASW sent a questionnaire to hundreds of social work organizations, some replies expressed hostility to the poverty program. "Neither the poor, nor anyone else except the 'inner circle' around the mayor and his appointees have been involved," one agency responded. Another shot back, "It is a politicians' program and social workers had to be asked to be involved." Other social workers independently complained about being excluded and insulted. The head of the Washington office of NASW grumbled about OEO's "pretty stiff hands-off attitude to what they call a 'hand-out' welfare program." He said, "We would like to demonstrate that they ought to start where they are and not go off in the wild blue yonder setting up some kind of high-powered community leadership group with business and labor and so forth that is going to solve the problem of poverty in a particular community."

Because OEO was designed in part to cut through the allegedly tired welfare bureaucracy, it was not surprising that Shriver never developed amicable relations with the social workers, who understandably protected their turf. And hostility from radicals like Saul Alinsky, who demanded that the poor themselves confront the power structure, was equally predictable. Alinsky branded OEO as a paternalistic ally of a welfare establishment that had always coopted the poor. In 1965 he blasted OEO as "the worst political blunder and boomerang of the present administration," as a "huge political pork barrel," and as "history's greatest relief program for the benefit of the welfare industry." Denouncing social workers as "pimps of the poor," he concluded, "The poverty program as it stands today is a macabre masquerade and the mask is growing to fit the face, and the face is one of political pornography."

Conservatives, too, predictably denounced OEO. Some Republicans grumbled, not without cause, that OEO jumbled together many old programs. In a searing minority report on the bill, senators Barry Goldwater of Arizona and John Tower of Texas called the bill a "Madison Avenue deal" and a "poverty grab bag." Community action programs, they charged (inaccurately), were "a sort of retread WPA." The Job Corps, like the old CCC, sought to give young men "sun tans and an appreciation for outdoor living." They objected especially to Shriver's "poverty czar powers," which would "dangerously centralize Federal controls."

Behind conservative arguments such as these lay two durable notions about poverty and welfare. First, poor people deserved their fate. "The fact is," Goldwater said, "that most people who have no skill have had no education for the same reason—low intelligence or low ambition." In the United States, people are rewarded by "merit and not by fiat." Goldwater asserted that the "mere fact of having little money does not entitle everybody, regardless of circumstances, to be permanently maintained by the taxpayers at a comfortable standard of living." The second notion followed from the first: welfare was wasteful. Conservatives pointed out that the nation had never been so affluent and that the economy would flourish if the government minded its own business. "The only solution to poverty," wrote the conservative columnist Henry Hazlitt, "is free enterprise and continued economic growth—those things which made America great."

Once OEO started spending money, in October 1964, conservative critics pounced on it. Indeed, OEO confronted the same kind of sniping that had damaged the WPA in the 1930s. Why was OEO money going to support the antiwhite plays of LeRoi Jones and the Black Arts Theater of Harlem? Or to Job Corps centers like the one at Camp Breckinridge, Kentucky, where enrollees were rioting? Or to the Child Development Group in Mississippi, which senators James Eastland and John Stennis charged was being used to organize black voters? Or to the community action program in Syracuse, which was employing the Alinsky-like tactics to confront local officials? Some of these complaints zeroed in on sloppy administration—the accounting procedures in Mississippi were open to criticism. Most reflected hostility from right-wing politicians who objected to leftists or blacks getting OEO money.

An article in *U.S. News and World Report* in 1965 typified the scattershot approach of conservative opposition. Entitled "Poverty War out of Hand?" it featured two anti-OEO cartoons and a photograph of young blacks loafing about a Jobs Corps center. It hit OEO for "administrative chaos, bureaucratic bungling, waste, extravagance, costly duplication of existing services, internal squabbling." It exposed the excesses of the Syracuse community action program, the allegedly excessive salaries in the Head Start program, and the Job Corps generally. It concluded with quotes from a black educator who described OEO as a "slaphappy, sloppy, wasteful procedure," and from a Republican representative who said, "This program could become not just a national disgrace, but a national catastrophe."

What hurt OEO most were grievances from state and local politicians who resented OEO's ideas of community action. The villains, as the politicos saw it, were Jack Conway, Shriver's deputy, and Conway's aide, Richard Boone. Conway had served on the task force since March 1964, when he had taken leave from the AFL-CIO. Boone, an activist who had worked with Hackett and the PCJD, had helped draft the sections of the antipoverty program that called for "maximum feasible participation" of the poor. During the drafting, most of the task force members had paid no attention to the phrase. Those who had, like Moynihan, had assumed it meant that southern communities should not exclude blacks. Or they saw it as a way of bypassing the bickering federal agencies and the social work establishment—what one planner called the "board ladies and bureaucrats." Few had anticipated that maximum feasible participation might lead to programs that placed the poor in power and challenged local authorities.

Few people in early 1964 quite appreciated the accelerating militancy of the civil rights movement and especially the anger of blacks in the urban ghettos. In the summer of 1964 the first of many riots by blacks broke out in Harlem. There and elsewhere, these decisively refuted the old stereotype of the apathetic poor. By late 1964, when OEO began dispensing money to a thousand communities across the country, activists were determined to take charge of the funds. Conway often agreed that established urban officials were excluding the activists from community action. Early in 1965, OEO withheld funds from New York, Los Angeles, Philadelphia, San Francisco, and Chicago on the grounds that their community action plans did not give the poor maximum feasible participation. Activism at the top had coincided with unrest at the grass roots to confound the expectations of the framers.

The protests from urban politicians ranged from reasoned discourses to screams of rage. Some officials merely pressed Shriver to define maximum feasible participation. Were the poor to dominate the community action boards? Must they be poor themselves or merely representatives of the poor? Did they have to be elected by the poor, or could they be appointed by city officials? Others openly opposed the notion of control by the poor. Mayor Robert Wagner of New York told a House subcommittee, "I feel very strongly that the sovereign part of each locality . . . should have the power of approval over the making of the planning group." The mayors of San Francisco and Los Angeles accused OEO of "fostering class struggle" and demanded that only elected officials be entrusted with antipoverty funds. Explaining this view, one city official grumbled, "You can't go to a street corner with a pad and pencil and tell the poor to write you a poverty program. They won't know how." Mayor Richard Daley of Chicago added that involving the poor as leaders "would be like telling the fellow who cleans up to be the city editor of a newspaper." Complaints such as these led the U.S. Conference of Mayors to pass a resolution in June 1965 urging OEO to recognize City Hall or existing relief agencies as the proper channels for antipoverty money.

Some state politicians, such as New York Governor Nelson Rockefeller, protested that antipoverty money was going only to Democrats. Senator Robert Byrd of West Virginia, an influential Democrat, countered that the OEO officials were "offering employment to persons who will change their registration from Democrat to Republican." Governor John Connally of Texas protested in 1965 to his friend Lyndon Johnson against a proposed amendment that would deprive governors of the right to veto antipoverty projects. The president assured his friend that the veto would remain, but governors remained unhappy. A top aide to Johnson, after attending the governors' conference in July 1965, reported, "I didn't talk with a single governor who approves of the way it is being handled in Washington and at the state level. Our closest friends are very much upset by the way it is being administered."

Johnson, alarmed, had already dispatched Vice President Hubert Humphrey to reassure the politicians. OEO, meanwhile, attempted to clarify what it meant by maximum feasible participation. The poor, it explained in February 1965, were to participate "either on the governing body or on a policy advisory committee" or have "at least one representative selected from each of the neighborhoods" involved. At least one-third of the representatives on local boards should be poor people elected by the poor. Although the issue remained controversial, these guidelines clarified some of the confusion for a time.

But giving the poor only one-third of the pie did not please activists. They feared that state and local politicians were winning the battle against Conway and Boone. Conway resigned in September 1965 and returned to the AFL-CIO. Congress, to ensure social peace in the cities, passed a series of amendments, removing the words maximum feasible participation and establishing procedures for poverty boards. Representation was to be one-third poor people, one-third local elected officials, and one-third local community groups. State or local governments were to design or approve of local poverty agencies, and increasingly large percentages of antipoverty money were earmarked for "safe" programs, such as Head Start, that were popular on Capitol Hill. A total of $846 million of the $1.17 billion OEO appropriation for fiscal 1967 was so earmarked. These actions effectively curbed community control. One scholar observed later, "Local initiative, which is presumed to rank just below motherhood on the political scale of values, was further circumscribed."

By then Johnson, who had stood by OEO in some of these fights, was losing heart. When he instructed Walter Heller to go "full tilt" in late 1963, he had seen himself as another FDR and the program as a popular monument to his humanitarian instincts. Instead, it had embroiled him in conflict with his own political allies. He wondered how Shriver had allowed himself to be surrounded by so many "kooks and sociologists." Increasingly absorbed in the Vietnam war, disillusioned by his venture into economic uplift, Johnson gave the OEO little presidential support after 1965.

The disaffection of politicians and the pressing fiscal demands of the war guaranteed that OEO would henceforth get low priority in Washington. Congress passed the Model Cities program in 1966, which competed openly with OEO by funneling funds for urban needs through existing city political organizations. Congress ultimately deprived OEO of its operating functions: Head Start went to HEW, the Job Corps to Labor, manpower training ultimately to local governments under the Comprehensive Employment and Training Act (CETA) of 1973. Community action programs survived until going to a new Community Services Administration in the 1970s. In 1974 OEO was dead, and the poverty war, such as it was, moved on from beachheads scattered through the federal bureaucracy.

Evaluating the war on poverty confronts manifold difficulties. First is the virtual impossibility of singling out the effect of OEO during a time of phenomenal economic progress and equally phenomenal growth in other public services. Between 1965 and 1970, OEO's peak years, the number of Americans defined as poor fell from 33 to 25 million. During these same years total federal spending for social welfare—including education, Social Security, health, and welfare—more than doubled. The war on poverty presumably contributed something to this broad fight against poverty, but how much was impossible to tell. As one scholar said in 1970, "The only strong statements that can be made are that poverty has dropped sharply since 1964, that the War on Poverty was associated with that drop, and that the extent of causation cannot at present be known."

Experts have also had trouble evaluating particular OEO programs. Despite its administrative problems, its record in delivering services under the auspices of community action was generally well regarded. The Head Start and Follow Through education programs reached more than two million young children during the late 1960s. The Neighborhood Youth Corps gave low-paying, make-work jobs to perhaps two million young people aged sixteen to twenty-one. Legal services provided under community action programs were estimated to serve almost 500,000 poor people in 1969, a peak year.

Whether these services enhanced the opportunity of the poor, however, was difficult to say; the answer depended heavily on the observer's expectations, political orientation, and standards of cost effectiveness. Early reports, for instance, suggested (probably wrongly) that Head Start did not improve the long-range educational performance of poor children who participated in it. Despite that unflattering reputation, Head Start continued to command support in Congress, which regarded it as an investment in long-range prevention of social deviancy and illiteracy. The Job Corps, which did help some young people find permanent employment, and which may therefore have been more cost effective, had a much cooler reception on the Hill.

It was particularly hard to evaluate the community action programs. With a thousand in operation at the peak of OEO, there were wide variations that defied easy generalizations. Some, as in Syracuse, excited conflict and controversy that led to counterattack from existing authorities. Others, as in Newark, paved the way for the rise of black political leaders and a shift in local leadership. The majority worked more or less harmoniously with existing institutions and concentrated on delivering educational, legal, and family planning services. In these places community action personnel augmented existing social service agencies and did not make dramatic changes in what had long been done.

These more-or-less traditional programs rarely paid more than lip service to the ideal of maximum feasible participation, but not because the organizers were cynical or engaged in a charade to pacify the poor. Rather, it was because MFP was as difficult to practice as it was to define. Some of the truly poor residents of a given area were, in Moynihan's words, "inarticulate, irresponsible, and relatively unsuccessful," and others were transients who did not identify with the "community." In areas divided by racial or ethnic tensions it was hard to mobilize the whole community as a group. For all these reasons, it was frequently difficult to involve the poorest members of a given neighborhood. The organizers of community action tended instead to be the more upwardly mobile near-poor, some of whom might have risen out of poverty without federal intervention; many wanted to escape the neighborhood, not to mobilize it. Some organizers were middle-class professionals who imposed structure from above. Although this sort of elitism sometimes worked fairly well to bring communities together and identify their problems, direction from above hardly approximated maximum feasible participation of the poor.

The results achieved by the relatively few community action agencies that were run by militants were dubious. The agency in Syracuse succeeded in rousing the poor but outraged public officials, who mobilized their formidable economic and political resources, fought back, and reestablished control. Militants did not always stop to ask: conflict for what? When it involved the poor, conflict perhaps lessened feelings of powerlessness, but did it promote community cohesion? And what was the point of arousing the poor, perhaps stimulating riotous behavior, if you could not gratify them? Of what use was power if it did not bring tangible economic rewards? A leftist critic of Alinskyism identified this dilemma as early as 1964. Organizers who attempted to challenge the power structure, he said, were like "unions who fight the boss at the shop level but fail to transform the fight into its political expression."

Some experts thought that the most promising community action programs were those in which determined reformers employed confrontational but nonviolent tactics. They were able to force authorities to grant poor people fairly broad participation in antipoverty boards. Evaluators believed that nonextreme forms of confrontation paid off in that poor people developed greater self-respect, and their feelings of powerlessness dissipated. One expert concluded later that community action programs of this type "changed the institutional structure in city slums and ghettos drastically and favorably." But evidence for such a judgment was short-run and anecdotal. What worked in one community did not work in another. And feelings like "self-respect" and "power" are not subject to very solid measurement. It remains unclear whether this sort of community action did more than more traditional efforts to change the opportunity, incomes, or psychological well-being of the poor.

It is possible to reach a few negative conclusions about community action. One refutes the notion that activity at the community level could ever accomplish very much. As one scholar commented, "The liveliest local participation . . . is futile without the resources and coordination appropriate to the problem." Another critic, Elizabeth Wickenden, emphasized that the "problems of poverty are only in limited instances localized in character. They are for the most part widely distributed, related to economic and social factors that operate nationwide, and would require more than local action for solution." In the absence of a very heavy financial commitment from federal funds, gaining control of a community was often a hollow victory. Community solutions to poverty, indeed, frequently represented romantic dreams reminiscent of the settlement house workers' faith in "neighborhood" at the turn of the century. It was not surprising, therefore, that conservatives during the Nixon years continued to support, though at modest levels of funding, the by then nonthreatening community action programs, which constituted a safe and inexpensive alternative to massive commitments of federal funds.

Another conceptual limitation of OEO was its almost exclusively urban cast. Like Riis and Hunter, like most people who rediscovered poverty in the 1960s, the OEO planners were virtually mesmerized by a vision of poverty in the cities and paid little attention to area redevelopment. Although the Appalachian program was part of the overall fight against destitution, it did not figure largely in the thinking of the task force that designed OEO. Aside from OEO's ill-financed rural loan program, the war on poverty did virtually nothing to alleviate destitution in the countryside, where almost 40 percent of the poor still lived in 1965, or to stem the South-to-North migrations that magnified the problems of the northern cities. Whether any program could have slowed these migrations is almost beside the point: no one much tried to develop one. James Sundquist concluded accurately that "when it comes to the solution of the poverty problem, a good many of the urban poverty thinkers have written off the rural areas and have concluded that the only way to deal with rural poverty is to let the people move and then handle them in the cities."

The greatest conceptual fuzziness concerned OEO's diagnosis of poverty. The program, like the contemporary rediscovery of the poor, depended at first on the structuralist insight that economic growth, however beneficial, could not pull all people out of poverty. Government transfer payments were therefore essential. But OEO then stressed the need to enhance opportunity. The contradiction is clear. If the poor included many who did not gain from economic growth—mostly people outside the labor market—then they probably needed handouts of some sort. The reluctance of planners to face that fact, and the refusal of Congress seriously to consider it, exposed again the resistance in America to costly programs that might sustain a permanent class of dependents on welfare.

Other negative conclusions concern the operation of OEO. Conceptual flaws aside, it never got much money to do what it proposed to do. Funding was low from the start, when Leon Keyserling had snorted, "It will hardly scratch the surface." After 1965 money became ever harder to get, and Shriver spent most of his time tramping the halls of congressional office buildings to preserve what funds he could. From 1965 until 1970 (after which time it no longer controlled most of the programs), OEO scrambled for an average of about $1.7 billion per year. The amounts never amounted to more than around 1.5 percent of the federal budget, or one-third of one percent of the gross national product. During these years the number of people officially regarded as poor never fell below 25 million. If all the OEO money had gone directly to the poor as income—and most of it did not—each poor person in America would have received around $50 to $70 per year.

Of course, OEO funds never went equally to every poor person. Most of the money went to community action areas or to Job Corps centers. Of the 600 poorest counties in the United States (one-fifth of all counties), 215 were not covered at all by a community action agency. And the war on poverty was never intended to reach those people who were not likely targets for greater opportunity: the aged, dependent children in female-headed families, the welfare poor. One expert, formerly an assistant director of OEO, concluded in a study for the Brookings Institution in 1970, "More than five years after the passage of the Economic Opportunity Act the war on poverty has barely scratched the surface. Most poor people have had no contact with it, except perhaps to hear the promises of a better life to come."

These serious limitations stood in cruel contrast to what had been promised. Johnson had foreseen a war against poverty; Shriver had assured everyone that he would abolish destitution in ten years. But Congress did not give him the tools. Perhaps no government program in modern American history promised so much more than it delivered. The contrast chastened theorists, who began to reconsider their utopian notions about the potential for social science and to lead a surge of neo-conservative thinking in influential journals like *The Public Interest.* The sociologist Nathan Glazer concluded as early as 1966, "There are limits to the desirable reach of social engineering." Moynihan added that social scientists "have no business prescribing. They don't know enough even to seriously consider attempting that." Wilbur Cohen, who remained eager for more reform, concluded in 1968 that OEO "tried to do too much at one time." More than any other program of Johnson's so-called Great Society, the war on poverty accentuated doubts about the capacity of social science to plan, and government to deliver, ambitious programs for social betterment.

The contrast between promise and performance infuriated some of the poor. This was perhaps the cruelest cut. The rhetoric of OEO in a mass media age did reach some poor people, especially the activist leaders. Some, notably blacks, were militant anyway for racial justice. When they got little in the way of tangible, secure benefits, they were disappointed, frustrated, outraged. One planner noted, "There was the assumption of regularly increased funding. Promises were made that way . . . the result was a trail of broken promises. No wonder everybody got mad and rioted." While such riots had deeper causes, notably racial discrimination, the most angry urban blacks tended to be those who raged at the gulf that separated reality from expanded expectations, which the poverty programs had helped to whet. When rioting hit Detroit, Mayor Jerome Cavanaugh blamed OEO and other federal programs. "What we've been doing, at the level we've been doing it, is almost worse than nothing at all . . . We've raised expectations, but we haven't been able to deliver all we should have."

In spite of these negative consequences of the war on poverty, in the longer run it is possible to conclude that some benefits, mostly unanticipated, came of it. One was the lessons experts learned from its failings. If some grew despondent about the potential of government and inclined toward a new policy of benign neglect, others reconsidered and recognized, first, that it was wrong to emphasize the apathy or even the powerlessness of the poor. Events of the late 1960s proved that needy people, far from being apathetic denizens of a culture of poverty, were capable of rage. Second, experts recognized the limited potential for rehabilitating the poor by opening up opportunity. The key was augmenting people's income by finding work for the employable, and giving welfare to the dependent poor. Beginning in 1965, these insights prompted a rapidly growing sentiment among experts for some form of guaranteed income maintenance for all Americans.

The war on poverty also had the unanticipated consequence of helping to arouse the poor. To some extent, that was happening anyway, thanks to the civil rights movement and to the general rise in expectations in the affluent 1960s. But the war on poverty, by promising government help, gave these expectations a shove in the same direction. Sundquist observed in 1969, "Out of the community action milieu are rising political candidates, public office holders, and entrepreneurs as well as agitators and prophets." The "most common phrase" of local authorities, he said, was "This town will never be the same again."

The legal services programs, which employed 1,800 lawyers in 850 law offices by 1969, probably did more than any other OEO service to encourage this change. The lawyers worked closely with community spokesmen to challenge discriminatory and stigmatizing aspects of welfare administration. In the long run, they contributed to the faith, widespread by the mid-1970s, in legal attacks on old practices. They also sharpened the political awareness of poor people. As early as 1966, they helped George Wiley, an activist, form the National Welfare Rights Organization, which stridently publicized the cause of the welfare poor. They aided in suits, ultimately supported by the Supreme Court, to overturn residency requirements and the absent father rule of AFDC. With such institutionalized support, previously poor Americans at last knew where to turn for help. If the militancy of these poor people was more unpredictable and short-lived than radical organizers wished, it was nonetheless more articulate and rights-conscious than at any time in the past. It was no longer easy to think that the poor were content to suffer.

The war on poverty, finally, dramatized the contemporary rediscovery of poverty, which might not have happened so rapidly without the involvement of Heller, of Kennedy, of Johnson. The result was to lift poverty from benign neglect to a place on the public agenda. That prominence prepared Congress to accept other programs helping the poor, notably federal aid to education and health insurance for the indigent, or Medicaid, in 1965. Those landmarks safely passed, the way lay open for Cohen and others to urge further liberalization of Social Security—on the somewhat novel basis that it would aid the poor. More directly, the focus on poverty was one of many elements that made public officials a little more responsive to the newly articulated demands of the poor. In this entirely unanticipated way, the rediscovery of poverty, and the OEO that institutionalized that discovery, contributed to one of the most astonishing developments of the 1960s: the explosion in welfare.

The Unraveling of America

ALLEN MATUSOW

Allen Matusow, Professor of History and Dean of Humanities at Rice University, is the author of *The Unraveling of America*, a volume in the New American Nation series. In his book, Matusow presents a critical interpretation of the policies and politics of American liberalism in the 1960s. Why did the liberals reject Johnson? What were the different factions within the party? What impact did the Tet Offensive have on the Vietnam debate?

I

In April 1965, three months after Lyndon Johnson made his decision to bomb North Vietnam, Democratic Senator Wayne Morse of Oregon predicted that Johnson's war policy would send him "out of office the most discredited President in the history of the nation." Given the popularity of both the war and the president at the time, Morse's prophecy seemed absurd on its face. But, as Vietnam dragged on month after month, it did indeed become an acid eroding Johnson's political base, until in the end it destroyed his presidency. The first constituency to be alienated by Vietnam—and the most dangerous opponent of Johnson's war policy—proved to be the liberal intellectuals.

At first glance the split between the president and the intellectuals seemed surprising. He was, after all, attempting to govern in the liberal tradition not only in his conduct of domestic policy but in foreign affairs as well. They must hate him, he came to believe, not really for anything he did but because of who he was—a crude Texas cowboy without a Harvard degree. What he failed to understand was that his liberalism and theirs—apparently so similar in 1964—thereafter rapidly diverged, his remaining rooted in the ideas of the 1950s, theirs moving far beyond.

The root of the difficulty was the breakup of the Cold War consensus. In the 1950s, of course, liberal intellectuals typically had embraced the Cold War as a holy crusade, becoming in the process staunch defenders of the American way of life. Even after Sputnik in 1957, when the intellectuals began denouncing the nation for its materialism and complacency, they did so primarily to goad the people into greater sacrifice for the struggle against world Communism. The first sign of restlessness began to appear around 1960. That was the year, for example, when Norman Podhoretz, a New York intellectual who had been a dutiful Cold War liberal but now felt the old ideas going stale, "going dead," became editor of the influential magazine *Commentary*. Daring to open his early issues to dissident voices, he discovered among the intellectuals who wrote for his magazine and read it "a hunger for something new and something radical." Radicalism was hardly the term to describe the outlook of the intellectuals in the Kennedy era, but they were more open to novelty, more willing to acknowledge the flaws in American society, than they had been for years. In 1963, when Kennedy and Khrushchev moved toward detente following the Cuban missile crisis, the international tension that for so long had sustained the Cold War mentality began to dissipate, the old obsession to bore. Liberal intellectuals supported Johnson's 1964 presidential campaign because they believed he shared not only their renewed commitment to social justice but their growing willingness to reach an accommodation with the Russians.

Strains in Johnson's relations with the liberals first appeared in February 1965 when Johnson launched his air war over North Vietnam. Immediately the *New Republic*, a leading journal of liberal opinion, and the Americans for Democratic Action (ADA), the leading liberal organization, condemned the bombing and called for a negotiated settlement. Johnson was perplexed by the criticism since he correctly believed that he was merely applying in Vietnam the doctrine of containment so recently espoused by the liberals themselves. He did not grasp that that doctrine had suddenly fallen from fashion. Among the prominent liberal intellectuals who attempted to account for the shifting views of their community were Hans Morgenthau, an academic specialist in foreign affairs, member of the ADA board, and an early and formidable war critic; Reinhold Niebuhr, the renowned theologian and a founder of ADA, ailing but still influential; Arthur Schlesinger, Jr., a historian, former White House aide to Kennedy and Johnson, half-hearted defender of the war in 1965, but a leading foe by 1966; John Kenneth Galbraith, the Harvard economist, Kennedy's ambassador to India, and in 1967 the ADA chairman; Richard Goodwin, a precocious speech writer for Johnson till September 1965, and a war critic by the following spring; and Richard Rovere, the prestigious political correspondent of *The New Yorker*, a late but important convert to the dove side of the war argument.

The liberal intellectuals did not apologize for their past support of the Cold War. So long as Communist parties everywhere had subordinated themselves to the malign purposes of the Soviet Union, every Communist gain threatened American security. But times had changed, the liberals said. The Communist world was now "polycentric" (many-centered), a situation resulting from the Sino-Soviet split and the emergence of conflicting national aspirations among Communist states. Wrote Schlesinger, "Communism is no longer a unified, coordinated, centralized conspiracy." According to Rovere, since Tito's break with Stalin in 1948, the U.S. should have known that "international Communism" was a myth, "that national interest was more powerful than ideology, and that while we might on occasion find it advisable to resist the outward thrust of certain Communist nations, it made absolutely no sense to have a foreign policy directed against an alliance that did not exist." In short, it was no longer necessary to oppose every Communist initiative on every part of the globe.

With the exception of Morgenthau, who favored recognizing spheres of influence, these intellectuals continued to advocate containing China. But they denied that the war in Vietnam followed logically from this policy. Secretary of State Dean Rusk's opinion to the contrary, China was not the enemy there. The war in South Vietnam, they argued, was primarily a civil war, pitting indigenous revolutionaries against the corrupt and repressive regime in Saigon. If the Communists won, Vietnam might well become a bulwark against the spread of Chinese influence in the region. As a practical matter, the U.S. could not win. Escalation on the ground in the South could easily be offset by the enemy and would do nothing to remedy the defects of the Saigon government. Bombing the North would merely strengthen the enemy's will to fight. If Johnson proceeded on the course of escalation, he would destroy the country he was trying to save or else provoke war with China.

The war, the liberals said, was not a result of American imperialism but a mistake of policy deriving from obsolete assumptions about international communism. Unfortunately, it was a mistake not easily remedied. Liberals rejected unilateral withdrawal on the grounds that it would mean abandonment of America's friends in the South, a blow to U.S. prestige, and maybe even the rise at home of a new Joe McCarthy to exploit the frustrations attending defeat. The liberal solution was a negotiated settlement—the middle course, they called it. Stop the foolish bombing in the North, since Hanoi demanded it as a precondition for negotiations. Convince Ho Chi Minh that the U.S. could not be dislodged by force. Offer the Vietcong a seat at the conference table and a role in the postwar political life of South Vietnam. It was possible, of course, that negotiations would fail. In that event, said Galbraith, "We must be prepared to defend for the time being the limited areas that are now secure." Indeed, on close inspection, it turned out that the liberals were waist deep in the Big Muddy along with LBJ and were no more certain than he of getting back to shore. The difference was that they thought the war was all a big mistake, and he was there on principle.

As opposition to the war among the intellectuals mounted, so did their impatience with the administration's response to the great racial and urban crisis that was tearing the country apart. As they never would have done during the American celebration that had characterized the heyday of the Cold War, liberals were now earnestly discussing the menace of corporate monopoly, redistribution of income, and a Marshall Plan for the cities. In its January 1967 issue *Commentary* ran both a long article by Theodore Draper attacking Johnson's foreign policy for its "willingness to use and abuse naked military power" and an essay by the Keynesian economist Robert Lekachman summarizing the case of many liberal intellectuals against the president's domestic policies. Lekachman wrote:

> Possibly Mr. Johnson went just about as far as a conservative politician in a conservative, racist country could have gone. The Great Society has distributed the nation's income even less equally than it was distributed before 1960. It has enlarged the prestige and influence of the business community. It has lost its token bouts with racism and poverty. The Great Society, never a giant step beyond the New Deal which was President Johnson's youthful inspiration, has ground to a halt far short of a massive attack on urban blight, far short of the full integration of Negroes into American society, and far short of a genuine assault upon poverty and deprivation.

Where liberal intellectuals led, liberal politicians usually followed. But politicians skeptical of the war in Vietnam initially hesitated to tangle with a president to whom most were bound by ties of party loyalty and whose vindictive character was legend. In 1965 even senators held their tongues, excepting of course Oregon's Wayne Morse and Alaska's Ernest Gruening, the lone opponents of the 1964 Gulf of Tonkin Resolution. Among those who privately worried but publicly acquiesced in Johnson's war policy were Senators Mike Mansfield, George McGovern, Frank Church, Joseph Clark, Eugene McCarthy, and J. William Fulbright. Fulbright was the pivotal figure. If he moved into the open against Johnson, the rest would follow.

A senator from the ex-Confederate state of Arkansas, Fulbright was a gentleman of inherited wealth, excellent education, and illiberal record on matters of race and social reform. But for more than twenty years, on matters of foreign policy, Fulbright had been the leading spokesman in Congress for the views of the liberal community. Though he had had his share of arguments with presidents, he was by nature a contemplative rather than a combative man, a Senate club member who played by the rules. Fulbright's early opinions on Vietnam were hardly heretical. In March 1964, in a wide-ranging speech attacking Cold War mythology, he paused over Vietnam long enough to make a few hawkish observations. The allies were too weak militarily to obtain "the independence of a non-Communist South Vietnam" through negotiations, he said. The only "realistic options" were to hasten the buildup of the regime in the South or to expand the war, "either by the direct commitment of large numbers of American troops or by equipping the South Vietnamese Army to attack North Vietnamese territory." In August 1964 Fulbright sponsored the Gulf of Tonkin Resolution, which gave Johnson authority to expand the war.

For reasons unknown, Fulbright had second thoughts about escalation once it actually began. Publicly in the spring of 1965 he backed Johnson's policy, though he called for a temporary bombing halt to induce Hanoi to negotiate. Privately, he warned his old friend in the White House against waging war on North Vietnam and tempted him with the vision of a Communist Vietnam hostile to China. Johnson seemed bored by Fulbright's conversation. Fulbright gave a Senate speech in June that both criticized the bombing and praised Johnson's statesmanship. In July Johnson began the massive infusion of ground troops into South Vietnam.

Fulbright's first real attack on the Johnson administration was occasioned not by Vietnam but by policy in the Dominican Republic. In April 1965 Johnson sent U.S. troops into the midst of a developing civil war, ostensibly to protect Americans but really to prevent a possible Communist takeover. Fulbright brooded over this intervention, held secret hearings on it, and finally in September delivered a powerful Senate speech attacking the administration's conduct as ruthless and lacking in candor. The president promptly ended all pretense of consulting the chairman of the Foreign Relations Committee and cut him socially.

As Fulbright edged toward open rebellion on the issue of the war, so did the other Senate doves, almost all of whom were liberal Democrats. This was probably one reason why Johnson halted the bombing of North Vietnam on Christmas Eve, 1965, and launched a well-advertised peace offensive allegedly to persuade Hanoi to negotiate. The State Department moved closer to Hanoi's conditions for negotiations in early January, and both sides scaled down ground action in South Vietnam. Diplomats in several capitals worked to bring the wary antagonists together. But on January 24, 1966, Johnson hinted to a group of congressional leaders that he might soon resume the bombing. Two days later fifteen senators, all of them liberal Democrats, sent a letter to Johnson urging him to continue the pause. Fulbright and Mansfield did not sign but were on record with similar views. On January 29, Johnson ordered the air attack to recommence. The episode convinced many liberals that Johnson's talk about peace masked his private determination to win total military victory.

In February 1966 Fulbright held televised hearings on the war. The scholar-diplomat George Kennan and the retired general James Gavin argued the case against it on grounds of American self-interest. Dean Rusk and General Maxwell Taylor parried the thrusts of liberal committee members now openly critical of Johnson's policy. Neither side drew blood in debate, but by helping legitimize dissent, the Fulbright hearings were a net loss for Johnson. Fulbright, meantime, was reading, talking to experts, and rethinking first principles. In the spring of 1966 he took to the lecture platform to hurl thunderbolts at orthodoxy. Revised and published as a book later in the year, Fulbright's lectures were a critique of American foreign policy far more advanced than any yet produced by the liberal academicians.

"Gradually but unmistakably America is showing signs of that arrogance of power which has afflicted, weakened, and in some cases destroyed great nations in the past," Fulbright said. Harnessing her might to a crusading ideology, America had overextended herself abroad and was neglecting vital tasks at home. Americans meant well overseas,

Fulbright conceded, but they often did more harm than good, especially in the Third World. A conservative people, Americans supported necessary social revolutions in traditional societies only if they were peaceful, that is, in "our own shining image." To violent revolutions, which "seem to promise greater and faster results," Americans reacted with automatic hostility or panic. Fulbright was hardly an apologist for revolutions, but neither would he oppose them, even if they were led by Communists. Fulbright dared to find much that was praiseworthy in Castro's Cuba and even extended sympathy to the aims of the Chinese revolutionaries, whose regime he would recognize de facto. In Vietnam, he said, the U.S. had blundered into a war against Communism in the only country in the world "which won freedom from colonial rule under communist leadership." Fulbright favored a negotiated settlement that would provide self-determination for South Vietnam through the mechanism of a referendum.

President Johnson had expected his main trouble to come from hawks who wanted to escalate faster than he did. Stung by the sweeping attacks of Fulbright and other doves, he resorted to a scoundrel's last refuge. Before a friendly audience of Democratic politicians in Chicago mid-May 1966, Johnson defended the war as a patriotic effort to secure lasting peace by punishing aggression and then said, "There will be some 'Nervous Nellies' and some who will become frustrated and bothered and break ranks under the strain, and some will turn on their leaders, and on their country, and on our own fighting men. . . . But I have not the slightest doubt that the courage and the dedication and the good sense of the wise American people will ultimately prevail." The attack failed to silence the critics. The majority of the people still backed the war, but not with the passion aroused by wars of the past. Fulbright continued to assault the premises of American foreign policy and, indirectly, the president who was acting on them. Confronted with irreconcilable views of world politics, members of the liberal public in ever-increasing numbers deserted the president and sided with the senator.

II

To make matters worse for Johnson, he faced a personal as well as an intellectual challenge to his party leadership. When Robert Kennedy emerged from mourning in early 1964, he discovered a remarkable fact.

Despite his squeaky voice, diffident public manner, private shyness, and reputation as a ruthless backroom operator, he was the sole beneficiary of his brother's political estate. In him resided the hopes of millions who believed in the myth of Camelot and longed for a Kennedy restoration. Robert Kennedy believed the myth himself and shared the longing. Lyndon Johnson, however, despised Kennedy personally and made himself the great obstacle to the younger man's ambitions. After Johnson denied him the vice-presidential nomination in 1964, Kennedy repaired to New York, where he successfully ran for the Senate. Soon there grew up around him what the political columnists called the Kennedy party—Kennedy loyalists still in the bureaucracy, some senators, New Frontiersmen out of favor, and lesser politicians, lawyers, and professors scattered around the country. Most of the Kennedy loyalists were liberals, but by no means all liberals were Kennedy loyalists. Robert Kennedy, after all, had been an ally of Joe McCarthy, an advocate of wiretapping, too zealous a pursuer of the Teamster chief Jimmy Hoffa, and a frequent offender of liberal sensibilities. But liberals unhappy with Johnson needed a popular leader, and Kennedy needed to broaden his party base. The one issue guaranteed to bring them together was Vietnam.

The issue posed problems for Kennedy. As a Cabinet officer, he had been an enthusiastic student of guerrilla warfare and strong supporter of his brother's counterinsurgency program in South Vietnam. When Johnson escalated in 1965, Kennedy questioned less the attempt to rescue South Vietnam by force of arms than the tendency to subordinate political to military considerations in fighting the war. Speaking at the graduation ceremony of the International Police Academy in July, he said, "I think the history of the last 20 years demonstrates beyond doubt that our approach to revolutionary war must be political—political first, political last, political always." To avoid offending Johnson, he excised from his prepared text the view that "victory in a revolutionary war is won not by escalation by by de-escalation." Kennedy waited one whole year after escalation before putting real distance between his position and Johnson's. It bothered Kennedy that, when Fulbright asked Rusk during the televised hearings of February 1966 to state the options other than "surrender or annihilation" that he was offering the Vietcong, Rusk had replied, "They do have an alternative of quitting, of stopping being an agent of Hanoi and receiving men and arms from the North." The war could go on forever if this was the American requirement for peace. So Kennedy decided to propose another option. On February 19, 1966, he became the first senator to suggest a negotiated settlement that would give the Vietcong "a share of power and responsibility"—in what he did not say. Assuming he meant the government of Vietnam, the administration dismissed the idea contemptuously. Kennedy's proposal, said Vice President Humphrey, would be like putting "a fox in the chicken coop" or "an arsonist in a fire department." Kennedy spent the next week clarifying and qualifying, and though he retreated some, he was clearly moving toward the peace wing of his party.

Strange things were happening to Bobby Kennedy. Perhaps prolonged grief deepened his social sympathies, perhaps he was trying in his own life to vindicate his brother's legend—or outdo it. Whatever the cause, Kennedy plunged into the currents of change that were swirling through America in the mid-1960s, currents that were altering the perspective of liberalism and passing Johnson by. Kennedy opened a running dialogue with students, made a friend of Tom Hayden, felt the yearnings of the poor and the black for power and dignity, and took unnecessary political risks. Blood donations for the Vietcong? Burial for a Communist war hero in Arlington Cemetery? Why not? he asked. Kennedy went to South Africa in mid-1966 to aid the opponents of apartheid. He attacked administration witnesses at Senate hearings in August for unresponsiveness to the poor. He flew to California to stand with Cesar Chavez in his fight to unionize the grape pickers. A man who risked his life scaling mountains and defying tropical storms on the Amazon, Kennedy was becoming an existentialist in politics, defining himself in action and moving where his heart told him to go.

As Kennedy and Johnson edged closer toward political combat, their personal relations worsened. In February 1967 *Newsweek* erroneously reported that Kennedy had brought back from a recent trip to Paris a peace feeler from Hanoi. The story enraged Johnson, who, believing it was planted by Kennedy, called him to the White House for a tongue lashing. According to *Time*'s colorful account, Johnson told Kennedy, "If you keep talking like this, you won't have a political future in this country within six months," warned him that "the blood of American boys will be on your hands," and concluded, "I never want to see you again." Uncowed, Kennedy called Johnson an s.o.b. and told him, "I don't have to sit here and take that—." Whether Kennedy really used vulgarity was a matter of some dispute, but there was no doubt that the gist of the conversation had been accurately reported. Less than a month later (March 2, 1967) Kennedy gave a major Senate speech calling for a halt to the bombing and a compromise settlement through negotiations. A few party malcontents, especially in the liberal wing, permitted themselves a small hope that maybe the crown prince of the Democratic party would claim his inheritance sooner than expected.

III

In the summer of 1967 gloom descended on the camp of the liberals. In August Johnson sent 45,000 more troops to Vietnam and asked for higher taxes to finance the war. And, though Defense Secretary Robert McNamara himself voiced public criticism of the bombing, day after day the bombs continued to fall. Liberals who had once viewed it merely as politically stupid watched in horror as the carnage mounted and now pronounced the war morally wrong as well. Meanwhile domestic insurrectionaries were gutting great American cities, the War on Poverty was bogging down, and the long-awaited white backlash finally arrived. Among those surrendering to despair that summer was Senator Fulbright. Speaking to the American Bar Association in August, he said, "How can we commend democratic social reform to Latin America when Newark, Detroit, and Milwaukee are providing explosive evidence of our own inadequate efforts at democratic social reform? How can we commend the free enterprise system to Asians and Africans when in our own country it has produced vast, chaotic, noisy, dangerous and dirty urban complexes while poisoning the very air and land and water?" Fulbright called the war "unnecessary and immoral" and blamed it for aggravating grave domestic problems. The country "sickens for lack of moral leadership," he said, and only the idealistic young may save us from the "false and dangerous dream of an imperial destiny."

Fulbright's charges about the damage done at home by the war were confirmed in the autumn. Driven by hatred of the war, new left students began acting out their guerrilla fantasies, and major campuses were threatened by chaos. No less disturbing to liberals was the fever of discontent rising in intellectual circles. Some of the nation's most brilliant writers and artists were concluding, as had their counterparts in France during the Algerian war, that they now had no choice but to resist the state.

From the beginning a minority of the nation's intellectual elite—call them radicals—saw the war as more than a blunder in judgment. Most of these radicals had life histories punctuated by episodes of dissent but had stayed aloof from politics during the Cold War. Vietnam brought them back to political awareness and gave focus to their inchoate alienation. To people like the novelists Norman Mailer and Mary McCarthy, the critics Susan Sontag and Dwight Macdonald, *New York Review of Books* editor Robert Silvers, the linguist Noam Chomsky, the anarchist writer Paul Goodman, and the poet Robert Lowell, America appeared to be in the hands of a technological elite that was debauching the American landscape and lusting after world dominion. Morally revolted by the imperial war against the peasants of Vietnam, the radicals found traditional politics insufficient to express their opposition. The war was a matter of conscience, and good men would act accordingly.

Their first impulse was to avoid complicity with the crime. Thus when Johnson invited a group of writers and artists to participate in a White House Festival of the Arts in June 1965, Robert Lowell refused to come. Scion of a distinguished American family, perhaps the best of living American poets, and a draft resister in World War II, Lowell sent a letter to the president, saying, "Every serious artist knows that he cannot enjoy public celebration without making subtle public commitments. . . . We are in danger of imperceptibly becoming an explosive and suddenly chauvinistic nation, and we may even be drifting on our way to the last nuclear ruin. . . . At this anguished, delicate and perhaps determining moment, I feel I am serving you and our country best by not taking part." Robert Silvers took the lead in circulating a statement in support of his friend Lowell and in two days attracted the signatures of twenty of the nation's most prominent writers and artists, among them Hannah Arendt, Lillian Hellman, Alfred Kazin, Dwight Macdonald, Bernard Malamud, Mary McCarthy, William Styron, and Robert Penn Warren. Johnson was so angry at "these people," these "sonsofbitches" that he almost canceled the festival.

By 1967 the radicals were obsessed by the war and frustrated by their impotence to affect its course. The government was unmoved by protest, the people were uninformed and apathetic, and American technology was tearing Vietnam apart. What, then, was their responsibility? Noam Chomsky explored this problem in February 1967 in the *New York Review*, which had become the favorite journal of the radicals. By virtue of their training and leisure, intellectuals had a greater responsibility than ordinary citizens for the actions of the state, Chomsky said. It was their special responsibility "to speak the truth and to expose lies." But the "free-floating intellectual" who had performed this function in the past was being replaced by the "scholar-expert" who lied for the government or constructed "value-free technologies" to keep the existing social order functioning smoothly. Chomsky not only enjoined the intellectuals once again "to seek the truth lying behind the veil of distortion"; he concluded by quoting an essay written twenty years before by Dwight Macdonald, an essay that implied that in time of crisis exposing lies might not be enough. "Only those who are willing to resist authority themselves when it conflicts too intolerably with their personal moral code," Macdonald had written, "only they have the right to condemn." Chomsky's article was immediately recognized as an important intellectual event. Along with the radical students, radical intellectuals were moving "from protest to resistance."

The move toward resistance accelerated through 1967. Chomsky announced in the *New York Review* that for the second consecutive year he was withholding half his income taxes to protest the war. Paul Goodman invited federal prosecution by acknowledging his efforts to aid and abet draft resistance. Mary McCarthy, back from a trip to Vietnam, said that "to be in the town jail, as Thoreau knew, can relieve any sense of imaginary imprisonment." On the cover of its issue of August 24, 1967, the *New York Review* put a diagram of a Molotov cocktail, while inside Andrew Kopkind, in the midst of dismissing Martin Luther King for having failed to make a revolution, wrote, "Morality, like politics, starts at the barrel of a gun." (Some intellectuals never forgave the *New York Review* for that one.) On October 12, 1967, the *New York Review* published a statement signed by 121 intellectuals and entitled "A Call to Resist Illegitimate Authority." The statement denounced the war on legal and moral grounds and pledged the signers to raise funds "to organize draft resistance unions, to supply legal defense and bail, to support families and otherwise aid resistance to the war in whatever ways may seem appropriate."

A few days later Stop the Draft Week began. This was an event whose possibilities excited radical intellectuals as well as radical students. Paul Goodman kicked the week off with a speech at the State Department before an audience of big business executives. "You are the military industrial of the United States, the most dangerous body of men at the present in the world," Goodman declaimed. On Friday, October 20, 1967, Lowell and Mailer spoke on the steps of the Justice Department prior to the efforts of the Reverend William Sloane Coffin to deliver to the government draft cards collected from draft resisters across the country earlier in the week. (This occasion provided evidence for later federal charges of criminal conspiracy against Coffin, Dr. Benjamin Spock, and three other antiwar activists.) Saturday began with speeches at the Lincoln Memorial ("remorseless, amplified harangues for peace," Lowell called them), and then the march across the bridge toward the Pentagon. Lowell, Mailer, and Macdonald, described by Mailer as "America's best poet? and best novelist??, and best critic???," walked to the battle together. Lowell wrote of the marchers that they were

> . . . like green Union recruits
> for the first Bull Run, sped by photographers,
> the notables, the girls . . . fear, glory, chaos, rout . . .
> our green army staggered out on the miles-long green fields,
> met by the other army, the Martian, the ape, the hero,
> his new-fangled rifle, his green new steel helmet.

At the Pentagon Mailer was arrested, much to his satisfaction, but Lowell and Macdonald failed of their object. Noam Chomsky, also present, had not intended to participate in civil disobedience, feeling its purpose in this occasion too vague to make a point. Swept up by the events of the day, Chomsky found himself at the very walls of the fortress, making a speech. When a line of soldiers began marching toward him, he spontaneously sat down. Chomsky spent the night in jail with Mailer.

In his brilliant book *The Armies of the Night*, Mailer probed for the meaning of these apocalyptic events. For him the siege of the Pentagon was a rite of passage for the student rebels, for the intellectuals, for himself. The few hundred fearful youths who sat on the Pentagon steps till dawn on Sunday were a "refrain from all the great American rites of passage when men and women manacled themselves to a lost and painful principle and survived a day, a night, a week, a month, a year." The battle at the Pentagon was a pale rite of passage, he thought, compared to that of the immigrants packed in steerage, Rogers and Clark, the Americans "at Sutter's Mill, at Gettysburg, the Alamo, the Klondike, the Argonne, Normandy, Pusan." But it was a true rite of passage nonetheless, the survivors having been reborn and rededicated to great purpose. On departing from jail Sunday morning, Mailer felt as Christians must "when they spoke of Christ within them." For Mailer and many other radical intellectuals, American institutions seemed so illegitimate that a moral man could find redemption only in resisting them. As for the liberals, they could only wonder what would happen to America if Lyndon Johnson was not stopped.

IV

Signs of a liberal revolt against Johnson's renomination were plentiful in the fall of 1967. Reform Democrats in New York, the liberal California Democratic Council, party factions in Minnesota, Michigan, Wisconsin, and elsewhere were preparing to oppose him. In late September the ADA national board implicitly came out against him by promising to back the candidate who offered "the best prospect for a settlement of the Vietnam conflict." The *New Republic* explicitly rejected his candidacy in an editorial that same week. And Allard Lowenstein, thirty-eight-year-old liberal activist and ADA vice-chairman, opened an office in Washington and began organizing a movement on campuses, in the peace movement, and among dissident Democratic politicians to "dump Johnson."

Lowenstein wanted Robert Kennedy to be his candidate. And the existentialist Bobby was tempted. Kennedy worried about the frustration building up in the antiwar movement and had himself come to view the war as morally repugnant. "We're killing South Vietnamese, we're killing women, we're killing innocent people because we don't want to have the war fought on American soil, or because they're 12,000 miles away and they might get 11,000 miles away," he said on *Face the Nation* late in November 1967. But Bobby the professional hated losing, and in his view he could not defeat Johnson in a fight for the nomination, and neither could anybody else. On that same TV program he stated flatly that he would not be a candidate. If he were, he said, "it would immediately become a personality struggle," and the real issues would be obscured. Asked about some other Democrat, such as Senator Eugene McCarthy of Minnesota, taking on the president, Kennedy replied, "There could be a healthy element in that." He would endorse neither Johnson nor McCarthy but support whoever was the eventual party nominee.

Eugene McCarthy had become convinced that someone would have to raise the issue of the war in the party primaries in 1968. When

Kennedy and other leading doves rejected Lowenstein's pleas to be the candidate, McCarthy agreed to run. Explaining his purpose at a press conference on November 30, 1967, he said, "There is growing evidence of a deepening moral crisis in America—discontent and frustration and a disposition to take extralegal if not illegal actions to manifest protest. I am hopeful that this challenge . . . may alleviate at least in some degree this sense of political helplessness and restore to many people a belief in the processes of American politics and of American government." In other words, McCarthy was offering his candidacy as an alternative to radicalism.

Only an unusual politician would undertake what no one else would dare. In truth McCarthy, who had spent eight months of his youth as a novice in a Benedictine monastery, was in the political world but not of it. He was a senator bored by the Senate, an office seeker who disdained intrigue and self-advertisement, a professional who valued honor more than influence. In recent years he had seemed more interested in Thomistic theology and writing poetry than in the business of government. His career, it appeared, would not fulfill its early promise. But the political crisis in the United States in late 1967 provided McCarthy with an opportunity perfectly suited to his self-conception. Like his hero Thomas More, he would play the martyr in a historic confrontation between conscience and power.

McCarthy's candidacy prospered beyond anyone's expectation, even his own. Though Johnson's rating on the Gallup poll was only 41 percent in November, the professionals were mesmerized by the cliche that no president could be denied renomination by his own party. The war was the biggest cause of Johnson's unpopularity. Hawks and doves disagreed on how best to end the war but otherwise had much in common: both disliked the war, wanted its early termination, and tended to blame Lyndon Johnson for dragging it on. It was the public's declining confidence in Johnson's ability to conclude the war that made him vulnerable to McCarthy's candidacy.

What little confidence still existed in the president's war leadership was shattered on January 31, 1968, when the Vietnamese Communists launched a massive attack in the midst of a truce called for the Tet holiday. Sixty-seven thousand enemy troops invaded more than one hundred of South Vietnam's cities and towns. The allies recaptured most urban areas after a few days and inflicted huge casualties on the attackers. But the Tet Offensive had astounded military men by its scope and daring. It showed that no place in South Vietnam was secure, not even the American embassy, whose walls had been breached in the first hours of the attack. And it temporarily derailed the pacification program in the countryside by drawing allied troops into the cities. Coming after recent administration assurances that the war was being won, the Tet Offensive dealt Johnson's credibility its crowning blow. When he and the U.S. commander in Vietnam, General William Westmoreland, issued victory statements after the offensive ended, few took them seriously, though militarily they were right. The chief political casualty of the Tet Offensive, therefore, was Lyndon Johnson.

In the six weeks after Tet, such pillars of establishment opinion as Walter Cronkite, *Newsweek*, the *Wall Street Journal*, and NBC News gave way and called for de-escalation. High officials in the government finally dared express their private doubts about the war to the president. The Gallup poll reported a seismic shift in public opinion: in February self-described hawks had outnumbered doves 60 percent to 24 percent; in March it was hawks 41 percent, doves 42 percent. And on March 10, two days before the New Hampshire primary, the *New York Times* set off waves of national anxiety by reporting a secret request from the generals to the president for 206,000 more troops for the war.

Meanwhile, in New Hampshire, the first primary state, McCarthy was proving an eccentric candidate. A lazy campaigner, he often did not return phone calls, would not court potential contributors, and avoided local politicians. His manner on the stump was uninspired, and even his references to the war were low-key. (McCarthy opposed unilateral withdrawal and advocated a negotiated settlement.) But McCarthy had an insight denied to his detractors: he mattered less in this campaign than the movement he represented. At the climax of the campaign there were so many student volunteers in the tiny state (3,000, or one for every 25 Democratic voters) that McCarthy's lieutenants begged potential workers to stay home. Scrubbed and shaven, the students ran a canvassing operation that was the envy of the professionals. Even McCarthy's peculiar style proved to be an asset. At a time when the country was fed up with politicians, shrill voices, and the hard sell, there was something reassuring in McCarthy's unhurried, dignified manner. He did not frighten people. He seemed safe.

Governor John W. King, one of the inept managers of Johnson's write-in campaign in New Hampshire, said in the beginning that McCarthy would get 5 percent of the vote. McCarthy himself predicted 30 percent. On March 12, 1968, 49 percent of New Hampshire's Democratic voters wrote in the name of the president of the United States, and 42 percent marked their ballots for a senator of whom days before few had heard. Poll data showed that more McCarthy voters in New Hampshire were hawks than doves. McCarthy's remarkable showing, then, was not a victory for peace, merely proof that Lyndon Johnson, who could neither pacify the ghetto, speak the plain truth, lick inflation, nor above all end the war, was a mighty unpopular president indeed.

McCarthy had done more than demonstrate Johnson's vulnerability. As he had hoped, his candidacy drained off some of the discontent flowing into illegal protest. Thousands of students who might otherwise have joined SDS got "clean for Gene." Intellectuals who had flirted with resistance a few months before became the senator's avid fans. McCarthy's traveling companion through much of New Hampshire was Robert Lowell—a symbolic relationship whose significance was probably lost on neither of these famous poets.

It had been a hard winter for Robert Kennedy. He realized after the Tet Offensive that his refusal to run had been a mistake. Throughout February 1968, while McCarthy's New Hampshire campaign was getting started, Kennedy and his advisers wrestled again with the problem of his candidacy. Kennedy was ready to go early in March and set in motion machinery for a campaign. But still he found reason to delay a public announcement. By the time he declared on March 16, 1968, the results of the New Hampshire primary had already electrified the country. Much of the constituency that would have been his now belonged to McCarthy. Lyndon Johnson, however, took Kennedy's candidacy more seriously than McCarthy's. He knew, even if the students did not, that Kennedy was the one man in the party who might beat him.

McCarthy refused to step aside for Kennedy and moved on to the Wisconsin primary, whose date was April 2. Early in March the president's men in Wisconsin had been confident of victory. But McCarthy arrived with more students, money, and prestige than he had had in New Hampshire, and by mid-month the Johnson managers knew their man was in trouble. On March 28 Postmaster Larry O'Brien, an old political pro, returned from a look around the state to tell Johnson that his cause there was hopeless.

While the political storms raged around them, Johnson and his advisers were deep into a momentous review of war policy. General Earle Wheeler, chairman of the Joint Chiefs of Staff, had blundered in late February when he privately requested 206,000 additional troops for

Vietnam. Since General Westmoreland was in no danger of being over-run, there was never much chance that Johnson would dispatch massive reinforcements. The tax money to pay for escalation was not there, and neither was the political support. Wheeler's request had one unintended result. By asking so much, it forced policy makers to resolve the basic ambiguity that had characterized America's policy since 1965. Militar-ily, Johnson had been seeking victory over the Vietcong. Diplomati-cally, he paid lip service to a negotiated settlement, which implied compromise. Since his generals were in effect telling him that they needed more troops than he could furnish to win, Johnson had no choice now except to opt for negotiation. Accounts differ on how John-son reached this conclusion in March 1968. But in the end those of his advisers urging some steps in the direction of de-escalation prevailed. On March 31 Johnson went on television to announce that he was stop-ping the bombing over most of North Vietnam and would end it entirely if Hanoi demonstrated comparable restraint. Johnson called on the North Vietnamese to respond to his partial bombing halt by accepting his invitation to negotiate. A few days later they did so.

Johnson announced another decision in this speech. For some time he had been dropping hints among friends and advisers that he might not run in 1968. Only at the last minute did he determine not to make his 1968 State of the Union Message the occasion for announcing his retirement. But his mood seemed to change after that, and he took steps to organize a re-election campaign. Even after the ambush in New Hampshire, Johnson authorized Larry O'Brien to meet with Cabinet of-ficers and give them marching orders for the political battle ahead.

Though most Johnson intimates believed he would run, he had compelling reasons not to. Exhausted, haunted by fear of another heart attack, bitter at the vilification he had suffered, the man had had enough. "The only difference between the [John F.] Kennedy assassina-tion and mine," he said in this period, "is that I am alive and it has been more torturous." There were other reasons too. Politically he faced a Congress opposed to his programs, a public that had lost confidence in his leadership, a defeat at the hands of McCarthy in the Wisconsin primary, and an uncertain contest with Robert Kennedy. On the diplo-matic front, he wished to take a step toward peace, which his oppo-nents, domestic and foreign, would probably dismiss as insincere if he remained a potential candidate. In his speech of March 31, Johnson spoke of "division in the American house" and declared his intention to keep the presidency above partisanship in this election year. "Accordingly," he told a stunned nation, "I shall not seek, and I will not accept, the nomination of my party for another term as your President." The liberals, with an assist from the peace movement, the attackers of Tet, and war-weariness, had dumped Johnson.

7

STALEMATE

The 1970s ushered in a period of uncertainty, frustration, and public cynicism. Many forces contributed to the pervasive mood of discontent—disillusion with Vietnam, anger at the abuse of presidential power, worry about persistent differences between the races. But one problem stands above all others: During the 1970s, the pillar of postwar American society—sustained economic growth—came to a crashing halt. A dramatic increase in oil prices subjected the United States and many other nations to fuel shortages, high inflation, and the worst economic slump since the 1930s. Inflation hit double digits in 1973 and 1974. During the period from 1972 to 1978, industrial productivity rose only one percent per year. From 1975 until 1980, the nation experienced for the first time what became known as "stagflation"—when unemployment and inflation increased simultaneously.

Neither political party seemed capable of providing leadership for the troubled times. Just two years after a smashing victory in the 1972 presidential contest, Richard Nixon was forced to resign in disgrace. His successor, former Michigan congressman Gerald Ford, never overcame public doubts about his competence to hold the nation's highest office. In 1976, the election of a former Georgia governor Jimmy Carter guaranteed Democrats control of Congress and the Presidency. But

Carter's vacillating leadership, a deeply divided party, and a poor economic climate prevented him from regaining the public's confidence.

Part of the confusion resulted from the decline of the Democratic Party and the break-up of the coalition that had sustained it. Thomas Edsall, a *Washington Post* reporter, attributes the party's decline to the emergence of controversial social issues, especially race, which alienated many white, middle-class voters. "The central conflict between liberalism and conservatism," he argues, "focused on the aggressive expansion of constitutional rights to previously disfranchised, often controversial groups." But Thomas Fergueson and Joel Rogers suggest a different interpretation. They contend that big business, threatened by sagging productivity and increased international competition, organized a successful assault against labor and Democratic social welfare programs.

Right Turn

THOMAS FERGUESON AND JOEL ROGERS

Thomas Fergueson teaches government at the University of Texas at Austin; Joel Rogers teaches law and sociology at the University of Wisconsin at Madison. In their provocative book, *Right Turn*, the authors criticized those who suggested that Democrats can recapture the presidency by acting more like Republicans. Democrats have failed, they suggested because they have been too beholden to the same constituency as the Republicans—namely, big business. Why did business decide to mobilize resources in the 1970s? Was their effort successful?

In a community as fragmented and decentralized as American big business, truly profound reversals of opinion usually require considerable time. Because such changes are as much processes as events, assigning a single date to them almost inevitably courts misunderstanding. But insofar as such an effort ever makes sense, it does for the terrible recession of the early 1970s. Lasting seventeen months, from November 1973 to March 1975, it was by far the longest and deepest economic downturn the United States had experienced since the Great Depression. It was then that the great developments that eventually drove American politics to the right became dramatically evident. And it was then that basic doubts about the whole New Deal began to spread throughout the American business community, including its multinational wing.

Deteriorating U.S. economic performance in an increasingly competitive and integrated world economy is the analytic key to the Democrats' decline. In a variety of ways, sagging growth and profits at home, and increased competition abroad, made the business community much more cost-sensitive. This stiffened business opposition to the growth of social spending and forced the Democrats to work within tighter fiscal constraints on their domestic programs. Pressures on the social side of the budget increased as growing U.S. involvement in the international economy, and in particular in the Third World, widened demands within the business community for increased military spending. Moreover, these competing demands on the budget could not be easily reconciled by simply raising taxes, for as profit margins sagged and intensified competition from abroad made it more difficult for corporations to pass taxes through to consumers, much of the business community was mobilizing in support of further tax reductions. Over the course of the decade, the convergence of these different pressures and demands produced a growing budget crisis in the United States, in effect forcing a choice between social and military spending.

For the Republicans, pressures to make this choice presented an enormous political opportunity. Unencumbered by a mass base, and devoted, as Office of Management and Budget (OMB) director David Stockman would later put it, to the principle that "government doesn't owe anyone anything," the Republicans were quite prepared to serve as a vehicle for tax and domestic-spending cuts and increased military outlays. For the Democrats, however, the growing trade-off between guns and butter forced the party to walk a political tightrope between the demands of its elite constituency and needs of its mass base. Even as the Democrats moved to the right over the course of the decade and the center of American party politics shifted, the tensions within the Democrats' ranks made them a less efficient vehicle for business aspirations than the Republicans. The GOP was thus the first beneficiary of America's right turn.

ECONOMIC DECLINE

While it was highlighted by the 1973–75 recession, the economic deterioration that drove this process began before, and continued after, that catastrophic event. In sketching some of its dimensions here, accordingly, we will refer back and forth in time. At the bottom line, profits of U.S. firms declined after 1965 and failed throughout the next fifteen years to regain their early 1960s levels. Annual net investment in plant and equipment followed suit, falling from an average 4 percent of GNP during 1966–70 to 3.1 over 1971–75 and 2.9 percent over 1976–80. As the baby-boom generation moved into the job market in the 1970s, the average annual growth rate of net fixed investment per worker dropped even more sharply, falling from 3.9 percent during 1966–70 to a bare 0.4 percent over 1976-80. Productivity suffered in turn, as the annual growth of output per worker employed in nonresidential business fell from 2.45 percent over 1948–73 to 0.08 percent over 1973–79. Not surprisingly, overall growth rates tumbled. Average annual growth in real GNP also tumbled, from 4.1 percent over 1960–73 to 2.3 percent over 1973–80.

For workers, the picture became particularly gloomy. After averaging 3.8 percent over 1965–69, unemployment rose to 5.4 percent over 1970–74 and 7 percent over 1975–79. Average real gross weekly earnings for private nonagricultural workers moved erratically in the late 1960s and early 1970s, rising 3 percent between 1965 and 1969, then dropping in 1970 below their 1968 level, then rising again to a postwar peak in 1972. After that they trended sharply downward, and by 1980 reached their lowest level since 1962. Real median family income also stagnated: after doubling between 1947 and 1973, it dropped 6 percent over 1973–80.

The international picture looked even worse. In the immediate postwar period, the United States had stood unrivaled as the world's hegemonic economic power. As the economies of Western Europe and Japan rebuilt, however, and parts of the Third World were more tightly integrated into the world capitalist system, the relative position of the United States declined. Between 1950 and 1960, the U.S. share of world GNP dropped from 40 to 26 percent, and its share of world trade fell from 20 to 16 percent. Over the next two decades, both shares continued to fall, dropping to 23 and 14 percent, respectively, by 1970, and to 21.5 and 11 percent, respectively, by 1980. America's largest firms were not excepted from this trend. In 1956, 42 of the world's top 50 industrial companies were U.S. firms. By 1970, the number had dropped to 32; by 1980, it was 23.

It should be noted that much of the early decline in the U.S. share of world GNP and trade simply reflected a correction of the peculiar situation that obtained at the close of World War II, when the economies of other major companies were still in ruins. At least after 1960, however, the gradual decline in the relative size of the U.S. economy was outpaced by the decline in trade. In dropping from 26 to 21.5 percent over 1960–80, the U.S. share of world GNP declined 17 percent. During the same period, the U.S. share of world trade dropped much faster, falling 31 percent. Quite apart from the growth of other economies, U.S. competitiveness was in decline.

This decline in competitive position was particularly evident in U.S. manufacturing. Overall, the U.S. market share of manufactures fell from 26 to 18 percent over 1960–80, and trade balance on non-R&D-intensive manufactures grew increasingly negative from the early 1960s on. Positive trade balances in R & D-intensive manufactures grew over the same period, but even here the U.S. lost its world market share in most of the top categories. As noted already, declining U.S. competitiveness eventually showed up in a negative balance on the merchandise trade account in 1971. With a brief interruption in the mid-1970s, the trade balance grew increasingly negative through the rest of the decade.

Even as it lost out in international competition, however, the United States became increasingly *integrated* into the world economy, a development that marked a virtual revolution in U.S. international economic relations. Together, exports and imports comprised only 7 percent of U.S. GNP in 1960, and as late as 1970 they comprised only 8.3 percent, or roughly the same share they had claimed forty years before. By 1980, however, their combined share had more than doubled, to 17.4 percent. Once again U.S. manufacturing provides the most dramatic evidence for this change, with both the exports and the imports of manufactures rising, by 1980, to more than 20 percent of domestic production. These, of course, are aggregate figures. In particular cases and sectors, import penetration and export dependence were considerably greater.

Even more important, such general measures of import and export flows can only suggest what may have been the single most important consequence of this convergence of declining competitiveness *and* increasing U.S. integration in the world economy—the fact that most U.S. firms (accounting for perhaps 70 percent or more of goods and services in the U.S.) now felt sharper competitive pressures from abroad, which in turn affected their own pricing policies. To a rapidly expanding degree, even big firms, including some of those that were maintaining market share, now operated in an environment in which prices were affected by international market forces beyond their immediate control. As a consequence, they tended to become "price takers" rather than "price makers," and were less capable of simply passing increased costs along to consumers.

The precise sources of the decline in U.S. domestic and international economic performance are matters of continuing dispute. There are many analyses, each with its (usually subsidized) proponents, and each with its favorite causal factor: the decline of the work ethic, a slowdown in innovation, new foreign strategies of international competition, a long-term crisis in work relations, excessive government regulation, increasing state or federal deficits, changes in relative prices resulting from the energy crisis, poor management. The list could easily go on.

Some of these explanations, such as the alleged slowdown in innovation or the popularly diagnosed decline of the Protestant ethic, rest on evidence so slender that they are hardly worth taking seriously. Others, which center on an alleged capital shortage in the 1970s or the "short-run" focus of U.S. managers, are almost equally implausible. More probably, in our view, the basic problem was a complex failure of investment, deeply rooted in the social organization of production in the United States, that was exacerbated by the emergence of the Third World as a major actor in the international economy. But we will not explore these matters here. No great agreement on the sources of U.S. economic difficulties is needed to recognize that those difficulties had profound political consequences in the United States, as domestic actors struggled to adjust to a radically altered environment. And it is those political responses, rather than the economic troubles that provoked them, that provide our focus here.

THE ATTACK ON LABOR

As the extent of U.S. economic deterioration became evident during the 1973-75 recession, business responded in predictable ways. Firms under pressure sought to cut costs, and while wages were already falling dramatically (so dramatically, indeed, that even many business spokespersons eventually conceded that wage costs were not the source of their continuing difficulties), for most firms the most natural place to begin cost cutting was with the price of labor.

These efforts took different forms. Continuing the pattern of the 1960s, many businesses operating in the Northeast and Midwest simply relocated production on a massive scale to areas where labor was cheaper and less organized. In some cases, firms located in the older industrial cities of those regions merely moved a few miles, from highly unionized central cities to less densely unionized, more hospitable neighboring suburbs. In many other instances, modern techniques for decentralized production made it possible to move operations (and, much more rarely, headquarters) to sites in the South and West or abroad.

Businesses also employed an arsenal of different strategies to improve their bargaining position with particular workers. In nonunion environments, flexible work schedules, elaborate individualized incentive schemes, and other attempts to forge a more "cooperative" system of industrial relations for the regulation of internal labor markets proliferated. Where workers persisted in attempts to form unions, a whole new class of labor-management consultants, skilled in the evasion or prudent violation of national labor law, found an expanding market among employers. Having risen in the mid-1960s after the downturn in profits, employer unfair labor practices against unions skyrocketed in the 1970s. The number of charges of employer violation of section 8(a)(3) of the Labor Management Relations Act, for example, which forbids employers to fire workers for engaging in union activity, doubled from 9,000 to 18,000 over the 1970–80 period. The number of workers awarded reinstatement or back pay by the NLRB rose from 10,000 to 25,000. By 1980, the number of illegal discharges for union activity had risen to about 5 percent of the total number of pro-union votes in representation elections before the Board. Put otherwise, by that time American workers faced a 1 in 20 chance of being fired for merely favoring unionization. Activists and in-shop organizers, of course, faced even greater risks.

The small minority of workers who were already unionized were better able to resist the general downward push on wages. As a result, the "union premium," or average differential between union and nonunion wages for comparable jobs, increased from 19 percent in the 1970–75 period to 30 percent during the second half of the decade. Again, however, such average figures disguise radically different particulars. In many cases union members suffered severe reductions in wages and benefits during the period. And many did not enjoy high wages to begin with.

More importantly, as emphasized in our discussion of the 1960s, wages alone do not tell the full story of union strength. Throughout the 1970s, as during much of the 1960s, labor continued to divide itself from its natural allies at home, while promoting aggressive U.S. foreign policies abroad. It failed to rejuvenate itself through aggressive organizing: the number of workers organized each year through NLRB elections declined 43 percent over 1970–80; the number lost through "decertification" elections more than doubled; the organized share of the civilian work force dropped from 25.7 to 20.9 percent. And its political influence waned. The decade began with Meany's successful move to block any Federation endorsement of George McGovern, the most liberal Presidential candidate in recent memory. It continued with labor twice (once under Ford, once under Carter) losing its fight to legalize "common situs" picketing, an issue of grave concern to embattled construction unions. And in what may have been its most spectacular postwar defeat, union leadership failed even to secure the modest changes in labor law and administration proposed in the Labor Law Reform Bill of 1977–78. There, in a replay of the fight over Taft-Hartley 14(b), a Republican-led filibuster killed the bill in the Senate, while another Democratic Administration looked on.

But while virtually all of American business pressed for wage reductions in the 1970s, and the employer offensive against unions and unionization hurt a major investor in the Democratic Party, the significance of the wage and unionization issues should not be overestimated in explaining America's right turn. By hurting labor, the employer offensive marginally hurt the Democrats' capacities of mobilization; it also weakened resistance within the party to the turn to the right. But the decline in labor's power in the 1970s only continued a long downward slide evident since at least the mid-1950s. It was not a new development, unique to the later period, that can be looked to as precipitating a general policy realignment.

Considered from the standpoint of the distribution of business "investment" between the two parties, moreover, the wage and labor issues look even less impressive as causal factors. As emphasized here repeatedly, the firms that provided the key support for the New Deal, and most of the major firms that later backed Kennedy and Johnson, were heavily capital-intensive. Labor costs for them were thus relatively less important than they were for labor-intensive firms. The latter, as a practical matter, had little choice but to become rock-ribbed Republicans, and had made this choice long before. Thus while the increased competitive pressures of the 1970s led virtually all firms to be more attentive to labor costs, and weighed especially heavily on labor-intensive firms already oriented toward the Republicans, the labor question alone probably squeezed comparatively few traditionally Democratic firms out of the party.

THE ATTACK ON REGULATION

What labor costs could not do by themselves, however, other features of the new world political economy the 1973–75 recession created could. Reeling from intense foreign competition, many sectors of big business, *including* several of the most capital-intensive multinational ones, such as pharmaceuticals, paper, and petrochemicals, lashed back at what they claimed were "unduly burdensome" government regulations—in particular "social" regulations of the environment and worker safety that fell particularly hard on these sectors. As one measure of business mobilization, statistical studies show that these regulated concerns were among those most likely to organize PACs during the period. They also launched major efforts to influence public opinion and attitudes of other elites. Many firms sponsored studies by academics and consultants that downplayed environmental risk. They cultivated ties with university researchers and scientists in the federal research laboratories. And they launched a broad campaign to influence the media. The pharmaceutical-related Smith Richardson foundation, the petrochemical-related Scaife funds, the chemical-related Olin foundation, and other lavishly funded institutions launched broad campaigns against government regulation and in support of "free enterprise." They supported "neoconservative" journals like *The Public Interest* or the American Enterprise Institute's antiregulatory *Regulation*. They poured enormous sums into a variety of "research institutes" such as Accuracy in Media that campaigned against alleged anti-business bias in the mass media. They supported conservative legal groups that brought suit against actions by the government and private parties that conservatives disapproved of. And they funded many campus newspapers and other projects oriented toward influencing students and other young people.

Contrary to myths of the spontaneous generation of conservative ideas, this effort was quite deliberate, and expensive. As prominent free-marketeer, former Nixon Treasury Secretary, and Olin Fund chair William Simon urged his corporate colleagues, business should provide funds "in exchange for books, books, and more books," extolling the merits of free markets:

Funds generated by business (by which I mean profits, funds in business foundations and contributions from individual businessmen) must rush by multimillions to the aid of liberty . . . to funnel desperately needed funds to scholars, social scientists, writers, and journalists who understand the relationship between political and economic liberty.

And rush they did. Olin provided major funding (on the order of $3 million a year by the end of the decade) to any number of free-market-oriented projects, ranging from the Law and Economics Center at Emory University, which emphasized the substitution of market incentives for legal controls in the "regulation" of business, to the New Coalition for Economic and Social Change, a conservative black alternative to the NAACP. Smith Richardson, also operating with a grants budget of about $3 million annually, provided support for the new movement of "supply-side" economics, which (among its other claims) emphasized the destructive effects of government regulation on savings and investment. The foundation was hailed by Jude Wanniski, a *Wall Street Journal* writer who promoted the movement, as *"the* source of financing in the supply-side revolution. . . . It's become the place to go if you have a project that needs money." Among the foundation's early grants in support of the supply-siders, offered on the advice of *Public Interest* editor Irving Kristol, was a $40,000 subsidy to Wanniski himself. It led to the publication of his *The Way the World Works*, a major popularization of supply-side thought. (Later the foundation would subsidize George Gilder's *Wealth and Poverty*, a book that emphasized the redemptive qualities of capitalist entrepreneurs, and that was widely described as the "bible" of the Reagan Administration). Scaife, in addition to its many other conservative grants, also joined in the promotion of anti-regulatory fervor. Between 1973 and 1980, Scaife funds provided $3 million to the Law and Economics Center, close to $4 million to the new (founded in 1973) Heritage Foundation, $2 million to various conservative media projects (including $900,000 to *The American Spectator*, $150,000 to Accuracy in Media, and $500,000 to Erie, Pennsylvania, TV station WQLN to help underwrite Milton Friedman's TV series "Free to Choose"), and close to $4 million to a variety of new "public interest" law firms attacking specific government regulations. (Between 1977 and 1982, Scaife would supply National Affairs, Inc., the publisher of *The Public Interest*, with $380,000.)

Such foundation activities, while very important, were only the tip of a massive wave of corporate subsidy to attacks on regulation. By the mid-1970s, U.S. firms were spending more than $400 million a year on "advocacy advertising," much of it directed against government constraints on business. By the end of the 1970s, total estimated corporate spending on advocacy advertising and grass-roots lobbying, again with much of the effort devoted to attacks on regulation, ran to $1 billion annually.

Though a few liberal, multinationally oriented Republicans remained committed to environmental and other regulation, the affinity of the Democrats for the environmentalists and other advocates of business regulation was stronger for both philosophical and financial reasons. Accordingly, the rising anti-regulatory, pro-"free enterprise" movement weakened the Democratic base in the business community and in the country at large. In addition, a range of regulatory restrictions—regarding the environment, pharmaceuticals, and dangerous (e.g., nuclear) technologies—specifically affected the Democrats' traditional base among firms doing large shares of business abroad. Particularly in the late 1970s, destructive competition among the major powers and the environmental perils of unrestrained Third World growth prompted some (very partial) multilateral efforts at environmental and other regulation—reflected in negotiations over the Law of the Sea Treaty, for example, or the Carter Administration's tightened policies on nuclear proliferation, or more aggressive enforcement by the Food and Drug Administration. As a result, companies that were anxious to sell untested drugs to the Third World, or export nuclear technologies, or engage in mammoth construction projects that degraded regional environments in other countries or offshore regions, sometimes found government in the way. Strongly identified with the Democrats, and backed by many of the same sectors (preeminently banking and other services) that promoted domestic environmental regulation, these international initiatives served to weaken support for the party among its other multinational supporters.

BUSINESS MOBILIZATION

By the mid-1970s the cumulative weight of all these factors—faltering domestic economic performance, lagging international competitiveness, the explosion of energy and other commodity prices, and pressures for increased military spending, along with a cost cutting in labor, regulation, social programs, and taxes—was immense. What might be termed the "old right" of the independent oil companies, protectionist sectors like textiles (whose leading spokesman was North Carolina senator Jesse Helms), and many raw-materials producers was on the march. Supplying millions of dollars of funds and other assistance to a wide variety of organizations—conservative publishing companies, foundations, think tanks, religious groups, and lobbying organizations—these groups vastly increased their national presence.

Simultaneously, in a process that was often mistaken for a "rightwing takeover" by the South and West, the center of gravity of American big business was also moving right. The Olin foundation—where William Simon was joined by the legendary John J. McCloy, a former backer of LBJ in 1964 and the recognized chairman of all things Eastern and established—several Scaife funds, Smith Richardson, Pew, Lilly, and other foundations, along with many corporations themselves, were spending hundreds of millions of dollars not only on promoting antiregulatory fervor and the virtues of "free" markets but on hard-line national security studies, general attacks on the welfare state and social spending, assaults on the progressive income tax, and detailed criticisms of past excesses of the "liberal" media on Vietnam, foreign news reporting, and other issues.

To the unaided eye, these activities appeared indistinguishable from those of the traditional right wing. But in fact several important differences did remain. In contrast to the "old right" that wrote import restrictions into the 1964 Republican platform, most of the multinational sponsors of this new right turn remained strongly committed to free trade. They also still shied away from direct, public attacks on organized labor, preferring to wait for the mass flight to the sunbelt (and the resurgent National Right to Work Committee) to take its toll. And, while they were prepared to fund moderate "evangelical" groups, they did not share the fundamentalism of the far right.

But the effect of this cultural turn was powerful all the same. Community organizations and liberal groups that had an easy time getting funds in the late 1960s and very early 1970s now struggled to find financing. Simultaneously the flock of conservative think tanks drawing vast business support—including the Heritage Foundation, American Enterprise Institute, Institute for Contemporary Studies, Hoover Institute, and National Bureau of Economic Research— were churning out the "books, books, and more books" that Simon called for, along with all manner of position papers, attacks on liberal "myths," and specific conservative policy suggestions. The network of "public interest" legal centers—including the Pacific, Capitol, Mountain States, Great Plains, Mid-America, and Southeastern legal foundations—were busy filing suits on issues ranging from welfare eligibility (to curb it) to environmental protection (to relax it). The boards of some of these newer groups, such as the San Francisco-based Institute of Contemporary Studies or the Washington, D.C.-based Heritage Foundation, mixed figures from multinationals that formerly bulwarked the older "liberal" establishment with representatives of far more conservative business interests.

The budgets of all sorts of business lobbying organizations were reviving. By this time, the Business Roundtable had emerged from the old Labor Law Study Group and other antecedents and began flexing the power that came of being an association of the CEOs of America's two hundred biggest firms. It was joined by a revitalized Chamber of Commerce, National Federation of Independent Business, National Association of Manufacturers, and scores of other trade associations. On a wide range of particular issues, these groups pressed forward with general business demands for tax relief, cuts in social outlays, and, in many cases, increases in military outlays.

The press also gradually shifted to the right. Though the TV networks and Eastern, multinationally oriented papers like *The New York Times* and *The Washington Post* remained well to the left of most nationally oriented conservative dailies and local TV stations in the South and West, they too came to reflect the new "mood." The shift at the *Times*, under new executive editor Abe Rosenthal, was later hailed by the Heritage Foundation's house journal, *Policy Review*:

> [W]hat we are witnessing now is a distinctly American comeback. The *New York Times*, America's greatest newspaper, is reaffirming its greatness by retreating from the radicalism of the last two decades and once again taking up responsible journalism. It is the first liberal institution to identify the excesses of liberalism, mainly its flirtation with Communism, and to see to correct them. Many *Times* readers feared that the newspaper did not have such resilience. Abe Rosenthal is proving them wrong.

What this meant, more concretely, is that the greatest of American newspapers now featured less intensive and less critical coverage of U.S. interventionism abroad; far more tales of Soviet aggression and the well-known miseries of life in the Eastern bloc; far less concern, in coverage as well as on the editorial page, with the less well-known miseries of the poor and working populations at home; and less support for progressive domestic policies in taxing and spending.

Chain Reaction

THOMAS EDSALL

Thomas Edsall, a Washington Post reporter, is the author of a number of books dealing with America's recent past. In *The New Politics of Inequality*, Edsall showed how post-Watergate reforms strengthened the influence of the wealthy and powerful and tilted government policy away from concern for the poor. *Chain Reaction*, which he wrote with the help of his wife Mary Edsall, examined how social issues precipitated the decline of the Democratic Party. Why was the issue of rights so politically explosive? Why did the white middle class abandon the Democrats in the 1970s?

In the aftermath of Richard Nixon's 1972 landslide victory over George McGovern, the investigation of the Republican break-in at the Democratic party headquarters—the scandal known as Watergate—provided the besieged forces of liberalism with an opportunity to stall the conservative ascendance. Watergate replenished forces on the liberal side of the political spectrum—the Democratic Congress, organized labor, civil rights groups, and the network of public-interest lobbying and reform organizations—supplying new leverage in what was otherwise rapidly becoming, in political terms, a losing ideological battle.

The central conflict between liberalism and conservatism since the late sixties had focused on the aggressive expansion of constitutional rights to previously disfranchised, often controversial groups. These included not only blacks, but others in relatively unprotected enclaves (mental hospitals, prisons, ghettos) as well as homosexuals (who increasingly resented being cast as deviant), ethnic minorities, and women—who had the strongest base of political support but whose movement, nonetheless, engendered substantial political reaction. Just as this expansion of rights had run into growing public and political opposition, the Nixon administration was itself caught flagrantly violating the core constitutional rights of "average" citizens—rights for which there was, in general, broad consensual support.

The official Republican sanction of the break-in of Democratic National Committee headquarters, the secret wiretapping of fourteen government officials and three newsmen, the burglary of anti-war activist Daniel Ellsberg's psychiatrist, and the extensive White House cover-up, constituted government-authorized violations of fundamental constitutional guarantees: due process, protection from illegal search and seizure, the separation of powers, and freedom of speech. The second article of impeachment against Nixon (the article receiving the greatest number of votes in the House Judiciary Committee, 28–10, in July 1974,) charged that in directing the FBI, CIA, IRS, and Secret Service to attack political adversaries, Nixon "repeatedly engaged in conduct violating the constitutional rights of citizens, impairing the due and proper administration of justice, and the conduct of lawful inquiries, or contravening the laws governing agencies of the executive branch."

The outcry against the actions of the Nixon White House effectively stifled for the moment public expression of the growing resentment toward the liberal revolution. Watergate "is the last gasp of . . . our partisan opponents," Nixon told his aide, John Dean. The Nixon administration had already been damaged by the forced resignation in October 1973 of Spiro Agnew, who, facing the possibility of a substantial jail term, resigned from the vice presidency, pleading *nolo contendere* to charges of accepting illegal payments from Maryland contractors.

For many liberal constituencies, Watergate provided the grounds to attempt to indict and convict the snowballing conservative counteroffensive. For Democratic members of Congress, and for the larger Democratic establishment, the procedural ruthlessness of the Nixon administration—the enemies lists, the attempts to use the IRS and Justice Department to harass political adversaries, the burglaries, and the illegal wiretapping—was part and parcel of a much broader and more threatening administration drive to assault the constitutional underpinnings of the liberal state.

For liberal interest groups, the appeal of Watergate was even more direct: "The election of Richard Nixon as President sent a shiver through the civil rights and anti-war movements—and the ACLU. A symbol of the cold war of the 1950s, Nixon appeared hostile to civil rights and to virtually all the recent gains in civil liberties," wrote Samuel Walker, in his 1990 book, *In Defense of American Liberties: a History of the ACLU*. After the national board of the American Civil Liberties Union (ACLU) voted to endorse impeachment of the president on September 29, 1973, when Congress was still very tentatively exploring the process, membership in the organization shot up. Ads, financed by such liberal bankrollers as General Motors heir Stewart Mott declared that "Richard Nixon has not left us in doubt . . . if he is allowed to continue, then the destruction of the Bill of Rights could follow," and produced a flood of cash and support. "Over 25,000 new members joined in 1973 alone, driving the ACLU's membership to an all-time high of 275,000."

The Watergate-inspired re-invigoration of the left effectively choked off the growth of conservatism from 1973 through 1976, but the suppression meant that instead of finding an outlet within the political system, rightward pressure built throughout the decade to explosive levels. The Democratic party experienced a surge of victory in 1974 and 1976, while developments in the economy, in the court-enforced enlargement of the rights revolution, in the expansion of the regulatory state, in rising middle-class tax burdens, and in the growth of crime and illegitimacy were all in fact working to crush liberalism.

Watergate resulted in a political system out of sync with larger trends. A host of groups on the left of the spectrum—Democratic prosecutors, the media, junior congressional Democrats, new reform organizations, and traditional liberal interest groups—gained control over the political agenda just when a selection of other key indicators suggested that the power of the right should be expanding:

- Family income after 1973 abruptly stopped growing, cutting off what was left of popular support for government-led redistributional economic policies. Inflation (driven in part by the first OPEC oil shock) simultaneously pushed millions of working and middle-class citizens into higher tax brackets, encouraging them to think like Republicans instead of Democrats. As low and middle-income voters began to view the taxes deducted from their weekly paychecks with rising anger, the number of welfare and food stamp clients continued to grow at record rates, forcing a conflict between Democratic constituencies that would lead, by the end of the decade, to a racially-loaded confrontation between taxpayers and tax recipients.

- In courts across the country, the drive by a wide range of civil liberties organizations—from the ACLU to the Mental Health Law Project to the National Gay and Lesbian Task Force—reached its height. These organizations were committed to winning new rights for recreational drug users, the mentally ill, gays, American Indians, illegal aliens and the dependent poor. Their success produced not only benefits for targeted populations, but also conservative reaction in communities in every region of the country.
- Crime rates continued to surge, intensifying public discontent with liberal Democratic support of defendants' and prisoners' rights.
- The movement to liberalize abortion laws, which had been making substantial political progress in state legislatures, succeeded with the Supreme Court's 1973 decision, *Roe v. Wade*; that decision, in turn, produced a political counter-mobilization that rapidly became a mainstay of the conservative movement. Equally important, *Roe* reflected the growing dependence of liberalism on court rulings. The legal arena provided liberal interest groups with a host of victories through the mid-1970s. Court rulings frequently lacked the political legitimacy and support, however, that comes from public debate and legislative deliberation. Liberal court victories reduced incentives for the left to compete in elective politics to win backing for its agenda, while sharply increasing the incentives for the right—both social and economic—to build political muscle.
- The Arab oil embargo of 1973 resulted in gas lines across the country, intensifying in some sectors hostility toward liberal foreign-policy positions seen as supportive of Third World interests. Covert and explicit hostility towards Third World countries intensified and fueled, in some cases, a resurgence of domestic nativism, and even a degree of racism.
- Legislation passed in the civil rights climate of 1965, liberalizing previously restrictive, pro-European immigration policies, produced a surge of Hispanic, Asian, and other non-European immigration; created new competition for employment and housing; increased pressure for public services; and generated a revival of pressures to restore restrictions on immigration.
- The Justice Department, the Equal Employment Opportunity Commission (EEOC), and the Office of Federal Contract Com-

pliance Programs (OFCCP) all capitalized on a sequence of legislative mandates, court rulings, and executive orders to sharply expand enforcement of affirmative action programs in the public and private sectors, increasing the saliency of the issue of quotas, an issue beginning to match busing in terms of the depth of voter reaction.

- Busing, in turn, by the early and mid-1970s, had become a legal remedy frequently imposed to correct school segregation in the North as well as in the South. The 1973 Supreme Court decision in *Keyes v. Denver School District No. 1* significantly increased the likelihood that a northern school system would be found guilty of illegal discrimination, and therefore subject to busing orders.
- In a number of major cities, black political gains were translating into the acquisition of genuine power. An inevitable outcome of the process of enfranchisement, the ascendancy of black politicians meant the loss of power for some white politicians, and in an increasing number of major cities competition for control of City Hall turned into racial confrontation. In 1967, Richard Hatcher and Carl Stokes won the mayor's offices in Gary, Indiana, and Cleveland, Ohio, respectively; in 1970, Kenneth Gibson became mayor of Newark; in 1974 Coleman Young and Maynard Jackson won in Detroit and Atlanta. These contests involved sharply polarized electorates (the only exception being the 1973 election of Tom Bradley, a black, in Los Angeles, where the mayoralty was won with more white than black votes). As Democratic black political power grew in the cities, Republican voting in white suburbs began to intensify, accelerating the creation of what political strategists would term "white nooses" around black cities.

There were forces at work in the 1970s, combining to produce an explosive mix—forces pitting blacks, whites, Hispanics, and other minorities against each other for jobs, security, prestige, living space, and government protection. As weekly pay fell, and as the market for working-class jobs tightened, government intervention in behalf of employment for minorities intensified; the doors opened for a wave of Latinos and Asians legally seeking jobs, at the same time that illegal immigration from across the Mexican border increased. Simultaneously, former civil rights lawyers and activists turned their attention to continuing the extension of rights to the ranks of the once-excluded.

This sequence of developments engendered a form of backlash within key sectors of the majority white electorate, backlash generating conservative pressures on an ambitious and threatening liberalism, conservative pressures which were only temporarily held in check by Watergate. The immediate political consequences of the investigation and prosecution triggered by the Watergate break-in lulled Democratic party leaders into ignoring the outcome of the 1972 presidential election—into thinking that their majority party status was secure, and that the ability of the Republican Party to dominate presidential elections with a racially and socially conservative message had been washed away in the outcry for official probity and reform.

Politicians, academics, and the media remained largely ignorant of the direction the country would, in fact, take by the end of the decade. Patrick Caddell, who had conducted polls for both McGovern in 1972 and Jimmy Carter in 1976, wrote in a post-1976 election memorandum to President-elect Carter: "When we turn to the Republicans, we find them in deep trouble. Their ideology is restrictive; they have few bright lights to offer the public. Given the antiquated machinery of the Republican Party, the rise of a moderate, attractive Republican in their primary process is hard to imagine. The Republican Party seems bent on self-destruction." Everett Carll Ladd, a political scientist expert in assessing the balance of power between the two parties, wrote in 1977:

> [W]e are dealing with a long-term secular shift, not just an artifact of Watergate. The Republicans have lost their grip on the American establishment, most notably among young men and women of relative privilege. They have lost it, we know, in large part because the issue orientations which they manifest are somewhat more conservative than the stratum favors. . . . The [Republican] party is especially poorly equipped in style and tone to articulate the frustrations of the newer, emergent American *petit bourgeoisie*—southern white Protestant, Catholic, black and the like."

In fact, it was the Democratic party that was continuing to lose its class-based strength. The forces pushing the country to the right exerted the strongest pressures on whites in the working and lower-middle class, and it was among these voters that Democratic loyalty was continuing to erode. Party leaders failed to perceive these trends because losses among low-to-moderate-income whites during the mid-1970s were compensated for by momentary gains among upper-income, normally Republican white voters who were most insistent on political reform in response to Watergate.

Among middle and low-status whites, voter turnout for Democratic congressional candidates in 1974, and for the Democratic presidential nominee in 1976, was lower than it had been in the 1960s, when the New Deal coalition was stronger.

Democrats at the height of Watergate had lost substantial levels of support among low-status whites, and had experienced a modest decline among middle-status whites. Only a surge of support among upscale whites compensated for the difference. A very similar pattern emerges in the comparison of the white Democratic vote for president in two very close elections, both won by Democrats, John Kennedy in 1960 and Jimmy Carter in 1976.

In effect, Democrats were winning in 1974 and 1976, just as the core of their traditional base among whites was crumbling. The party became dependent on upscale, traditionally Republican voters whose new found loyalty would disappear as economic and foreign-policy issues regained their saliency, and as the memory of Watergate faded.

In the buildup of conservative, anti-liberal sentiment in the electorate, the most important development was the fact that 1973, the year the Senate set up a special committee to investigate Watergate, was also the year that marked the end of a sustained period of post–World War II economic growth. Hourly earnings, which had grown every year since 1951 in real, inflation-adjusted dollars, fell by 0.1 percent in 1973, by 2.8 percent in 1974, and by 0.7 percent in 1975. Weekly earnings fell more sharply, by 4.1 percent in 1974 and by 3.1 percent in 1975. Median family income, which had grown from $20,415 (in 1985 inflation-adjusted dollars) in 1960, to $29,172 in 1973, began to decline in 1974, when family income fell to $28,145, and then to $27,421 in 1975.

Steady economic growth, which had made redistributive government policies tolerable to the majority of the electorate, came to a halt in the mid-1970s, and, with stagnation, the threat to Democratic liberalism intensified. In a whipsaw action, the middle-class tax burden rose with inflation just as the economy and real-income growth slowed. The tax system was losing its progressivity, placing a steadily growing share of the cost of government on middle and lower-middle-class voters, vital constituencies for the Democratic party. In 1953, a family making the median family income was taxed at a rate of 11.8 percent, while a family making four times the median was taxed at 20.2 percent, nearly double. By 1976, these figures had become 22.7 percent for the average family, and 29.5 percent for the affluent family. In other words, for the affluent family, the tax burden increased by 46 percent from 1953 to 1976, while for the average family, the tax burden increased by 92.4 percent. Not only were cumulative tax burdens growing, but they were also shifting from Republican constituencies to Democratic constituencies.

At the same time, one of the most painful elements of the federal income-tax structure, the marginal rate system, had begun to impinge on the vast majority of voters, not just on the affluent. As recently as the early 1960s, 90 percent of the population was effectively exempt from steeply rising marginal tax rates that applied only to those in the top 10 percent of the population. For 90 percent of the population, there were only two marginal rates, 20 percent for nearly half of all taxpayers, and 22 percent for a quarter of the entire population, as the bottom fifth paid no taxes whatsoever. By 1979, however, this same 90 percent of the population faced ten different marginal tax rates. Routine pay hikes regularly pushed taxpayers into higher marginal brackets and, worse, rising inflation meant higher marginal rates without any increase in real income. At the same time, Congress also approved steadily higher Social Security taxes. From 1960 to 1975, the maximum annual Social Security tax liability grew from $144 to $825, a 473 percent increase. During the same period, per capita income grew by only 166 percent, so that the Social Security tax was taking an increasingly large bite out of wage and salary income.

In political terms, the damage was most severe to the Democratic party. Democratic-approved Social Security tax hikes fell much harder on those making less than the median income, voters who had traditionally tended to vote Democratic by higher margins than those above the median. In 1975, for example, a worker with taxable income of $14,100 paid $825, or 5.85 percent of his income, to Social Security, while someone making $75,000 paid the same $825, or just 1.1 percent of income.

These economic developments became one-half of an equation that functioned to intensify racial divisions within the traditional Democratic coalition. The other half of the equation was that taxpayer-financed welfare, food stamps, and other expenditures for the poor were growing exponentially. In the decade from 1965 to 1975, the number of families receiving benefits under Aid to Families with Dependent Children (AFDC), grew by 237 percent. Until that point, the national caseload had been growing at a *relatively* modest pace—from 644,000 households in 1950 to 787,000 in 1960 to 1,039,000 in 1965, an increase over fifteen years of 61 percent.

From 1965 to 1970, the number of households on welfare more than doubled to reach 2,208,000, and then grew again by more than one million, reaching 3,498,000 families in 1975. The Food Stamp program, which was initiated on a small scale in 1961 and then greatly enlarged in 1970, provided benefits to 400,000 people in 1965, 4.3 million in 1970, and increased four-fold, to 17.4 million recipients in 1975. Throughout the 1970s, the illegitimacy rate for both blacks and whites grew significantly, but for blacks, the decade saw illegitimate births begin to outnumber legitimate births. For whites, the illegitimacy rate rose from 5.7 percent of all live births in 1970, to 7.3 in 1975, to 11.0 in 1980; for blacks, the rate went from 37.6, to 48.8, to 55.2 percent in the same period.

The tensions growing out of these economic and social trends were compounded by the substantial conflicts growing directly out of the expansion of the civil rights movement into the broader rights revolution. Lawyers who had been trained in the trenches of the South—often funded by liberal, tax-exempt organizations and foundations, just as civil rights litigation projects had been—moved, in the late 1960s and early 1970s, into the broader rights arena. They developed litigation strategies designed to remedy the longstanding denial of rights to groups in unprotected enclaves (psychiatric hospitals, immigrant detention camps, Indian reservations, jails), and also to social "victims" (homosexuals, the disabled, the indigent). Particularly powerful was the evolving idea that conditions of birth or chance—ranging from gender to race to skin color to sexual orientation to class origin to ethnicity to physical or mental health—should not place any American at a social or economic disadvantage, insofar as it was possible for the state to offer protection and redress. "The rights revolution was the longest-lasting legacy of the 1960s," writes Samuel Walker in his history of the ACLU. "Millions of ordinary people—students, prisoners, women, the poor, gays and lesbians, the handicapped, the mentally retarded and others—discovered their own voices and demanded fair treatment and personal dignity. The empowerment of these previously silent groups was a political development of enormous significance."

The rights movement had already found political expression within the Democratic party, which had not only endorsed a broad spectrum of human rights at its 1972 convention, but which was granting specific recognition to a network of separate caucuses for blacks, women, and homosexuals within the Democratic National Committee.

It was not until the mid-1970s, however, that the rights revolution reached its full power, changing some of the most fundamental patterns and practices of society. As these changes began to seep into public consciousness, the political ramifications slowly became felt throughout the majority electorate—an electorate under economic siege and rapidly losing its tolerance for the rapid redistribution of influence, as well for the redistribution of a host of economic and social benefits.

Just as the economy was beginning to stagnate, as oil producing countries were demonstrating their power to hold the energy-hungry United States hostage (with the price of imported oil rising from $1.80 a barrel in 1970 to $14.34 in 1979), and as the shift from manufacturing to services was forcing major dislocations in the job market, the rights revolution assaulted the traditional hierarchical structure of society, and in particular the status of white men.

The strongest of the rights movements was, in fact, the drive for the equality of women, who were included as beneficiaries of the equal employment provisions of the original 1964 Civil Rights Act. Political support for women's rights remained strong, symbolized by the congressional approval in 1972 of the Equal Rights Amendment (ERA) and by a series of legislative victories throughout the 1970s. At the same time, the women's movement—in combination with financial pressures making the one-earner family increasingly untenable—produced a major alteration in family structure, as labor force participation among married women grew steadily, from 35.7 percent in 1965, to 41.4 in 1970, to 45.1 percent in 1975, to 50.7 percent in 1980.

The changes that were taking place in the workplace, in family relationships, and in the balance of power between men and women were not cost-free. The number of divorces, which had remained relatively constant from 1950 through 1967, began to escalate sharply. In 1967, the divorce rate for every 1,000 married women was 11.2; by 1975, the rate had grown to 20.3; and in 1979, the divorce rate reached its height, 22.8—more than double the 1967 level. At the same time, the annual number of children of parents getting divorced grew from 701,000 in 1967, to 1.12 million in 1975, to 1.18 million in 1979.

The more outspoken leaders of the women's rights movement, many of whom cut their teeth in the civil rights and anti-war movements, adopted rhetoric and tactics that exacerbated the anxieties of a host of men already facing diminished job prospects, eroding family incomes, and a loss of traditional status in their homes. "Lesbian sexuality could make an excellent case, based on anatomical data, for the extinction of the male organ," Anne Koedt wrote in "The Myth of the Vaginal Orgasm," an essay subsequently reprinted in an estimated twenty different anthologies of feminist writings.

The women's rights movement was reinforced by the Supreme Court in *Roe v. Wade*, as the Court took the expanded right to privacy established in *Griswold v. Connecticut*, a case involving the sale of contraceptives, and extended the reasoning to establish a woman's right to terminate pregnancy during the first trimester. The sum of these developments—the entry of women into the workforce, the rising divorce rate, and the doubling of the number of reported abortions, from 586,800 in 1972 to 1.2 million in 1976—as well as the halving of the fertility rate between 1960 and 1975—contributed to the building of a conservative response.

The anti-abortion movement and the massive growth of parishioners attending fundamentalist Christian churches during the 1970s were in many ways powerful reactions to the emergence of the women's rights movement. "[T]he danger signs are quite evident: legislation on the national level reflects widespread acceptance of easy divorce, abortion-on-demand, gay rights, militant feminism, unisex facilities, and leniency towards pornography, prostitution and crime. . . . In short, many religious leaders believe that America may soon follow the footsteps of Sodom and Gomorrah," wrote Tim LaHaye, organizer of fundamentalist Christian voters, in his book, *The Battle for the Mind*.

The surge of women newly entering the job market, women now empowered with unprecedented control over their reproductive and sexual lives, coincided with the opening of the nation to another source of competition for employment and, in the Southwest and West, for political power: Hispanic and Asian immigration. Legislation enacted in 1965, growing out of the general climate surrounding the civil rights revolution, ended the racially restrictive immigration policies that had been on the books since the Immigration Act of 1924. The 1965 law opened the door to a wave of new immigration, primarily from Mexico and the Caribbean. The total number of legal immigrants and refugees from Central and South America, rose from 183,717 in the 1950s, to 751,060 in the 1960s, to 1,555,697 in the 1970s. These figures do not include the movement of United States citizens in Puerto Rico to the mainland, nor do they include illegal immigration, nor do they reflect the population growth following immigration—with the total Hispanic population of the United States growing from 9.07 million in 1970 to an estimated 22.4 million in 1990. The rising tide of legal Hispanic immigration was matched by Asian immigration, which grew from 186,671 in the 1950s, to 447,537 in the 1960s, to 1,798,861 in the 1970s. Overall, the Asian population in the United States also grew rapidly—from 1.34 million in 1970 to 7.3 million in 1990.

The drive to achieve equality for women and the abandonment of racially exclusionary immigration policies, in tandem with the civil rights movement, were consistent with the evolution of an egalitarian American political culture. But each evolutionary development contributed in turn to a growing conservative backlash or reaction, which was strengthened in turn by the increasing momentum of the more controversial rights movements. In 1974, the gay rights movement persuaded the American Psychiatric Association to remove homosexuality from its list of mental illnesses; between 1973 and 1975, the movement won approval of gay rights ordinances in eleven cities and counties, barring discrimination on the basis of sexual orientation; by 1989, the drive had produced legal prohibitions against discrimination against gays in housing, employment, and in the provision of other services in sixty-four municipalities, sixteen counties, and thirteen states.

The early 1970s also produced a movement to win legal rights for the mentally ill and for the mentally retarded, accelerating the nationwide process of deinstitutionalization. In 1975, the mental health rights movement won, in *O'Connor v. Donaldson*, a decision by the Supreme Court barring involuntary institutional confinement of non-dangerous patients. *Donaldson* was followed by a series of decisions in state and federal courts establishing stringent procedural safeguards for those facing forced commitment, including the right to a formal hearing, the right to appeal, the right to be represented by a lawyer, and proof from committing authorities that confined individuals were dangerous either to themselves or to others. The general public approved these rights in principle, but the practical reality—particularly the lack in every jurisdiction of taxpayer support for costly community-based alternative care—led to the abandonment of large numbers of emotionally fragile men and women to the streets, subways, parks, and storefronts of the nation, where routine commuting, recreational, and shopping experiences became disturbing and often frightening for significant numbers of voters.

8

DECLINE OF HEGEMONY

The United States in 1945 controlled over half of the world's gross national product. Of course this position of strength was artificial. How to deal with America's relative decline in the decades that followed constituted one of the United States' two main foreign policy challenges in the post war world. The other and even more dominant theme remained the confrontation between the United States and its allies on the one hand, and the Soviet Union and its client states on the other.

It is no exaggeration to say that American policy-makers viewed all foreign policy issues within the Cold War prism. The Kennedy and Johnson administrations continued the post-war policy of depending on Western Europe to buttress the American position against the Soviet Union. The creation of NATO, our first entangling alliance, in 1949, set the stage for a permanent American military presence in Europe. For the first fifteen years after the war the United States clearly dominated the alliance both economically and militarily. But after 1960 Western European countries had recovered sufficiently to seek some independence from the United States. Further, France and West Germany, together with the Benelux countries and Italy, had in 1957 formed the European Economic Community. Initially operating only as a tariff free-zone, its founders intended that the Common Market lay the ground work for a united Europe. While all American administrations welcomed this development, American diplomats found themselves increasingly at odds with members of the European Community on agricultural, and in the case of France, military matters.

Richard Nixon came to the White House in 1969 carrying staunch cold warrior credentials. Together with his Secretary of State, Henry Kissinger, he presided over a strategic evolution of American foreign policy. Relations with the Soviet Union, while improved from the naked confrontation of the Cuban Missile crisis of 1962, had remained tense. Nixon and Kissinger inaugurated a policy of detente with Moscow while at the same time ending the two-decade long non-recognition of the People's Republic of China. Simultaneously Nixon, appreciating the decline in American economic strength, set forth the Nixon Doctrine which called for regional powers to absorb defense responsibilities formerly borne by the United States.

While arming surrogate states such as Iran seemed sensible at the time, this particular decision bore bitter fruit after Jimmy Carter became President in January 1977. As Gaddis Smith makes clear, the question of the nature, purpose and meaning of foreign policy had long been debated in this country. Yet Carter's principles collapsed, shattered by a double blow. Rejecting the policy of detente, the Soviet Union invaded Afghanistan. In Iran, the long-standing American buttressing of a repressive government dominated by the Shah of Iran contributed to a fundamentalist revolution led by the Ayatollah Khomeini and the humiliating hostage crisis when fifty-one American embassy workers were held in Tehran for fourteen months. The ashes of Carter's presidency lay in the fulcrum of these two crises.

Pax Americana

DAVID CALLEO

David Calleo, professor of history at Johns Hopkins University, has long delineated the evolving challenges to American foreign policy-makers. In this excerpt from *Beyond American Hegemony* he explains the interconnections between the American created Atlantic Alliance and the global system. Were the tensions between the United States and its allies inevitable? Should the United States have encouraged more autonomy among its allies?

To conceive of anything so abstract as a world system calls for imagination of a specialized nature. The teeming complexity of international relations has to be squeezed into some sort of conceptual model—giving, at best, a highly selective approximation of reality. Such a model invariably reflects the vantage point and preoccupations of the analyst. Its usefulness depends on whether it helps separate superficial happenings from the deeper forces that shape events. Insofar as it does, past and present scenarios may be more clearly understood and future events may be anticipated or even shaped.

From an American perspective, it is the all-pervasive role of the United States that distinguishes the world system after World War II from what preceded it. Since 1945, the United States has clearly been the leading power over much of the world and, in many spheres, has acted as a sort of managing director of the international system. So central has the American role been in creating, conceptualizing, and sustaining the postwar global order that this order may reasonably be described as a *Pax Americana*, with the United States playing the role of hegemonic power.

To call a system hegemonic, however, is not to indict it as coercive or exploitative. Many styles of hegemony exist among nations, just as many fashions for leadership can be found among individuals. Elements of exploitation and coercion necessarily exist in any international system, but the question of who profits and who pays is generally complex. Sustaining its world role in the present system costs the United States a great deal. To some extent, America's allies are free riders on the benefits of that American effort. In that respect, it is they who exploit the United States.

Determining coercion is no less problematic. Even in the Warsaw Pact—NATO's Soviet counterpart, where the disparity of power between the hegemon and its allies is enormous—Russian leadership involves considerable persuasion and concession. NATO reveals hegemonic leadership in a far subtler mode. Several of America's Atlantic allies are themselves important political, economic, and military powers. When they accept American leadership, they do so because, on balance, it seems in their own interest. Their own strength, as well as the variety and intricacy of transatlantic entanglements, compel discussion and bargaining. Multilateral institutions are natural structures for regulating such relationships. If the United States has played the leading role in many of the postwar multilateral institutions, it has by no means always had its own way. In short, to call an international system hegemonic means that one power generally takes the initiative in structuring and managing. It does not necessarily mean that the role results in exploitation or springs from coercion.

Not only is America's hegemony strongly qualified—even among countries with whom it has the most intimate connections—but its weight varies greatly from one region of the globe to another. This postwar international system, even if viewed as a *Pax Americana*, is extremely diverse in its parts and is probably becoming more so. The system's overall character depends on the relationships among these diverse parts, and the relationships have been changing significantly.

For convenience, it has grown customary to divide the postwar system into three broad state groupings, or "worlds." The United States, together with the other NATO states, the rest of "Free Europe," Japan, and the white British Commonwealth make up one obvious grouping: a core of liberal, democratic, advanced industrial states that are closely linked to each other. This First World forms what can be called the Near Empire of the *Pax Americana*. Aside from the United States itself, the most important part of this inner core is Western Europe, and the most important relationship, upon which the whole structure depends, is the Atlantic Alliance.

Beyond the pale of the *Pax Americana* is the alien Second World of the Soviet sphere—initially limited to a vast continental bloc including Eastern Europe and China. The Russians, attempting to rival the Americans, have extended their influence and have become entangled with a variety of other far-flung clients. Meanwhile, the Chinese defection has removed a giant chunk from the original Eurasian empire.

While the Soviet role in the postwar system has often been described as a threat to be contained, the relationship between Second and First worlds is clearly more complex than that description would imply. The Russians and their allies are increasingly entwined in the general international system. Eastern Europe and even the Soviet Union itself have been drawn into a nascent pan-European system of growing economic, cultural, and political significance. At the same time, Soviet strategic rivalry with the United States has become rather structured over the years, particularly through the arms limitation agreements.

Finally, everyone speaks of a Third World of highly diverse states in Asia, Africa, and Latin America. Many of these countries were once parts of Europe's formal or informal colonial empires. Many are still military clients or economic dependencies of the Americans or Western Europeans. A few—Cuba, North Korea, Vietnam—are Soviet clients. The biggest states—China and India—are militarily nonaligned.

Most Third World states are poor by Western industrial standards, although several have immense natural resources and some have had remarkably rapid industrial growth. With the exception of vast and still autarchic China, most Third World states are closely integrated into a world political economy that depends heavily on conditions and policies in the United States, Western Europe, and Japan. Hence, if Europe, America, and Japan are the Near Empire of the *Pax Americana*, the Third World is the Far Empire.

The international system has not only distinct geographical parts but also distinct functional dimensions. To name the most obvious, the *Pax Americana* has both a military and an economic dimension. Even if these realms are more related than is often believed, particularly by those expert in one and uninformed about the other, each is usually analyzed by discrete sets of experts and managed by distinct bureaucracies. Each has its own set of multilateral institutions through which international relations are structured.

Within these separate military and economic institutions, the political relationships between the United States and its allies are markedly different. NATO's formal organization, for example, is forthrightly hegemonic. In many respects, Western Europe seems an American military protectorate. All members, even those with nuclear deterrents of their own, depend on the American strategic deterrent to balance the immense Soviet nuclear force. Most, including the Federal Republic of Germany, have no other strategic defense. In addition, NATO vests the United States with organizing and leading Europe's territorial defense. Thus an American general is NATO's Supreme Allied Commander (SACEUR), and an American ground force of ten divisions is either stationed in West Germany or waiting to be sent there if needed. A large American tactical air force guards European skies, and a large American fleet is permanently stationed in the Mediterranean.

As Europeans have grown stronger, they have not supplanted the Americans within NATO so much as developed independent national military capabilities outside it. Among the major European states, France has gone the furthest in this direction. France has a completely independent national nuclear deterrent and has formally withdrawn its armed forces and territory from the American-directed NATO command. France remains, however, within the alliance and still cooperates selectively in military arrangements. Moreover, geography ensures that France, like the rest of Western Europe, will continue to enjoy the advantages of American protection.

Thus while NATO preserves the forms of American hegemony, the reality has grown more complex, with a substantial part of Europe's own military strength outside the NATO framework.

In the multilateral institutions that seek to organize economic relations in the First World, the formal pattern is far less hegemonic. The most obvious institutional difference lies in the establishment, in 1958, of the powerful European Economic Community (EEC), where Europeans meet without Americans not only to regulate the intimate and interdependent economic relations within Europe but also to try to form a common position for dealing with the rest of the world.

This differentiation between military and economic relations can be seen as a sort of transatlantic compromise. As the Europeans recovered from the war and grew stronger, they built their own independent organization for economic relations but chose to remain militarily dependent within an American-dominated alliance. Thus, while Western

Europe remains an American protectorate militarily, it has organized itself into an economic bloc that has become not only America's biggest single customer but also its biggest industrial and financial rival. As is often said, Europe has become an economic giant while remaining a military dwarf.

The tensions of such an ambivalent dual relationship have been rising in recent years. Trade and monetary relations have grown highly political. The United States has become increasingly inclined to invoke its military role while demanding economic concessions. While the "affluent allies" have grown more critical of American economic "mercantilism" and "mismanagement," Americans have increasingly resented European free riding on their heavy defense spending, a burden that weakens the American economy while protecting the physical security of its principal competitors.

Japan illustrates the consequences of this dual pattern of military dependence and economic competition even more sharply than does Europe. After the war, the Japanese renounced not only nuclear weapons but also any kind of substantial military establishment. Japan's singleminded pursuit of civilian industrial prowess has yielded a rich harvest of economic success, but the country's continuing military dependence has also left it open to an increasingly blatant use of American hegemony to exact economic concessions. Japan's recent moves toward rearmament, while presumably prompted by American demands for sharing the military burden, may well result in growing economic resistance and diplomatic independence.

Relations within the First World are closely affected by the separate and increasingly distinctive American, European, and Japanese relations with the other worlds. As previously noted diverging American and European relations with the Soviet and Third Worlds, primarily for the effect this conflict has on NATO's own durability. Such divergences have often been reactions to changes in the global context, changes that alter relations among the three worlds and then reverberate back to affect relations within the First World.

American relations with the Second, or Soviet, World are mostly with the Soviet Union itself and are primarily concerned with security matters. Attempts to develop Soviet-American economic relations have foundered on recurring American efforts to bargain trade for political concessions or fears that trade would strengthen Soviet war-making capabilities. The Russians themselves have a natural tendency to emphasize the military relationship. It is the only sphere where they are, in any sense, equal to the Americans. In commercial weight or cultural prestige, they are notably inferior to the United States as well as to the major European states and Japan.

This bilateral Soviet-American preoccupation with security questions reinforces a tendency in both to see world politics in military terms and, as a result, to exaggerate each other's role in shaping world events. In Washington as well as in Moscow, international politics can still be seen as a global duel—a zero-sum game where all events are significant only insofar as they represent a gain for one or a loss for the other. Since bipolar competition is thought to be the underlying reality, conflict in one geographical region is seen as tied to conflict in another. Such "linkage politics," or "horizontal escalation," is a characteristic tendency of American policy.

One consequence is the manic-depressive American reaction to détente diplomacy, the latest round of which was discussed earlier. Those inclined to blame the Soviets for most of the world's troubles tend to overestimate the likely gains from more cordial diplomatic relations. They are equally ready to react strongly when détente brings no significant diminution in the world's revolutionary turbulence or in Russian attempts to take advantage of it. For all its fixation on duopoly, however, American diplomacy has never been willing to offer the Soviets the equal global status they presumably crave. But while the United States has never been willing to appease Russia by acknowledging it as a comanager of the international system, neither has it been willing to persist with confrontation. Each time the Americans turn in anger from détente, the consequent political, diplomatic, and economic strains eventually return them to it. Hence, the continuing cycle of fresh hope and fresh disappointment that characterizes Soviet-American relations.

The Western Europeans have broader and, in many respects, more intimate relations with the Second World, the Eastern European states in particular, than do the Americans. European détente diplomacy has concentrated less exclusively on military questions than on trade, investment, cultural communication, travel, and emigration. Such relations tend to penetrate more deeply and directly into the societies and economies of the Eastern bloc.

Behind Europe's détente diplomacy lies a basic geopolitical strategy for gradually reconstituting a pan-European system, but without accepting Soviet hegemony, renouncing American protection, or constructing an indigenous European balance of power. The strategy builds on Western Europe's own anomalous position as a group of highly advanced states, loosely linked together, which remain simultaneously military dependents and economic competitors of the Americans.

As loyal American allies in NATO, Western Europeans enjoy a certain collective anonymity in their military dealings with the Russians. Their national diplomacy with the East can therefore focus on more promising economic, cultural, and diplomatic relationships. The low politics of trade, investment, and cultural exchange thus serve the high politics of promoting pan-Europeanism. The Russians, it is hoped, can gradually be led out of their paranoiac isolation into a prosperous and liberal European family. The process may also persuade the Russians to loosen their grip on the other states of Eastern Europe.

Few Western European governments expect, or probably want, sudden or dramatic success from this strategy. Many have seen perceptible progress over recent years, and few see any alternative approach. Pan-Europeanism poses considerable practical difficulties, however, for the Atlantic Alliance, as well as provocative long-range implications for the international system in general.

In the opinion of many analysts, however, these long-range implications are likely to remain merely theoretical, for Europe's strategy is hamstrung by too many drawbacks. Progress in opening up the Eastern sphere tends, for example, to revive old divisions among the major Western European states themselves. The more the Western states succeed in their Eastern strategy, the more they tend to quarrel among themselves. Recurring French nervousness about supposed German tendencies toward Finlandization is a perennial symptom. And the more the Europeans are divided among themselves, the more their détente strategem risks becoming an invitation to Soviet hegemony.

A second drawback to Western Europe's Russian strategy lies in the very rigidity of Soviet hegemony and the domestic incompetence of most communist regimes, not least that of the Soviet Union itself. A Western European policy based on promoting peaceful liberalization through prosperity is forever stymied by national communist bureaucracies too inflexible to permit the freedom needed for economic prosperity and often unable to govern at all without brutal and alienating repression. The greater the popular discontent, the more the heavy-handed Soviets can be counted on to block reform. The problems of Poland are an obvious illustration.

Periodic confrontation between the superpowers also upsets Western Europe's détente strategem. The experiment requires making the continent a sort of safe zone where pan-European relations can develop while insulated from East-West conflicts elsewhere. For obvious reasons, America's manic-depressive détente cycle, combined with the tendency toward linkage politics or horizontal escalation, is a particular threat. The détente phases of American policy raise fears of a superpower condominium, cemented by a shared desire to keep Europe divided and subordinate. American enthusiasm for détente also generally corresponds with lessened military spending, which leads to deterioration of the bipolar military balance, either at the strategic level or in the European region itself. Western Europe's strategy depends on being able to operate from a position based both on Europe's own economic and political superiority and on military strength borrowed from the Americans. When American military protection falters, Europe's comfortable détente strategy falters with it. In short, Europe's policy requires a delicate balance between deterrence and cooperation, and America's oscillations inevitably cause unwelcome reverberations.

Aside from the difficulties of managing so delicate a strategy, there is the longer-range danger that Europe will be so drawn into the Soviet embrace as to lose or abandon its American protection. Unable to borrow America's military strength, Europe would become Finlandized. Its resources would fall under Soviet hegemony, and the *Pax Americana* would end. Such a view assumes that Europe would be unable to produce its own substitute for American military protection. Here, the greatest danger is probably not any dearth of Western European military capabilities, nor illusions about dealing with the Soviets from a position of military inferiority. Rather, it is the internecine conflicts that would arise if the Western European states began building a military coalition of their own. Such a coalition would require a major strengthening of West Germany's forces and would raise the question of Germany's nuclear protection. Rather than face these issues, European governments have much preferred that military problems be handled via an American protectorate organized through NATO, an arrangement that sustains a military balance at minimal economic and political cost to themselves and, despite increasing American protest, still leaves their hands relatively free for conciliatory and productive economic relations with the East. Insofar as this military dependence grows more delicate and discordant, the triangular American-European-Soviet relationship becomes a point of vulnerability not only for the Atlantic Alliance but for the postwar order in general.

Differing American, European, and Soviet relations with the Third World add another complex dimension to the postwar system. A far more diverse category than either the Atlantic or Soviet worlds, the states of the Third World offer a bewildering variety of climates, cultures, religions, races, internal conditions, and international relationships. Except for China and the handful of states in the Soviet orbit, such as Cuba or Vietnam, most Third World states are caught up in varying degrees of economic and political dependence on the United States and its major allies of the Near Empire. These relationships reflect the economic and political patterns that have succeeded the old imperial systems that died in World War II.

Through diverse alliances, subsidies, and indirect as well as occasionally open interventions, the United States took the early lead in shaping this postwar Third World. American policy promoted rapid decolonization and an open international economy. In its theory, the American formula for decolonization was not unlike that championed by the British Liberals of the last century. All nations were to have formal political independence, but within an international economic system that opened their raw materials and markets to trade. Advanced manufacturing nations would continue to enjoy economic access to the world's less developed regions, but would have no direct political or administrative control over them. Like the nineteenth-century British Liberals, twentieth-century Americans believed that if comparative advantage were permitted to work its beneficial magic, the global economy could be expected to prosper. With trade open to all, the world could also avoid these mercantilist wars over economic access that, as Adam Smith taught long ago, were as unnecessary as they were destructive.

Critics often call this formula "free-trade imperialism," the natural ideology of countries so advanced that they fear no competitors. Protectionism, by contrast, has typically been sought by developing industrial countries, like Germany or the United States in the mid-nineteenth century, trying to shield their infant industries from the rigors of superior competition—at that time, British. Classic protectionist theory did point ultimately to free trade among equally developed economies; in other words, to a pluralist liberalism. Britain's free-trade imperialism, however, was seen as a premature and hegemonic form of liberalism, really a mercantilist ideology for perpetuating Britain's historical advantage.

Colonialism came to be defended as a sort of systemic analogue to domestic protectionism. Unable to compete in an open world system, where another power is still dominant, an industrializing state seizes and directly controls some portion of the non-Western world, thereby guaranteeing itself access to the raw materials, markets, or profitable investments it needs for its own development. A world thus divided into several colonial empires can be said to reflect a plural balance within the international system, with no single dominant economic and military power. This theory was amply demonstrated in practice. As other industrial powers rose to challenge Britain in the later nineteenth century, they turned to imperialism as well as protectionism. Free trade was abandoned, and the scramble for colonial empires began. Britain did better than other countries in the scramble, but to have to annex territory hitherto dominated informally was, in itself, a sign of Britain's decline from world hegemony.

The United States after the Second World War occupied the same overwhelming economic and military predominance as Britain had in the mid-nineteenth century. A policy of liberal free trade and anticolonialism thus came naturally to the Americans. In an open system, with weakened European and Japanese competitors ejected from their privileged colonial sanctuaries, America would predominate. From such a perspective, commonplace in Europe, America's decolonization seemed merely an ideological cover for replacing Europe's colonial empires with America's new global hegemony. In some circles, European bitterness was considerable and still has not been entirely forgotten. But since the cause of reestablishing Europe's colonial empires could not generate sufficient moral, political, or military force to defeat the forces of Third World nationalism, decolonization had to be accepted, gracefully by the British, painfully by the French, Dutch, Belgians, and Portuguese.

Americans had little sympathy. Europe's best interest lay in rebuilding its own domestic economies to compete successfully in the open world America was fostering. Europe's lingering colonialism was hopelessly out of step with the insistent nationalism that the war had triggered everywhere in the Third World. Americans feared Europeans would embroil themselves in a series of militarily hopeless and morally indefensible wars opposing Third World independence. European attempts to link the defense of their empires to the containment of communism were countered by American fears that the Russians would be made to seem champions of national independence. The irresistible nationalism of the Third World would thus be linked with the Soviet model for national development. The great challenge, as the Americans saw it, was to join the Third World's nationalism to political and economic liberalism rather than to totalitarian and protectionist communism. Hence a liberal-national model for Third World development became vitally important in postwar American policy.

Creating a development model to suit Third World nationalism extracted serious concessions from America's free-trade liberalism. Third World countries, sensitive about free-trade imperialism, wanted not only formal political independence but also modernization. This meant developing an indigenous industrial economy rather than merely providing food and raw materials for the industrial West. Soviet and Chinese communism offered a mercantilist autarchic model for achieving that industrial goal. In response, American development theory, although continuing to stress free trade and private multinational investment, quickly came to encompass a substantial degree of state planning, subsidy, and trade concessions. European development theories generally have gone even further in this direction.

As in the Near Empire, multilateral institutions and international bureaucracies have managed much of the system's business. Institutions like the World Bank, the General Agreement on Tariffs and Trade (GATT), and, later, the United Nations Conference on Trade and Development (UNCTAD) became the contexts within which American, European, and Third World interests have played out and reconciled their competing claims. For the United States to remain the predominant global power, it has had to adjust its ideas to the increasingly assertive and effective demands from both Third World countries and its own Western and Japanese allies. Where it has lagged, its hegemony has grown less acceptable.

In many respects, this Far Empire of the *Pax Americana* has been a notable success. Despite the immense transformations and dislocations bound up with decolonization and modernization, many countries in the non-Communist Third World have achieved remarkable economic growth.

Success in the Third World has also tended to reinforce ties within the First World. While disputes over the colonial legacy continued to sour transatlantic relations in the 1950s, European states, while losing their colonial domains, gradually realized that the economic objectives of the old empires could be achieved far more cheaply within the more universal system of the *Pax Americana*. Japan's postwar position presents the most striking illustration. For Japan, losing the Second World War meant giving up an Asian "coprosperity sphere" but gaining access to a much wider range of markets throughout the whole world, including the American domestic market.

Under the broad mantle of the *Pax Americana*, Europe and Japan have refashioned something of their old global influence. For Third World countries, leery of too-intimate patronage from a superpower, Europe and Japan have been alternative sources of capital, markets, and arms. Through its various trade and aid policies, the Common Market has been a powerful instrument of European diplomacy. Both France and Britain, moreover, have maintained a substantial military capability in various regions, legitimized by a range of alliances, including constitutional links with former colonies.

In the 1950s, and occasionally thereafter, French diplomacy vainly sought to structure an American-British-French global directorate— presumably as a way to exert greater leverage on American global policy. From time to time, NATO has sought to coordinate "out of area" policy. While formal attempts at structured cooperation generally have failed, American and European policies toward the Third World, even where competitive, came to terms easily enough through most of the 1960s. Europeans, like Americans, wished to limit Soviet global influence. Since the late 1960s, however, transatlantic consensus on global matters has been undermined by wars in Vietnam and the Middle East and, in the 1970s, by the oil crisis. Europeans, while demanding consultation, have often distanced themselves from particular American policies toward the Third World.

As the United States has grown less able to control events in the Third World, Europeans have increasingly sought their own special relationships and arrangements, often in rather ostentatious disagreement and competition with the Americans. This has been particularly noticeable since the oil crisis of 1973. A secure flow of cheap energy was a major benefit of the early *Pax Americana*. With the United States seemingly less able to guarantee that flow, American prestige suffered while Europe and Japan grew more aggressive in preserving their own positions. Just as American success in the Third World had reinforced transatlantic interdependence, its diminishing sway beyond Europe provoked transatlantic separation.

Surveying this postwar system in its various elements gives rise to somewhat conflicting reactions. America's postwar leadership, and the Atlantic partnership that has sustained it, has given the world a prosperous peace of impressive duration. For all its obvious blemishes, this postwar order has been a dazzling success. Few governments seriously want to overturn it, even if many would prefer a more favored position within it. But there are now strong trends undermining the system's stability, not least within the Atlantic world itself.

To suppose the present international system incapable of rejuvenation seems premature. Among the states with the most to lose are those of Western Europe, which have enjoyed a prosperous security unprecedented in this century. Whatever the accumulating irritations, the Atlantic Alliance still has a powerful geopolitical logic, reinforced by compelling cultural bonds and roughly four decades of institutional cooperation. The United States, with its enormous wealth and vitality, not to mention an impressive heritage of civic decency and self-discipline, is unlikely to be thrown over by the Europeans in favor of adventures with the Soviet Union or the Third World. The Alliance's underlying strength has long been so obvious that its tensions have been complacently pushed aside. But looking at these tensions within the larger context suggested here leads to a more troubling evaluation, particularly when the economic dimension is considered alongside the military and political.

The Paths of American Diplomacy

GADDIS SMITH

The split between the so-called realist and idealist schools of American foreign policy making was never as apparent as in the Carter administration. In this excerpt from *Morality, Reason and Power*, the seminal book on the Carter administration, Yale University professor Gaddis Smith traces the historical antecedents of the basic debate over the nature and purpose of American foreign policy, a debate which continues to this day. What should be the goals of a nation's foreign policy? In the "real world" is it possible to have a moral foreign policy?

American foreign policy during the four years of Jimmy Carter's Presidency (1977–81) was a whirlpool of disagreement over the fundamental nature of national and world security. President Carter, his advisers, supporters, and critics attempted to define that security and set an appropriate course for the United States. During some past Administrations, a single current of thought and action had prevailed, allowing policy to glide on a smooth stretch of consensus. For example, during the early years of the Cold War, the nation was agreed on the "zero-sum game" approach to the Soviet Union. Whatever made the United States stronger and the Soviet Union weaker was good. But during the Carter years a combination of world events, political developments within the United States, and decisions by the Administration brought multiple currents more visibly into conflict than at any time since the United States became a world power.

A quartet of philosophical problems pervaded the foreign policy of the Carter Administration and tied those years to the broad sweep of history. The problems were not new. They had been confronted repeatedly by Americans during the twentieth century. As long as nations compete with or threaten each other, these problems will never be ultimately resolved.

First, is preservation of moral principle or enhancement of material power the primary objective of foreign policy? Which is the end and which the means? Should moral principle be sacrificed when questions of power are at stake? Always? Sometimes? Never? Is the United States ever justified in using methods abroad which would be immoral or illegal at home? Should the moral character of foreign leaders and nations influence American decisions to extend or withhold support? Or is the only test of a relationship whether the other nation can be of material benefit to the United States? Conversely, should the United States ever make a sacrifice for moral principle? How great a sacrifice, and on whom, specifically, should it fall? And if these questions have no clear answers, what rules of reason should a government follow in seeking a viable balance? Should those rules be spelled out in advance, perhaps by Congress, or should the President and his advisers make decisions case by case?

Second, is foreign policy dictated by external threats which are real and undeniable; or are alleged external threats merely the excuse for actions driven by internal forces? Throughout American history, all commentators on and makers of foreign policy have been primarily externalists or internalists in their analysis of what is wrong and what needs to be done. Externalists emphasize the hostile intent of other nations. President James K. Polk was an externalist in 1846 when he said that Mexico had shed American blood on American soil. Franklin D. Roosevelt was an externalist in 1941 when he said that the defense of all nations under attack by Germany was vital to the United States. Ronald Reagan was an externalist in 1982 when he said the Soviet Union was the source of evil in the modern world. Externalists are usually people in power and their supporters.

Internalists, on the other hand, have generally been critics outside of government or politicians trying to win office (if they do win, they often become externalists). They argue that foreign policy is too often the result of unworthy internal forces—e.g., selfish economic interests, ruthless politicians putting personal advantage over the general welfare —and is therefore wrong and even immoral. Internalists offer an easy solution: Americans need only repent, reform and throw the rascals out. The democratic process will solve all problems. Internalists have been relatively ill informed about conditions outside the United States, but confident that externalists misrepresent and exaggerate foreign threats. Abolitionists who said the greed of slaveowners for more territory caused the war with Mexico, isolationists who said Roosevelt in 1941 wanted to become the supreme ruler of the world, and most opponents of the Vietnam war were internalists. The voice of reason would suggest that externalists and internalists are both right and wrong. The nation has faced real external threats and has acted against other countries for inappropriate internal reasons. But can reason tell, case by case, where lies the dividing line between appropriate and inappropriate internal motives, between real and concocted threats?

Third, should it be a rule for the United States to abstain from foreign quarrels unless vital interests are clearly threatened; or should the presumption be on the side of intervention lest an unfavorable development, no matter how remote, grow into a threat? Was George Washington's warning against entangling alliances useful advice only for a young, weak nation, or was it wisdom for all time? Is the world a seamless web with no limit to or prioritization of American interests, or is it a collection of zones and spheres, some of which have little or no meaning for American security? At one end of this debate stood outright isolationists, and at the other the advocates of the "domino theory"—i.e., the fall of any nation to unfriendly influence could lead to the fall of all, including the United States itself. The strict isolationist position became untenable after Pearl Harbor in 1941, and the extreme interventionist position fell into disrepute after the United States lost the war in Vietnam. It was the task of the Carter Administration to try to find solid ground on shifting terrain. In an unstable world, both abroad and at home, this task proved beyond the Administration's intellectual and political means.

Fourth, should the United States be concerned primarily with prevailing over particular hostile nations, specifically the Soviet Union? Or should an enlightened foreign policy focus on universal problems of the human condition: violations of human rights, the shortage of energy and other resources, the threat of proliferating arms, both nuclear and conventional? Should foreign policy, like a football game, be controlled by "the logic of conflict" or by an effort to create a more beneficial world order? Is the traditional objective of maintaining a favorable balance of power permanently valid? Or is the old objective part of the problem in that it obscures deeper dangers, such as the worldwide spread of armaments, uncontrolled technology capable of producing nuclear weapons, inadequate sources of energy, the maldistribution of wealth, damage to the environment? Advocates on one side of this debate said that the failure to attend to global problems could make the earth uninhabitable. Traditionalists, on the other hand, said that a failure to contain the Soviet Union would render the United States powerless to save itself or the world. The world-order advocates generally stressed the priority of North–South relations over those of East and West. They said it was more important to ask if a nation was rich (the North) or poor (the South) than to inquire if it was in the political sphere of the United States (the West) or the Soviet Union (the East). This division ran like a fault line through the Carter Administration and all discussion of the wisdom or folly of its particular decisions.

The Ghost of Woodrow Wilson

In 1917, six decades before Jimmy Carter was inaugurated, President Wilson made military power the servant of moral principle when he led the nation into war against Germany, not to protect specific American interest, but "for the ultimate peace of the world and . . . for the rights of nations great and small and the privilege of men everywhere to choose their way of life." He said the United States had "no selfish ends to serve . . . We are . . . champions of the rights of mankind." But any government denying those rights, any autocratic government, "could not be trusted to keep faith . . . or observe its covenants." Arching over Wilson's thought and program was the conviction that the moral injunctions of Jesus Christ were equally applicable to nations as to individuals. Whatever was sinful for a person was sinful for a nation.

Wilson's principles contained an irresolvable contradiction and a cluster of political problems. How could the United States pledge to respect the right of every nation to determine its own way of life and at the same time insist that such a way of life imitate American ideals of human rights? If human rights were violated within another nation, must the United States abandon the principles of non-intervention and self-determination in order to rectify or punish that violation? Must the United States be invariably hostile to "autocratic" governments, refusing to seek a range of mutual interests, lest recognition and negotiation taint moral principle? Must the United States expend resources without limit in a crusade for a morally perfect world? Was there any room for choice of policy when the nation was faced with a moral issue? And if so, who would decide what the choice was? The President alone? The Congress?

The role of weapons and military force was ambiguous in Wilson's world view. In the ageless discussion over whether weapons are a cause of insecurity or neutral instruments capable of either furthering or deterring aggression, Wilson seemed to come down on the side of those who saw weapons as evil in themselves. He adhered to the international equivalent of support for domestic gun control. He would have disagreed with the implication of the slogan, favored by those who oppose control, that "guns do not kill people; people kill people." The fourth of Wilson's "Fourteen Points" of January 1918 called for "Adequate guarantees given and taken that national armaments will be reduced to the lowest point consistent with domestic safety." On another occasion, he advocated "that moderation of armaments which makes of armies and navies a power of order merely, not an instrument of aggression or selfish violence." But when one nation's "order" seemed "selfish violence" to another, who could distinguish between weapons of peace and weapons of aggression? Wilson assumed that issues of right and wrong would always be clear and that if any nation was guilty of wrongdoing it would be punished by the collective, democratic will of mankind as interpreted under American leadership in the new League of Nations.

Wilson assumed that democracies by their nature had no selfish purposes. They would always respect human rights and act peacefully. When he said the United States was going to war to make the world "safe for democracy," he meant as well safe through democracy. He believed that wars were plotted by autocrats or small groups of conspirators to advance their selfish purposes against the true interests of the people. Democracy would reject the use of spies, secrecy, lying, war itself.

The great irony is that the President who exalted the democratic process as inseparable from a moral foreign policy was defeated by that process. In 1919, the United States Senate refused to approve American membership in the League of Nations on Wilson's terms. In 1920, the American people agreed with the Senate's decision and elected Republican Warren G. Harding. It was the opinion of the majority, expressed through democratic means, that the United States should make no permanent commitments to other nations or to a world security system, moral or otherwise, and should remain free to decide every course of action in terms of the nation's interests in each case.

Wilson died in 1924, and the remnant of Wilsonian true believers dwindled in number and influence until, by the early 1930s, there was close to a national consensus in favor of isolationism, defined as almost total non-involvement in the political affairs of nations outside the Western Hemisphere. The defeat of Wilson's vision was also a victory for an enlarged congressional role in foreign policy, and Congress during the 1920s and 1930s put severe limits on Presidential power. Isolationists were vehement internalists. They denied that other nations had the capacity to injure the United States, as long as the United States refrained from intervening in their affairs. They asserted that the United States had gone to war in 1917, not to make the world safe for democracy and from autocracy, but to serve the interests of bankers and munitions makers who had an investment in a victory for Great Britain, France, and Russia over Germany. As the historian and political activist Charles A. Beard argued, it should be the obligation of the American government to establish the "open door" of equal opportunity for all Americans at home, rather than intervene around the world to protect the "open door" to trade and investment profits for selfish interests.

But the outbreak of the European war in 1939 made it increasingly difficult to argue that the United States faced no external threat. Isolationists found themselves on the defensive, and after the Japanese attack on Pearl Harbor, they were quite undone. The American people were virtually unanimous in approving the nation's entry into war against the Axis (Germany, Japan, and Italy). Never before or since has there been such support for a cause: the complete defeat of the enemy.

COLD WAR "REALISM"

The death of isolationism did not, however, mean the rebirth of Wilsonian moralism. Although political leaders after 1941 paid graceful tribute to Wilson's memory, those who provided the new guiding assumptions for American foreign policy were more fundamentally anti-Wilsonian than the isolationists. As adherents to the newly embraced assumptions of "realism" and "geopolitics," they agreed that the United States should be involved in world affairs, but the reasons involved power, not morality. In the words of Nicholas Spykman, an influential academic exponent of the new geopolitics, nations should make the "preservation and improvement of their power position" the primary objective of foreign policy. "The statesman who conducts foreign policy can concern himself with values of justice, fairness, and tolerance only to the extent that they contribute to or do not interfere with the power objective. They can be used instrumentally as moral justification for the power quest, but they must be discarded the moment their application brings weakness."

The "realist" view of the world guided American leaders during the Second World War, easing the pain of sending men to their deaths and of inflicting enormous casualties on the enemy. The decisions to develop atomic bombs and drop them on Japan were made in that spirit. "Realism" also facilitated the transition from war against the Axis to Cold War. The principles of geopolitics ordained that the alliance between the United States and Great Britain on the one hand and the Soviet Union on the other was an expedient and temporary measure directed against Hitler. Geopoliticians argued that, after the destruction of German power, it was inevitable that the two remaining great powers, the United States and the Soviet Union, would come into conflict. The fact that the Soviet Union was a grim totalitarian state, with many characteristics reminiscent of Nazi Germany, added intensity to the perception of inevitable hostility. Even those who, in the euphoria of victory over the Axis, dreamed of resurrecting a Wilsonian world order through the United Nations or some form of world government were converted to an anti-Soviet position because of the Soviet Union's use of the veto in the United Nations and its patent violations of human rights. The creation of an ideal world would have to wait until Russia ceased to be simultaneously powerful and totalitarian.

The philosopher of the "realist" attack on Wilsonian moralism was the theologian Reinhold Niebuhr. In 1932, Niebuhr published *Moral Man and Immoral Society*, a closely reasoned critique of the assumption, so dear to Wilson, that moral standards for individuals and for nations could be the same. Niebuhr said that an individual could, by an act of supreme moral selflessness, sacrifice his or her interests, even life itself, in service to a higher good. But nations existed to protect their members. They could not act except in terms of their interests, interests which often conflicted with those of other nations and which made strife inevitable. Twenty years later, at the height of the Cold War, Niebuhr applied this argument specifically to American foreign policy. In *The Irony of American History*, his most widely read book, he stressed the tragic necessity of making "conscious choices for the sake of good. If men or nations do evil in a good cause; if they cover themselves with guilt in order to fulfill some high responsibility; or if they sacrifice some high value for the sake of a higher or equal one they make a tragic choice. Thus the necessity of using the threat of atomic destruction as an instrument for the preservation of peace is a tragic element in our contemporary situation."

Niebuhr and some of his more thoughtful contemporaries warned that the United States must not become so obsessed with fighting the evils of communism that it decided that any weapon was justified. In this way, said Niebuhr, Americans could become as ruthless as the enemy. But this warning was a minor note in the orchestrating of American power against the Soviet Union. The major theme, by the late 1940s, was containment through military means, resting on economic strength.

The makers and spokesmen of Cold War foreign policy were all externalists. Their creed began with the conviction that the principal, proper, and necessary obligation of the American government was to maintain and be prepared to use military superiority against the foe. No other obligation could be allowed to interfere. The foe, the Soviet Union, was an aggressive, totalitarian force bent on world domination, oblivious to any reasoned appeals, responsive only to force. Conflict between the United States and the Soviet Union was irreconcilable and would continue until one side prevailed, with or without general war. Fundamental cooperation between the two nations was impossible, although each might adopt a transient cooperative posture for tactical reasons, but in the end the Soviets could never be trusted. The only way for the United States to deter war or mitigate its worst consequences was through the maintenance of military superiority. The existence of nuclear weapons reinforced and in no way invalidated this principle. To accept limits on American armed force because of a desire to avoid offending the Soviet Union was naive and dangerous. Arms-control agreements were also dangerous unless they clearly increased the relative power of the United States over the Soviet Union.

Those who believed in this creed were so sure of their own righteousness and so convinced of the utter evil of the Soviet Union that they denied there was any danger of corrupting American ends through the use of immoral means. The issue was explicitly addressed in early 1950 by the authors of National Security Council document 68–NSC-68, as it is generally known. This long memorandum, written principally by and under the guidance of State Department official Paul Nitze and formally approved by President Harry S. Truman, is the single most important statement of the creed of containment and the "zero-sum game" approach to the Soviet Union. Although the actual text remained secret until 1975 (largely because of information in it on atomic weapons), the ideas were proclaimed by the government on every occasion and used as guides for policy. NSC-68 called for subordinating all other concerns to increasing American power and diminishing the relative power of the Soviet Union. Did that mean the United States should be prepared to use any means? The answer is yes, said NSC-68. "Our free society, confronted by a threat to its basic values, naturally will take such action, including the use of military force, as may be required to protect those values. The integrity of our system will not be jeopardized by any measures, covert or overt, violent or nonviolent, which serve the purposes of frustrating the Kremlin design, nor does the necessity for conducting ourselves so as to affirm our values in actions as well as words forbid such measures, provided only they are appropriately calculated to that end and are not so excessive or misdirected as to make us enemies of the people instead of the evil men who have enslaved them." Despite the weak closing qualification, the statement was a justification for employing any means—secrecy, lying, covert interference in the affairs of other nations, sabotage, assassination—for a self-proclaimed end; in short, for doing all those things which Woodrow Wilson once thought could never be done by a democracy.

Indeed, the philosophy of NSC-68 was fundamentally antidemocratic and skeptical of the capacity of American society to survive unless it accepted limits on free discussion. As the document said: "The democratic way is harder than the authoritarian way because, in seeking to protect and fulfill the individual, it demands . . . that he exercise discrimination: that while pursuing through free inquiry the search for truth he knows when he should commit an act of faith; that he distinguish between the necessity for tolerance and the necessity for just suppression. A free society is vulnerable in that it is easy for people to lapse into excesses—the excesses of a permanently open mind wishfully waiting for evidence that evil design may become noble purpose, the excess of faith becoming prejudice, the excess of tolerance degenerating into indulgence of conspiracy."

"Suppression" meant not only a voluntary act by the individual; it meant something the government was justified in doing to individuals and groups. Senator Joseph R. McCarthy achieved national attention in February 1950, just as NSC-68 was being drafted, with his public crusade to suppress communists and other dangerous thinkers in America. The sophisticated men who wrote and approved NSC-68 considered McCarthy and his methods crude and malodorous. But the difference between McCarthyism and the arguments of NSC-68 were matters of tone and style, not substance.

If the Cold War "realists" harbored doubts about the viability of democracy in the United States, how viable was democracy in the rest of the world—where Wilson had once said that only democratic nations were qualified for membership in the community of the righteous? In the Cold War climate of 1950, the diplomat-historian George F. Kennan had an answer to that question. During a tour of Latin America, he concluded that liberal leaders in countries without a tradition of strong democratic government appeared to lack the capacity to resist communism. This meant, said Kennan in a report to Secretary of State Dean Acheson, that the United States ought not insist on fulfillment of democratic niceties. "We cannot be too dogmatic about the methods by which local communists can be dealt with . . . Where the concepts and traditions of popular government are too weak to absorb successfully the intensity of communist attack, then we must concede that harsh governmental measures of repression may be the only answer; that these measures may have to proceed from regimes whose origins and methods would not stand the test of American concepts of democratic procedure; and that such regimes and such methods may be preferable alternatives, and indeed the only alternatives, to further communist successes."

For two decades, from the late 1940s until the late 1960s, the foreign policies of the men (and they were all men) who followed the creed of NSC-68 enjoyed almost total support from Congress and the people. Whether a Democrat or a Republican was in the White House made no fundamental difference. There was an overwhelming consensus behind the policies of reviving and rearming Western Europe, organizing a string of anti-Soviet alliances around the world, fighting the Korean war, maintaining a hostile face toward communist China, and forever building superiority in nuclear weapons over the Soviet Union. The secret aspects of these policies were known in broad outline to those attentive to foreign affairs: the overthrow with CIA assistance of Mossadegh in Iran (1953) and Arbenz in Guatemala (1954), manipulation of elections in other countries, bribery, spying, perhaps assassination. Such operations were criticized only when they failed—as with the attempt to overthrow Fidel Castro of Cuba through the ill-fated Bay of Pigs invasion of 1961. The attitude of Congress during these years was that the President knew best; the responsibility of Congress was to provide the money and ask no embarrassing questions. The historically minded believed congressional restrictions on foreign policy during the 1930s had made German aggression easier and thus had contributed to the Second World War. Few congressmen wanted to make that mistake again.

"The best and the brightest" (to use David Halberstam's phrase) of those years considered themselves moral beings. Some of them read Reinhold Niebuhr. They believed they were capable of avoiding excess while accepting the tragic necessity of doing evil in a good cause. But the sense of restraint—slight as it had been early in the Cold War— eroded. Suppression of the truth became more common, and so did covert action against other governments. Bonds were strengthened between Washington and harsh, repressive dictators. And the United States entered the Vietnam war.

America and the Third World: Lessons from Iran

JAMES A. BILL

The American experience in Iran easily serves as a paradigm of American relations with Third World countries. From the 1953 CIA led coup which reinstated the Shah of Iran until the Shah's inglorious decline in the United States during 1980 and the release of the American hostages some months later, the United States played an important role in Iran's foreign and domestic affairs. Indeed, most Iranians saw the United States as the hidden power in Iran, whether as Iran's free-world benefactor or as the "great Satan." In this selection from his book *The Eagle and the Lion*, James Bill summarizes what he sees as the twelve lessons from this ultimately tragic encounter. How did our preoccupation with the Cold War affect our relationships with other countries? To what extent should human rights issues influence our relationships with otherwise loyal allies?

The overall lesson for U.S. foreign policy that follows from an analysis of the Iranian-American imbroglio is that the fundamental problem is systemic. A complex network of interrelated, reinforcing factors resulted in an outcome that seriously damaged American national interests. A summary analysis suggests twelve separate but related recommendations for future American foreign policy-making with respect to the Third World.

1. *Any unquestioned, dominant policy premise in Washington should be treated with skepticism and subjected to careful and continual questioning.*

Such "shared attitudes" or "party lines" have a tendency to become entrenched with time, and vested interests provide them with private and public political protection. The longer such premises prevail, the more difficult it is to challenge them. Therefore, the U.S. position with respect to a particular Third World country should be subject to constant review and reconsideration based on changing political realities. This recurring reexamination should take place at the highest levels of the organizations involved in the formation of U.S. foreign policy. The Iranian-American debacle resulted largely from the Pahlavi invincibility premise that existed in Washington during the administration of every U.S. president since John F. Kennedy. In a world challenged fundamentally by forces of change, the United States can ill afford to lock itself irrevocably into a particular policy perspective.

2. *The influence of private interests that seek to promote a particular foreign policy must be exposed and controlled.*   As demonstrated by the influential Pahlavite lobby in America, powerful informal political elites can exert critical pressure in making U.S. foreign policy. The reasons for such private pressure may be personal, political, economic, ideological, or emotional. Yet this form of lobbying does not necessarily promote American national interests. Although it is certainly possible that private interests may coincide with national public interests, they often do not. In this situation, foreign policy-making should be determined by public officials professionally qualified to perform this task.

A corollary of this proposition involves private interests within the government itself that link up with external groups in pursuit of shared foreign-policy goals. This "privatization" of foreign policy-making was evident in the Iran-Contra affair when zealous staff members in the NSC such as Lt. Col. Oliver North secretly pursued initiatives that ran counter to policy enunciated by the U.S. Congress and the Department of State.

3. *Important foreign-policy decisions should not be made primarily on the basis of domestic political exigencies.*   American political leaders are always sensitive to the need to win reelection, and they often seem to support any foreign policy that they feel will maximize these chances. Whether such a position is itself of benefit to overall American interests or whether it is a wise long-term policy are sometimes considered secondary issues by national leaders. In the case of the president, for example, scholars have argued that key foreign policy decisions are made on the basis of their domestic political utility for the chief executive himself. It was partly because of this danger that John F. Kennedy once stated: "Domestic policy can only defeat us; foreign policy can kill us." During the Carter administration, domestic political considerations played a minor role in the disastrous decision to admit the shah into the United States and a major role in the policy developed to deal with the hostage crisis. The priority of domestic political considerations is also related to the informal private elite and its promotion of a particular political premise in Washington. This elite has not been above using its considerable influence in the American political scene as leverage for a preferred foreign policy.

4. *In a world of multiple crises, U.S. policymakers must beware of focusing all attention on one or another issue at the expense of other more volatile and strategically more costly crises.*   Just as domestic political considerations can be a diverting influence, so too can international crises, which occur increasingly frequently in this interdependent world. As a superpower on the international stage, the United States often finds itself embroiled simultaneously in numerous crises around the world. In attempting to attend to one crisis, U.S. decision makers have a tendency to turn their backs on others, thereby inviting foreign policy disaster in these other contexts. In the case of the Iranian revolution, President Carter and his most experienced and sensitive advisers were deeply preoccupied by the Arab-Israeli issue and the Camp David agreement. By the time they turned their attention to Iran, it was late, and policy decisions had already been preempted by other bureaucratic offices, in this case the National Security Council. Debilitating international diversions can paradoxically reinforce domestic political priorities, since certain international issues are selected for attention because of their domestic American implications.

5. *American policymakers must focus their attention less on the Soviet role in Third World upheaval and more on the deepening class conflict and vibrant new forms of populist religion that increasingly energize much of the Middle East, Africa, Asia, and Latin America.*   For years, American policymakers have maintained such a fixation with Soviet intentions and activities that they have presumed Soviet involvement in upheaval whenever and wherever it occurs. This Sovietcentric point of view has resulted in distorted U.S. understanding of social forces at work in much of the Third World. In the Middle East, the Arab-Israeli/Palestinian issue was not created by the USSR; neither Nasser nor Qaddafi was a product of Soviet machinations; Anwar Sadat's assassin was not a communist; the Lebanese imbroglio was not conceived by the Soviet Union. Most pertinently, the Iranian revolution was home-grown. Despite some imaginative early attempts by certain officials and scholars to link Khomeini to the Soviet Union and the extremist student-revolutionaries to a communist-controlled faction of the Palestine Liberation Organization, the Soviet Union had precious little to do with the revolution. Like the United States, it was caught unaware by the speed and thoroughness of the movement. This Sovietcentric view of the world also contributed to the problem of international diversions as American officials turned their attention especially to crises considered to be specifically related to Soviet aims.

6. *The United States must resist the early resort to military force to administer to crises born of political and economic causes.*   Instead, sophisticated, sensitive, and creative new methods of diplomacy are essential to the successful formulation of foreign policy in contexts resistant to the clumsy and sometimes counterproductive application of force. In the Middle East, this lesson is seen in the consequences of the 1982 Israeli invasion of Lebanon, the 1983 disaster of American marines sent into Lebanon, and indeed by the costly Soviet military occupation of Afghanistan. In Iran, the shah's regime, backed by one of the most powerful military machines in the Third World, collapsed in the face of a massive popular uprising in which millions of citizens marched in the streets during a year of generally peaceful demonstrations. The fact that the Pahlavi armed forces were backed by the American military establishment only highlights the limits of military power. Political power in the form of diplomacy, intellectual power in the form of understanding, and ideological power in the form of principles all carry special strengths. In confronting the challenges of Third World societies torn by turbulent change, brainpower is at least as important as firepower. This emphasis on military methods is closely related to the Sovietcentric mind-set discussed above. It is in response to the Soviet challenge that the United States has felt it necessary to respond with an increasing early emphasis on the force of arms.

7. *The United States foreign policy-related organizations must institutionalize an emphasis on language and area studies.*   Although the Foreign Service Institute, given its resources, does what it can to prepare diplomats for new assignments, serious inadequacies remain. It may indeed be true that Iran represents an especially severe case of debilitating embassy inadequacies; and at the same time, it does expose an area badly in need of fundamental reform. In order to understand other cultures, especially those alien to the American-European system, it is necessary to have both the proper tools and the proper attitude. Although American officials have been quite aware of the problem they term "localitis," they have not always been as sensitive to the basic lack of understanding based on weak area preparation and a narrow range and shallow level of contacts. In this situation, the American eagle, with its increasing concern for a sharpened beak and talons, risks a weakened capacity to see, hear, sense, and understand when flying in unfamiliar environments. This limited capacity to communicate and understand Third World societies is partially a result of the preoccupation with military power. On the other hand, the distorted understanding of complex social and political forces can at the same time promote the emphasis on physical force. In Iran, by viewing the society from the top down, American officials maintained a somewhat simplistic view of political realities, a view that promoted policy that stressed the efficacy of military force. The United States draped its interests around the royal shoulders of the shah, whose own existence was supposedly guaranteed by his powerful military establishment.

8. *American diplomats must become conversant with all levels and sectors of the societies to which they are posted.*   Since all diplomats are charged with the task of remaining informed, it is essential that they throw their information-gathering nets as far as possible across the social and political waters of their host countries. Below-par area training is part of a process that promotes the constricted nature of U.S. contacts in foreign countries. This, of course, must be done carefully, professionally, and tactfully. As indicated in considerable depth in the chapters above, in Iran there was an intelligence failure of considerable proportions. The Iranian-American relationship was largely bound and determined at the very top—it was an elite-to-elite connection. This failure to know and to understand because of limited contacts directly reinforced the area training inadequacies. By associating primarily with selected, English-speaking elites who inhabit the uppermost reaches of the power structures, there is little incentive to spend time in the difficult struggle for language competence and in-depth area understanding.

9. *American diplomats must be carefully, selectively, and professionally chosen for their particular assignments.* This is especially true in the case of the ambassadorial selection, since this personal representative of the president of the United States establishes the style and shapes the perspective of the entire embassy that he or she directs. Also, such selection must carefully consider the sensitivities of the government and peoples of the receiving country. An analysis of the history of Iranian-American relations reveals a number of particularly poor ambassadorial choices. Perhaps the most obvious error was Richard Nixon's appointment of former CIA chief Richard Helms as U.S. ambassador to Iran during the critical 1973–77 period. Given the history of CIA activities in Iran and the strong negative feelings among Iranian citizens from all walks of life about the CIA's real and purported roles in the country, this was a most unfortunate decision. Many Iranians believed that this appointment was an arrogant act by the United States to move the CIA into a position of direct, on-the-spot control of their country. And it was deeply and extensively resented. Helms's competence, which was considerable, was beside the point. An ill-suited ambassador, therefore, can reinforce and even exacerbate the problems of inadequately prepared officials with shallow understanding and limited contacts.

10. *The flawed official understanding of Third World societies can be improved by seriously consulting the analyses available in nongovernmental sources.* There has been a tendency to overemphasize classified materials or materials gathered only through governmental channels. As indicated above, much of this information is flawed by inaccuracies that flow from biased sources. That information is classified does not necessarily mean that it is either more accurate or more valuable than what is available in published sources. On the contrary, scholars, journalists, businessmen, and others carry two major advantages over official observers. First, since they are not government employees, they are generally more trusted and carry more credibility in foreign lands. This enables them to tap a broader range of perspectives and at the same time to gain information that is not necessarily biased in the same manner as that available to government sources. Second, scholars in particular have more time to dig and more space for all-important analysis. Harried diplomats work under heavy time pressure and are often overwhelmed by crisis. Former CIA chief Stansfield Turner has written that on taking that important post, he soon realized that "there was excessive use of secret data as opposed to open information." In terms of the Iranian revolution, he has pointed out that "there was relatively little secret information that was pertinent." This reluctance to consult external sources systematically only reinforced the views presented by official sources, sources often inadequate to the task and directed by diplomatic leaders unsuitable for their posts.

11. *American foreign policy-making must increase its emphasis on long-range analysis and institutionalize a planning process that is seriously consulted by leading decision makers.*   America lacks theoretical guidelines to enable its policymakers to come to grips with the challenge of fundamental global change. In Iran, the United States failed badly when faced with a genuinely revolutionary situation. In the words of diplomat Charles Naas: "Let's face it, this was a massive revolution. As individual foreign service officers and certainly as a government as a whole, we had very little experience of how to handle such a situation. As a result, once again we were badly equipped intellectually to move in the post-revolutionary situation." Improved analytic capabilities are essential if the United States is to move beyond crisis management and into the more complex field of crisis avoidance. According to a former director of the CIA, "Analysis, especially political analysis, is the Achilles heel of intelligence." This weakness in analysis cuts across all American foreign policy-making agencies. The roots of problems must be exposed and remedies suggested in this context. Only informed analysis can lead to the development of effective policy that will serve American national interests in the long term. The traditional lack of attention to the external sources that tend to place more stress on analysis, of course, has only exacerbated this problem.

12. *Finally, bureaucratic conflict and rivalry must be moderated in order to insure the more efficient determination of high-quality information and the more sensitive formation of policy.*   Professionalism must take precedence over the personal and political struggles to which organizations are so very susceptible. More specifically, the increasingly institutionalized National Security Council-Department of State schism must be repaired. The foreign policy disaster of Iran demonstrates its seriousness. At the time of the Iranian revolution, the NSC, the organization with the least understanding of the forces brewing in Iran, was precisely the group that had most influence on the president's policy preferences. This conflict continued after the revolution until it ruptured publicly with the 1986 revelations concerning the NSC-sponsored arms sales to Iran. In his introduction to the Tower Commission Report, R.W. Apple summarizes the NSC as "led by reckless cowboys, off on their own on a wild ride, taking direct operational control of matters that are the customary preserve of more sober agencies." Yet this problem of bureaucratic conflict pervaded all U.S. governmental organizations that dealt with Iran. Their effectiveness was partially smothered both by their conflict with other organizations and by their own intramural rivalries and feuds. This severe bureaucratic tension contributed greatly to many of the other problem areas isolated and briefly discussed above. Most important, it impeded analysis and weakened the capacity of diplomats and foreign policy-makers to do their jobs.

These twelve problem areas overlap and interlock in a system that highly resists reform. They comprise a linked chain, each twisted link contributing directly to the strength of the one before it. Foreign policy analysts have often called attention to one or several of these problems. The Iran-America case has the peculiar "advantage" of reflecting an unusually broad range of foreign policy weaknesses. Most of the problems that have plagued U.S. foreign policy over the years have made their appearance, to one degree or another, in this story. More important, the Iran case demonstrates how these problems reinforced one another and how they constituted a highly resilient system of errors. This finding has profound implications for any attempts at reform. Revisions or improvements in any one area are unlikely to alter significantly the overall system. Only a conscious attempt to transform the system is likely to yield significant results.

On the other hand, a close examination of the weaknesses indicates that some areas may be more sensitive to reform than others. The denominator most common to the widest range of problem areas—in nine of the twelve—is the fundamental failure of understanding. Whether because of diversionary influences, personal or economic self-interest, or just plain ignorance, the United States failed to understand the culture, religion, and broad range of social and cultural forces at play in Iran. Although U.S. officials generally had adequate knowledge of the shah and his civilian and military elite, they never really understood the orientations, motivations, and fundamental power of the masses. Although understanding does not automatically result in improved policy, it is certainly a necessary beginning. In Iran, if the realities had been grasped, it is considerably more likely that U.S. policy would have been more enlightened and therefore more successful.

Iran is in many ways very special. A Shi'i Muslim society ruled by an absolute monarch, Iran had a long history of foreign intervention into its internal affairs. The manner in which American leaders entangled themselves with the Pahlavi elite approached a degree seldom seen elsewhere. Early blatant interventionary successes (the Musaddiq episode), which set the stage for later failure, were also relatively rare in American diplomatic history. Finally, the system of U.S. foreign policy-making seemed particularly inept and flawed in Iran.

Despite this, at a more general level Iran is representative of many Third World societies: an authoritarian political system in a society with pronounced class divisions confronted by the unsettling challenge of modernization. At a time when the Third World looms increasingly large on the international political horizon, the United States must learn to develop new relationships based on trust and mutual respect with the peoples and classes that will direct these developing societies in the years ahead. In order to create such new patterns, it shall be essential to address the problems identified above. Otherwise, the string of dramatic foreign policy defeats that began with China and continued through Cuba and Vietnam shall not end with Iran.

In a world torn by inequality, weakened by misunderstanding, and convulsed by violence, the American eagle needs to do more than strengthen its wings and sharpen its talons. It must also improve its qualities of perception, its communication skills, and its moral credibility. Its painful experience with the Iranian lion in the Persian Gulf can prove to be a valuable learning experience. If so, the sometimes confused and ruffled American eagle can regain its capacity to soar in respected splendor and dignity across the turbulent international landscape.

9

HAVE WE OVERCOME?

Three decades have passed since Martin Luther King stood in the shadow of the Lincoln Memorial and voiced his dream that his "children will one day live in a nation where they will not be judged by the color of their skin, but by the content of their character." In the intervening years, African-Americans have made enormous strides toward realizing King's dream. Americans have witnessed a vast increase in African-American political power, the elimination of overt forms of discrimination, and greater integration in the workplace.

But King's dream of a truly integrated society has remained elusive. In 1989, an exhaustive examination of 22,000 neighborhoods in sixty cities, including ten major metropolitan areas that contain 29 percent of the nation's African-American population, concluded that "racial segregation in this country is deeper and more profound than previous attempts to study it had indicated." The emergence of a large and growing African-American underclass, confined to the inner cities, removed from mainstream society, and burdened by crime, drug addiction, and alcoholism has cast a dark shadow over African-American hopes for economic equality.[1]

[1]Douglas S. Massey and Nancy A. Denton, "Hypersegregation in U.S. Metropolitan Areas: Black and Hispanic Segregation Along Five Dimensions," *Demography*, 26. (August, 1989), 373–91.

In the early stages of the civil rights struggle, African-Americans and whites shared a common faith that all Americans deserved equal access to public facilities and the right to vote. Later, the emergence of more controversial issues such as busing and affirmative action helped erode that consensus. A poll commissioned by the NAACP Legal Defense and Educational fund in 1989 found that African-Americans and whites were "worlds apart" in their perception of race relations. Most whites believed that African-Americans are treated equally in America while large numbers of African-Americans disapproved. African-Americans, by an overwhelming majority-supported a larger government with many services; whites preferred a smaller government with fewer services. This ideological gap between African-Americans and whites has created "wedge issues" which provide an ideal vehicle for conservatives to raise issues of taxation, welfare spending and the general role of government that split the Democratic coalition along racial lines. "Direct appeals to racial prejudice may no longer be acceptable in American politics," a journalist observed, "but race, in an indirect and sometimes subliminal way, remains a strong undercurrent in presidential politics and a driving force in the battle today between Republicans and Democrats."[2]

The 1988 presidential campaign served as a chilling reminder of the saliency of racial issues in American politics. Republican nominee George Bush's most effective advertisement showed an African-American rapist, Willie Horton, furloughed from a Massachusetts prison. The spot featured a stark, black-and-white scene of inmates walking through a revolving door, as an ominous voice announced that Dukakis had allowed many prisoners to escape. "This is not racism in a sheet and a hood," wrote Tom Wicker. "It is race consciousness in a white as well as a blue collar."[3]

The selections that follow provide unique insight into the ambiguous legacy of race in America. A *Common Destiny*, the first comprehensive study of black-white relations since Gunner Mydal's pioneering *An American Dilemma*, concludes that "many black Americans remain separated from the mainstream of national life under conditions of

[2]Lee Sigelman and Susan Welch, *Black American's Views of Racial Inequality* (Cambridge: Cambridge University Press, 1991). Thomas Edsell and Mary Edsell "Race" *Atlantic* (May, 1991) 53.
[3]*New York Times*, November 18, 1988.

great inequality." "The American dilemma," the authors concluded, "has not been resolved." Robert Weisbrot, in his lucid account of the civil rights struggle, balances the modest gains of African-Americans with the utopian goals of the civil rights movement. Steven Lawson provides a historical perspective on the relationship between the civil rights struggle and the development of African-American electoral power.

A Common Destiny

GERALD JAYNES AND ROBIN M. WILLIAMS

Published in 1990, twenty years after the Kerner Commission released its report on the causes of racial rioting, A *Common Destiny* attempted to reassess the state of African-Americans. Edited by Gerald
Jaynes and Robin M. Williams, much of the research was conducted
under the auspices of the Committee on the Status of Black Americans. What is the "new" American dilemma? Why has so little progress been made toward achieving African-American equality?

Just five decades ago, most black Americans could not work, live,
shop, eat, seek entertainment, or travel where they chose. Even a quarter century ago—100 years after the Emancipation Proclamation of
1863—most blacks were effectively denied the right to vote. A large
majority of blacks lived in poverty, and very few black children had the
opportunity to receive a basic education; indeed, black children were
still forced to attend inferior and separate schools in jurisdictions that
had not accepted the 1954 decision of the Supreme Court declaring
segregated schools unconstitutional.

Today the situation is very different. In education, many blacks
have received college degrees from universities that formerly excluded
them. In the workplace, blacks frequently hold professional and man-
agerial jobs in desegregated settings. In politics, most blacks now participate in elections, and blacks have been elected to all but the highest
political offices. Overall, many blacks have achieved middle-class status.

Yet the great gulf that existed between black and white Americans
in 1939 has only been narrowed; it has not closed. One of three blacks
still live in households with incomes below the poverty line. Even more

blacks live in areas where ineffective schools, high rates of dependence on public assistance, severe problems of crime and drug use, and low and declining employment prevail. Race relations, as they affect the lives of inhabitants of these areas, differ considerably from black-white relations involving middle-class blacks. Lower status blacks have less access to desegregated schools, neighborhoods, and other institutions and public facilities. Their interactions with whites frequently emphasize their subordinate status—as low-skilled employees, public agency clients, and marginally performing pupils.

The status of black Americans today can be characterized as a glass that is half full—if measured by progress since 1939—or as a glass that is half empty—if measured by the persisting disparities between black and white Americans since the early 1970s. Any assessment of the quality of life for blacks is also complicated by the contrast between blacks who have achieved middle-class status and those who have not.

The progress occurred because sustained struggles by blacks and their allies changed American law and politics, moving all governments and most private institutions from support of principles of racial inequality to support of principles of racial equality. Gradually, and often with much resistance, the behaviors and attitudes of individual whites moved in the same direction. Over the 50-year span covered by this study, the social status of American blacks has *on average* improved dramatically, both in absolute terms and relative to whites. The growth of the economy and public policies promoting racial equality led to an erosion of segregation and discrimination, making it possible for a substantial fraction of blacks to enter the mainstream of American life.

The reasons for the continuing distress of large numbers of black Americans are complex. Racial discrimination continues despite the victories of the civil rights movement. Yet, the problems faced today by blacks who are isolated from economic and social progress are less directly open to political amelioration than were the problems of legal segregation and the widely practiced overt discrimination of a few decades past. Slow overall growth of the economy during the 1970s and 1980s has been an important impediment to black progress; in the three previous decades economic prosperity and rapid growth had been a great help to most blacks. Educational institutions and government policies have not successfully responded to underlying changes in the society. Opportunities for upward mobility have been reduced for all lower status Americans, but especially for those who are black. If all racial discrimination were abolished today, the life prospects facing many poor blacks would still constitute major challenges for public policy.

SUMMARY OF MAJOR FINDINGS

This report summarizes and interprets a large body of data and research analyses concerning the position of blacks in American society since the eve of World War II. We write at a time 20 years after the Kerner Commission, following the summer riots of 1967, warned that ours was becoming a racially divided and unequal nation. We write 45 years after Gunnar Myrdal in *An American Dilemma* challenged Americans to bring their racial practices into line with their ideals. Despite clear evidence of progress against each problem, Americans face an unfinished agenda: many black Americans remain separated from the mainstream of national life under conditions of great inequality. The American dilemma has not been resolved.

The new "American dilemma" that has emerged after the civil rights era of the 1960s results from two aspirations of black Americans: equal opportunity—the removal of barriers to employment, housing, education, and political activities—and the actual attainment of equality in participation in these sectors of life.

Central to the realization of these aspirations are national policies promoting equality of opportunity for the most disadvantaged blacks (especially in areas such as employment and education) and the preservation among black people of attitudes and behaviors toward self-help and individual sacrifice that have enabled them to benefit from such opportunities. Black-white relations are important in determining the degree to which equal opportunity exists for black Americans. Whites desire equality of treatment in social institutions and in governmental policy; however, many whites are less likely to espouse or practice equality of treatment for blacks in their personal behavior. Thus, at the core of black-white relations is a dynamic tension between many whites' expectations of American institutions and their expectations of themselves. This state of relations is a significant improvement from 45 years ago when majorities of white people supported discrimination against blacks in many areas of life. But the divergence between social principle and individual practice frequently leads to white avoidance of blacks in those institutions in which equal treatment is most needed. The result is that American institutions do not provide the full equality of opportunity that Americans desire.

Foremost among the reasons for the present state of black-white relations are two continuing consequences of the nation's long and recent history of racial inequality. One is the negative attitudes held toward blacks and the other is the actual disadvantaged conditions under which many black Americans live. These two consequences reinforce each other. Thus, a legacy of discrimination and segregation continues to affect black-white relations.

In the context of American history, this continuing legacy is not surprising. Racial and ethnic differences have had crucial effects on the course of American history. In particular, black Americans' central role in several constitutional crises—their past status as slaves and the debates over slavery during the Constitutional Convention of 1787; the fighting of the Civil War; the denial of blacks' basic citizenship until the civil rights movement of the 1950s and 1960s—has frequently focused international attention on black-white relations in the United States. In view of this history, race is likely to retain much of its saliency as a feature of American society for some time.

Indeed, as the twenty-first century nears, demographic conditions will increase Americans' awareness that theirs is a multiracial society. The Bureau of the Census projects that the black population will increase from 11.7 percent of the U.S. total in 1980 to 15 percent in 2020; blacks will be nearly 1 of 5 children of school age and 1 of 6 adults of prime working age (25–54). Rising numbers of blacks will be represented both in influential occupations and positions, and among the poor, the least educated, and the jobless. At the same time, immigration trends are also increasing the numbers and proportions of Asian-Americans and Hispanics in the U.S. population. Thus, the importance of racial and ethnic minorities in general to the nation's well-being is growing.

We can summarize our main findings on the status of blacks in America in the late 1980s succinctly:

- By almost all aggregate statistical measures—incomes and living standards; health and life expectancy; educational, occupational, and residential opportunities; political and social participation—the well-being of both blacks and whites has advanced greatly over the past five decades.
- By almost all the same indicators, blacks remain substantially behind whites.

Beyond this brief picture lies a more complex set of changes that affect the *relative* status of black Americans:

- The greatest economic gains for blacks occurred in the 1940s and 1960s. Since the early 1970s, the economic status of blacks relative to whites has, on average, stagnated or deteriorated.
- The political, educational, health, and cultural statuses of blacks showed important gains from the 1940s through the 1960s. In addition, some important indicators continued to improve after the early 1970s.
- Among blacks, the experiences of various groups have differed, and status differences among those groups have increased. Some blacks have attained high-status occupations, income, education, and political positions, but a substantial minority remain in disadvantaged circumstance.

These patterns of change have been largely determined by three factors:

- Political and social activism among black Americans and their white allies led to changes in governmental policies; particularly important were sweeping improvements in the legal status of blacks.
- Resistance to social change in race relations continues in American society.
- Broad changes in overall economic conditions, especially the post-1973 slowdown in the nation's economic growth, have significantly affected social and economic opportunities for all Americans.

The rest of this section explicates these main findings and their causes. The next section presents a summary of the committee's detailed findings for the various areas we studied. The final section presents the committee's conclusions and some projections for the future.

BLACKS AND WHITES IN A CHANGING SOCIETY

Two general developments in the status of black Americans stand out; each is reflective of a near-identical development in the population at large. First, for the period 1940–1973, real earnings of Americans improved steadily, but they stagnated and declined after 1973. Similarly, over these same periods, there was a clear record of improving average material status of blacks relative to whites followed by stagnation and decline. Second, during the post-1973 period, inequality increased among Americans as the lowest income and least skilled people were hurt most by changes in the overall economy. Similarly, there were increasing differences in material well-being and opportunities among blacks, and they have been extremely pronounced.

These developments may be understood as consequences of four interdependent events that have altered the status of blacks, relative black-white status, and race relations in the United States. These events were the urbanization and northern movement of the black population from 1940 to 1970; the civil rights movement that forced the nation to open its major institutions to black participation during the same three decades; the unprecedented high and sustained rate of national economic growth for roughly the same periods; and the significant slowdown in the U.S. economy since the early 1970s.

The civil rights movement, blacks' more proximate location near centers of industrial activity, and high economic growth enabled those blacks best prepared to take advantage of new opportunities to respond with initiative and success. Increases in educational opportunities were seized by many blacks who were then able to translate better educations into higher status occupations than most blacks had ever enjoyed. Black incomes and earnings rose generally, with many individuals and families reaching middle-class and even upper middle income status. The new black middle class moved into better housing, frequently in the suburbs, and sometimes in desegregated neighborhoods. Despite much confrontation between whites and blacks as blacks abandoned traditional approaches to black-white relations, race relations eventually advanced closer to equal treatment.

At the same time, many blacks were not able to take advantage of the new conditions that developed: some were still located in areas relatively untouched by the changes; some lacked the family support networks to provide assistance; for some, better opportunities simply did not arise. Those who were left behind during the 1960s and 1970s faced and still face very different situations than poor blacks immediately before that period.

A major reason is the performance of the economy. Real weekly earnings (in constant 1984 dollars) of all American men, on average, fell from $488 in 1969 to $414 in 1984; real weekly earnings of women fell from $266 in 1969 to $230 in 1984. For the first time since the Great Depression of the 1930s, American men born in one year (e.g.,

1960) may face lower lifetime real earnings than men born 10 years earlier. Among the myriad and complex responses to these economic conditions have been rising employment rates among women, but falling rates among men, while the unemployment rates of both men and women have been on an upward trend for three decades.

A generation ago, a low-skilled man had relatively abundant opportunity to obtain a blue-collar job with a wage adequate to support a family at a lower middle class level or better. Today the jobs available to such men—and women—are often below or just barely above the official poverty line for a family of four. For example, black males aged 25–34, with some high school but no diploma, earned on average $268 weekly in 1986; in 1969, black male dropouts of that age had averaged $334 weekly (in constant 1984 dollars). For white men of the same age and education, work conditions have been better, but changes over time cannot be said to have been good: in the years 1969 and 1986, mean weekly earnings were $447 and $381. Thus, among men who did not complete high school, blacks and whites had lower real earnings in 1986 than in 1969.

Obtaining a well-paying job increasingly requires a good education or a specific skill. Many young blacks and whites do not obtain such training, and the educational system in many locations is apparently not equipped to provide them. Recent reports on the state of American education sound great alarm about the future status of today's students. One in six youths dropped out of high school in 1985, and levels of scholastic achievement are disturbingly low by many measures. Young men with poor credentials, finding themselves facing low-wage job offers and high unemployment rates, frequently abandon the labor force intermittently or completely. Some choose criminal activity as an alternative to the labor market.

Greater numbers of people are today susceptible to poverty than in the recent past. With some year-to-year variation, the percentage of Americans living in poverty has been on an upward trend: from 11.2 percent in 1974 to 13.5 percent in 1986. In addition, the poor may be getting poorer in the 1980s: the average poor family has persistently had a yearly income further below the poverty line than any year since 1963.

More and more of the poor are working family heads, men and women who are employed or seeking employment but who cannot find a job that pays enough to prevent their families from sliding into or near poverty. For the more fortunate, reasonably secure from the fear of poverty, such middle-class advantages as a home in the suburbs and the ability to send their children to the best college for which they qualify are goals that were reached by their parents but may be unattainable for many of them.

Perhaps the most important consequences of the stagnating U.S. economy have been the effects on the status of children. Many members of the next generation of young adults live in conditions ill suited to prepare them to contribute to the nation's future, In 1987, 1 of 5 (20 percent) American children under age 18—white, black, Hispanic, Native American, and Asian-American—were being raised in families with incomes below official poverty standards. Among minorities the conditions were worse: for example, 45 percent of black children and 39 percent of Hispanic children were living in poverty. During the 1970s, approximately 2 of every 3 black children could expect to live in poverty for at least 1 of the first 10 years of their childhood, while an astounding 1 of 3 could expect at least 7 of those 10 years to be lived in poverty.

We cannot emphasize too much the gravity of the fact that in any given year more than two-fifths of all black children live under conditions of poverty as the 1980s draw to a close. As fertility rates decrease, the total youth population of the United States will contain a larger proportion of comparatively disadvantaged youths from minority ethnic and racial groups This change may in turn lead to major changes in labor markets, childbearing, the armed forces, and education.

Under conditions of increasing economic hardship for the least prosperous members of society, blacks, because of their special legacy of poverty and discrimination, are afflicted sooner, more deeply, and longer. But the signs of distress that are most visible in parts of the black population are becoming more discernible within the entire population. This distress should be viewed in the context of the underlying changes within American society that affect not only black-white differences, but all disadvantaged blacks and whites who face the difficult economic conditions of the late 1980s.

DETERMINANTS OF BLACK STATUS

One major determinant of black status has been noted in the previous sections: the stagnation of the U.S. economy since 1973, which has particularly hurt lower class blacks. In this section we note two other determinants: organizational and individual resistance to change, intended and otherwise, that has erected and maintained barriers to black opportunities; and the policies of governments and private organizations aimed at improving blacks' position, which have resulted in large measure from black activism, initiative, and self-identity.

Barriers and disadvantages persist in blocking black advancement. Three such barriers to full opportunity for black Americans are residential segregation, continuance of diffuse and often indirect discrimination, and exclusion from social networks essential for full access to economic and educational opportunities. These barriers also existed for blacks who overcame them in earlier decades, but those successes were achieved in an economy that was growing rapidly and providing good wage opportunities even to low-skilled and less educated job seekers. In the 1960s, blacks seeking to help themselves also were benefited by a society more willing to expend energy and resources toward improving opportunities for the poor and minorities.

The past five decades have shown that purposeful actions and policies by governments and private institutions make a large difference in the opportunities and conditions of black Americans. Such purposeful actions and policies have been essential for past progress, and further progress is unlikely without them. Many blacks attained middle-class status because government and private programs enabled them to achieve better educations and jobs, through employment and education programs and government enforcement of equal employment opportunity.

Black initiative and identity have increasingly played primary roles in bringing about changes in government and private institutions and improvements in blacks' economic, social, and political status. This is of course evident in blacks' leadership of the civil rights movement and in their response to industrial opportunity during the great rural-to-urban migration of 1940–1970. But is is also evident in the strivings of individuals to finish high school or attain higher education; to enter a predominantly white factory, secretarial pool, or corporate law office; or to desegregate an entire institution, such as a professional sport, military combat corps, or legislative body.

Many blacks who have not succeeded live in environments in which social conditions and individual behavioral patterns are often detrimental to self-improvement. Such behaviors may be natural responses to group conditions and social forces perceived as beyond personal control. One-half of black families with children must manage their affairs with only one parent—almost always a mother. These families are overwhelmingly poor (59 percent were below the poverty line in

1987), have high rates of dependence on family assistance benefits, and live in areas with a high percentage of families in similar circumstances. Why do such behaviors and conditions persist? There are no simple answers to this crucial question and no answers that can be validated as scientific findings. We can say, however, that the evidence does not support some popular hypotheses that purport to explain female-headed households, high birth rates to unmarried women, low labor force participation by males, or poor academic performance solely on the basis of government support programs or, more generally, on the existence of a "culture of poverty" among the black poor. Black-white cultural differences have narrowed since 1960, not widened.

Our analysis of the problem does identify a number of important contributory factors. Discrimination plays an important role in the lives of many blacks, and even in the absence of discrimination the opportunities of many blacks are limited. Black youths in poor environments probably anticipate little payoff from working for academic achievement and may underestimate their opportunities. Those in poorly staffed, dilapidated schools populated with underachieving students can easily fall into the trap of perceiving the pursuit of academic excellence as a poor investment. Inequalities in economic status to a large extent cause and interact with other status features to maintain overall black-white differences in status. Consequently, status gaps between blacks and whites will remain as long as blacks' economic status lags behind that of whites. For example, differences in black-white voting patterns result from persistent economic and social inequalities that impede electoral participation regardless of race; individual blacks now participate as much or more than whites of comparable socioeconomic status. Similarly, differences in socioeconomic status account for the entire black-white difference in high school dropout rates. In health, differences in black and white infant mortality are similarly linked to differences in economic status. In the criminal justice system, much of the differential sentencing of blacks and whites can be attributed to differences between sentences for defendants of higher and lower economic status.

Yet the status of blacks is determined by the presence of both racial stratification and class (position within the socioeconomic structure of society). Changes in black-white relations and social opportunities do not affect blacks of different status in similar ways. For example, because of higher geographic concentrations of poor households among blacks, segregated residential areas affect the quality of schools and medical care available to low-income blacks more than they affect the availability of these resources to higher income blacks or low-income whites. And we have already noted that changes in the national economy have had particularly negative effects on lower status Americans, white and black. But changes have been most detrimental to the fortunes of blacks, and opportunities were curtailed most for blacks of lowest status.

Freedom Bound

ROBERT WEISBROT

Robert Weisbrot, Professor of History at Colby College, is the author
of two books dealing with civil rights: *Father Divine and the Struggle for
Racial Equality*; and, *Freedom Bound: A History of America's Civil
Rights Movement*, from which this excerpt is adapted. What does he
believe are the chief successes of the civil rights movement? How has
it fallen short of the expectations of its leaders?

It is now clear that the more expansive hopes for civil rights
progress were markedly inflated. Residential segregation, seen in the
persistence of inner-city black ghettos and lily-white suburbs, has easily
survived federal fiats against housing discrimination. De facto segregation of churches, social centers, and private schools also remains routine, suggesting that in important respects the society's newfound
emphasis on interracial harmony has been more rhetorical than real.
Wealth, too, is largely segregated along racial lines; the median family
income of blacks is barely half that of whites, and blacks are three times
as likely to be poor. As for black political power, it is still embryonic
with regard to national office holding and access to the circles that
make foreign and domestic policy. In all, the roots of racial inequality
have proved too deeply embedded in centuries of American history to
be washed away by a decade's liberal reform.

Race relations have changed at a glacial pace in much of the rural
South, where only the hardiest civil rights activists could weather the
repressive social climate. Southern whites understandably regard black
militancy as an urban malady, for only in the cities have blacks developed
an independent business and professional class able to lead sustained

protests. In many outlying towns, where whites monopolize credit and own the farms and textile mills that provide crucial jobs, the etiquette of racial deference persists.

Unwritten rules of segregation in small Southern communities still have the force of law. Harassment and occasional beatings discourage blacks from approaching the polls on election day, whatever the language of federal statutes. Blacks also know to avoid restaurants where they will draw stares instead of service, hotels that will always be "fully booked," and golf courses where management sand traps will foil their bids for access. Even white physicians who treat persons of both races commonly route their patients into separate waiting rooms with pre-1960 firmness. Here progress in race relations often comes in rudimentary concessions to black dignity, as in the recent removal of a chain-link fence dividing black and white plots in a Georgia county cemetery. Until that headline-making decision, black funeral processions had entered the cemetery through a back gate.

Challenges to old racial mores can bring spiraling retaliation. In Ludowici, Georgia, where students picked separate white and black homecoming queens until 1984, an argument in the high school lunchroom over interracial dating degenerated into an interracial brawl. Discipline was swift and selective: several students were expelled, all of them black. After local black leaders protested, hooded Klansmen visited the town, and within hours the home of a civil rights activist was burned to the ground. Fire marshals blamed faulty wiring, but Joseph Lowery of the Southern Christian Leadership Conference thought it absurd to deny the real problem: faulty white racial attitudes. The former SNCC worker Charles Sherrod observed, "Those people who shot at us, and blew up churches and all that 20 years ago, they haven't gone anywhere. The attitudes are still there. Their behavior has changed because we have got a little power. They won't do anything they can't get away with."

Few officials anywhere in the South still defy civil rights laws openly, for events in the 1960s showed the futility of shrill racist posturing. Softer sabotage, however, still limits the impact of federal guarantees. After passage of the Voting Rights Act in 1965, whites generally acquiesced in the registration of blacks but devised ways to undermine the new electorate. Testimony in 1982 before the Senate Judiciary Committee revealed that nearly half the counties of Alabama, Georgia, Louisiana, and South Carolina had disregarded the act's "preclearance" requirement by changing electoral laws—often for transparent racial reasons—without first obtaining federal approval. Cities with large black populations imported white voters by annexing adjacent suburbs, and cities with a few predominantly black areas discarded district elections for at-large voting. Legislators have also excluded black voters from communities through redistricting schemes of rare cartographic cunning. The understaffed Justice Department has trailed such infractions at a discouraging distance. An amendment to the North Carolina constitution, designed to gerrymander away the influence of new black voters, escaped challenge from federal attorneys until 1981, fourteen years after it was illegally implemented.

Outside the South racism treads more softly but still sequesters most blacks in ghettos. Blacks formed 6 percent of the suburban population in 1980 (up from 5 percent in 1970), and even this figure was inflated by spillover into older, industrial suburbs that white flight turned into segregated enclaves. Federal studies show pervasive discrimination by white realtors and residents, resulting in hundreds of census tracts in New York, Cleveland, and other metropolitan areas that contain no nonwhites. Nor is housing bias entirely covert. Obscene phone calls, curses, threats, firebombings, and rocks and bricks crashing through windows are among the dozens of incidents that each year impart a rough frontier quality to black settlement in white neighborhoods. Such experiences confirm that the open-housing legislation of the 1960s has meant little beside the resolve of whites to maintain property values and "ethnic purity" in their communities.

Racial violence and harassment, a central target of civil rights protest, still occurs daily in every region of the country. The Justice Department conservatively recorded a rise in racist attacks from 99 in 1980 to 276 in 1986; the count by individual cities is more extensive. New York City's police department charted an increase in bias-related clashes from four a week to ten a week in early 1987. Chicago reported 240 episodes of racially motivated violence and harassment in 1986, an increase for the third consecutive year. The spark is often no more than the presence of a black person in a store, on the street, in a new home. For dejected white students at the University of Massachusetts at Amherst, the defeat of the Boston Red Sox in the 1986 World Series was enough reason to beat a black New York Mets fan unconscious and injure several others. Several months earlier, at Howard Beach, New York, three black "outsiders" fled an attack by eleven whites; one of the blacks, twenty-three-year-old Michael Griffith, was killed when he ran onto a parkway of speeding cars in his attempt to escape a beating. Kevin Nesmith, a black student at the Citadel Military School, in Charleston, South Carolina, resigned after whites in Klan robes burst into his room at two in the morning shouting racial slurs and hazing him. Something akin to a freedom ride befell black students returning from Newton North High School to their homes in Boston when whites smashed the bus windows with stones and a tire iron. These and other recent episodes do not approach the systematic, officially sanctioned terror against blacks that once scarred American history. They nonetheless point to the continued difficulty blacks face in securing basic civil rights.

Police each year kill dozens of blacks, including children. Defenders of police conduct stress the extreme danger facing officers in some ghetto neighborhoods, their need to use deadly force on occasion to survive, and their able protection of blacks, notably during civil rights marches that have drawn white hecklers. Still, cases abound of unprovoked, cold-blooded police shootings of ghetto residents that almost invariably go unpunished.

The criminal justice system is less blatantly harsh toward blacks than in the past, but patterns of punishment still appear skewed by racial prejudice. Blacks average longer prison terms than whites for the same offense and are the primary victims of capital punishment. Criminals of any race, moreover, are treated more severely for victimizing whites. In 1987 a case that challenged the death penalty as being tainted, in practice, by racial bias showed that in Georgia, even after accounting for 230 other factors, killers of white persons were four times more likely to be executed than killers of blacks. Despite corroborating evidence of prejudice in meting out capital punishment, the Supreme Court narrowly upheld the death penalty. The majority opinion asserted, in language shades removed from *Plessy v. Ferguson*, that the treatment of black and white prisoners was admittedly different but not discriminatory.

Failure to include blacks fully in the nation's prosperity is the most glaring limitation of the movement for racial justice. In the South two-thirds of all black workers, compared with one-third of all whites, hold low-income jobs. The national economy today relegates more than half of all black workers to menial jobs, perpetuates a black underclass of deepening antisocial bent, and confines even educated blacks to the margins of wealth and opportunity. These problems can be traced to various causes—racial differences in family structure, education, and job experience among them—but they are also rooted in both past and persistent discrimination.

Title VII of the 1964 Civil Rights Act did not end bias in employment but drove it behind closed office doors. Managers commonly assigned blacks to dead-end jobs, minimized their executive role, scrutinized them more harshly than comparably trained whites, and excluded them from the after-hours fraternizing that can advance careers. In 1982 only one in thirty black men (compared with one in ten whites) filled management or administrative jobs, reflecting a ten-year increase so minute that it was probably a matter of statistical error. No black headed a corporation in *Fortune* magazine's top 1,000, and few had risen above the level of vice-president in any major firm. Tokenism thus became more intricate in the era of affirmative action, permitting a greater minority presence in the office but seldom in the conference suites where deals, promotions, and salaries are decided.

An aura of the closed medieval guild still surrounds craft unions, which have countered civil rights laws with subtler means of racial exclusion. One AFL-CIO union, representing New York City's electrical contractors, avoided punishment for racist practices by devising an "outreach training program" for minorities in 1971. Over a decade later state investigators charged that the program required black and Hispanic trainees to work eleven years before they could reach class A journeyman status, compared with five years for white apprentices. Nonwhite trainees were also taught a curriculum separate from that of whites, with obsolete textbooks and without the fifth year of classroom instruction needed to pass the union exam and obtain work at journeymen's wages. Many other AFL-CIO locals have also been exposed for turning affirmative action programs into a permanent racial obstacle course for minorities.

Despite a minutely detailed skein of evidence that shows racism permeating the economy, Americans frequently cite two apparent exceptions—the entertainment industry and professional sports—as proof that merit, not color, determines success. It is true that the presence of black athletes, and in some sports their predominance, is now taken for granted. So, too, is the celebrity of black television and film stars such as Bill Cosby, Richard Pryor, and Eddie Murphy. Even in these fields, however, blacks have strained against a color line placed well before the limits of their talent and drive.

While blacks have fared better in films and on television than before the civil rights movement, they still receive few parts not written specifically for a black. Leading roles are confined mainly to escapist "situation comedies" that affirm their right to be caricatured as sharply as whites. The versatile Broadway performer Ben Vereen complained that casting directors too often envisioned him in the role of janitor. A Hollywood agent confirmed that Vereen's experience was the norm for black actors: "They're looking for druggies, athletes or men struggling out of the ghetto." Regarding black actresses, the agent said, "If you're beautiful, you can play a prostitute; if you're fat, you can play a mother; and if you're ugly, you can play a maid." Bill Cosby, among the few blacks to transcend such stereotyping, has refused to appear as an Oscar-night presenter because this industry just does not represent [black] America."

As in all of American life since the civil rights movement, Hollywood executives express their prejudices (or reflect those of their audience) mainly in sub rosa messages. One NBC memorandum on how to promote a show with an ethnically mixed cast warned against highlighting its most seasoned performer, Debbie Allen, because of racial considerations: "On *Fame*: Spot you sent has to be more generic and less black. . . . [Show] VARIOUS TEACHERS. CAN USE LYDIA BUT ALSO NEED WHITE TEACHERS." Similar indiscretions confirm that the advance of tolerance since the heyday of "Amos 'n' Andy" can still be measured in degrees.

Athletics, too, has seen blacks advancing in powerful strides but still unable to leap the highest racial hurdles. Fans now glory in black triumphs—the speed of Edwin Moses, the airborne agility of basketball's Michael Jordan, the destructive power of the boxer Mike Tyson. But there are limits. Racist loyalties are easily stirred, as boxing promoters have shown by building up white contenders of often limited skill, for the box office appeal of a "great white hope" battling a black champion. And while black physical skills are no longer disparaged, as in the days when athletic leagues were segregated, blacks have yet to receive recognition for mental and leadership qualities in any American sport.

Forty years after Jackie Robinson entered the major leagues, jobs as managers and administrators are nearly beyond the reach of blacks. The Los Angeles Dodgers vice-president Al Campanis explained on television in April 1987 that this was due not to racism but to the fact that blacks lacked the "necessities" for these executive positions. The seventy-year-old Campanis, unaccustomed to the media spotlight, was immediately fired for his expression of views doubtless known to his colleagues over many decades. Yet the policy of tokenism in baseball's upper echelons continued.

Racial stereotyping pervades other sports as well. "Thinking" and leadership positions in football, such as those of quarterback and coach, are generally reserved for whites no matter how many blacks stand out elsewhere in the lineup. And in basketball, where blacks hold nearly every record except that for frequency of promotion to administrative roles, it is common to see five black players huddled around a white coach.

More ominous for blacks than the racism in sports and entertainment is the public view that these fields provide broad avenues of mobility for blacks with initiative. In fact they permit no more than a trickle of talented individuals to escape poverty, which would be true even if all professional athletes and entertainers were black. The visibility and lucrative contracts of several hundred media heroes belie the misery of millions in the black underclass, whose lot has generally worsened since the height of civil rights protest.

Flaming buildings in Watts brought the ghettos into national view in 1965. Twenty years later a study of Watts commissioned by the city and county of Los Angeles revealed isolated improvements amid systemic decay. Watts in 1985 featured a new hospital, a civic center, better bus service, and a shopping center named for Dr. King that featured the first full-service supermarket built since the riot. But unemployment, a major cause of the riot, had risen from under 12 percent at the time of the 1960 census to nearly 20 percent in 1980. The estimated actual jobless rate in Watts, including those no longer seeking work and those who never entered the labor force, was 30 percent for adults and 50 percent for teenagers.

"There ain't no middle class right now—either you're up or you're down," said Duane Randolph, one of many Watts residents hurt by the loss of low-skilled factory jobs to automation and to suburban settings. Randolph formerly worked as a warehouse laborer and as a janitor for day-care centers but had held no job since the late seventies. "I've been on hold for a long time now," he said. "I'll be 29 next month, and my good thing ain't come around right now." More fortunate was a resident who traveled up to two hours from Watts to his job, and back again, as a housekeeping porter at a hospital north of downtown Los Angeles. The slim rewards of such ambition could at best send mixed signals to other young black males seeking meaningful employment.

Government services since the riot have fallen further behind the need for better jobs and education. In 1985 not one comprehensive job-training or placement program operated in Watts. Existing programs were poorly coordinated and were further hurt when state officials closed the local office overseeing fair employment and housing. Public schools have also lost ground since the sixties. Overcrowding has forced year-round sessions, and the refusal of veteran teachers to accept assignment to Watts has led to staffing hundreds of classrooms with a series of temporary teachers. According to the government report, educational problems "remain critical and may be growing worse."

As in 1965, Watts today encapsulates the outlook of urban black America. There are nearly ten million poor blacks—more than in 1960—and their numbers are growing faster than are those of the middle class. In 1960 three-quarters of all black men were employed, but barely half held jobs in 1980. Even this count was optimistic, for the Census Bureau was unable to find an additional 15 to 20 percent of all black men twenty to forty years old, who were presumed to have neither employment nor permanent residences. A realistic estimate, then was that more than half of all black adult males did not have jobs, a figure twice the national unemployment level during the Great Depression.

The unraveling of family ties has accompanied and aggravated this descent into the underclass. The proportion of single-parent, female-headed households grew from one-fifth of all black families in 1960 to nearly one-half in 1986, accounting for about 75 percent of all black children raised in poverty. This is not a black problem alone; since 1970, births to single women have become more prevalent throughout American society, more than doubling among whites, to 14.5 percent in 1985. But among blacks the incidence of such births reached 60 percent. It is a disastrous trend in a society where female-headed families, regardless of race, are four times as likely to be poor as all other families. In 1986 the median income for households headed by women was $13,647, compared with $32,805 for two-parent families of all races.

Diminishing choices for young black men in particular have sharpened their survival skills, which take them outside the regular economy and, in many cases, the law. Young blacks in prison—over 56,000 males twenty to twenty-four years old in 1984—exceed by more than 25 percent the number of young blacks living in college dormitories.

Violence in ghetto neighborhoods has grown with the burgeoning drug economy that produces immense wealth for major suppliers, affords "negative idols" for the young, and generates wars that recognize no bystanders as innocent. Adult prison gangs in Watts now deploy youth gangs as street troops to sell cocaine and murder rivals. Teens are increasingly armed and deadly to anyone caught in gang shootouts. Forty thousand gang members patrolled Los Angeles County in 1985, an increase of twelve thousand from 1980, and a number rising by 10 percent each year.

For black males in the inner city, prison rather than college or career speeds the coming of age. The Harlem-born novelist Claude Brown observed that young blacks view the prospect of imprisonment with "nothing more than the mild apprehension or anxiety that attends, for instance, a bar mitzvah, joining the Marines or any other manhood initiation ritual in any normal society. One goes into the Marines as a young boy and comes out a 'real man.' It is the same with going into the 'joint,' as prison is called."

At New Jersey's Trenton State Prison, Brown spoke with a black inmate, not quite old enough to shave, who was serving fifteen years—a "dime and nickel" sentence—for armed robbery. Brown painted for the youth a future of certain tragedy if he continued to pursue his criminal ways. Each time he went on the prowl for a victim or an establishment, there was a 60 percent likelihood of his being killed, permanently maimed, or ending up doing a long "bit" in jail. Even if he successfully carried off nine or ten robberies for $1,000 or more, in a few days to a week at most he'd be back where he started. The boy responded,

> I see where you comin' from, Mr. Brown, but you got things kind of turned around the wrong way. You see, all the things that you say could happen to me is dead on the money, and that is why I can't lose. Look at it from my point of view for a minute. Let's say I go and get wiped [killed]. Then I ain't got no more needs, right? O.K., supposin' I get popped, shot in the spine and paralyzed for the rest of my life—that could happen playin' football, you know. Then I won't need a whole lot of money because I won't be able to go no place and do nothin', right? So, I'll be on welfare, and the welfare check is all the money I'll need, right? Now if I get busted and end up in the joint pullin' a dime and a nickel, like I am, then I don't have to worry about no bucks, no clothes. I get free rent and three squares a day. So you see, Mr. Brown, I really can't lose.

The logic, at once murderous and suicidal, left Brown relieved that the youth was serving a fifteen-year sentence: "It would be twice as comforting to know that this young cynic was doing a 30-year bit." Still, as Brown realized, the problem reached beyond the fate of one prisoner, to racial legacies that neither time nor civil rights laws alone could redeem.

A RECORD OF CHANGE

Like other reform movements the crusade for racial justice inevitably fell short of the utopian goals that sustained it. Still, if America's civil rights movement is judged by the distance it traveled rather than by barriers yet to be crossed, a record of substantial achievement unfolds. In communities throughout the South, "whites only" signs that had stood for generations suddenly came down from hotels, rest rooms, theaters, and other facilities. Blacks and whites seldom mingle socially at home, but they are apt to lunch together at fast-food shops that once drew blacks only for sit-ins. Integration extends equally to Southern workers, whether at diner counters or in the high-rise office buildings that now afford every Southern city a skyline.

School desegregation also quickened its pace and by the mid-1970s had become fact as well as law in over 80 percent of all Southern public schools. Swelling private school enrollments have tarnished but not substantially reversed this achievement. A privileged 5 to 10 percent of all Southern white children may find shelter from the *Brown* verdict at private academies; but the words "massive resistance" have virtually disappeared from the region's political vocabulary.

Hate groups once flourished without strong federal restraint, but the civil rights movement has curbed the Ku Klux Klan and other extremist threats. Beginning in 1964 the FBI infiltrated the Klan so thoroughly that by 1965 perhaps one in five members was an informant. During the 1980s, amid a rise in racial assaults, synagogue bombings, and armed robberies to bankroll fringe groups, the federal government mounted the largest campaign against organized subversion since World War II. In 1987, members of the Florida Realm of the United Klans of America were convicted of illegal paramilitary training exercises, and leaders of the Identity Movement, which preaches a theology of hatred toward Jews and blacks, were indicted for conspiring to overthrow the government. Federal action has encouraged private lawsuits, including one that bankrupted the United Klans of America. After a black teenager in Mobile, Alabama, was murdered by Klansmen and left hanging from a tree in 1981, the boy's family won a $7 million judgment. To pay damages the Klan had to cede its two-story national headquarters, near Tuscaloosa, Alabama, to the black litigants. Reeling from legal and financial adversity, Klan membership declined from 10,000 in 1981 to less than 5,500 in 1987, the lowest since the early seventies.

Protection of voting rights represents the movement's most unalloyed success, more than doubling black voter registration, to 64 percent, in the seven states covered by the 1965 act. Winning the vote literally changed the complexion of government service in the South. When Congress passed the Voting Rights Act, barely 100 blacks held elective office in the country; by 1989 there were more than 7,200, including 24 congressmen and some 300 mayors. Over 4,800 of these officials served in the South, and nearly every Black Belt county in Alabama had a black sheriff. Mississippi experienced the most radical change, registering 74 percent of its voting-age blacks and leading the nation in the number of elected black officials (646).

Black influence in electoral politics acquired a compelling symbol during the 1980s with the emergence of the Reverend Jesse Jackson of Chicago as a presidential contender. As a young aide to Dr. King from 1966 to 1968, Jackson had stood out for his eloquence, élan, and ambition. In the 1970s Jackson won national acclaim for spurring ghetto youths to excel in school, but his denunciations of American society as racist, capitalist, and imperialist kept him on the fringes of public life. Over the next decade, however, as blacks increasingly protested President Reagan's neglect of minorities and the poor, Jackson began to temper his revolutionary message in hopes of forging a revitalized reform coalition.

Jackson campaigned in the 1984 Democratic presidential primaries, drawing large crowds and intense media coverage with his mixture of evangelical fervor, nimble wit, and self-conscious identification with minority hopes. He spoke of a "Rainbow Coalition" that would transcend racial lines, though his campaign chiefly focused on mobilizing black voter registration and turnout with the aid of Negro churches. This strategy enabled Jackson to win nomination contests in South Carolina, Louisiana, and Washington, D.C., and to finish third in delegates at the Democratic National Convention. Partly offsetting this achievement was Jackson's failure to draw even 5 percent of the white voters, whether because of his race, radical image, or suspect character.

(Jews in particular recoiled at Jackson's ties with the Black Muslim Louis Farrakhan, who had branded Judaism a "gutter religion.") Despite these weaknesses Jackson's campaign legitimized Black Power to the American people in a way that Stokely Carmichael and others in the 1960s had vainly tried to do from outside the political mainstream.

In 1988 Jackson hewed closer to the political center and reached well beyond his core supporters, in a second bid for the Democratic presidential nomination. The now seasoned candidate trimmed his radical rhetoric, conciliated many who had thought him opportunistic and divisive, and emphasized broadly appealing liberal themes of economic opportunity for all citizens. Jackson's approach, which this time afforded him second place among seven competitors, reflected and fostered a new openness toward blacks in the Democratic party and in the nation. An especially prominent landmark of political change was Jackson's Michigan primary victory, with 54 percent of the vote, just twenty years after that state's Democratic contest had gone to the Alabama segregationist George Wallace. The candidate's progress, as in 1984, remained in key respects exceedingly personal, for it did not appreciably change his party's stand on key issues nor dispel racism as a factor in national politics. Still, more than any black leader since Martin Luther King, Jr., Jackson had inspired Americans with the faith—crucial to every reform movement—that the decisive stage of America's democratic odyssey lay just ahead.

Despite unsettling parallels with the aftermath of Reconstruction, the modern civil rights movement should prove better able to resist the undoing of black gains. A salient difference is the greater reluctance in recent times to risk convulsing society by spurning the ideal of equality. Blacks during Reconstruction had exerted relatively minor influence over the white leadership that instituted—and then abandoned—measures for racial justice. By contrast blacks a century later shook whole cities with mass demonstrations, demanded and secured sweeping changes in federal law, and reshaped the political agenda of two strongminded chief executives. These protests brought a new respect for Afro-Americans, breaking forever the comfortable myth that blacks were content with a biracial society and proving that they had the rare courage needed to challenge it.

New currents in world affairs have reinforced the consensus to guarantee black civil rights. During the late nineteenth century Americans were largely indifferent to the nonwhite world except for the growing possibilities of colonizing or otherwise controlling it. The European nations that most influenced this country were themselves indulging in imperialism based on racial as well as national interests. Global pressures today are vastly different. Competition for the support of nonwhite nations and the near-universal ostracism of South Africa, which asserts a racist ideology, require American society to pay at least nominal homage to racial equality.

Pluralism is also more firmly rooted in American values than ever before. The black revolution stimulated others, including women, homosexuals, Hispanics, native Americans, and Asians, who frequently modeled their actions on the values and tactics popularized by Martin Luther King, Jr. Each emerging movement, while pursuing a discrete agenda has bolstered the principle that government must guarantee equal rights and opportunities to all citizens.

Racism lost more than legal standing with the triumph of civil rights campaigns; it lost social standing. Even the Daughters of the American Revolution, an organization known for its racially exclusive character, apologized in 1982 for having spurned the singer Marian Anderson over four decades earlier. The DAR's president general, a native of Beulah, Mississippi, invited Anderson to perform at the organization's ninety-first convention in Constitution Hall. The eighty-year-old singer was by then too frail to attend, but the black soprano Leontyne Price, who treated the DAR to a concert ending with "The Battle Hymn of the Republic," assured her interracial audience that Anderson was "here in spirit."

The deepening interest in racial harmony has encouraged recognition of the black experience as central to American history. The 1977 television drama "Roots," which engaged audiences in the trauma of racial slavery and the struggle for freedom, became the most widely viewed special series in the history of the medium. Six years later Congress created a holiday to honor Martin Luther King, Jr., and by extension the civil rights movement he symbolized. Such a tribute had eluded Thomas Jefferson, Andrew Jackson, both Roosevelts, and other giants of American history. President Reagan, who had originally opposed enacting a holiday for King as an unwise "ethnic" precedent, signed the popular bill into law while standing alongside King's widow, Coretta.

In the South, as in the rest of the nation, few whites seriously contemplate returning to the state of race relations before 1960. This outlook differs strikingly from Southern intransigence after Reconstruction and reflects the disparate ways in which the two eras of racial change occurred. Reconstruction came as a sudden, violently imposed up-heaval in Southern race relations that virtually nothing in the region's history had prepared it to accept. The civil rights movement instead ad-vanced nonviolently, secured small gains over decades, and fostered progress from within the region. The campaigns that ended legalized segregation in the sixties marked the culmination of this gradual change. Many white Southerners had by then reconciled themselves to reforms that seemed inevitable and even, perhaps, beneficial.

Freed from the albatross of defending Jim Crow at the expense of national respect and regional peace, Southerners could focus on tasks of economic and social modernization. Mississippi's leading journal, the *Jackson Clarion-Ledger*, offered a glimpse into this revolution in priori-ties. After the March on Washington in 1963, a front-page story re-ported that the capital was "clean again with Negro trash removed." Twenty years later the paper won a Pulitzer Prize in public service for exposing the need for fuller desegregation and better funding of public schools.

Southern memories of black protests have mellowed to the point where both races treat them as parts of their history to be proud of. Montgomery motorists now drive down the Martin Luther King, Jr. Ex-pressway, and the Dexter Baptist Church, where King was pastor, has become a national landmark. The prison cell King occupied in Bir-mingham is set aside as a library for inmates, his "Letter from a Birming-ham Jail" framed on the wall. In Georgia's capitol a portrait of King hangs near a bust of Alexander Stephens, the Confederate vice-president. One elderly black tour guide, assigned to interpret these landmarks of the past, ignored the bust of Stephens, and beamed, "Here is Nobel Prize winner Martin Luther King, Jr. He was born and bred right here in Atlanta on Auburn Avenue."

Political calculation has sealed this acceptance of racial change. Over a quiet bourbon and branch water in his Senate office, Mississippi's arch-segregationist James Eastland confided, "When [blacks] get the vote, I won't be talking this way anymore." Later Eastland was among the many officials who jettisoned their tested appeals to prejudice, learned to pronounce "Negro" in place of more casual epithets, and prefaced the names of newly valued black constituents with the once forbidden appellation "Mister."

Even the past master of race baiting, Alabama's George Wallace, was struck color-blind on the road to Montgomery in his 1982 gubernatorial campaign. Wallace, who like most politicians believed above all in winning elections today, tomorrow, and forever, spent much of his hard-fought contest kissing black babies and humbly supplicating their parents' support, assuring them of his reborn attitudes on race matters. (He won the campaign with the aid of forgiving black electorate and welcomed several blacks to positions in his cabinet.) Whatever Wallace's deepest sentiments, his actions were a striking testament to the legacy of the civil rights protests that he once vowed to crush but that instead have left an indelible imprint on the nation's moral landscape.

The full impact of civil rights campaigns has yet to be felt. The movement could not wholly sweep away old Jim Crow hierarchies, but rather superimposed new patterns of behavior on a still race-conscious society. Cities like Selma, Alabama, where black activists battled white supremacists in the 1960s, today reflect two eras of race relations at once, giving no final sign of which will prevail.

Segregated neighborhoods persist in Selma, along with segregated social patterns. The Selma Country Club has no black members and until 1983 would not allow a black dance band inside. Elks Club members attend separate white and black chapters. Nearly a thousand white students attend two private academies founded with the express purpose of excluding blacks. Racial lines run through the city's economy: the overall jobless rate in Selma in 1985 was 16 percent but nearly twice as high for blacks as for whites. And in politics, residents tend to make racial choices for public office. The black community leader Frederick Reese won 40 percent of the mayoral vote in 1984 but only a handful of white supporters; Joseph Smitherman received 10 to 15 percent of the black vote but stayed in office with nearly 100 percent of the white vote.

Yet race relations in Selma have noticeably changed since the city's landmark civil rights demonstrations in 1965. The onetime "moderate segregationist" Smitherman began to tend an image as a facilitator of black mobility. In 1984 Smitherman observed proudly that 40 percent of the police force was black, including the assistant chief, several lieutenants, captains, and key department heads. The city's personnel board had three blacks and two whites, the eight-person library board was evenly composed of blacks and whites, and the school board had five blacks to four whites. Asphalt pavement, which had often stopped short of black neighborhoods, now stretched for miles throughout the town, covering over dirt roads and, with them, an era of flagrant neglect of black residents.

Perhaps most important to Selma's blacks and many whites, the movement reduced ignorance, fear, and hate. The black lawyer and civil rights activist J.L. Chestnut remarked in 1985, on the twentieth anniversary of his city's civil rights marches, that new attitudes were taking root: "My children don't think of white children as devils, and I don't think white children see my kids as watermelon-eating, tap-dancing idiots. If there is hope, it is in the fact that children in Selma today don't have to carry the baggage that Joe Smitherman and J.L. Chestnut carry. And that means they will never be scared the way we used to be scared." Teenagers at Selma's integrated public high school knew about the events of "Bloody Sunday" but viewed them as a mystery from another time. "Kids today, they're used to the way things are," explained Karyn Reddick, a black student. "Try as you can, you can't believe that white people once treated black people that way. It seems like something that happened long, long ago."

From Boycotts to Ballots

STEVEN F. LAWSON

Steven F. Lawson is Professor of History at the University of South
Florida and the author of two books on African-American voting
rights: *Black Ballots: Voting Rights in the South, 1944–1965*; and *In Pursuit of Power: Southern Blacks and Electoral Politics*. Professor Lawson
originally presented this paper in 1988 as part of a conference entitled
"New Directions in Civil Rights Studies," held at the University of
Virginia's Center for the Study of Civil Rights. Has political empowerment improved the lives of most African-Americans?

In 1946 southern black soldiers returned from having fought in
World War II, only to encounter white racism at home. A Georgia veteran expressed the sentiments of black GIs throughout the region,
many of whom marched to county courthouses demanding their right
to vote. "Peace is not the absence of war," he declared, "but the presence of justice which may be obtained, first, by your becoming a citizen
and registered voter." The following decade, as the pace of the civil
rights movement was quickening, some 25,000 people rallied at the
Lincoln Memorial in Washington, D.C., to celebrate a "Prayer Pilgrim-
age for Freedom." On 17 May 1957 the Reverend Martin Luther King,
Jr., who had recently led a pathbreaking bus boycott in Montgomery,
Alabama, emphasized suffrage as the key weapon for black liberation.
"Give us the ballot," King predicted, and African-Americans would use
it to secure their basic rights, ensure justice, and guarantee responsible
government. Over a quarter of a century later, more than ten times the
number of people who heard King in 1957 assembled in the same location to honor his memory and listen to one of his disciples update his

message. On August 27, 1983, with the ballot long won, the Reverend Jesse L. Jackson proclaimed: "We can have change through elections and not bloody revolution. Our day has come. From slaveship to championship . . . [f]rom the outhouse to the courthouse to the White House, we will march on."

These expressions of the black veteran, minister, and presidential candidate represented separate but interconnected dimensions of black politics. Each sought to combine traditions of protest with the use of the franchise to achieve racial equality. For African-Americans the ultimate aim of politics, either protest or electoral, has been liberation. Seeking emancipation form the bondage of white supremacy, disfranchised southern blacks challenged the political system for admission, even as they hoped to transform it by their participation. Toward this end marches, rallies, and demonstrations became political instruments to obtain a share of power to shape public policy, just as casting a ballot was aimed at making the political process more responsive to their demands.

Scholars of the civil rights struggle have furnished a full but as yet incomplete picture of the political aspects of the black freedom movement. For over twenty years political scientists, sociologists, historians, and journalists have filled library shelves with volumes investigating the origins of the movement, the individuals who led it, the groups that mobilized it, the tactics they employed, and the legislation and litigation they pursued. In general, the literature in the field can be divided according to the scholarly discipline of the researchers. Sociologists have concentrated on analyzing the civil rights phenomenon, including its political ramifications, within the framework of the formation and development of other social protest movements. Political scientists, who have written most extensively about black politics, have tended to focus on minority electoral behavior and the responses of the executive, legislative, and judicial branches to civil rights pressures. For their part, historians have written biographies of major leaders, the organizations they guided, and the issues they pursued, and most recently they have begun to examine case studies of the movement as it originated and matured in various communities throughout the South. Drawing upon many of these works, this chapter offers a historical perspective on the development of black electoral politics and its relationship to civil rights protest.

During the post-World War II period, black southerners have moved through four stages of political development: reenfranchisement, mobilization, competition, and legitimacy. Judged by voter registration, participation at the polls, campaigning, and officeholding, the overall gains have been impressive. Yet one must remember that these advances have occurred unevenly and at different rates. In some areas blacks already have passed through all four phases of this political cycle, whereas in others they have barely moved beyond reacquiring the suffrage. In most places, southern black political development has fallen somewhere along the spectrum short of full legitimacy. The civil rights movement has never taken root in many locations and has been abandoned prematurely in others; but where it has operated, blacks generally have gained increased influence to affect or power to mold decisions vital to their lives.

However, with the legal barriers to political participation mainly overcome, many African-Americans still have found their economic hardships resistant to cure through the ballot box. Though political empowerment has meant a great deal to most southern blacks, it has been much less successful in lifting the burdens of class from their shoulders. Ironically, the political advances of the civil rights struggle, which have most benefited the burgeoning black middle class, have heightened differences between the most affluent and the more impoverished segments of the black community. This interplay of race and class concerns remains the most vexing issue for both practitioners and students of black politics.

Civil rights proponents have long believed that blacks could not be free without obtaining the right to vote. At the turn of the century, W.E.B. Du Bois set the standard for rejecting racial solutions that excluded the exercise of the franchise. Attacking Booker T. Washington for his strategy of postponing black participation at the ballot box, Du Bois insisted that the right to vote was intimately connected to first-class citizenship. Without it blacks would never command respect, protect themselves, and feel pride in their own race. To Du Bois, a scholar of the freedom struggle after the Civil War, Reconstruction provided vital evidence that black elected officials could transform the lives of their constituents. From this experience they derived the historical lesson, summarized by Eric Foner, that "it was in politics that blacks articulated a new vision of the American state, calling upon government, both national and local, to take upon itself new and unprecedented responsibilities for protecting the civil rights of individual citizens."

The end of Reconstruction and the subsequent disfranchisement of blacks did not extinguish the yearning of African-Americans to regain the right to vote and once again become active political agents. Beginning in 1910, the National Association for the Advancement of Colored People, with Du Bois among its leaders, launched a judicial attack on various techniques aimed at depriving southern blacks of their ballots. Following an early victory against the grandfather clause, the association waged a protracted campaign that eventually succeeded in overturning the white primary in 1944. By gaining a voice in the process of choosing candidates in the one-party Democratic South, blacks secured access to the only election that counted. Assessing the potential implications of this decision, a prominent black lawyer concluded that the "Supreme Court released and galvanized democratic forces which in turn gave the South the momentum it needed toward ultimate leadership in American liberalism."

Unfortunately this triumph fell short of such optimistic expectations. Instead of the white primary, southern states employed a variety of surrogates—literacy tests, poll taxes, and the discriminatory administration of voter registration procedures—that kept the overwhelming majority of blacks from the ballot box. On both the national and local levels suffragists struggled to remove the remaining political obstacles. In 1957 and 1960 the NAACP, together with its liberal white allies, persuaded Congress to enact legislation challenging discriminatory registration practices. Meanwhile, black southerners themselves were organizing to recover the franchise. NAACP branches filed lawsuits and sponsored voter registration drives and voter education workshops. Independent civic leagues often joined in these enterprises, as did freedom-minded clergy who used their pulpits to preach the virtues of the ballot. When the Reverend Mr. King and his ministerial colleagues formed the Southern Christian Leadership Conference in 1957, they immediately launched a "Crusade for Citizenship" to sign up three million new voters in two years.

The long history of the struggle to obtain the right to vote suggests the strength of the consensus of civil rights advocates that reenfranchisement constituted the decisive step toward political equality. Participation at the polls was expected to yield the kinds of basic benefits that groups exercising the franchise customarily enjoyed. Yet for black Americans much more was at stake. With their systematic exclusion from the electoral process, the simple acquisition of the vote constituted an essential element of liberation from enforced racial subordination. The political scientist Charles V. Hamilton, who studied the voting rights struggle both as a participant and scholar, found this passion for the ballot very understandable. "White America had spent so much effort denying the vote to blacks," he observed, "that there was good reason to believe that they must be protecting some tool of vast importance. Perhaps it was reasonable to put so much emphasis on the one fundamental process that clearly distinguished first-class from second-class citizens."

In focusing on reenfranchisement, blacks sought to validate the principles of the American creed. To this extent, their aims were easily comprehensible to white Americans. By working for the suffrage, blacks committed themselves to the established rules of electoral politics, thereby seeking to make them work in their own behalf. Rather than attempting to overthrow the liberal ideology of republican self-government, black suffragists tried to gain admission to the democratic polity as an equal participant. As long as they moved in this direction, social change, by implication, would be seen as coming from the ballot box rather than from the barrel of a gun. In emphasizing the vote, therefore, blacks tacitly agreed to enter a political contract with the ruling order. Grievances could be settled slowly, peacefully, and with little disruption. Armed with the ballot, blacks would achieve respect and begin to compete for the fruits of the equal opportunity previously denied them.

Yet while sharing the values of liberal democracy, some black suffragists also held a more radical vision of political emancipation. The Student Nonviolent Coordinating Committee survived less than a decade, but it had a profound effect on shaping an alternative approach to black political empowerment. Founded in 1960, SNCC operated mainly in the rural, black-belt areas of the South, where racial oppression usually was most extreme and well entrenched. Living amid abject poverty and vigilante violence, SNCC field-workers came to see the ballot more as a means of transforming existing political institutions than as merely gaining access to them. They viewed the suffrage not as an end in itself but as an instrument for organizing local communities. Through voter registration efforts, SNCC members hoped to identify indigenous leaders who could then mobilize friends and neighbors to join in actively addressing the issues directly affecting them. Their vision of participatory democracy was premised on collective involvement in determining policies. In SNCC's scheme of community-oriented decision making, political governance signified more than the right of individuals to cast an unfettered vote; it meant the power of the group to define and execute its own agenda.

Those touched by SNCC and recruited for grass-roots leadership shared both traditional and radical notions of the suffrage. They combined a faith in the possibility of the ballot's potential to improve their individual lives with the hope that it would enable them to collaborate in overcoming their oppression. Bob Moses, SNCC's architect of voter registration in Mississippi during the early 1960s, built his community-organizing approach around the suffrage, because "every person, every black person, felt it was right." He believed strongly that civil rights organizers should take their cues from local people, who would then respond more favorably to their efforts. A seventy-year-old minister in Greenwood, Mississippi, experienced a personal transformation in reaching the decision to become a registered voter. "I am tired of being a second-class citizen," he told a SNCC field-worker. "All of my life I have wanted to go [to register] and I ain't been able to. I am glad you are here. I am going to register to vote." Fannie Lou Hamer, who in 1962 had been evicted from her job on a plantation in Sunflower County, Mississippi, for attempting to register, ruminated on the relationship between racial esteem and the ballot. Before she obtained the franchise, she said, "some white folks . . . would drive past your house in a pickup truck with guns hanging up on the back and give you hate stares." But now this had changed because she and the majority of blacks in her community had become empowered to vote. In words that echoed Du Bois's views half a century earlier, she asserted: "These same [white] people now call me Mrs. Hamer, because they respect people who respect themselves."

Voter registration campaigns connected electoral and protest politics. Though in the early days SNCC's members split over the relative merits of conducting direct-action demonstrations and canvassing for black suffrage enrollment, the distinction between the two rapidly faded. In many areas of the Deep South, registration drives themselves became a form of mass protest. In the rural black belt and in cities like Birmingham, Alabama, attempting to register voters led to violent white responses. Mass marches then ensued and produced confrontations and arrests that focused a national spotlight to their plight. In fact, voter registration drives brought civil rights activists into closer contact with individuals than was usually the case in protest demonstrations. Franchise workers went directly into people's homes, where they observed firsthand the daily problems of racism and poverty. Thus, as a vehicle for rallying blacks to engage white racism directly and expose it to public scrutiny, voter registration drives took their place alongside sit-ins, freedom rides, and other forms of nonviolent protest.

Electoral politics also reinforced a variety of protest tactics. The Montgomery bus boycott of 1955, for instance, was preceded by increased black voter registration and participation. Black ballots had begun to influence the outcome of some local contests and raise expectations about the improvements that voting would bring. When the pressure of the black vote failed to convince white officials to resolve the bus problem voluntarily, black political activists like E.D. Nixon and Jo Ann Robinson took the lead in organizing the boycott. Similarly, in 1957 in Tuskegee, Alabama, those most actively involved in voter registration activities launched a boycott to protest a racially motivated legislative gerrymander. Three years later, the sit-in movement began in Greensboro, North Carolina, a city that several years earlier had elected a black man to serve on the municipal council. The successful sit-ins, August Meier observed, "almost invariably occurred in places where Negroes formed a significant share of registered voters." Electoral activities helped to heighten awareness among blacks that they could organize to challenge Jim Crow. Yet scholars have scarcely explored the connection between the two. For example, under what conditions did local blacks redirect their energies away from conventional political efforts at the polls to direct-action protests in the streets?

Combining protest and electoral activities, civil rights proponents thus waged more than a moral struggle; they conducted a political movement. They did not limit their appeals to matters of conscience but depended on the political techniques at their disposal to force changes in the status quo. Persuasion without provocation was not enough, and conversion without power did not work. As Adam Fairclough has written about Dr. King, the civil rights leader "explicitly rejected the notion that blacks . . . could overcome their subjugation through ethical appeals and rational argument: they also needed an effective means of pressure." As a political struggle, the civil rights movement, through protest, electoral activity, or a combination of the two, attempted to exert the necessary force to restructure power relationships between the races.

Inevitably, the reenfranchisement of black southerners gave impetus to the political mobilization of African-Americans. The hundreds of voter registration drives throughout the South in the early 1960s, especially under the auspices of the Voter Education Project, succeeded in signing up some 688,000 black registrants. The proportion of eligible blacks registered jumped from approximately 29 percent in 1962 to 43 percent two years later. Subsequently, the battle to register blacks in Selma, Alabama, in the face of severe repression by obstructionist white officials focused national attention on the distress of the disfranchised throughout Dixie and culminated in the passage of the Voting Rights Act of 1965. Having won this landmark piece of legislation through the persistent pressure of collective action, blacks could not take their hard-earned voting rights for granted. Rather, they had to continue mobilizing people to register and go to the polls in order to gain real power.

The Voting Rights Act suspended literacy tests in specified jurisdictions and provided the federal government with the option of dispatching examiners to register blacks in designated counties in seven southern states. This landmark law produced dramatic results. Within four years about three-fifths of the eligible black population managed to register. Nevertheless, Washington left the job of promoting voter registration to the civil rights organizations that had done so in the past, placing a heavy burden on grass-roots civil rights organizations.

Although civil rights groups lacked adequate finances and personnel to complete the task, they had created the foundation for mobilizing the black electorate. For generations the South had buttressed its structural obstacles to voting with extralegal violence and intimidation, creating a well-founded fear among blacks concerning the costs of trying to become involved in politics. Civil rights associations provided a source of solidarity, a sense that individuals did not have to feel so alone and vulnerable in the face of danger; consequently, they helped to reduce the level of fear to manageable proportions. This, in turn, boosted black confidence in removing the political barriers that impeded racial advancement.

The campaigns yielded impressive results. After 1965 the gap between white and black registration shrank. In 1966 the proportion of adult whites registered in the seven states originally covered by the Voting Rights Act exceeded that of blacks by a margin of nearly 30 percent; in 1982 the differential had closed to an average of about 9 percent. The estimated difference in turnout in presidential elections was even less. In 1968 black participation in the South lagged behind whites' by 10 percent, but in 1984 blacks trailed by only 5 percent.

Even more striking than the narrowing of this racial divide, blacks actually engaged in political activities at a much higher rate than would have been predicted from their socioeconomic profile. Because a larger portion of blacks than whites occupied the lower end of the income and educational scales, they lacked the resources usually associated with high levels of political involvement. Yet blacks showed a greater incidence of political participation compared with whites of similar socioeconomic status.

This surprising finding can be attributed in large measure to the heightened black consciousness aroused by the civil rights movement. Collective action had demonstrated the power of oppressed groups to reshape their political world, and the racial pride that developed convinced blacks that politics concerned them as much as it did whites. In Mississippi, where the black registration figure jumped from 6 percent in 1964 to 60 percent in 1971, a black observer touring the Magnolia State remarked "that we are casting aside the feelings of inferiority and shame and realizing what a strong and beautiful people we are." In conducting voter registration drives, erecting citizenship schools, holding mock elections, and directing protests, civil rights groups mobilized black southerners, many of them impoverished and poorly educated, to overcome these handicaps and band together for increased political action.

Along with the civil rights movement, the federal government also played a significant role in galvanizing group consciousness and black political mobilization. The power of Washington in economic and diplomatic affairs had expanded steadily during the New Deal and World War II; from 1944 on, the civil rights movement diverted some of that influence to the cause of racial equality. Reformers aimed to tip the balance of power in the federal system from the southern states to the national government. Because the states typically regulated the areas of education, public accommodations, law enforcement, and voter registration requirements, civil rights groups needed federal force to destroy racist practices in the South. Demonstrations were designed to disturb the racial peace, create crises, and compel federal intervention on the side of civil rights protesters. Generally, this strategy worked. Presidents John F. Kennedy and Lyndon B. Johnson helped convince liberal foundations to sponsor and sustain the most important collaborative suffrage enterprise in the South, The Voter Education Project, which joined the NAACP, SNCC, SCLC, and Congress of Racial Equality. Furthermore, the Justice Department filed suits against discriminatory registration practices, and in 1965 the passage of the Voting Rights Act resulted in the enrollment of the majority of blacks.

The extension of federal responsibility that emerged out of the civil rights struggle carried over to the implementation of legislation as well. After the Supreme Court interpreted the Voting Rights Act as ranging beyond unfair voter registration procedures to the prohibition of discriminatory election procedures, the federal bureaucracy expanded its surveillance of the South and began investigating the biased use of at-large elections, multimember districts, reapportionment, and municipal annexations. Under the 1965 law, all changes in electoral rules had to be submitted to the Justice Department for approval. Despite the increasingly conservative outlook of successive presidential administrations in the 1970s and 1980s, voting rights enforcement became an institutionalized and regular feature of the political process. Scholars disagree about whether the Justice Department's civil rights overseers have monitored discriminatory electoral practices strongly enough, but there is little doubt that government officials scrutinized state action to a degree unthought of a generation earlier.

Nevertheless, the civil rights movement caused a reallocation of power in the federal system without undermining it. In general, Washington acted cautiously, choosing to interfere in state affairs only as a last resort. The national government refused to intervene to shield civil rights activists from the racist intimidation and terror they experienced on a daily basis in well-known southern locales. Neither federal marshals nor troops stormed into the South until massive violence occurred and it was clear that local officials could not or would not maintain order. Even after passage of the Voting Rights Act, federal registrars went into only some threescore of the most recalcitrant counties, leaving most of Dixie untouched. Furthermore, the Justice Department allowed the overwhelming majority of southern electoral laws submitted for its prior clearance to stand. Whatever increased authority the national government possessed was administered in a spirit of cooperation with the states.

This federal sensitivity to states' rights unintentionally spurred the growth of black consciousness, the driving force behind political mobilization. Ironically, by failing to heed the appeals of suffrage workers for increased federal protection in the South, a move that would have shifted law enforcement from local to national hands, Washington radicalized civil rights activists. Disappointment with white liberals prompted some of the most dedicated civil rights proponents to rethink their strategy and goals. Out of this reexamination, groups such as SNCC and CORE moved away from supporting integration with whites to building autonomous political bases within their own communities. This emphasis on black power, whatever negative, antiwhite connotations it carried, reflected the positive growth of heightened black solidarity. The black power impulse served to mobilize the newly enfranchised to become politically active and advance their collective racial interests.

With federal law guaranteeing reenfranchisement and black racial consciousness becoming increasingly politicized, African-Americans sought to compete for electoral power. In the past, the minority of southern blacks who had the freedom to vote, including those in scattered cities like Atlanta, Durham, and Tuskegee, used their ballots to support moderate white candidates against their race-baiting opponents. Now as a result of the increased availability of the suffrage and the intense struggle needed to secure it, black southerners looked to members of their own race to represent their interests. This was especially true in areas with a large number of blacks among the eligible voters, where the chances of electing a black candidate were high. Just as acquisition of the ballot furnished a necessary step toward advancing first-class citizenship, so too did the election of blacks serve as a badge of equality. "A race of people excluded from public office," a black political leader in South Carolina asserted, "will always be second class." The running of black candidates both reflected growing racial pride and presented a stimulus to further black political mobilization. The election of a black candidate to a post in a rural county in Mississippi, the winner declared, "will give the Negro race the feeling . . . like they can progress, and this in itself [will make] more people run for public office."

The extension of the suffrage and the racial esteem that accompanied it broke the hold of whites over selecting black political leaders and setting their agendas. According to Louis Martin, a prominent black journalist and presidential adviser, the Voting Rights Act ushered in a new breed of minority politician who understood "that political power is generated in the black precincts and does not come from the hands of the great white father." Many of the black contestants and elected officials had participated in some aspect of the civil rights struggle and viewed their role as an extension of the movement. In contrast to the white officials they challenged or replaced, they typically considered politics an arena for continuing the transformation of black communities that the civil rights movement had sparked. As Fannie Lou

Hamer put it, she expected black officials to respond "to human needs" and "save [their] people."

However, the transition from civil rights to electoral politics did not necessarily move this smoothly. Mass demonstrations depended on emotional appeals, tended to be episodic, and soon lapsed after resolution of the particular crisis. In contrast, the competition for public office, as a political scientist has observed, "is more mundane and requires both long-term political skills and the ability to consistently draw the black electorate." Candidates had to get elected by spending long hours campaigning door-to-door and shepherding large numbers of people to the polls. Once elected, they had to master the techniques of bargaining and compromise, often settling for solutions hammered more out of pragmatism than morality. Despite the humanistic concerns they often brought to their positions, black elected officials had to accommodate to the constraints imposed upon them by the political system they entered.

Operating within these limitations, black public officials nonetheless achieved notable accomplishments. Their candidacies stimulated increased black political mobilization, and their elections have provided significant minority access to city halls and county courthouses, where most black officials hold power. They also succeeded in opening up jobs and allocating government contracts to their black constituents, improving the quality of municipal services, and reducing racist rhetoric and violence. Reaping tangible and symbolic gains, they helped tear down the psychological and physical walls that kept blacks in confinement. A retired worker in Tuskegee, Alabama, clearly recognized the difference they made: "Everything's better. In the old days, before black officials ran the county, most black people steered clear of white enclaves. They used to arrest you over there if you went through," but not anymore.

Still, the attainments have fallen short of the needs. Perhaps the limitations of the ballot were clearer to black officeholders than to those who put them in office. As Richard Arrington, the black mayor of Birmingham, Alabama, remarked, "there are the expectations of the black community that expects you to do more than you can do." In most cities and counties of the South (and the rest of the country as well) black elected officials have been in the minority and thus could not deliver political rewards without the cooperation of white colleagues. Even in those rural, black-belt areas where blacks controlled a majority of government positions, the blacks lacked the economic resources to affect significantly the material conditions of the impoverished population. Even in more prosperous major cities presided over by black mayors, such as Atlanta, Birmingham, and New Orleans, economic power remained in white hands. "Blacks have the ballot box," an Atlanta newspaper editor admitted, "and whites have the money." Consequently, urban black politicians aligned with white businessmen to promote downtown redevelopment projects and gentrification of their cities, resulting in the displacement of poor residents from their neighborhoods, making it harder for them to find adequate housing and jobs.

The failure to achieve further success stemmed in part from the inability of blacks to win a greater share of elected positions. The number of black elected officials in Dixie has skyrocketed since 1965, leaping from less than 75 in 1965 to 3,685 in 1987. Yet, of the more than 80,000 elected officials in the former Confederate states, only 4.6 percent were black by the latter year, far less than the proportion of blacks in the population of the region. Moreover, in twenty-one of eighty counties where blacks constituted a majority of the population in the original seven states covered by the Voting Rights Act, no member of their race held elective office in 1980.

Reenfranchised southern blacks failed to realize their electoral potential for a variety of reasons. In some places, they had not yet acquired the economic resources and political skills to mount effective campaigns. The civil rights movement, which had been so instrumental in mobilizing political participation, scarcely operated in many areas of the South and failed to stay long enough in others. Furthermore, blacks encountered resistance from whites who attempted to weaken the strength of their newly acquired ballots. The existence of such electoral procedures as at-large elections and multimember districts diluted minority voting power, making it more difficult for blacks to elect representatives of their own choosing.

The numerical underrepresentation of black elected officials did not necessarily leave them without important political leverage. If they wished, blacks could use their votes to help elect white representatives and gain concessions from them. Indeed, increased black electoral participation served to make outspoken racist appeals in political contests a thing of the past and forced aspiring white candidates to campaign for black ballots. However, black citizens wanted not only influence but power, a condition they associated with the election of African-Americans to represent their communities.

This issue of fair representation brought to the surface tensions within the civil rights coalition over individual versus group-centered goals. "At a time of rising civil rights consciousness," the political scientist Abigail M. Thermstrom commented, "the question of proper representation for at least certain groups—those defined by race, ethnicity, and political marginality—was bound to arise." The Voting Rights Act furnished the opportunity for blacks to cast their ballots, but it did not guarantee their election. Traditionally, liberals believed that the chief aims of the civil rights struggle were to eliminate discriminatory barriers to equality under the law and to utilize the Constitution as a color-blind instrument. Having achieved these goals with the legislative victories of the 1960s, many whites deserted the civil rights coalition in opposition to race-conscious entitlements that treated blacks not as individuals but as members of a historically exploited group. With respect to the franchise, critics of affirmative action policies worried that "categorizing individuals for political purposes along lines of race and sanctioning group membership as a qualification for office may inhibit political integration." According to this view, as long as blacks were free to cast their votes and influence the outcome of elections, the constitutional guarantee of equal opportunity for all citizens was fulfilled.

In contrast, civil rights leaders redefined liberal norms. While eschewing advocacy of official quotas mandating proportional representation, they argued that in a society in whose institutions racism persisted, it was appropriate to fashion remedies that took race into account. It did not suffice to give blacks the right to vote and then tolerate supposedly neutral electoral rules that had the effect of diluting the impact of their ballots. Forged through collective action, the communitarian outlook of the freedom struggle shaped blacks' political aspirations. For most of American history elected positions had been reserved for whites by virtue of their race. After years of struggle and sacrifice, African-Americans claimed legal and moral justifications for a larger share of the electoral representation than they possessed.

Blacks also waged this battle for representation within the structure of the Democratic party. Though not entirely successful, they managed to pry open its doors to more extensive black participation. They accomplished this as a direct consequence of the civil rights movement in the South. In 1964, when the SNCC-inspired Mississippi Freedom Democratic party contested for delegate seats at the Democratic national convention, it set in motion a process that transformed the party organization. The MFDP did not gain official recognition that year, but national party leaders promised to bar discrimination within their southern ranks and to ensure that blacks had ample opportunity to participate in the selection of Democratic functionaries in the future. In 1968 party leaders kept their word and awarded seats at the convention to a biracial delegation from Mississippi, as well as to those from several other southern states. Within the next four years, reform reached its peak as the party adopted affirmative action guidelines requiring "representation of minority groups on the national convention delegation in reasonable relationship to the group's presence in the population of the State."

The effects were impressive. In four years the percentage of black convention delegates had more than doubled, to 14.6 percent. For the most part, the delegations at the 1972 convocation containing the highest ratio of blacks came from states designated by the Voting Rights Act. Mississippi led the way with 56 percent, and in each of the covered states the proportion of black representatives equaled or exceeded the percentage of blacks in the population. The Democratic party had been so much altered by the addition of blacks and other traditionally underrepresented groups, such as women and young people, that one older, white male delegate could barely recognize it. "I never thought I'd see the day," he exclaimed, "that middle-aged white males would be our biggest minority." Though the figures for black delegate representation dropped at subsequent conventions, they continued to reflect the greatly increased presence of blacks in the Democratic party—and nowhere more then in the land of Dixie, the center of the civil rights movement.

As blacks gained increased representation in governmental and partisan institutions, minority participation in the political process acquired added legitimacy. Where African-Americans won public office, including those instances where they captured a majority of the available positions, whites generally accepted the validity of their rule. This is not to suggest that whites completely abandoned their efforts to hamper or subvert blacks from exercising power, especially in those rural, black-belt counties of the South traditionally most hostile to racial equality. But in most locales whites either resigned themselves to or actively cooperated with black governance. White businessmen found black officials supportive of their plans for economic modernization, and because of their overwhelming population advantage in most communities and in every state, whites learned that fears of living under black domination had been greatly exaggerated. For those whites who refused to concede the legitimacy of black political rights, the enforcement of the Voting Rights Act kept their resistance in check.

Yet white cooperation with black participation in the political process stemmed from more than self-interest or federal coercion. Segregationists had an increasingly difficult time defending disfranchisement in a political culture that considered the right to vote essential to republican government and that viewed restrictions founded on race as unacceptable. It was true that basic principles of the democratic ethos had not changed between the end of Reconstruction and the beginning of World War II, the period during which the South had encountered relatively little opposition from the national government in circumventing the guarantees of the Fifteenth Amendment. However, the subsequent wartime struggle against Nazi fascism and the ensuing Cold War campaigns to line up nonwhite nations behind America's anti-Soviet foreign policy helped undermine the racist premises upon which black disfranchisement had been sustained in the South. Furthermore, whereas other civil rights issues like school desegregation and fair employment generated serious disagreement, protection of the suffrage encountered fewer objections. Clearly, the struggle for enfranchisement produced legislative conflicts in Washington and fierce hostility in the South, but overall, Americans accepted the principle of majority rule and the sanctity of free elections. In sum, whites have largely recognized the legitimacy of black political representation, as Peter Eisinger noted, "by explaining it as a product of democratic processes" and the norms of fair play.

At the same time, by adopting electoral competition as the chief means of pursuing racial advancement, African-Americans have stamped their own legitimacy on the established political order. With ballots in hand, blacks resorted less often to the kinds of protest activities that were the only methods available for influencing policy when they were disfranchised. "Black political participation," one observer declared, "is to the civil rights movement what the protest movement was in the 1960s." In this vein, elected officials became "the principal agents of implementation" of the benefits blacks obtained through the political system. As a consequence, more disruptive forms of agitation seemed anachronistic. "There was no longer a need to march in the streets against the policies of big city mayors," Manning Marable concluded, "because blacks were now in virtually every municipal administration across the nation."

The process of black political legitimization has further served to absorb into the electoral mainstream some of the most radical impulses of the civil rights era. The experience of the Mississippi Freedom Democratic party provides a case in point. As the organizers of the MFDP conceived of this group, it represented economically dispossessed sharecroppers and domestic workers. Reflecting the philosophy of SNCC, they did not just desire delegate recognition from the national Democratic party; rather they sought also to transform political and economic relations in the Magnolia State. "We want to be in on the ground level, where the decisions are made about us," Bob Moses asserted. "We don't want to [be] mobilized every four years to vote. We want to be in the actual running of things." Their challenge rejected in 1964, they did see blacks gain representation in the Democratic party, albeit in altered form. In 1968 the biracial Loyalist delegation that gained the seats at the national convention consisted of fewer MFDP veterans than four years before. They had been replaced by more moderate blacks and whites. By the end of the 1970s, this Loyalist faction exchanged its national recognition for incorporation with the mostly white Democratic regulars, who controlled the party apparatus within Mississippi. Little remained of the original spirit or membership of the MFDP by the time of fusion. Although unity accorded blacks acceptance as political partners within the Democratic party, the progressive goals that the early civil rights militants had envisioned remained unfulfilled.

As the influence of protesters gave way to the power of professional politicians, black elected officials increasingly entered coalitions with whites. At the local level, in those places where blacks constituted a majority of the electorate they needed fewer white votes to triumph. Nevertheless, throughout the South (as well as the North), blacks needed white allies to govern effectively. Where African-Americans had numerical strength, they still lacked control of economic resources. Without the cooperation of white businessmen and financiers—and this was as true in rural Lowndes County, Alabama, as in metropolitan Atlanta, Georgia—black officials could not raise the funds to carry out their programs. Consequently, they had to devise policies to improve black living conditions without threatening white community elites. For example, in 1981 Birmingham mayor Richard Arrington explained: "What I had to decide as mayor was not whether I was going to pursue civil rights goals, but how to do it. If I alienated all the white leadership, I began to realize that it was going to be twice as hard to achieve the goals."

Under such circumstances, whites often played a pivotal role in shaping black politics. As black candidates began competing with each other in areas containing black majorities, the minority white electorate helped determine the outcome. In Atlanta and New Orleans, for example, some victorious black officials have failed to win a majority of black votes but clinched their election by capturing the bulk of white ballots. These politicians faced the delicate task of representing black interests without offending the whites who had tipped the balance of electoral power in their favor. In many areas of the South, particularly in small towns and rural areas, blacks still assumed that whites only voted for blacks to manipulate and control them. In one such hamlet, a losing black candidate expressed his skepticism about his black opponent who received most of the white votes: "Doc is not classified as black to me. You black when black folks elect you. White folks don't vote for black folks."

At the state level, where blacks everywhere were in the minority, they necessarily had to forge coalitions with whites. In most instances this meant black support for white candidates; in the former Confederacy, only in Virginia has a black won statewide election to the top executive post of governor. Blacks won a rising share of seats in state legislatures, but they remained outnumbered by white lawmakers and therefore had to form biracial alliances to obtain benefits for their constituents. As a rule, they have joined forces with moderate white "New South" politicians, who supported both desegregation and the expansion of industrial and commercial ventures. These policies favored middle-class whites and blacks, leaving the poor of both races behind. In general, the representatives of impoverished blacks and whites failed to construct biracial coalitions along common class lines. As in the past, very different perspectives on race continued to divide those most economically depressed. A recent study by a team of political scientists confirmed this point: "Nearly all . . . white subgroups opposed the positions on current racial issues that are preferred by majorities of southern blacks."

Yet the widespread participation of black voters in the South also altered the racist outlook of the Democratic party in the region. With the growth of the Republican party within Dixie and its appeal among conservative white voters, Democratic politicos scrambled for black votes to compensate for white flight from their ranks. A senior Democratic officeholder in Mississippi remarked: "When the blacks stay with the Democrats, we can just about win, but when they leave, we can't." In return for this support, white southern Democratic lawmakers increasingly took positions favorable to their black constituents. The shift in backing for civil rights legislation was especially striking. In 1975 and 1982 southern white Democratic congressmen lined up solidly behind renewal of the Voting Rights Act, reversing the situation of a decade earlier when the overwhelming majority had opposed the measure. In 1987 the defeat of Robert Bork for nomination to the Supreme Court hinged on the refusal of key southern Democratic senators to approve it. Blacks perceived Bork's judicial philosophy as endangering the civil rights advances they had so recently made. As Senator Richard C. Shelby of Alabama, who owed his election to the black electorate, declared: "In the South, we've made a lot of progress. We do not want to go back and revisit old issues."

At the same time, white southern Democrats still tended to be more conservative on economic and class-related issues than their northern counterparts. The significance of the black electorate notwithstanding, whites composed from three-quarters to over four-fifths of the registered voters in the South. With the changing racial complexion of his party, a white Democratic official from South Carolina warned about the perils of ignoring this white majority. "Within a short time," he remarked in early 1988, "we could be a black party in the South, deserted by the whites, a band of hopeless people waiting for favors from Washington." To defeat Republicans, the Democrats had to hold onto the bulk of black votes while obtaining a substantial minority of white electors. Because whites held much more conservative opinions than did most blacks, Democratic politicians had to balance their positions somewhere between the liberal and conservative ends of the spectrum. As a result, successful southern white Democrats typically cast themselves as moderates.

In the American political system, perhaps the ultimate sign of legitimacy comes in the presidential arena. In this respect, the campaigns of Jesse L. Jackson for the Democratic nomination in 1984 and 1988 indicated the arrival of blacks as active agents in national electoral politics. In the past, the black electorate had contributed winning margins to Democratic standard-bearers—most recently for Jimmy Carter in 1976. But never before had a black candidate mounted as strong a challenge for the top office in the land as did Jackson. Building upon a solid foundation of black votes, especially in the South, Jackson attempted to fashion what all national politicians must ultimately create: a winning coalition. For him this meant an alliance with whites as well as with other exploited minorities. Though Jackson's campaigns emerged from the tradition of protest and reenfranchisement in the civil rights era South, they have become part of the respectable electoral mainstream. His platform included not only social and economic issues of special interest to blacks but also foreign and domestic policies that mattered to whites. Born out of the reawakened racial consciousness of the freedom movement, the Jackson candidacies tried to construct a "Rainbow Coalition" that united people of all races around common economic and political concerns. His two defeats notwithstanding, the Reverend Mr. Jackson helped confer on black political aspirations a renewed measure of legitimacy.

Despite some splendid accomplishments, the acquisition and utilization of the ballot did not solve some fundamental problems. The ballot has proved a necessary but insufficient tool for achieving racial equality in theory as well as practice, and black political power is wider than it is deep. Entry into politics had limited effectiveness in relieving the economic distress that blacks endured disproportionately to their presence in the population. Whereas the poverty rate among black families declined over the decade of the 1970s (from 41 percent to 30 percent), the percentage of impoverished blacks was still more than four times that of whites (7 percent). Blacks experienced a higher incidence of unemployment than did whites, and the figures for young black male adults reached depression-era levels. In Lowndes County, Alabama, one of the first places in the rural South where blacks came to political power, their median family income rose slightly in comparison with that of white residents (from 33 percent to 41 percent); nevertheless, the median family income of blacks, $7,443, trailed far behind that of whites, $18,350. Accordingly, in 1985 the black sheriff of the county, John Hulett, summed up the obvious lesson: "Until people become economically strong, political power alone won't do. For most people, it's like it was sixteen years ago."

The economic news was not all bad. Expanding opportunities resulting from desegregation and affirmative action programs swelled the size of the black middle class. From this group, with its access to economic resources and educational skills, new black political leaders emerged. Only recently risen from the lower rungs of the economic ladder, these middle-class black politicians tended to identify with the plight of those less fortunate. In addition, their newfound upward mobility was not entirely secure, and they remained more vulnerable than their white counterparts to downswings in the economy. For this reason and because they were products of the same emancipatory forces that shaped the racial consciousness of poor blacks, middle-class blacks continued to share with them mutual concerns associated with race.

In the long run, this growing class stratification in black communities may erode racial solidarity, though to what extent remains unclear. During the civil rights era, southern blacks, no matter what their economic class, encountered a monolithic structure of racial segregation. Conflicts over tactics and strategy existed among various civil rights organizations, but they usually managed to subordinate their rivalries to the common fight against Jim Crow and disfranchisement. Having achieved many of their aims, blacks became freer to divide politically along conventional lines of class, section, generation, and gender. Even Jesse Jackson's presidential bid in 1984 failed to unite black elected officials. Those black politicians most closely tied to national Democratic party affairs were more likely to support one of the established white candidates in the primaries than those who operated chiefly on the local political stage and supported Jackson, the acknowledged outsider. The degree to which the political cleavage among blacks is occurring and the forces behind it offer rich possibilities for future research.

This process of fragmentation was slowed down by the enduring significance of race in American politics. The United States has not yet become a color-blind society, and race looms large as a category for determining political choices. Public opinion surveys indicated that blacks and whites disagreed sharply over a broad range of policy issues, especially those that deal with federal efforts to reverse the economic and social effects of past racial discrimination and seem to give preferential treatment to blacks. "Even those blacks who have 'made it' economically," Thomas Cavanagh reported, "are more likely to support the views of poor blacks than those of well-to-do whites." Furthermore, racial polarization accompanied reenfranchisement. The emergence of southern blacks into the electorate initially sparked a political countermobilization of southern whites to sign up to vote. While blacks flocked into the Democratic party in the South, whites deserted to the Republican party and joined newly transplanted northerners to turn it into a competitive force in the traditionally one-party region. In presidential elections, a majority of white southerners have not supported a

Democratic presidential candidate since 1964, in contrast to the over-whelming mass of black voters. In addition, this sharp racial split at the polls also existed in local contests where black and white candidates directly competed against each other.

10

REAGAN
REVOLUTION?

In 1980, Ronald Reagan, a former movie actor and two-term California governor, capitalized on voter dissatisfaction with incumbent Jimmy Carter to score a stunning triumph in the presidential election. Promising to lower taxes, raise military spending, and cut wasteful social programs, Reagan won 489 electoral votes to Carter's 49, and helped his party make major gains in Congress. For some observers, Reagan's victory represented the demise of the New Deal coalition and inevitable triumph of Richard Nixon's conservative majority. "Like a great soaking wet shaggy dog, the Silent Majority—banished from the house during the Watergate storms—romped back into the nation's parlor this week and shook itself vigorously," observed William Safire.

The new President moved quickly to push Congress to enact the major pieces of his conservative agenda. In May 1981, the president pushed through Congress a budget resolution that called for deep cuts in many social programs and increased spending for the military. In August, Congress passed Reagan's tax plan which included a 25 percent reduction in tax rates over three years. Some observers favorably compared Reagan's success in enacting his conservative agenda to Roosevelt's achievement during the early days of the New Deal. "With a gift for political theater, Mr. Reagan has established his goals faster, communicated a greater sense of economic urgency and come forward with more comprehensive proposals than any new president since the first 100 days of Franklin D. Roosevelt," concluded one journalist.[1]

Though many commentators applauded Reagan's legislative skill, many questioned the wisdom of his policies. Liberals charged that Reagan's tax policy favored the rich while his budget cuts hurt the poor. "Under the Reagan dispensation, shame is banished, greed enshrined, and the political supremacy of private wealth celebrated as frankly as it was in the Gilded Age," declared the partisan *New Republic*.[2] Critics also charged that the President's expanded military spending created crippling budget deficits, while his lax enforcement of civil rights and environmental rules reduced the quality of life of millions of Americans. Conservatives, on the other hand, praised the President for revitalizing the economy, stifling inflation, cutting unnecessary regulation, and restoring a sense of pride in government.

Because his administration ended so recently, it is impossible to evaluate Reagan's long-term impact. Will the Republican majority that he forged signal the beginning of an enduring conservative coalition? What impact will the budget deficits have on the nation's economy in the 1990s? Will Reagan's conservative judicial appointees rewrite laws on affirmative action and abortion?

In the selections that follow, two insightful observers attempt to assess Reagan and his presidency. Lou Cannon, a *Washington Post* reporter who followed Reagan from his early days in California politics to his last day in the White House, shows how Reagan's early career in Hollywood shaped his presidency. Cannon depicts the president's fantasy world which "had been created in Hollywood, out of material he brought with him from the Middle West." Kevin Phillips, an influential political advisor to Richard Nixon, argues that however uninformed the president may have been, his policies had a dramatic impact on American society. By favoring society's most fortunate, Reagan widened the cleavage between rich and poor. "The 1990s," he wrote, "were a triumph of upper America."

---

[1]Steven R. Weisman, "Reagan's First 100 Days," *New York Times Magazine* (April 216, 1981), 23.
[2]"The New Gilded Age," *New Republic* (August 15, 1981), 5–6.

President Reagan:
The Role of a Lifetime

LOU CANNON

Lou Cannon, who covered the White House for the *Washington Post*, is the author of two best selling books about Ronald Reagan. His most recent book, *President Reagan: The Role of a Lifetime*, received wide praise for its comprehensive and balanced treatment of the Reagan presidency. Cannon benefited from nearly a quarter century of covering Reagan, and from the close cooperation of many of the President's key advisors. The result is an insightful and critical analysis of the inner-workings of the Reagan White House. How did Reagan's experience in Hollywood influence his conduct in office?

And believe me, Bedtime for Bonzo *made more sense than what they were doing in Washington.*

—RONALD REAGAN, MAY 25, 1982

Ronald Reagan's cinematic visions and theatrical gifts were better suited to the grander stage of Washington than to Sacramento. He had skated through as governor, relying on his charm and negotiating skills and upon aides who had survived by learning the ways of the legislature. On balance he was a good governor, though not a great one. His second term, which ended in 1974, was marked by constructive welfare, education and tax legislation that owed at least as much to these no-longer-novice aides and to the Democratic leadership of the legislature as to his own abilities. But eight years as governor had taught Reagan that he performed best when he attended to larger visions. Once he settled in as governor, he became indifferent to the everydayness of government and unconcerned about his lack of fundamental civics knowledge. He learned to let others, particularly Edwin Meese III, do the heavy lifting and to rely upon his directors, as he had done in Hollywood. Reagan saved himself for the big scenes. By the time he reached the White House in 1981, after three tries at the presidency, Reagan felt free to draw upon the themes, examples and anecdotes of his movie days. He had real-life movies in his head and a surer sense of his own role in the production of the Reagan presidency. He knew what he wanted to accomplish, and what he wanted to be. What he wanted to be, and what he became, was an accomplished presidential performer.

Reagan never forgot the gibes about his acting that he endured during his first campaign for public office and periodically throughout his political career. He owed a debt to his acting experience, but he was circumspect about acknowledging it. Not until his final weeks in the White House, when no one any longer cared if he was role-playing, did Reagan publicly discuss the link between his careers as performer and president. ABC's David Brinkley gave him the opportunity a month before he left the White House by asking if he had learned anything as an actor that had been of use to him in the presidency. "There have been times in this office when I've wondered how you could do the job if you hadn't been an actor," Reagan replied. The comment amused Nancy Reagan, who had heard it many times before. And it prompted Reagan's friend George Will to write, "I do not know precisely what he meant, and he probably doesn't either, but he was on to something." What Reagan was on to, in Will's view, was the importance of the "theatrical element" in politics, an awareness, Will said, that Reagan shared with such democratic leaders as Churchill, de Gaulle and Franklin Roosevelt and with such dictators as Hitler, Mussolini and Castro.

While a theatrical element certainly permeated the Reagan presidency, "being an actor" meant more to Reagan than theatrics. Unlike the leaders cited by Will, he had practiced acting as a vocation and allowed it to become his principal mode of behavior. He had learned to play himself on screen, and he had also learned to remain on camera when the shooting stopped. Furthermore, he thought of actors as among the noblest people on earth. In his early days as a banquet speaker he had served as a self-appointed defense committee for the moral standards of the stars, who he thought had been maligned because of the loose lifestyles of a few celebrities. When I asked Reagan three days before he left the White House what he had meant by his answer to Brinkley, he answered me by hitting the button of an old mental cassette filled with his thoughts on the wholesomeness of Hollywood. A passage of this mental tape is a quotation from a column by Irwin S. Cobb, another defender of the filmland faith, who was chiding someone who had accused actors of taking a "childish approach" to life. With a dreamy smile, Reagan recited Cobb for a small group of reporters in the Oval Office who had been expecting to hear about the achievements of his presidency. "He said, if this be true, and if it also be true that when we approach the final curtain that all men must bear in their arms that which they have given in life, the people of show business will march in the procession carrying in their arms the pure pearl of tears, the gold of laughter and diamonds of stardust they spread on what might otherwise have been a rather dreary world," Reagan said. "And when they reach the final stage door the keeper will say, open, let my children in."

Later, after he had left the White House, I put the Brinkley question to Reagan again. This time he skipped the lyricism and gave a multitude of more specific answers. He said that being an actor had taught him to understand the feelings and motivations of others. He said being an actor had "the practical side" of preparing people to face batteries of cameras and questions from the press. He also claimed that bad reviews and "undeserved criticism" prepared an actor for the rough exchanges of politics, although Reagan could be as thin-skinned and sensitive to criticism as any novice politician. Most important, he said, actors find themselves being called upon to perform on the spot at public gatherings. Reagan, while often dependent on cue cards to discuss the most mundane of issues, was proud of his performances in such moments. He knew what to say when a microphone was thrust at him. Directors could be confident, as television critic Tom Shales observed, that when the camera "cut to reaction shots of Ron and Nancy . . . they'd both be ready with a capital R." Reagan believed, with some insight, that his life as an actor had prepared him for new roles, new challenges and new performances in the world outside Hollywood. "You can't always dictate the stage of life upon which you will perform," he said. But when the spotlight swung to him, Reagan was usually ready.

He also steadily sought new stages. In his moviemaking days Reagan's peers soon recognized that he had interests beyond acting. It showed up in his involvement in the Screen Actors Guild, of which he served as president during six turbulent years. And it showed up, too, in early expeditions into politics for such candidates as Minnesota Democrat Hubert Humphrey, in his first race for the U.S. Senate in 1948, and

Los Angeles Mayor Fletcher Bowron, a nonpartisan officeholder supported by liberals and organized labor in 1953. Even on the movie set, Reagan took a broader interest in what went on than most actors. He learned to see things from a director's viewpoint, and he was interested in staging and lighting techniques. "You knew you weren't talking to a bubblehead," said Fred De Cordova, who directed *Bedtime for Bonzo* and was impressed both with Reagan's interest in public affairs and his conduct on the set. "He would make suggestions as many actors do, but what I found with Ronnie is that the suggestions were helpful and not particularly self-serving. He was willing to give up a line not to help himself but to make the scene play better." De Cordova did not see a potential president in "Ronnie," but he believed that Reagan would graduate from the acting ranks to management, perhaps becoming head of a studio or an executive in a talent agency.

Reagan never lost his interest in production, but he kept it in proportion. White House aides who despaired of ever engaging him in a substantive discussion of issues learned they could involve him by discussing the scripts and scenes of the presidency. As on the set of *Bonzo* and other films, Reagan was willing to express ideas that had the potential of improving the script or the production. But he thought of himself as the leading man, not the producer or the director, and he usually counted on his aides and sometimes on his wife to know what was best for him. Reagan thought in terms of performance, and those closest to him approached his presidency as if it were a series of productions casting Reagan in the starring role. The chief impresario of Reagan's first term as president was Michael K. Deaver, a canny public relations man who had been with Reagan since his first campaign. Operating with the understated title of deputy chief of staff, Deaver became the grand producer of the Reagan presidency. He tried to see to it that the script, staging and lighting of each scene provided Reagan an opportunity to give a smashing performance. Every Deaver decision was based on whether it would show Reagan to best advantage. Deaver lacked Hollywood experience, but he had helped produce the Reagan governorship and knew the strengths and limitations of the leading man. And Deaver was also especially adept at dealing with leading lady Nancy Reagan, whom many in the White House considered a better actor than her husband. One of Deaver's tasks was to see that she was happy with her role in the production but didn't make too many changes in the script.

Deaver's attempt to craft each scene of the Reagan presidency proved contagious. Others who observed that he was successful in his work and highly popular with the Reagans because of it copied his methods, sometimes obsessively. Little was left to chance. Reagan was so fond of the phrase "God bless you" that he would have been apt to say it to an atheist, but aides began writing the line into scripts for closing the most trivial of meetings. Since the words were written down for him, Reagan read them instead of remembering them. The scripts usually were written on "half sheets" of heavy bond paper that in the White House substituted for the four-by-six cards Reagan favored in stump speeches. The words were written in oversize type that compensated for Reagan's severe nearsightedness, which in his campaign days had prompted him to switch on most occasions from three-by-five cards to the four-by-six cards. Overuse of the cards and half sheets was bothersome to old friends, who knew that Reagan ad-libbed easily and did not need a piece of paper in his hand to carry on a serious conversation. But his stage managers recognized that Reagan preferred the comfort of the cue cards, and they saw no reason to take chances. "He was an actor and he worked from a script," said Rhett Dawson, the White House chief of operations in the closing years of the Reagan presidency. "If you gave him a script, he would do it."

Over time the cinematic approach became so woven into the fabric of the Reagan presidency that subordinates schooled in economics or statecraft routinely used Hollywood terminology to direct Reagan in his daily tasks. It could be an unsettling practice to those unaccustomed to it. One White House aide recalls that Secretary of State George P. Shultz, huddling with Reagan in the secure vault of the American ambassador's residence in Moscow during the 1988 summit, coached him for his meeting with Soviet leader Mikhail Gorbachev by telling him what to do "in this scene." Schultz proceeded through a series of precise directions in stage terminology, telling Reagan where to stand and what to say. The aide was horrified that the secretary of state would treat the president as a man who "didn't have the intellectual wherewithal to be able to think or act on his own." But Reagan was not offended. He himself saw the meeting with Gorbachev as a significant performance, and he valued the services of a good director.

White House Chief of Staff Kenneth Duberstein, who saw Reagan safely off the stage in the last act of his presidency, also took a benign view of what he called "the performance part of the presidency." Duberstein, who had worked as congressional liaison under White House Chief of Staff James A. Baker III in the first term, shared De Cordova's view that Reagan was an actor with a larger vision of the role in which he was engaged. Assessing what acting meant to Reagan as president, Duberstein said, "Certainly, it's the communication, the ability to communicate, the ability to find the right words in his prepared speeches. But more times than not, also in his ad libs, to find the right expression or the right anecdote. It is the ability to have people looking at you and you lead comfortably. It is the ability to be assured that sometimes you're playing to a much bigger house than you expected. It is proving yourself each day as an actor, because you have another performance. In the day there are many scenes and you have to get through them. . . . It's welcoming another head of state as another leading actor who is going to share the billing with you, but you know that you always have top billing. It's Reagan graciously sharing top billing. It's how to deal with the bit players in the cameo appearances, and the cameo actors who drift through. It's knowing that there is a final curtain. It's knowing that everything isn't hunky-dory. Sometimes there are tragedies, and you have to do that, too. It's speaking to the families of the Marines who were killed in Lebanon or the families of the soldiers on the USS *Stark*."

Reagan was good at doing all of these things, as even such adversaries as Tip O'Neill acknowledged. But his actor's approach to the presidency required a staff that understood a performer's needs. "You need to have a very strong stage manager-producer-director," said Duberstein, who returned with Howard Baker to the White House in 1987 as part of the production team that sought to salvage the Reagan presidency after the Iran-contra fiasco. "You need to have very good technical men and sound men at all times." When such technical help was lacking, in Duberstein's view, everything "falls apart because the actor-president isn't prepared. He isn't prepared because the people around who are managing, directing, producing are not up to speed and therefore he can't walk into a situation using his years of experience and function effectively."

To those who took a more traditional approach to the presidency, Reagan almost never seemed prepared. He had a handful of bedrock convictions and a knack of charming people of any rank or station. Occasionally, he also demonstrated a useful policy impulse. But Reagan lacked a technical grasp of any issue, and he was usually bored by briefings. While he valued compromises and had the temperament of a negotiator, he rarely knew enough about the substance of a dispute to be able to understand the sticking points. Most of his aides thought of him as intelligent, but many also considered him intellectually lazy. Reagan

wanted, whenever possible, to have the pros and cons of an issue set out
in single-page summaries, dubbed "mini-memos" when his then Chief
of Staff William P. Clark created them in California. He preferred to
have "the boys," as he called the middle-aged and elderly men who
were his advisers, settle differences on issues among themselves and
bring a consensus recommendation to him for approval. When the boys
could not reach a consensus and brought a contentious matter to him
for resolution, he asked few questions and often responded to carefully
constructed arguments with anecdotes, frequently off the point.

Republican congressional leaders found Reagan uninterested in political strategy, although he was always willing to place a call to a waver-
ing congressman if provided with the script of what he ought to say.
What animated Reagan was a public performance. He knew how to edit
a script and measure an audience. He also knew that the screenplay of
his presidency, however complicated it became on the margins, was
rooted in the fundamental themes of lower taxes, deregulation and
"peace through strength" that he had expounded in the antigovernment
speech he had given in 1964 for Goldwater. The Speech was his bible,
and Reagan never tired of giving it. Its themes and Reagan's approach to
government were, as his friend William F. Buckley put it, inherently
anti-statist." When a White House discussion even remotely turned to
the idea that government was too big or too inefficient, Reagan would
participate by drawing examples from the portfolio of antigovernment
horror stories he had accumulated during a quarter century of campaigning. But on other issues, especially when the discussion was over his
head, Reagan's participation was usually limited to jokes and cinematic
illustrations. This is not surprising, as Reagan spent more time at the
movies during his presidency than at anything else. He went to Camp
David on 183 weekends, usually watching two films on each of these
trips. He saw movies in the White House family theater, on television
in the family quarters and in the villas and lavish guest quarters accorded presidents when they travel.

On the afternoon before the 1983 economic summit of the world's
industrialized democracies in Colonial Williamsburg, White House
Chief of Staff James Baker stopped off at Providence Hall, where the
Reagans were staying, bringing with him a thick briefing book on the
upcoming meetings. Baker, then on his way to a tennis game, had carefully checked through the book to see that it contained everything
Reagan needed to know without going into too much detail. He was

concerned about Reagan's performance at the summit, which had attracted hundreds of journalists from around the world and been advertised in advance by the White House as an administration triumph. But when Baker returned to Providence Hall the next morning, he found the briefing book unopened on the table where he had deposited it. He knew immediately that Reagan hadn't even glanced at it, and he couldn't believe it. In an hour Reagan would be presiding over the first meeting of the economic summit, the only one held in the United States during his presidency. Uncharacteristically, Baker asked Reagan why he hadn't cracked the briefing book. "Well, Jim, *The Sound of Music* was on last night," Reagan said calmly.

Nevertheless, Reagan's charm and cue cards carried him through the summit without incident. By the third year of his presidency the leaders of the democracies were also growing accustomed to Reagan's anecdotes and to his cheerful sermons about the wonders of the market system and lower taxes. They were awed at what they saw as his hold on the American people. One regular participant in the annual summits said the other leaders would stare at Reagan with rapt attention when he spoke, as if trying to divine the secret of his success. When the leaders took breaks in their meetings for the inevitable "photo opportunities," they clustered around Reagan so they could be photographed with him. In the halcyon days of his presidency Reagan seemed to have no need of briefing books. And even on those occasions when he read them, he was more apt to find solutions in the movies he watched religiously each weekend in the White House or at Camp David.

Sometimes the movies and the briefing books pointed in the same direction. By mid-1983 the U.S. and Soviet governments were beginning to emerge from the mutual acrimony that had prevailed between them since the Soviet invasion of Afghanistan in Christmas week of 1979. Guided by Reagan's impulses and Schulz's diplomacy, the U.S. government was beginning to explore what would ultimately become, after the ascension of Gorbachev, a more optimistic and productive era in U.S.-Soviet relations. But arms control enthusiasts on Capitol Hill were skeptical about Reagan's intentions toward the nation he had called "the evil empire." The administration had been able to persuade a swing group of moderate Democrats to join with Republicans in supporting limited deployment of the MX missile only after Reagan pledged that he would also diligently pursue arms control opportunities. On the first weekend in June 1983, while Democratic support for the

MX remained very much in question, Reagan went to Camp David with a briefcase full of option papers on arms control. He made a few personal phone calls, scanned the material in the folders and put them aside. After dinner Reagan was in the mood for a movie, as he usually was on Saturday night. The film that evening was *War Games*, in which Matthew Broderick stars as a teenage computer whiz who accidentally accesses the North American Aerospace Defense Command (NORAD) and almost launches World War III. It was an entertaining antiwar film with a clear message, intoned in the movie by an advanced computer: the only way to win the "game" of thermonuclear war is not to play it.

Two days later Reagan met at the White House with several of the Democratic congressmen who had backed the MX in exchange for the president's arms control commitment. He began the meeting by reading from cue cards tailored to congressional concerns. "I just can't believe that if the Soviets think long and hard about the arms race they won't be interested in getting a sensible agreement," Reagan said. Then he put the cue cards aside and his face lit up. He asked the congressmen if any of them had seen *War Games*, and when no one volunteered an answer launched into an animated account of the plot. The congressmen were fascinated with Reagan's change of mood and his obvious interest in the film. "Don't tell the ending," said one of them. "It was really funny," said Congressman Vic Fazio of California after the meeting. "I was sitting there so worried about throw weight [a measure of a missile's lifting power] and Reagan suddenly asks us if we've seen *War Games*. He was in a very good humor. He said, 'I don't understand these computers very well, but this young man obviously did. He had tied into NORAD!'" Reagan continued with his impromptu review by saying he had found a little bias in the casting of the high school teacher in the movie as "a wimp." Then he turned to Army General John W. Vessey Jr., chairman of the Joint Chiefs of Staff, and said with a smile, "They portrayed the general as this slovenly, mean, unthinking guy." Vessey's face reddened. It was clear to the congressmen that the veteran infantry combat officer did not like being compared by his commander in chief to a celluloid caricature of an unstable military man who couldn't tell a war game from a Soviet nuclear attack.

Reagan at least knew that *War Games* was a film. At other times he related cinematic scenes of heroism as if they were historical events. He also gave historical import to World War II propaganda stories that lodged in his mind as fact. The most famous of these is a story he told

on several occasions during the campaigns of 1976 and 1980 and repeated on December 12, 1983, to the annual convention of the Congressional Medal of Honor Society, meeting in New York City. Reagan
called it "a thrilling story of heroism," as indeed it was. During the
course of a bombing raid over Europe during World War II, a B-17 was
hit by antiaircraft fire. The young ball-turret gunner had been severely
wounded, and other crew members were unable to get him out of the
turret. As the B-17 returned over the English Channel, it began to lose
altitude and the commander ordered the men to bail out. "And as the
men started to leave the plane, the last one to leave—the boy, understandably, knowing he was left behind to go down with the plane, cried
out in terror—the last man to leave the plane saw the commander sit
down on the floor," Reagan said. "He took the boy's hand and said,
'Never mind, son, we'll ride it down together.' Congressional Medal of
Honor, posthumously awarded."

This report provoked Lars-Erik Nelson, the Washington bureau
chief of the *New York Daily News*, to do some checking. He went
through the 434 citations of Medal of Honor winners during World
War II, found no such award and wrote a column about it. Readers responded to the column, and one of them said that Reagan's story reminded him of a scene in a 1944 movie, *A Wing and a Prayer*, which
was set in the South Pacific and starred Dana Andrews. In this scene
the pilot of a Navy torpedo bomber with a three-man crew rode the
plane down with his wounded radioman after the gunner bailed out.
"We'll take this ride together," the pilot said. But another reader was
equally certain that Reagan must have found the story in *Reader's Digest*, and Nelson did some more checking on that. It turned out that the
magazine had indeed printed a similar story, abridged from an account
written by reporter Jack Tait in the *New York Herald Tribune*. Tait's
original story was datelined "A Flying Fortress Base, England, Feb. 1,
1944," and was similar to the one Reagan told except that it was another gunner, not the pilot, who went down with the wounded crew-
man. In Tait's story the last man to jump heard the gunner say, "Take it
easy, we'll take this ride together." But Tait was unable to verify the accuracy of the story, which he described as one "circulating at this base
that has almost become a legend." This disclaimer was omitted in the
abridged *Reader's Digest* account, which was part of a typical package of
stories celebrating the World War II heroism of America's fighting men.

Because of the similarities in the working and the setting, Nelson
concluded that Reagan most likely had remembered the *Reader's Digest*

account rather than the film. He was offended because Reagan had told a mythical story of heroism to America's most honored heroes, all of whom had impressive and substantiated stories of their own. When Nelson called the White House speechwriting office and asked if anyone bothered to check the accuracy of accounts presented as factual in presidential speeches, he was told by a researcher that it was a story Reagan had told many times before and had brought with him to the White House.

For their part, White House aides could not understand why reporters were making such a fuss about the facts. "If you tell the same story five times, it's true," said White House spokesman Larry Speakes when he was asked about the accuracy of Reagan's story, repeating a rural drollery of his Mississippi boyhood that had become a standard saying among government flacks. Reagan had indeed brought emotional stories of wartime heroism with him to the White House, and his aides thought he had the license to tell them. Long before he spoke to the Medal of Honor winners, the aides had adopted Reagan's own standard of judging stories by their impact rather than their accuracy. The only serious debate within the White House was whether Reagan knew what he was doing when he told a made-up story or whether he had reached a point where he actually could not distinguish films from facts. Many years later Reagan further blurred the issue by acknowledging to reporters that he had seen *A Wing and a Prayer* but also remembered "reading a citation" during his Army days that recommended a medal for a pilot who had ridden his plane down rather than leave a wounded crew member to face death alone. This "citation" may have been the account in *Reader's Digest*, of which Reagan was a faithful reader. But Reagan's comforting comment to Charles McDowell, when the columnist told him a mythical story he believed to be true, suggests that Reagan recognized at some level that he told stories without regard for factual accuracy. After he left the White House, Reagan admitted as much. Discussing the military buildup he had pushed as a top priority, Reagan told Landon Parvin, "Maybe I had seen too many war movies, the heroics of which I sometimes confused with real life, but common sense told me something very essential—you can't have a fighting force without an esprit de corps. So one of my first priorities was to rebuild our military and, just as important, our military's morale." Reagan's stories of heroism were a tool for carrying our this objective. It mattered little to him if the stories he told had been invented by wartime writers and filmmakers or if they had actually occurred.

War movies and the analogies that Reagan took from them would prove to have enormous consequences in his presidency, particularly in Central America. But peace films such as *War Games* also occupied a crucial compartment in Reagan's emotional arsenal—and would prove even more significant. More than half a century earlier, in a Eureka College production of Edna St. Vincent Milay's antiwar play, *Aria da Capo*, Reagan had portrayed a shepherd who is strangled to death, and he remembered the role in precise detail. In Hollywood he became an avid science-fiction fan, absorbed with a favorite theme of the genre: the invasion from outer space that prompts earthlings to put aside nationalistic quarrels and band together against an alien invader. Reagan liked this idea so much that he tried it out on Gorbachev in their first meeting at Geneva in 1985, saying that he was certain the United States and the Soviet Union would cooperate if Earth were threatened by an invasion from outer space. Reagan's idea was not part of the script, and it startled his advisers. It may also have startled Gorbachev, who did not have at his fingertips the Marxist-Leninist position on the propriety of cooperating with the imperialists against an interplanetary invasion. In any event, Gorbachev changed the subject. Reagan thought this meant he had scored a point, and he proudly repeated what he had said to Gorbachev to a group of Maryland high school students after he returned to the United States. He also repeated it to his advisers, to mixed reactions. Conservative National Security Council staff member Fritz Ermarth, after hearing Reagan deliver a 1987 version of this "romantic fantasy," wrote an angry memo to Colin Powell, then the deputy national security adviser, saying that Earth had in fact been invaded by a devil who forced all the nations of the earth to unite against him. The devil was called Hitler. The memo observed that the great powers had united and defeated him but had not in the process resolved the differences between the United States and the Soviet Union or between democracy and communism.

Powell did not reply to the memo. He knew more than he had ever wanted to know about Reagan's preoccupation with what Powell called "the little green men," and he struggled diligently to keep interplanetary references out of Reagan's speeches. Powell was convinced that Reagan's unique proposal to Gorbachev had been inspired by a 1951 science-fiction film, *The Day the Earth Stood Still*, starring Michael Rennie and Patricia Neal. It was a film with a peace message, one that in a Hollywood still quivering from Red-hunting congressional committees would probably have been permitted only in science fiction. The alien hero of the film, portrayed by Rennie, is an envoy from a benign and highly advanced civilization that has tamed its own violent tendencies by turning peacekeeping duties over to an interplanetary force of robots who are programmed to destroy nations that resort to war. This civilization has been monitoring scientific developments on Earth, with growing alarm. The advanced civilization fears that Earth nations that have penetrated the secrets of the atom will also acquire the means of space travel and carry their weapons and "petty quarrels" into the galaxy. The alien has come to put the planet on notice. His mission is to urge the Earth nations to work together in peace—and to warn them that they will be destroyed by the robotic police force if they do not. For his troubles, the alien is greeted as "a menace from another world" and pursued and eventually killed by U.S. troops. After a miraculous resurrection he gives a departure speech to scientists assembled outside his flying saucer and tells them, "The universe is getting smaller every day. There must be security for all, or no one is secure." The alien then warns the earthlings that they must "join us and live in peace" or be obliterated. "We shall be waiting your decision," he declares before flying away in his saucer. "The decision rests with you."

Reagan's dream of a peaceful, unified planet did not vanish with the departure of this cinematic spaceship. He had been idealistic enough to join the United World Federalists at the end of World War II. He had a horror of nuclear weapons, which he proposed banning altogether in his 1986 meeting with Gorbachev in Reykjavik, and particularly of the reliance of the superpowers on "mutual assured destruction" (MAD) to keep the peace. Reagan also believed in the probability of life on other planets. The fantasy of an interplanetary invasion that would force the nations of the world to cooperate seemed to him a useful and dramatic way of making the point that mankind has a shared interest in world peace.

The president's advisers shared neither Reagan's fantasy nor his belief in the efficacy of the interplanetary analogy. Powell, a conspicuous success in a job where many failed during the Reagan administration, was a distinguished combat officer who was fond of the president and possessed a military man's respect for his commander in chief. He was also among the most moderate, realistic and thoughtful of Reagan's aides. While he would change his stand during the Bush administration, in which he served as chairman of the Joint Chiefs of Staff, Powell during his tenure as national security adviser reinforced Reagan's view that military action in Panama would be resented throughout Latin America. Powell was also one of the few high-ranking administration officials to recognize that the CIA-armed contras lacked much support either in Nicaragua or on Capitol Hill, and he helped engineer the compromise providing "nonlethal aid" to the rebels so that they would neither be wiped out nor cause a wider war on Reagan's watch. But the president's casual references to invasions from outer space made Powell uneasy. He worried that people might think Reagan was really concerned about interplanetary invasions if he kept raising the issue. When the subject came up, Powell would roll his eyes and say to his staff, "Here come the little green men again."

But it was difficult, particularly toward the end of the presidency, to deter Reagan from using favorite stories in a speech. While the president was usually willing to say anything his advisers put in his hands, he liked adding personal touches and dramatic flourishes to important speeches. One of these occasions was Reagan's address to the United Nations General Assembly in 1987, scheduled less than two months before the superpower summit in Washington at which he and Gorbachev would sign the Intermediate Nuclear Forces (INF) treaty. Reagan's speeches to the United Nations were a measure of the distance he had traveled in dealing with the Soviet Union. In 1982, when he gave his first speech to the international body, the United Nations was a forum from which to challenge the Soviets. But in his second term the United Nations became a place for peace speeches, and especially so in this year when Gorbachev was coming to America. When the draft of the 1987 U.N. speech was circulated, Reagan saw another opportunity to draw upon his fantasy of interplanetary invasion. He scribbled out a passage with a version of the story that he had told Gorbachev in Geneva, knowing full well that Powell and Secretary of State Shultz thought the reference naïve. Reagan did not care about that. Maybe there were little green men on other planets and maybe not, but Reagan knew that his story was a transcendent and understandable way of expressing the primacy of world peace and the necessity of cooperation between the superpowers. Powell, who had kept similar passages out of other speeches, realized that the example was important to Reagan and yielded.

"In our obsession with antagonisms of the moment, we often forget how much unites all the members of humanity," Reagan told the U.N. General Assembly on September 21, 1987. "Perhaps we need some outside, universal threat to make us recognize this common bond. I occasionally think how quickly our differences worldwide would vanish if we were facing an alien threat from outside this world. And yet, I ask you, is not an alien force already among us? What could be more alien to the universal aspirations of our peoples than war and the threat of war?"

This was Reagan at his most idealistic, the Reagan who abhorred war and who questioned the foundations of modern deterrence by proposing to the leader of the Soviet Union that all nuclear weapons be abolished. It was the Reagan who proposed "my dream" of an antimissile space shield and who offered to share with the Soviets the technology he believed would make it possible. It was the Reagan who believed, along with the alien in *The Day the Earth Stood Still*, that "there must be security for all or no one will be secure." It was the visionary Reagan, leaving Red Square to proclaim the end of the Cold War and the beginning of a new era in superpower relations.

And it was also the real Reagan, performing as peace president in the role that suited him best. This role dismayed many of his conservative supporters, who preferred his message of freedom to his message of peace. Reagan thought the message was indivisible, and he realized sooner than most of his supporters that the Communist system was on the ropes. Reagan believed that freedom would triumph. He believed in heroism, in the triumph of goodness, in happy endings. He believed in peace through strength, but he also believed in peace.

Most Americans believed in these things, too, and Reagan knew they believed in them. It was not surprising that he drew inspiration and examples from war movies and science-fiction films. Hollywood excels in these, or once did, and Hollywood had been the center of Reagan's life from the time he was twenty-six years old until after he turned fifty. Even when he was gone from Hollywood, Hollywood was never gone from him. He watched movies whenever he could, and the movies were the raw material from which he drew scenes and sustenance. He converted movie material into his own needs. And he remained an actor as well as a moviegoer. He thought of himself as a performer, and he believed that his performances had a purpose. He was an actor, in the White House and out of it. Acting was what he did best.

The Politics of Rich and Poor

KEVIN PHILLIPS

In 1969, Kevin Phillips, then a young Republican political strategist, published his prescient *The Emerging Republican Majority*, which suggested that by championing the cause of social conservatism, Republicans could make serious inroads into the Democratic coalition. More than twenty years later, in *The Politics of Rich and Poor*, Phillips warns that, by pursuing policies that benefited the rich at the expense of the poor and middle class, the Republican Party under Ronald Reagan had provided Democrats with a chance to regain the presidency by running on a platform of economic populism. If Reagan's policies helped only the rich, why did so many other people vote for him?

The reduction or elimination of federal income taxes had been a goal of all three major U.S. capitalist periods, but were now a personal preoccupation for Ronald Reagan, whose antipathy toward income taxes dated back to World War II, when a top rate of 91 percent made it foolish to work beyond a certain point. Under Reagan, the top personal tax bracket would drop from 70 percent to 28 percent in just seven years. In 1987 the Congressional Budget Office showed just who was getting the cream from these reductions: the top 1 to 5 percent of the population.

In 1861 a Republican administration and Congress imposed the first U.S. income tax to finance the Civil War. After two wartime increases, the federal levy was terminated in 1872, abetting the mushrooming fortunes of the Astors, Carnegies, Morgans and Rockefellers.

Later, as postwar laissez-faire collapsed into populism and progressivism, public doubts about excessive wealth resurged, and with them came income tax pressures. In 1894, after the prior year's unnerving stock market panic, Congress passed a tax of 2 percent on incomes over four thousand dollars, which the U.S. Supreme Court declared unconstitutional in 1895. A constitutional amendment solved the problem in 1913. As Europe marched to war in 1914, joined by the United States in 1917, the demand for income tax revenue soon repeated itself. Levies climbed quickly, and by 1920, the top rate was 73 percent.

As a result, postwar federal revenues exceeded peacetime needs and discouraged peacetime enterprise. When the Harding administration took office in 1921, tax rates were quickly reduced, in four stages, to a top bracket of just 25 percent in 1925. As Reaganite theorists would recall six decades later, cutting income taxes amidst gathering commercial prosperity helped create the boom of the 1920s. The prime beneficiaries were the top 5 percent of Americans, people who rode the cutting edge of the new technology of autos, radios and the like, emerging service industries (including new practices like advertising and consumer finance), a booming stock market and unprecedented real estate development. As federal taxation eased, especially on the upper brackets, disposable income soared for the rich—and with it conspicuous consumption and financial speculation.

By the crash of 1929, striking changes had occurred in the distribution of both taxes *and* wealth. The bottom-earning 80 percent of the population, never much affected, had been cut off the income tax rolls entirely. As a result, the top 1 percent of taxpayers were paying about two thirds of what the Treasury took in. Even so, because the top rate had fallen from 73 percent to 25 percent, federal taxation was taking less and less of booming upper-bracket incomes and stock profits. By contrast, many farmers and miners, and some workers, hurt by slumping commodity prices, found themselves with lower real purchasing power than they had enjoyed in the placid decade before World War I. Tax policy was not the only source of upward redistribution, but it contributed greatly to the polarization of U.S. wealth and the inequality of income, which peaked between 1927 and 1929.[1]

[1]This maldistribution is often cited as a factor in the 1929 crash and subsequent depression. One scholar goes so far as to contend that the lower 93 percent of the nonfarm population actually experienced a 4 percent decline in real disposable per capita income between 1923 and 1929 (Charles F. Holt, "Who Benefitted from the Prosperity of the Twenties?" *Explorations in Economic History* 14, July 1977, pp. 277–89).

But Democrats, soon back in control of Congress and then the White House, preferred to afflict rather than nurture concentrated wealth. Now the direction or redistribution moved *downward*. To achieve that, the top tax rate reached 63 percent by 1932, 79 percent by 1936 and soared to 91 percent during World War II, the incentive-less bracket that so offended Ronald Reagan and his Hollywood friends. Ninety-one percent remained the nominal top rate until 1964, when it fell in two stages to 77 percent and then 70 percent.

If not for the war in Vietnam, there might have been further cuts in the late sixties, but the war was costly, sustaining a high rate structure and even requiring a surtax from 1968 to 1970. More perversely, wartime outlays generated an inflation that lifted more and more middle-class citizens into what had long been *upper-class* brackets. So by the late 1970s, with the war over but with inflation still intensifying, cyclical demand for tax reduction gathered momentum. After nearly fifty years, proposals for deep rate reductions were back on the national agenda. Though Republican politicians aroused little interest in the Kemp-Roth tax cuts of 1978, this lack of support was only temporary.

Over the next two years, a new conservative outlook took shape in Washington, entrenched in 1980 by Reagan's election. The 1981 Economic Recovery Tax Act, passed by a surprisingly willing Congress, offered far more than relief for middle-class bracket creep. Supply-side proponents of individual rate cuts and business-organization lobbyists for capital formation and corporate depreciation allowances shared a half-trillion-dollar victory.[2] For the first time since the New Deal, federal tax policy was fundamentally rearranging its class, sector and income-group loyalties.

Corporate tax rates were reduced and depreciation benefits greatly liberalized. By 1983 the percentage of federal tax receipts represented by corporate income tax revenues would drop to an all-time low of 6.2 percent, down from 32.1 percent in 1952 and 12.5 percent in 1980. For individuals the 1981 act cut taxes across the board—by 5 percent in 1981, then 10 percent in 1982 and another 10 percent in 1983. Another highly significant change trimmed the top bracket from 70 percent to 50 percent. Taxation of *earned* income had been capped at a 50 percent top rate since 1972. Now the same treatment would be extended to *unearned* income, an enormous boon to the small percentage

---

[2]That was the estimated cost of the 1981 tax cuts over the next five years.

of the population deriving most of its income from rents and interest. Meanwhile, the top rate on capital gains was effectively cut to 20 percent, having earlier been dropped form 49 percent to 28 percent by the Steiger Amendment reductions of 1978. Conservative tax-reduction supporters predicted a surge in savings, venture capitalism and entrepreneurialism. Liberal economists, disheartened, prophesied more inflation and mounting inequality. Both predictions only half proved out. The savings rate didn't grow, and neither did inflation, but enterprise *and* inequality did—an old story.

Critics of emerging income polarization would eventually cite the increasingly benign treatment between 1978 and 1981 of property income (interest, dividends and rents) and capital gains, a benefit that flowed mostly to a small stratum of taxpayers. According to a 1983 Federal Reserve Board survey, families in the top 2 percent owned 30 percent of all liquid assets (from checking accounts to money market funds), 50 percent of the corporate stocks held by individuals, some 39 percent of corporate and government bonds and 71 percent of tax-exempt municipals. And applying a broader measurement of upper-income status, the wealthiest 10 percent owned 51 percent of liquid assets, 72 percent of corporate stocks, 70 percent of bonds and 86 percent of tax-exempts.

The inflation of the late 1970s and then subsequent post-1981 disinflation would affect different economic strata in different ways. At first, under inflation, blue-collar wages stagnated, at least in real terms, but a fair percentage of reasonably well off property owners benefited from increased bank CD interest rates, real estate values, precious metals, jewelry, art and rents. When disinflation took over in 1981–82, the big benefit shifted to the more truly rich. Real interest rates soared, and as that happened, upper-bracket holders of financial assets—mostly stocks and bonds—chalked up the greatest gains. Data compiled by the Economic Policy Institute in 1988 spelled out the much larger 1978–86 gain in property income (up 116.5 percent) compared with wage, salary and other labor income (up 66.6 percent). Lightened levies on capital gain and property income, coming just around the time when those categories were climbing, helped fuel upper-bracket wealth and capital accumulation more or less as conservative tax strategists and entrepreneurial theorists had hoped.

The second big redistributive spur was Washington's decision to let Social Security tax rates climb upward from 6.05 percent in 1978 to

6.70 percent in 1982-83, 7.05 percent in 1985 and 7.51 percent in 1988–89—a schedule originally voted in 1977 under Carter—while income tax rates were coming down. By 1987, however, Maine Democratic senator George Mitchell complained that "as a result, there has been a shift of about $80 billion in annual revenue collections from the progressive income tax to the regressive payroll tax. The Social Security tax increase in 1977 cannot be attributed to the current administration. But the response in the 1980s—to make up for a tax increase disproportionately burdening lower-income households with a tax cut disproportionately benefiting higher-income households—*can* be laid to the policies of this administration." Mitchell was hardly overstating the new reliance on Social Security. Between 1980 and 1988, the FICA tax on $40,000-a-year incomes doubled from $1,500 to nearly $3,000. The portion of total annual federal tax receipts represented by Social Security rose from 31 percent to 36 percent while income tax contributions dropped from 47 percent to under 45 percent.

After his reelection in 1984, Reagan moved to replicate the full reduction of the Harding-Coolidge era and succeeded in doing so when the 1986 tax reform cut top individual rates from 70 percent in 1981 to just 28 percent as of 1988—effectively matching the 1921–25 reduction from 73 percent to 25 percent. Democrats were largely uncritical; as we have seen, their acquiescence in such reversals is typical of capitalist heydays.

Taxpayers would not feel the final effects of the 1986 tax reductions until April 1989, and 1988 tax-distribution data couldn't be officially analyzed for several years thereafter, well past the president's departure from office. Yet the debate over who had gained and lost under Reagan intensified. Reaganites and their critics both had a substantial case. Supply-siders and other advocates of bracket reduction could show that the upper-tier rate cuts had not increased the *proportion* of taxes paid by the poor and middle classes. During the Reagan years the percentage of total federal income tax payments made by the top 1 percent of taxpayers actually rose, climbing from 18.05 percent in 1981 to 19.93 percent in 1983, 21.9 percent in 1985 and 26.1 percent in 1986. And this could have been predicted. As we have seen, their share of national income was increasing by similar proportions. When wealth concentrates at the top of the pyramid, lower rates *do* bring larger receipts than the higher rates of the preconcentration period. Coolidge-era precedents, invoked by supply-siders from the first, had been even more lopsided. Because the upper-bracket rate cuts of the 1920s also removed most lower- and lower-middle-income families from the rolls, the percentage of total taxes paid by the top 1 percent actually climbed from 43 percent in 1921 to 69 percent in 1926. Early supporters of a tax rollback—not least Coolidge—were quick to boast of this, and assigned credit to the rate cuts. The same boasts were made in the 1980s.[3]

The statistical deception, of course, was that the increased ratios of total tax payments by high-income persons were not an increased burden. Overzealous supply-siders were way too insistent that Reagan's tax policy "soaked the rich," promoted "economic justice," and that "the Reagan years have been, contrary to the conventional wisdom, an age of benevolent Robin Hoodism." Claims that the tax cuts had helped promote prosperity under Coolidge and Reagan were plausible, although more plausibly these cuts *overlapped* rather than caused the two capitalist heydays. That the rich were "soaked" during the 1980s was, however, untrue, as anyone walking down Rodeo Drive could see. It was precisely such exaggerations that undermined supply-sider credibility.

Under Reagan, as under Coolidge, the clear evidence is that the net tax burden on rich Americans as a percentage of their total income *shrank* substantially because of the sweeping rate cuts. The surge in actual tax payments was the result of higher upper-bracket incomes. To measure the benefits, imagine a businessman who had made $333,000 in salary, dividends and capital gains in 1980, and paid $120,000 in federal income taxes. As prosperity returned in 1983, his income climbed to $500,000. Yet with the applicable rates reduced, he might well have paid, say, $150,000 in taxes, *more actual payment*, of course, but *less relative burden*. That many blue-collar and middle-class Americans had lost their jobs in 1981–82 (when unemployment briefly neared 11 percent) also helps explain why the top 1 percent of 1983 taxpayers—disproportionate beneficiaries of a surging stock market—wound up shouldering a higher portion of the overall federal income tax burden. They were gaining while the bottom half of the population was losing. "Soaked" is hardly the term to describe what happened to millionaires paying out lower percentages of sharply rising incomes.

[3]In his 1928 message to Congress, for example, President Coolidge observed that tax rate cuts stimulated business production to the extent that total tax revenues increased: "Four times we have made a drastic revision of our internal revenue system, abolishing many taxes and substantially reducing almost all others. Each time the resulting stimulation to business has so increased taxable incomes that a surplus has been produced" (John D. Hicks, *Republican Ascendency*, 1921–33 [New York: Harper Brothers, 1960], p. 107).

In 1987, to plot the rearrangement of effective *overall* tax rates, the economists at the Congressional Budget Office took *all* federal taxes—individual income, Social Security, corporate income and excise—and calculated the change in their combined impact on different income strata after 1977. Families below the top decile, disproportionately burdened by Social Security and excise increases and rewarded less by any income tax reductions, wound up paying *higher* effective rates. The richest families, meanwhile, paid lower rates, largely because of the sharp reduction applicable to nonsalary income (capital gains, interest, dividends and rents).

These shifts go a long way to explain both the surge in consumption *and* the rising inequality of income. America's richest 5 percent (and richest 1 percent, in particular) were the tax policy's new beneficiaries. Nor did the CBO's 1988 projections anticipate a significant reversal from the 1986 tax reform, with its unusual combination of further rate reductions (down to a 28 percent top bracket) partly balanced by elimination of credits and deductions. Effective tax rates for 1988 *would* fall slightly for the bottom 20 percent relative to 1984, the CBO found, but not by enough to restore 1977's lower combined-impact levels. Middle and upper groups, in turn, would find their effective rates slightly higher in 1988 than in 1984. For these brackets, a part of the 1981 cut was recaptured. However, the *overall* net effect of the 1977–88 tax changes would be different for *middle-class* versus *top-tier* taxpayers. For Mr. and Mrs. Middle America, the changes during Reagan's second term had the effect of canceling out the minor benefits of 1977–84 reductions. Escalating Social Security rates were a principal culprit. *Upper-echelon taxpayers alone were projected to benefit from a large net reduction in effective overall federal tax rates for the entire 1977-88 period.*

Some of the anomalies of the redesigned tax burden were extraordinary, not least the "bubble" that imposed a marginal income tax rate of 33 percent on family incomes of $70,000 to $155,000 in contrast to the 28 percent rate that applied above these levels. In 1988 a $90,000-a-year family with two husband-and-wife breadwinners making $45,000 each found itself in a 40.5 percent marginal federal tax bracket—a 33 percent income tax rate plus a 7.5 percent Social Security levy—in contrast to the 28 percent marginal rate of a millionaire or billionaire.

Policy at the federal level wasn't unique. During 1988 a collateral thesis began to emerge that state-level tax changes during the 1980s were also aggravating the trend to inequality. Citizens for Tax Justice, a

group financed by labor unions and various liberal organizations, calculated that rising state sales taxes were falling disproportionately on poor
families. And a 1988 study contended that half the states with income
taxes had made them less fair for many low- and middle-income residents in 1986–87. The 1986 federal revisions required modification of
state tax laws. The complaint was that those modifications were biased.
Critics, however, lacked the documentation rapidly proliferating on the
federal level, and in any event, *federal fiscal policy was the main issue*.

The irony was that Democratic election-year presidential politick-
ing did not recognize that importance. Opinion polls in April 1988-tax
time-revealed public skepticism of tax reform, its fairness and its wisdom. Yet Dukakis avoided the subject. Upper-bracket increases were
rejected at the Democratic National Convention. Tax issues were ignored in 1988 as they had been 1928.

What was also ignored—perhaps because of its complexity—were
the data, contrary to widespread belief, showing that non-Social Security taxes for all Americans as a percentage of GNP had been significantly cut during the 1980s. Conservative insistence that the overall
federal tax burden hadn't been reduced was deceptive. Certain revenue
ratios *did* decline. Between 1 and 2 percent of GNP that had been gathered in taxes for *general* public sector purposes under Eisenhower and
Nixon—some $40 billion to $80 billion a year in 1988 dollars—was
routed back to the private sector under Reagan, enlarging the federal
budget deficit, and thereby affecting federal spending and interest rate
outlays, also with redistributive effects.4 It was true, that *total* federal
tax receipts remained roughly constant as a percentage of Gross National Product, but Social Security receipts were rising sharply, disguis-
ing a relative decline in *other* revenues, reducing Washington's ability
to fund non-Social Security programs from schools to highways.

Other postwar Republican administrations had not sought this kind
of fundamental reversal in government's role. Under Eisenhower, on

4Harvard professor Benjamin Friedman reaches a similar conclusion a bit differently: "It was only in
the 1980s under Reagan's new fiscal policy, that this long-standing relationship changed. Because of
Kemp-Roth, the share of individuals' income paid in taxes of all kinds other than Social Security contributions *declined* between 1979 and 1986. After including the hike in Social Security, the total tax
payments of individuals was still 18.2 percent. In the meanwhile, government transfer payments kept
on rising in relation to income, reaching 13.4 percent in 1986. The balance left to pay for all other
government services was down to just 4.8 percent of income, fully two percentage points below what it
was on average from the fifties to the seventies" (Benjamin Friedman, *Day of Reckoning* [New York:
Random House, 1988], p. 156.

average, non-Social Security federal receipts—principally from personal income, corporate income and excise taxes—had represented 15 percent of GNP, enabling the government to run without deficits. By the late 1960s federal deficits were a fact of fiscal life. Ironically, bracket creep in the late 1970s was perversely helpful—non-Social Security receipts expanded to 14 percent of GNP, reducing deficits again, compared with mid-decade figures.

But the 1981 tax cuts, along with rising military outlays, tight Federal Reserve Board policy and the cost of the 1981–82 recession, sent the federal deficit soaring to 5 to 6 percent of GNP, the highest peacetime levels since the Depression. Non-Social Security revenues in the range of 12 percent of GNP simply were not enough to run the U.S. government in the late 1980s, no matter what the stimulus of tax cuts might be. Part of the slack was made up by money borrowed at home and abroad at high cost. But how long could this go on? Tax relief and incentive economics meant not only income polarization but a frightening buildup of debt.

11

THE END OF THE
COLD WAR

Ronald Reagan came to the presidency pledged to reassert American power and prestige. He did so but at a cost Americans would continue to pay throughout the nineteen nineties: the longest peace-time economic expansion combined with a highly expensive military buildup led to a definitive victory in the Cold War but left a legacy of accelerating economic decline.

Although some commentators had long maintained that the Soviet Union's economic strength would not stand the test of time, no one could have predicted the rapid disintegration that actually occurred. In 1985 Mikhail Gorbachev took charge of the Soviet Union determined to resuscitate the Soviet system. He proclaimed the twin programs of *glasnost* (freer speech) and *perestroika* (economic reforms). Instead of saving his country, the attempted changes destroyed the Soviet Union. Galloping disruption and economic dislocation led Gorbachev in 1989 to allow the Soviet satellites in Eastern Europe to go their own way. Having cut off the limbs to save the patient, Gorbachev found that the illness had spread too far. The secession of the Baltic states led to a fragmentation of the Soviet Union, a process which reached its end point on Christmas Day 1991 when Gorbachev resigned as president of the Soviet state. With that action the Soviet

Union, born in revolution in 1917, disappeared. In its place were fifteen republics, eleven of which then loosely combined to form the Commonwealth of Independent States.

While euphoria reigned in the United States so did caution. Americans could take pleasure from their "victory" but remained cautious knowing that the fragile new successor nations needed to defeat economic and political chaos in order to survive. Further, the sobering thought of thirty thousand nuclear weapons in none-too secure hands tempered by optimism.

The horror of contagious nuclear proliferation contributed to the American decision to go to war in January 1991. Saddam Hussein, the dictator of Iraq, had long been a bully but only in 1990, when Iraqi forces invaded neighboring Kuwait, a major supplier of oil to the United States, did the American government decide that Hussein was an unalloyed adversary. Our swift victory over Hussein in February 1991 helped reassure the United States of its strength but ultimately did little to stabilize the Middle East, long a pressure cooker.

As the triumphal glow faded, new doubts assailed the United States. An economic recession, mounting domestic problems and an apparently ever-stronger Japan caused many Americans to worry seriously about the position of the United States in the next century. The Cold War had passed into history but the American people remained uncertain as to the nature of the new world order and their place within it.

America in Decline?

PAUL M. KENNEDY

No one book better summed up American anxiety during the second half of the nineteen eighties than did *The Rise and Fall of the Great Powers* by Yale professor Paul Kennedy. With the evidence of growing German and (especially) Japanese prosperity increasingly evident, Americans looked for explanations for this dramatic turnabout. In Kennedy's work they found persuasive answers to their questions. Is America really in decline? Why do these kinds of issues raise doubts as to the nature of American decision making?

It is worth bearing in mind the Soviet Union's difficulties when one turns to analyze the present and the future circumstances of the United States, because of two important distinctions. The first is that while it can be argued that the American share of world power has been declining *relatively* faster than Russia's over the past few decades, its problems are probably nowhere near as great as those of its Soviet rival. Moreover, its *absolute* strength (especially in industrial and technological fields) is still much larger than that of the USSR. The second is that the very unstructured, laissez-faire nature of American society (while not without its weaknesses) probably gives it a better chance of readjusting to changing circumstances than a rigid and *dirigiste* power would have. But that in turn depends upon the existence of a national leadership which can understand the larger processes at work in the world today, and is aware of both the strong and the weak points of the U.S. position as it seeks to adjust to the changing global environment.

Although the United States is at present still in a class of its own economically and perhaps even militarily, it cannot avoid confronting the two great tests which challenge the *longevity* of every major power that occupies the "number one" position in world affairs: whether, in the military/strategical realm, it can preserve a reasonable balance between the nation's perceived defense requirements and the means it possesses to maintain those commitments; and whether, as an intimately related point, it can preserve the technological and economic bases of its power from relative erosion in the face of the ever-shifting patterns of global production. This test of American abilities will be the greater because it, like Imperial Spain around 1600 or the British Empire around 1900, is the inheritor of a vast array of strategical commitments which had been made decades earlier, when the nation's political, economic, and military capacity to influence world affairs seemed so much more assured. In consequence, the United States now runs the risk, so familiar to historians of the rise and fall of previous Great Powers, of what might roughly be called "imperial overstretch": that is to say, decision-makers in Washington must face the awkward and enduring fact that the sum total of the United States' global interests and obligations is nowadays far larger than the country's power to defend them all simultaneously.

Unlike those earlier Powers that grappled with the problem of strategical overextension, the United States also confronts the possibility of nuclear annihilation—a fact which, many people feel, has changed the entire nature of international power politics. If indeed a large-scale nuclear exchange were to occur, then any consideration of the United States' "prospects" becomes so problematical as to make it pointless—even if it also is the case that the American position (because of its defensive systems, and geographical extent) is probably more favorable than, say, France's or Japan's in such a conflict. On the other hand, the history of the post-1945 arms race so far suggests that nuclear weapons, while mutually threatening to East and West, also seem to be mutually unusable—which is the chief reason why the Powers continue to increase expenditures upon their *conventional* forces. If however, the possibility exists of the major states someday becoming involved in a nonnuclear war (whether merely regional or on a larger scale), then the similarity of strategical circumstances between the United States today and imperial Spain or Edwardian Britain in their day is clearly much more appropriate. In each case, the declining number-one power faced threats, not so much to the security of its own homeland (in the United States' case, the prospect of being conquered by an invading army is remote), but to the nation's interests abroad—interests so widespread that it would be difficult to defend them all at once, and yet almost equally difficult to abandon any of them without running further risks.

Each of those interests abroad, it is fair to remark, was undertaken by the United States for what seemed very plausible (often very pressing) reasons at the time, and in most instances the reason for the American presence has not diminished; in certain parts of the globe, U.S. interests may now appear larger to decision-makers in Washington than they were a few decades ago.

That, it can be argued, is certainly true of American obligations in the Middle East. Here is a region, from Morocco in the west to Afghanistan in the east, where the United States faces a number of conflicts and problems whose mere listing (as one observer put it) "leaves one breathless." It is an area which contains so much of the world's surplus oil supply; which seems so susceptible (at least on the map) to Soviet penetration; toward which a powerfully organized domestic lobby presses for unflinching support for an isolated but militarily efficient Israel; in which Arab states of a generally pro-western inclination (Egypt, Saudi Arabia, Jordan, the Gulf emirates) are under pressure from their own Islamic fundamentalists as well as from external threats such as Libya; and in which all the Arab states, whatever their own rivalries, oppose Israel's policy toward the Palestinians. This makes the region very important to the United States, but at the same time bewilderingly resistant to any simple policy option. It is, in addition, the region in the world which, at least in some parts of it, seems most frequently to resort to war. Finally, it contains the only territory—Afghanistan—which the Soviet Union is attempting to conquer by means of armed force. It is hardly surprising, therefore, that the Middle East has been viewed as requiring constant American attention, whether of a military or a diplomatic kind. Yet the memory of the 1979 debacle in Iran and of the ill-fated Lebanon venture of 1983, the diplomatic complexities of the antagonisms (how to assist Saudi Arabia without alarming Israel), and the unpopularity of the United States among the Arab masses all make it extremely difficult for an American government to conduct a coherent, long-term policy in the Middle East.

In Latin America, too, there are seen to be growing challenges to the United States' national interests. If a major international debt crisis is to occur anywhere in the world, dealing a heavy blow to the global credit system and especially to U.S. banks, it is likely to begin in this region. As it is, Latin America's economic problems have not only lowered the credit rating of many eminent American banking houses, but they have also contributed to a substantial decline in U.S. manufacturing exports to that region. Here, as in East Asia, the threat that the advanced, prosperous countries of the world will steadily increase tariffs against imported, low-labor-cost manufactures, and be ever less generous in their overseas-aid programs, is a cause for deep concern. All this is compounded by the fact that, economically and socially, Latin America has been changing remarkably swiftly over the past few decades. At the same time, its demographic explosion is pressing ever harder upon the available resources, and upon the older conservative governing structures, in a considerable number of states. This has led to broadbased movements for social and constitutional reforms, or even for outright "revolution"—the latter being influenced by the present radical regimes in Cuba and Nicaragua. In turn, these movements have produced a conservative backlash, with reactionary governments proclaiming the need to eradicate all signs of domestic Communism, and appealing to the United States for help to achieve that goal. These social and political fissures often compel the United States to choose between its desire to enhance democratic rights in Latin America and its wish to defeat Marxism. It also forces Washington to consider whether it can achieve its own purposes by political and economic means alone, or whether it may have to resort to military action (as in the case of Grenada).

By far the most worrying situation of all, however, lies just to the south of the United States, and makes the Polish "crisis" for the USSR seem small by comparison. There is simply no equivalent in the world for the present state of Mexican-United States relations. Mexico is on the verge of economic bankruptcy and default, its internal economic crisis forces hundreds of thousands to drift illegally to the north each year, its most profitable trade with the United States is swiftly becoming a brutally managed flow of hard drugs, and the border for all this sort of traffic is still extraordinarily permeable.

If the challenges to American interests in East Asia are farther away, that does not diminish the significance of this vast area today. The largest share of the world's population lives there; a large and increasing proportion of American trade is with countries on the "Pacific rim"; two of the world's future Great Powers, China and Japan, are located there; the Soviet Union, directly and (through Vietnam) indirectly, is also there. So are those Asian newly industrializing countries, delicate quasi-democracies which on the one hand have embraced the capitalist laissez-faire ethos with a vengeance, and on the other are undercutting American manufacturing in everything from textiles to electronics. It is in East Asia, too, that a substantial number of American military obligations exist, usually as creations of the early Cold War.

Even a mere listing of those obligations cannot fail to suggest the extraordinarily wide-ranging nature of American interests in this region. A few years ago, the U.S. Defense Department attempted a brief summary of American interests in East Asia, but its very succinctness pointed, paradoxically, to the almost limitless extent of those strategical commitments:

> The importance to the United States of the security of East Asia and the Pacific is demonstrated by the bilateral treaties with Japan, Korea, and the Philippines; the Manila Pact, which adds Thailand to our treaty partners; and our treaty with Australia and New Zealand—the ANZUS Treaty. It is further enhanced by the deployment of land and air forces in Korea and Japan, and the forward deployment of the Seventh Fleet in the Western Pacific. Our foremost regional objectives, in conjunction with our regional friends and allies, are:
>
> —To maintain the security of our essential sea lanes and of the United States' interests in the region; to maintain the capability to fulfill our treaty commitments in the Pacific and East Asia; to prevent the Soviet Union, North Korea, and Vietnam from interfering in the affairs of others; to build a durable strategic relationship with the People's Republic of China; and to support the stability and independence of friendly countries.

Moreover, this carefully selected prose inevitably conceals a considerable number of extremely delicate political and strategical issues: how to build a good relationship with the PRC without abandoning Taiwan; how to "support the stability and independence of friendly countries" while trying to control the flood of their exports to the American market; how to make the Japanese assume a larger share of the defense of the western Pacific without alarming its various neighbors; how to maintain U.S. bases in, for example, the Philippines without provoking local resentments; how to reduce the American military presence in South Korea without sending the wrong "signal" to the North.

Possibly this concern about the gap between American interests and capabilities in the world would be less acute had there not been so much doubt expressed—since at least the time of the Vietnam War—about the *efficiency* of the system itself. Since those doubts have been repeatedly aired in other studies, they will only be summarized here; this is not a further essay on the hot topic of "defense reform." One major area of contention, for example, has been the degree of interservice rivalry, which is of course common to most armed forces but seems more deeply entrenched in the American system—possibly because of the relatively modest powers of the chairman of the Joint Chiefs of Staff, possibly because so much more energy appears to be devoted to procurement as opposed to strategical and operational issues. In peacetime, this might merely be dismissed as an extreme example of "bureaucratic politics"; but in actual wartime operations—say, in the emergency dispatch of the Rapid Deployment Joint Task Force, which contains elements from all four services—a lack of proper coordination could be fatal.

In the area of military procurement itself, allegations of "waste, fraud and abuse" have been commonplace. The various scandals over horrendously expensive, *under*performing weapons which have caught the public's attention in recent years have plausible explanations: the lack of proper competitive bidding and of market forces in the "military-industrial complex," and the tendency toward "goldplated" weapon systems, not to mention the striving for large profits. It is difficult, however, to separate those deficiencies in the procurement process from what is clearly a more fundamental happening: the intensification of the impacts which new technological advances make upon the art of war. Given that it is in the high-technology field that the USSR usually appears most vulnerable—which suggests that American *quality* in weaponry can be employed to counter the superior Russian *quantity* of, say, tanks and aircraft—there is an obvious attraction in what Caspar Weinberger termed "competitive strategies" when ordering new armaments. Nevertheless, the fact that the Reagan administration in its first term spent over 75 percent more on new aircraft than the Carter regime but acquired only 9 percent more planes points to *the* appalling military-procurement problem of the late twentieth century: given the technologically driven tendency toward spending more and more money upon fewer and fewer weapon systems, would the United States and its allies really have enough sophisticated and highly expensive aircraft and tanks in reserve after the early stages of a ferociously fought conventional war? Does the U.S. Navy possess enough attack submarines, or frigates, if heavy losses were incurred in the early stages of a *third*

Battle of the Atlantic? If not, the results would be grim; for it is clear that today's complex weaponry simply cannot be replaced in the short times which were achieved during the Second World War.

This dilemma is accentuated by two other elements in the complicated calculus of evolving an effective American defense policy. The first is the issue of budgetary constraints. Unless external circumstances became much more threatening, it would be a remarkable act of political persuasion to get national defense expenditures raised much above, say, 7.5 percent of GNP—the more especially since the size of the federal deficit (see p. 390) points to the need to balance governmental spending as the first priority of state. But if there is a slowing-down or even a halt in the increase in defense spending, coinciding with the continuous upward spiral in weapons costs, then the problem facing the Pentagon will become much more acute.

The second factor is the sheer variety of military contingencies that a global superpower like the United States has to plan for—all of which, in their way, place differing demands upon the armed forces and the weaponry they are likely to employ. This again is not without precedent in the history of the Great Powers; the British army was frequently placed under strain by having to plan to fight on the Northwest Frontier of India *or* in Belgium. But even that challenge pales beside the task facing today's "number one." If the critical issue for the United States is preserving a nuclear deterrent against the Soviet Union, at *all* levels of escalation, then money will inevitably be poured into such weapons as the MX missile, the B-1 and "Stealth" bombers, Pershing IIs, cruise missiles, and Trident-bearing submarines. If a large-scale conventional war against the Warsaw pact is the most probable scenario, then the funds presumably need to go in quite different directions: tactical aircraft, main battle tanks, large carriers, frigates, attack submarines, and logistical services. If it is likely that the United States and the USSR will avoid a direct clash, but that both will become more active in the Third World, then the weapons mix changes again: small arms, helicopters, light carriers, an enhanced role for the U.S. Marine Corps become the chief items on the list. Already it is clear that a large part of the controversy over "defense reform" stems from differing assumptions about the *type* of war the United States might be called upon to fight. But what if those in authority make the wrong assumption?

A further major concern about the efficiency of the system, and one voiced even by strong supporters of the campaign to "restore"

American power, is whether the present decision-making structure permits a proper grand strategy to be carried out. This would not merely imply achieving a greater coherence in military policies, so that there is less argument about "maritime strategy" versus "coalition warfare," but would also involve effecting a synthesis of the United States' long-term political, economic, and strategical interests, in place of the bureaucratic infighting which seems to have characterized so much of Washington's policymaking. A much-quoted example of this is the all-too-frequent *public* dispute about how and where the United States should employ its armed forces abroad to enhance or defend its national interests—with the State Department wanting clear and firm responses made to those who threaten such interests, but the Defense Department being unwilling (especially after the Lebanon debacle) to get involved overseas except under special conditions. But there also have been, and by contrast, examples of the Pentagon's preference for taking unilateral decisions in the arms race with Russia (e.g., SDI program, abandoning SALT II) without consulting major allies, which leaves problems for the State Department. There have been uncertainties attending the role played by the National Security Council, and more especially individual national security advisers. There have been incoherencies of policy in the Middle East, partly because of the intractibility of, say, the Palestine issue, but also because the United States' strategical interest in supporting the conservative, pro-Western Arab states against Russian penetration in that area has often foundered upon the well-organized opposition of its own pro-Israel lobby. There have been interdepartmental disputes about the use of economic tools—from boycotts on trade and embargoes on technology transfer to foreign-aid grants and weapons sales and grain sales—in support of American diplomatic interests, which affect policies toward the Third World, South Africa, Russia, Poland, the EEC, and so on, and which have sometimes been uncoordinated and contradictory. No sensible person would maintain that the many foreign-policy problems afflicting the globe each possess an obvious and ready "solution"; on the other hand, the preservation of long-term American interests is certainly not helped when the decision-making system is attended by frequent disagreements within.

All this has led to questions by gloomier critics about the overall political culture in which Washington decision-makers have to operate. This is far too large and complex a matter to be explored in depth here. But it has been increasingly suggested that a country needing to reformulate its grand strategy in the light of the larger, uncontrollable changes taking place in world affairs may not be well served by an electoral system which seems to paralyze foreign-policy decision-making every two years. It may not be helped by the extraordinary pressures applied by lobbyists, political action committees, and other interest groups, all of which, by definition, are prejudiced in respect to this or that policy change; nor by an inherent "simplification" of vital but complex international and strategical issues through a mass media whose time and space for such things are limited, and whose *raison d'être* is chiefly to make money and secure audiences, and only secondarily to inform. It may also not be helped by the still-powerful "escapist" urges in the American social culture, which may be understandable in terms of the nation's "frontier" past but is a hindrance to coming to terms with today's more complex, integrated world and with *other* cultures and ideologies. Finally, the country may not always be assisted by its division of constitutional and decision-making powers, deliberately created when it was geographically and strategically isolated from the rest of the world two centuries ago, and possessed a decent degree of time to come to an agreement on the few issues which actually concerned "foreign" policy, but which may be harder to operate when it has become a global superpower, often called upon to make swift decisions vis-à-vis countries which enjoy far fewer constraints. No single one of these presents an insuperable obstacle to the execution of a coherent, long-term American grand strategy; their cumulative and interacting effect is, however, to make it much more difficult than otherwise to carry out needed changes of policy if that seems to hurt special interests and occurs in an election year. It may therefore be here, in the cultural and domestic-political realms, that the evolution of an effective overall American policy to meet the twenty-first century will be subjected to the greatest test.

The final question about the proper relationship of "means and ends" in the defense of American global interests relates to the economic challenges bearing down upon the country, which, because they are so various, threaten to place immense strains upon decision-making in national policy. The extraordinary breadth and complexity of the American economy makes it difficult to summarize what is happening to all parts of it—especially in a period when it is sending out such contradictory signals.

The first of these is the country's relative industrial decline, as measured against world production, not only in older manufactures such as textiles, iron and steel, shipbuilding, and basic chemicals, but also—although it is far less easy to judge the final outcome of this level of industrial-technological combat—in global shares of robotics, aerospace, automobiles, machine tools, and computers. Both of these pose immense problems: in traditional and basic manufacturing, the gap in wage scales between the United States and newly industrializing countries is probably such that no "efficiency measures" will close it; but to lose out in the competition in future technologies, if that indeed should occur, would be even more disastrous. In late 1986, for example, a congressional study reported that the U.S. trade surplus in high-technology goods had plunged from $27 billion in 1980 to a mere $4 billion in 1985, and was swiftly heading into a deficit.

The second, and in many ways less expected, sector of decline is agriculture. Only a decade ago, experts in that subject were predicting a frightening global imbalance between feeding requirements and farming output. But such a scenario of famine and disaster stimulated two powerful responses. The first was a massive investment into American farming from the 1970s onward, fueled by the prospect of ever-larger overseas food sales; the second was the enormous (western-world-funded) investigation into scientific means of increasing Third World crop outputs, which has been so successful as to turn growing numbers of such countries into food *exporters*, and thus competitors of the United States. These two trends are separate from, but have coincided with, the transformation of the EEC into a major producer of agricultural surpluses, because of its price-support system. In consequence, experts now refer to a "world awash in food," which in turn leads to sharp declines in agricultural prices and in American food exports—and drives many farmers out of business.

It is not surprising, therefore, that these economic problems have led to a surge in protectionist sentiment throughout many sectors of the American economy, and among businessmen, unions, farmers, and their congressmen. As with the "tariff reform" agitation in Edwardian Britain, the advocates of increased protection complain of unfair foreign practices, of "dumping" below-cost manufactures on the American market, and of enormous subsidies to foreign farmers—which, they maintain, can only be answered by U.S. administrations abandoning their laissez-faire policy on trade and instituting tough countermeasures. Many of those individual complaints (e.g., of Japan shipping below-cost silicon chips to the American market) have been valid. More broadly, however, the surge in protectionist sentiment is also a reflection of the erosion of the previously unchallenged U.S. manufacturing supremacy. Like mid-Victorian Britons, Americans after 1945 favored free trade and open competition, not just because they held that global commerce and prosperity would be boosted in the process, but also because they knew that they were most likely to benefit from the abandonment of protectionism. Forty years later with that confidence ebbing, there is a predictable shift of opinion in favor of protecting the domestic market and the domestic producer. And, just as in that earlier British case, defenders of the existing system point out that enhanced tariffs might not only make domestic products *less* competitive internationally, but that there also could be various external repercussions— a global tariff war, blows against American exports, the undermining of the currencies of certain newly industrializing countries, and a return to the economic crisis of the 1930s.

Along with these difficulties affecting American manufacturing and agriculture there are unprecedented turbulences in the nation's finances. The uncompetitiveness of U.S. industrial products abroad and the declining sales of agricultural exports have together produced staggering deficits in visible trade—$160 billion in the twelve months to May 1986—but what is more alarming is that such a gap can no longer be covered by American earnings on "invisibles," which is the traditional recourse of a mature economy (e.g., Great Britain before 1914). On the contrary, the only way the United States can pay its way in the world is by importing ever-larger sums of capital, which has transformed it from being the world's largest creditor to the world's largest debtor nation *in the space of a few years*.

Compounding this problem—in the view of many critics, *causing* this problem—have been the budgetary policies of the U.S. government itself. Even in the 1960s, there was a tendency for Washington to rely upon deficit finance, rather than additional taxes, to pay for the increasing cost of defense and social programs. But the decisions taken by the Reagan administration in the early 1980s—i.e., large-scale increases in defense expenditures, plus considerable decreases in taxation, but *without* significant reductions in federal spending elsewhere—have produced extraordinary rises in the deficit, and consequently in the national debt, as shown on the next page.

**U.S. Federal Deficit, Debt and
Interest, 1980–1985**
(billions of dollars)

	Deficit	Debt	Interest on Debt
1980	59.6	914.3	52.5
1983	195.4	1,381.9	87.8
1985	202.8	1,823.1	129.0

The continuation of such trends, alarmed voices have pointed out, would push the U.S. national debt to around $13 *trillion* by the year 2000 (fourteen times that of 1980), and the interest payments on such debt to $1.5 *trillion* (twenty-nine times that of 1980). In fact, a lowering of interest rates could bring down those estimates, but the overall trend is still very unhealthy. Even if federal deficits could be reduced to a "mere" $100 billion annually, the compounding of national debt and interest payments by the early twenty-first century will still cause quite unprecedented totals of money to be diverted in that direction. Historically, the only other example which comes to mind of a Great Power so increasing its indebtedness in *peacetime* is France in the 1780s, where the fiscal crisis contributed to the domestic political crisis.

These American trade and federal deficits are now interacting with a new phenomenon in the world economy—what is perhaps best described as the "dislocation" of international capital movements from the trade in goods and services. Because of the growing integration of the world economy, the volume of trade both in manufactures and in financial services is much larger than ever before, and together may amount to some $3 trillion a year; but that is now eclipsed by the stupendous level of capital flows pouring through the world's money markets, with the London-based Eurodollar market alone having a volume "at least 25 times that of world trade." While this trend was fueled by events in the 1970s (the move from fixed to floating exchange rates, the surplus funds flowing from OPEC countries), it has also been stimulated by the U.S. deficits, since the only way the federal government has been able to cover the yawning gap between its expenditures and its receipts has been to suck into the country tremendous amounts of liquid funds from Europe and (especially) Japan—turning the United States, as mentioned above, into the world's largest debtor country by far. It is, in fact, difficult to imagine how the American economy could have got by *without* the inflow of foreign funds in the early 1980s, even if that had the awkward consequence of sending up the exchange value of the dollar, and further hurting U.S. agricultural and manufacturing exports. But that in turn raises the troubling question about what might happen if those massive and volatile funds were pulled out of the dollar, causing its value to drop precipitously.

The trends have, in turn, produced explanations which suggest that alarmist voices are exaggerating the gravity of what is happening to the U.S. economy and failing to note the "naturalness" of most of these developments. For example, the midwestern farm belt would be much less badly off had not so many individuals bought land at inflated prices and excessive interest rates in the late 1970s. Again, the move from manufacturing into services is an understandable one, which is occurring in all advanced countries; and it is also worth recalling that U.S. manufacturing *output* has been rising in absolute terms, even if employment (especially blue-collar employment) in manufacturing industry has been falling—but that again is a "natural" trend, as the world increasingly moves from material-based to knowledge-based production. Similarly, there is nothing wrong in the metamorphosis of American financial institutions into *world* financial institutions, with a triple base in Tokyo, London, and New York, to handle (and profit from) the great volume of capital flows; that can only boost the nation's earnings from services. Even the large annual federal deficits and the mounting national debt are sometimes described as being not too serious, after allowance is made for inflation; and there exists in some quarters a belief that the economy will "grow its way out" of these deficits, or that measures will be taken by the politicians to close the gap, whether by increasing taxes or cutting spending or a combination of both. A too-hasty attempt to slash the deficit, it is pointed out, could well trigger off a major recession.

America and the
New World Order

PAUL NITZE

Paul Nitze is one of the most noted American diplomats of the twentieth century. As an architect of NSC–68 he helped create the national security state in which we live. No one knows what will be the right solutions to the problems we now confront but Nitze provides an excellent enumeration of the issues facing us. What are the dangers from increasing nationalism? Why did a staunch cold warrior hope that the Soviet Union would remain intact? How have events subsequent to this article altered the key issues?

Each of us has experienced the phenomenal central European revolution of 1989, its preliminaries in Poland and its continuing aftermath, particularly in Germany and the Soviet Union. But each has done so from his or her own window on the world.

Having spent much of my life as a policy planner, I tend to focus on the future, on what lies ahead, on what is desirable and perhaps practical, and on what policies would most successfully help to bring about these aims. I also tend to translate this forward-looking perspective into American terms: What should we in this country view as our role in collaboration with others in moving the world toward this desired future?

In charting a road to the future, it is sometimes wise to look back on relevant turning points of the past. For over forty years the foreign and defense policies of the United States have been guided by a central theme, a well-defined basic policy objective. That goal, throughout the Cold War, was for the United States to take the lead in building an international world order based on liberal economic and political institutions, and to defend that world against communist attack.

The political-strategic situation is now changed. We are in an important period of transition. Our postwar policies appear to have achieved their principal objective, and a new conception of our foreign and defense policies is required as we face a future less dominated by an ideologically driven U.S.S.R. Before we can formulate a new strategy, however, it is first in order that we review our postwar policy of containment, its origins and rationale, and where and the degree to which it has succeeded.

By 1981 both the United States and the Soviet Union had shifted their primary focus in negotiations to the issue of elimination, or at least control, of intermediate-range nuclear forces (INF). This issue was of crucial importance to the European members of the NATO alliance. The United States had agreed with its NATO partners to deploy Pershing II and ground-launched cruise missiles in Europe in order to offset the Soviet Union's earlier deployment on the continent of longer-range nuclear missiles with multiple warheads. The Soviet aim in these negotiations was now to block the U.S. deployment, without giving up their own missiles. If successful in this objective, the Soviets would have shattered the NATO alliance and isolated the United States.

NATO did not flinch, however, despite a concerted Soviet propaganda campaign and Moscow's walkout from the INF talks. This check to Soviet policy was a crucial point in the long, continuous Western effort to contain Soviet expansionism. It provided clear evidence to a new generation of Soviet leaders that old tactics of intimidation would not work. Led by Mikhail Gorbachev, the Soviets were now prepared to reconsider their former policies and methods.

In a meeting in Moscow in 1987 with Secretary of State George Shultz, Gorbachev recalled that when he first became general secretary of the Communist Party he did not begin from a standing start. He and Nikolai Ryzhkov were appointed to the Politburo in 1982 and, Gorbachev recounted, it was then that they exchanged views on the serious internal problems facing the Soviet state—the political structure of the party, the backwardness of the economy, the excessive allocation of resources to defense, and more. After these discussions, Gorbachev said, they appointed a hundred teams composed of the brightest minds they could find to analyze these problems and come up with suggestions for solutions.

When I heard these statements by Gorbachev, it seemed to confirm that our policy of containment had indeed achieved its basic aim;

Soviet leaders were forced to look inward, and they did not like what they saw.

Containment has thus been largely successful, the Cold War is waning and communist ideology may well be in its final decline, much as Nazism and fascism were at the end of World War II. The non-Soviet part of the Warsaw Pact has now lost its strategic significance. It is time therefore to reexamine containment, our longstanding central policy objective, with the goal of making a transition to a new conception of U.S. policy, one better suited to a changing future.

I

A time of transition is bound to be a period of uncertainty; old guideposts are gone or quickly fading and new landmarks need to be sorted out and established. The United States cannot possibly ensure that global stability will follow this period of transition. The most we can do is to use our influence to move world events in a direction of peace.

We first need to break down the problem into its relevant parts—political, economic, military, regional, environmental, etc.—and reach tentative conclusions about sensible policy in each category, testing from time to time the coherence of an overarching line of policy that integrates these various components. Thus while thinking through the long-term measures that we hope will lead to global stability, we must also deal concurrently with the immediate problems before us. It is only by successfully handling these problems that we keep our long-range planning from losing touch with the practical world as it is evolving.

What are our current issues?

—First, should we continue to focus our policy toward the Soviet Union on helping Gorbachev preserve his base of power, or should we focus more on our longer-term relations with whatever regime may emerge in control of the Russian people and those willing to remain associated with them?

We need to walk a fine line on this question. It is in the U.S. interest that Gorbachev remain in charge. He is a known quantity and his policies, with all their faults, are probably preferable to those we could currently expect from any likely successor.

On the other hand, we should not tie ourselves so closely to Gorbachev that we undermine our ability, should he lose power, to work with those who will follow. We made that mistake with Chiang Kai-shek in China and the shah in Iran. We cannot afford to repeat it with Gorbachev in the Soviet Union.

—Should we seek a prompt conclusion to the Strategic Arms Reduction Talks (START) along the lines suggested in the communiqué at the U.S.–Soviet summit in June 1990, or should we reassess the possibility and desirability of a deeper set of stabilizing reductions?

I believe it is in our interest to seek deeper and more stabilizing cuts in strategic forces than those contemplated by the summit communiqué. These cuts should focus on landbased missiles with multiple warheads, particularly the Soviets' heavy intercontinental ballistic missiles (ICBMS). As long as these missiles exist, their great destructive capability will poison our political and military relations with the Soviet Union. These missiles will cause us to take costly and undesirable countermeasures to assure that there is no possibility of the Soviet Union exploiting their enormous potential. It would be far better for all if the Soviet Union were to eliminate its heavy ICBMS as part of an agreement under which both it and the United States eliminated land-based, multiple-warhead missiles and placed equal ceilings on remaining strategic nuclear warheads.

Specifically, I suggest the draft START treaty be amended as follows:

— to ban land-based missiles with multiple warheads;
— to relax or even eliminate the limit of 1,600 on the number of weapon systems for each side, as this would remove the necessity for either to deploy destabilizing, multiple-warhead systems;
— to limit the weight of individual warheads to 200 kilograms or less in order to prevent the deployment of new large special-function nuclear warheads, such as those the Soviets are suspected of planning to deploy on their new SS-18 Mod 6; and
— to reduce the number of existing strategic warheads by at least twice that contemplated by START, i.e., by approximately 75 percent as opposed to approximately 35 percent.

If all ground-based, multiple-warhead nuclear missiles were banned, the remaining systems permitted to each side would be highly survivable against a first-strike nuclear attack. These remaining systems would include single-warhead, fixed or mobile, ground-based nuclear missiles; submarine-launched nuclear ballistic missiles and nuclear cruise missiles; long-range air-launched nuclear cruise missiles; and bombers armed only with gravity bombs and short-range attack missiles limited to less than 600 kilometers.

If the nuclear systems permitted to each side were inherently highly survivable and unable to attack more than a single target, there would be no point in either side's attempting to improve its position by initiating an attack on the strategic forces of the other. Three to five thousand such systems on each side would suffice to make undetected cheating or the capabilities of other nuclear powers—now and in the foreseeable future—insufficient to upset the inherent stability this type of arrangement would bring to the nuclear relationship between the United States and the U.S.S.R.

I believe the opportunity for a radical and mutually beneficial solution is better now than it would be if the issue were postponed. We should therefore insist now on a truly stabilizing treaty, rather than being satisfied with the half-measures currently proposed.

—Should we encourage Lithuania and the other Baltic states seeking greater independence to postpone or scale back their demands in order to relieve the pressure on Gorbachev, or should we support our long-held position that the absorption of these states by Stalin through an unsavory deal with Hitler was improper?

This is of course one of the issues important to Gorbachev's prospects. In the case of the Baltic states, however, I believe other considerations must prevail. The United States has never recognized the propriety of Soviet annexation of the Baltic states, and to change our position now would be inconsistent with our values and counterproductive in the long term. It is thus sensible to encourage negotiations between Moscow and the Baltic states, but we should allow the Baltic governments to decide for themselves what negotiating position to take.

—What should our attitude be toward a united Germany and NATO?

The United States and NATO continue to have an important role in maintaining stability on the European continent and contributing to stability elsewhere on the globe. Other organizations, such as the 35-nation Conference on Security and Cooperation in Europe (CSCE), may play useful supporting roles, but could not possibly substitute for NATO, at least as far as the United States is concerned. It is important that NATO include the powerful political, economic and military forces that a unified Germany will represent. I also believe that Soviet security interests will be better served by a Germany united within

NATO than by a neutral Germany. Recent negotiations suggest that Gorbachev has also come around to this view. Clearly, an isolated Germany is potentially more dangerous than one cooperating as a valued member of a community of nations.

—What are our primary economic concerns and what should we do about them?

Economic problems abound worldwide, from the collapse of the Soviet economy, to the struggles of the East European countries to convert to free-market economies, to the ordeal of Third World nations seeking to emerge from overwhelming debt. In considering the panoply of global economic problems and possible solutions, I think we must first concentrate on getting our own house in order. The U.S. budget deficit, coupled with our balance-of-payments problems, is limiting our ability to aid the new democracies of Eastern Europe and Central America, to help fund solutions to global environmental problems and to otherwise bring our economic clout to bear on world problems of great interest to everyone. If we are to suggest sacrifices by others attempting to shift to market economies, pay off their debts and remedy sources of ecological damage, then we must also be prepared to reduce excessive consumption and heal our own economy.

The United States must also deal with other domestic problems currently exacerbating international difficulties. A stepped-up campaign against drug use should be undertaken in an effort to reduce the U.S. demand that is such a major factor in the worldwide drug trade. Separately, strict enforcement of the clean air law is necessary to help reduce the U.S. emissions that are major contributors to worldwide environmental deterioration.

—How should we deal with problems that transcend national boundaries, such as global environmental decay?

Many problems we now face cut across national boundaries and affect many cultures. Economic and environmental problems are but two categories; others include terrorism and drugs. Still other problems that face many individual nations, such as hunger, can best be addressed through concerted international efforts.

These types of problems can generally be handled more efficiently and effectively by supranational institutions than by individual governments acting in the absence of some central coordinating body. Any grant of authority to a supranational body, however, implies some loss by nations of sovereign choice. We must therefore be careful to balance

the gains of centrally directed efforts against the costs of reduced freedom of choice for individual nations. The gains to be derived from a
supranational authority most clearly outweigh the costs in environmental issues. One nation's efforts to reverse the growing damage to the
world ecology can easily be undercut by the negligence of other countries. A coordinated international effort is certainly required if we are to
save our environment.

II

Returning to the question of an overall policy line, a strategic concept
to guide our approach to the panoply of issues we face and to give our
individual policies larger coherence. The new strategic concept I propose is captured in the following four sentences:

—The central theme of the policy of the United States should be the accommodation and protection of diversity within a general framework of
world order.
—Our aim should be to foster a world climate in which a wide array of
political groups are able to exist, each with its own and perhaps eccentric ways.
—Supranational institutions, such as the United Nations and its organs,
NATO, the European Community, CSCE and the Organization for Economic Cooperation and Development, should be given the role of providing stability and forward movement on important global and regional
issues that transcend national or ethnic boundaries.
—The United States, with inherent political, economic, cultural and military strengths, and no territorial or ideological ambitions of its own, can
and should play a unique role in bringing its powers to the support of order
and diversity among the world's diffuse and varied groups.

The emphasis on diversity derives from one of the most important
lessons of the past few years: the near impossibility of erasing cultural
ties, ethnic identities and social practices in a world where communications and ideas cannot be suppressed. Despite the efforts by communist
leaders for decades to impose a common culture and society on their
subjects, a Europe with a rich mix of nationalities and cultures is once
again reviving. A similar process is occurring on other continents as
well. Not only are the aspirations of individuals and ethnic groups once
again being realized, but this constellation of the cultures promises to
enrich us all.

While there is much to learn from the ways of others, diversity also creates problems. The tensions that diversity had generated in the past have arisen once more—between Hungarians and Romanians, Bulgarians and Turks, Serbs and Albanians, and among the many nationalities throughout the Soviet Union. Such tensions may be the primary threat to peace in the years ahead.

Diversity therefore presents us with mixed blessings. As a democratic nation that honors freedom, we protect the right to dissent and to be different, as well as the rights of minorities from discrimination, and thus the United States supports this movement toward greater diversity. As a people who can learn from the ways of others, we welcome the opportunity to do so. As students of history, we understand that the aspirations of various peoples to realize their heritage cannot in any event be long suppressed.

As realists, however, we must recognize and try to contend with the dangers that accompany excessive nationalism and threaten to destroy the general peace. The assertion that the United States has no ideological ambitions does not mean we are without strong values; it means only that we should not impose these values on others. Just as we can learn from other peoples, they too can learn much from us, but we must realize that cooperative efforts among nations are generally more effective in achieving this end. The central element of my theme is thus the accommodation and protection of diversity within a framework of global order.

III

The emphasis on a global role for the United States is perhaps controversial. Many Americans argue that the current mood favors a withdrawal from a leading role in international affairs. Their reasoning is that a great threat is no longer evident, and the United States is therefore free to turn inward and tend to its domestic concerns.

This outlook is shortsighted. As the issues I have addressed above indicate, there remain numerous international problems that deeply affect American interests. New problems of this same nature are bound to arise. The United States remains uniquely capable of contributing in conjunction with others to the effective solution of these problems. No other nation can do the job as well.

The Soviet Union, for example, even with the reductions I have advocated for a START treaty, will retain thousands of nuclear warheads and remain a potential threat to the United States and its allies. The current instability in that country only exacerbates the problem; no one can be sure into whose hands these weapons may eventually fall. No other country is capable of relieving the United States of the burden of deterring the use of these weapons, and none is likely to be able to do so in the future. Nor would we want any other country to deploy the nuclear arsenal needed to assume that role alone.

Similarly, should nationalist tensions in Europe erupt into civil or cross-border conflicts, no other country would seem as well qualified to play the role of honest broker in facilitating, with others, a peaceful resolution of these differences and terminating hostilities. In the absence of the United States from Europe, Germany would seem to have the greatest military, political and economic power on the continent, and thus leadership would fall to it in such a situation. Germany, however, is not well suited for such a role. Suspicion of German intentions, justified or not, remains too high among the nations of Europe for Germany to be effective in the role of honest broker.

The United States therefore must remain in a position to contribute to the continent's stability should European nations, including Germany, wish us to do so. This does not necessarily mean the continued presence of large numbers of American troops in Europe; we will only keep such forces there as are wanted and only for such a time as they are wanted. A constructive U.S. role in European affairs can be derived from more than simply the number of troops deployed; potential power can be symbolized even by the presence of forces of limited size.

Similar examples of problems meriting a U.S. role exist in other regions of the world. In the Middle East, the strategic importance of which is obvious, the United States is currently actively supporting the peace process, attempting to work with Israel, Egypt and the Palestine Liberation Organization. It is not evident that any other country has the clout necessary to assume this role effectively.

In time our leading role in the Far East could perhaps be assumed by Japan. But this would raise considerable concern among other Asian nations, especially those who have fallen under Japanese domination in the past. It is further doubtful that the Japanese would find it feasible to consider the interests of others comparable to their own.

All of these cases argue for the American role I have proposed. But let me also make clear the constraints on this role. I am proposing active U.S. participation in cooperative efforts with varying groups of sovereign nations to deal constructively with common problems; I am not proposing unilateral U.S. action. I am suggesting we act internationally where the common interest can be served; I am not suggesting unduly impinging upon the sovereignty of others. Our engagement on the world scene should therefore be carefully selective, based on our new objective of tolerating and strengthening diversity around the globe.

The Basis for America's Future

ROBERT HORMATS

That money provides the sinews of war as well as the basis for a sound peace has long been a truism. In this article former diplomat, now banker, Robert Hormats details the American economic position at the end of the Cold War and discusses possible reforms which would help ensure a more economically secure future. What steps could be taken to rectify American problems at the close of the twentieth century? What are the political and economic obstacles to such reforms?

In the aftermath of the war to liberate Kuwait, it is worthwhile reflecting on the conditions at home that made it possible for the United States to mobilize more than 500,000 troops, deploy an enormous armada of ships, planes and equipment halfway around the world, and wage a war of stunning technological intensity. America's capacity to execute such a vast campaign was no accident. Nor was it simply the result of the buildup of a great arsenal in the 1980s, although that helped to equip U.S. forces with the firepower to get the job done.

Such success was made possible by an underlying economy able to turn out great volumes of extremely advanced military equipment and software as well as men and women skilled in operating them. The U.S. economy would not have been capable of doing this but for a history of high American savings and enormous investment in education, industry, science, technology and the infrastructure to link these elements together. Savings and investments of earlier years were not intended primarily to bolster America's capacity to send well-equipped forces overseas, but they had the derivative effect of making that possible and, more generally, of strengthening the foundations of American global power—political and economic, as well as military.

It is an ominous sign for the future, then, that today U.S. domestic savings are close to a historical low and that investment in education, industry, infrastructure and vanguard technologies is inadequate. While the United States is likely to maintain military preeminence for years to come, savings and investment shortfalls raise concerns about America's future capacity to produce the resources, technologies and trained people necessary to maintain its current overwhelming military edge. Consequently, there is reason for alarm about this country's ability a decade or two from now to fight a gulf-type war—or any other war—so successfully and with so few casualties. Without this confidence the United States could become reluctant to act decisively, and other nations might become more willing to challenge American interests.

But even if the probability of the United States ever again having to take military action abroad were to fall to zero, domestic economic problems would still pose a serious threat to vital American interests. Economic strength will become an increasingly important aspect of national power, and in many cases the decisive aspect, in what promises to be a more competitive global commercial and financial environment. Geoeconomic competition will contend with, and perhaps surpass, geopolitical competition as the driving force in international relations.

The financing of the Gulf War is also grounds for concern. It was altogether appropriate for the United States to call on other members of the international coalition to underwrite a large portion of the war's costs, because they too had a vital interest in the success of Operation Desert Storm. It is nonetheless a fact that this was the first U.S. military operation in this century that America felt unable to pay for by itself. Without significant financial assistance from abroad, either a new tax increase or added government borrowing would have been required, as in past wars. That would have slowed an economy already in recession in early 1991; the very notion that these unpopular measures would have been necessary could have turned a few critical votes in Congress against the president, perhaps enough to deny authorization to use force in the gulf.

The United States ultimately received pledges of over $50 billion from its allies. But there can be no assurance that in the future U.S. intervention will be called for in areas of the world where so many other wealthy nations have parallel or common interests and will thus be willing to foot so large a share of the bill. Of course future U.S. leaders are likely to seek to mobilize coalitions to support their actions, but they will not wish to feel unable to move militarily without passing the hat.

If America's economy does falter, so will the underlying source of its international power. Thus this nation's central foreign policy priority in coming years and its central domestic priority must be the same: strengthening the American economy. Unless the United States reinvigorates in this decade the economic roots of its international power, it risks an erosion of self-confidence and of its international leadership at the turn of the century. With a weak economy and a society in conflict over how to allocate slowly growing resources, this nation would find it increasingly difficult to achieve its essential global objectives.

I

Walter Lippmann once cautioned that American foreign policy "consists in bringing into balance, with a comfortable surplus of power in reserve, the nation's commitments and the nation's power." If commitments exceed power, "insolvency" results; that leads to political dissension. It might be tempting to balance the equation by seeking to reduce commitments. But America will continue to have significant global responsibilities—even if it can achieve greater burden-sharing—that it cannot shed without compromising important interests.

America's commitments abroad are not simply a drain on its economy; many are vital to it. The United States exports 13 percent of its GNP, 20 percent of its manufactured goods and 30 percent of its farm production; millions of U.S. jobs depend on sales abroad; production by their foreign subsidiaries is integral to the success of many American corporations; intracompany cross-border trade is critical to the profitability of a wide range of U.S. businesses; and imported oil and commodities are vital to the U.S. economy. Political stability abroad, open sea-lanes, the sanctity of borders, stability of supplies and the ability to secure greater openness in the economies of trading partners all serve important U.S. economic and strategic interests.

To remain a preeminent economic, political and military power the United States cannot shrink from its essential international purposes and objectives; it must maintain an economy strong enough to attain them.

Conventional wisdom correctly holds that its people are a nation's greatest resource. Like other resources, they can be underutilized. That is the case in America today. The difference between vigorous and weak economic growth for the United States in the 1990s will be its effectiveness in developing and mobilizing the skills and creativity of a far greater portion of its citizens.

If 15 percent of all the nation's factories or forests were destroyed in an earthquake or fire, the country would be in a state of crisis; yet for years the talents of roughly that portion of working age Americans have been wasted due to illiteracy, inadequate training or poor motivation—and this is treated with complacency.

The United States is in the midst of a dramatic demographic transformation. Hispanics, blacks and Asians together will account for more than half the growth in the U.S. labor force over the next decade. Almost nine million immigrants entered the United States during the 1980s, accounting for 40 percent of the nation's labor force growth, and the pace continues. Women of all racial groups and origins now account for over 60 percent of new work-force entrants.

At the same time, the number of working-age people in the United States will grow more slowly in the future than in the 1980s, as the 77 million baby boomers born between 1946 and 1964 are followed by a smaller number of labor-force entrants. Because the ratio of retirees to active workers will increase steadily, the productive output of new workers will have to increase significantly in coming years just to maintain current national living standards.

America has not done well at incorporating blacks and Hispanics into the work force or tapping their full productive potential. Yet significant increases in American growth in the 1990s—as well as a reduction in the size of the nation's economic underclass and improved social cohesion—will be difficult to achieve without higher levels of labor-force participation and productivity by men and women in both groups, many of whom are now on the economic sidelines. They, indeed all Americans, will have to perform knowledge- and technology-driven jobs to higher and higher standards in coming years.

The task of productively engaging a broader spectrum of citizens—minorities, disadvantaged youths from all groups and the elderly—challenges America's political, social and corporate structure. Together they must develop a comprehensive "life-cycle" strategy for investment in and better utilization of the nation's human resources, starting at childhood and running through an individual's productive years. Three related objectives demand priority attention: support for children early in life; improvement of education and training practices; and better engagement of older Americans in the workplace.

SUPPORT FOR YOUNG CHILDREN

American society stands out from other industrialized democracies with respect to the deteriorating family structure and the number of poor one-parent households. The 1987 Metropolitan Life Study of the American Teacher found that among the most serious impediments to learning were parents leaving children alone after school, poverty at home and single-parent families. These factors put children at an early disadvantage, force the educational system to serve as a parental substitute and divert time from teaching basic skills.

One out of five children in America lives in poverty; many suffer from hunger and health problems; immunization is erratic, leading to the revival of childhood diseases once considered virtually eradicated. All these factors seriously impair learning. Programs to prevent unwanted teenage pregnancies, enhance prenatal and infant care and broaden childhood health care are basic.

Large numbers of needy children in the United States have no access to preschool programs; low pay and low status hamper the staffing of many centers. A dollar invested in preschool education saves six times the amount otherwise spent on special education, welfare and law enforcement. In France preschool for three- to five-year-olds is free; 98 percent of the country's children attend such schools, more than three times the American figure; preschool teachers hold the equivalent of a masters degree; directors are often pediatric nurses trained in public health and child development.

Even if moral considerations do not compel greater attention to young children, economic self-interest should. Today's neglected children are bound to impose an economic burden on American society for decades to come.

EDUCATION AND TRAINING

The weakness of this nation's primary and secondary education system is widely recognized as an impediment to productivity growth. One observer puts the point succinctly: "The accumulated data on comparative education . . . point up two trends. First, compared with their peers in Asian and European countries, American students stand out for how little they work. Second, compared with Asians and Europeans, American students stand out for how poorly they do."

American secondary education is especially deficient in preparing students for jobs. In Germany the apprentice system serves as a transition from school to the workplace; more than one million young people annually enter a three or four year program in which they attend vocational schools part time while working part time for a company. In the United States the large number of high school dropouts and inadequately prepared graduates, particularly among minorities, means that many of America's future workers will lack the necessary skills to succeed.

Productively absorbing a steady flow of new immigrants in the 1990s will be especially important to the success of many of the world's industrial economies. Millions of political and economic immigrants are likely to flow into western Europe from the Soviet Union, eastern Europe and northern Africa. U.S. immigration will come primarily from Latin America, but Soviets and East Asians are also expected in large numbers. Even Japan, heretofore unwilling to accept workers from elsewhere in Asia, is likely to need the labor they could provide.

Having incorporated tens of millions of immigrants into its economy for over three centuries, America should be able to take significant advantage of new flows relative to countries such as Japan with greater social rigidities and less immigration experience. But the United States can realize this advantage only if its educational and social systems can assimilate new refugees as effectively in the future as in the past.

An increasingly open global economy poses another dimension to the challenge of education. The reduction of trade barriers since World War II, improved transportation and the global diffusion of technology mean that factories producing standardized goods can be built nearly anywhere and their output shipped inexpensively around the world. Workers in industrialized nations producing such goods compete against lower-wage workers in Thailand, Brazil or India who use basically the same equipment. Such competition compresses profits and wages. Jobs in such industries therefore are decreasing in the United States; where they do exist, companies keep salaries low in order to survive.

Less-educated workers—many of whom tend to work in these industries—have been especially hard hit. Since 1983 the unemployment rate among high school dropouts has been 10 to 14 percentage points higher than those with a high school diploma. That translates into a wider income gap between skilled and unskilled Americans, and more problems for the country's economic underclass. In a global economy workers can command high wages and obtain good jobs only by adding greater value then their counterparts abroad; to do so they must bring higher skills and knowledge to their work.

The global economy imposes additional pressure on business, since virtually any American advantage can sooner or later be duplicated abroad. A company and its workers must create a moving target for competitors; a product or technology needs constant improvement to sustain a margin of advantage. Because knowledge, as a component of virtually every product, is far greater than a decade ago, both workers and managers must not only enter their jobs with high-level skills but constantly upgrade those skills throughout their careers.

A comprehensive set of reforms is needed to strengthen the capacity of the U.S. educational system to turn out larger numbers of skilled workers and managers. These should include: giving students a greater choice among competing schools and programs; allowing "alternative providers," such as universities or corporations to operate and sponsor schools; expanding the number of merit-based schools in which success leads to bonuses for teachers and failure to closure; and emphasizing co-operative problem solving rather than lectures. In some German schools the same teachers stay with students for several grades to build close re-lationships—an experiment worth trying in the United States. A case can also be made to expand the U.S. school year. Currently it is 180 days; in Japan it is 240 days, in Germany 230.

Financing reforms cannot be left entirely to individual localities. America today is increasingly segregated by income groups. Poor areas often cannot afford to improve local schools; if not helped to do so, their students will fall further behind wealthier areas, exacerbating edu-cational and subsequently wage gaps. Net new expenditures for edu-cation could be held to a minimum by realizing cost savings from "debureaucratization." Private school administrative costs are consider-ably lower than those of public schools; in the public schools, teachers made up 65 percent of staffs in 1960, but only 53 percent in 1988. If ad-ditional funds are still needed, dedicated education taxes would be jus-tifiable as an investment in the future.

RETIREMENT

American retirement programs were established for the most part when men and women did not live, or remain economically productive, for as long as they do today. At that time the U.S. work force was growing so rapidly that the economy as a whole could afford to support a group of early retirees. A concerted effort is now required by business and government to provide more flexibility in Social Security regulations, retiree benefits and working conditions to encourage older Americans to participate longer in the productive economy.

Mobilizing the growing pool of retired business people, engineers, computer experts and skilled workers to serve as instructors in secondary schools would help the educational system better prepare students for careers. These retirees also can help to replace the nearly 40 percent of public school teachers who will retire this decade. To fill this gap nearly half of all college graduates would have to become teachers; only ten percent now plan to do so.

Americans over the age of 65 receive nearly half of noninterest, nondefense government spending—up from one-third in 1965—through programs such as Medicare and Social Security. By using their expertise to train and thus increase the earning power of future workers, retirees would increase the tax flows available to support programs that ultimately benefit them.

II

Defects in America's educational system and a general lack of investment in human resources are part of a broader national myopia. Deep philosophical differences divide American public opinion on such issues as income distribution, taxes and the size and scope of government programs. The focus has been primarily on satisfying the immediate needs of competing constituencies. Budget politics in recent years have often been characterized by a "we versus they" debate among interest groups—frequently diverting attention from long-term priorities.

Lack of orientation toward the future is not limited to government. U.S. private savings during the first quarter of this century averaged over 16 percent of GNP; from 1950 to 1979 they dropped to an average of about seven percent; during the past decade they fell to roughly five percent. Per capita consumption, the other side of the coin, hovered between 56 and 60 percent of GNP from 1950 to 1970; over the last 20 years it has risen to a range of 62 to 66 percent of GNP. Higher per capita consumption has coincided with a surge in consumer debt. From 1960 to 1987 home-mortgage debt was between 36 and 46 percent of the value of owner-occupied real estate; in the last three years, beginning before the fall in real estate values, it soared to over 57 percent.

Many U.S. businesses behaved in a similar fashion—leveraging themselves through massive borrowing. Corporate debt in 1982 amounted to $1.40 for every dollar of GNP; by 1990 that figure had reached $1.90. Since 1982 corporate debt has grown at a rate of 10.8 percent annually while pretax profits have risen at a rate of only 7.7 percent. These are not sustainable relationships. A major deleveraging of the U.S. economy, characterized by a slower rate of borrowing and greater use of equity financing, is inevitable.

As borrowing was increasing, U.S. investment in plant and equipment relative to GNP was falling from its levels of the 1950s and 1960s; its percentage of GNP is now below that of most other major industrialized nations. For years America's competitors have devoted a larger percentage of their GNP to investment. In 1989, for the first time since World War II, another nation, Japan, outinvested the United States in absolute terms. And it is projected to do so for at least the next several years.

Nonmilitary research and development in the United States has risen substantially, up by 140 percent from over a decade ago. But as a percent of GNP it is still below levels attained in the 1960s and is smaller than in Germany or Japan. A 1990 National Science Foundation report expressed concern that for the first time in 14 years U.S. research and development expenditures did not keep pace with inflation.

Consider also the state of infrastructure. Between 1965 and 1985 U.S. public spending on roads, bridges and railways dropped from 2.2 percent of GNP to 1.0 percent; it remains at about that level, among the lowest in the industrialized world. Japan and Germany spend an average of 5 percent and 2.5 percent, respectively, on infrastructure. In this country deteriorating highways alone are estimated to cost the economy $35 billion in delayed interstate commerce.

On the other hand, U.S. manufacturing productivity presents a far brighter picture. It grew almost three times faster in the 1980s than in the 1970s due to the successful restructuring programs of many American corporations and their increased attention to international competitiveness. U.S. manufacturing productivity has either kept pace with or outpaced other major industrial competitors. But weakness in U.S. investment places this country in danger of being overtaken in this area as well.

Intergenerational conflict will be one of the consequences of sluggish investment. Younger workers whose incomes grow slowly due to deficiencies in their education, or in corporate and public infrastructure, will resent being forced to transfer more and more money through payroll or income taxes to retirees. Many are already at a relative disadvantage because large numbers of older Americans have been the beneficiaries of a big rise in home prices in the 1970s and 1980s and enjoy low fixed-rate mortgages. In contrast, significant numbers of younger workers face the prospect of higher housing prices and higher mortgage rates. On average their salaries are likely to grow more slowly than those of their parents, limiting their ability to accumulate wealth. Poorer workers will object to paying taxes for Social Security. Medicare and other support programs requiring no needs test, meaning that the benefits will go to people better off than they.

Because voting strength will shift increasingly in their favor, the elderly will be in a strong position to resist large cuts in their benefits. Intergenerational struggle for resources—of which America got a taste in the 1990 budget debate—could be long and perhaps bitter. And if the problems of the underclass worsen, there will be an intense tug of war between advocates of that group and those of America's elderly. Middle-class working Americans, caught between the two, will claim with increasing justification that the government asks too much of them and provides too little.

Intergenerational and interclass resource allocation, and relative tax burdens, are likely to constitute central and divisive domestic political issues for years to come, without vigorous economic growth. The resulting social friction could sap America's international strength. The political and legislative compromises reached are likely to draw discretionary resources away from long-term investment requirements as well as from future defense, foreign assistance or other international needs.

III

The country as a whole has not experienced the sort of crisis or shock that a democracy frequently requires to focus a critical mass of public opinion on the need for bold change. Its problems have come on gradually. Despite the savings and loan crises, the October 1987 stock market crash, plus a host of underlying concerns, a sense of urgency about or commitment to substantial alterations in policy or practice appear lacking.

For a number of years political leaders at federal, state and local levels have tended to shy away from controversial decisions on tough economic issues. Many political compromises of recent years have been widely understood in advance to fall far short of their claims to resolve major problems they purport to address: successive fictional "budget deals" from the start had no chance of reducing the deficit; "energy independence policies" and "anti-drug policies" promised but simply had not the content to produce significant results.

The country has come to accept a version of "no report card" politics: controversial decisions are often shunted off to commissions answerable to no one or to courts outside the reach of voters. Political preservation has spawned an aversion to telling voters bad economic news, confessing mistakes or cutting popular programs that no longer serve priority interests or are too expensive to fund. Citizens, in turn, have come to expect little candor from their leaders on economic matters. Much of this is of course not new; it is, however, damaging to the national interest when fundamental changes are required.

Breaking out of this pattern of shortsighted policymaking will require a systematic national effort to identify long-term national goals around which public opinion and private energies can coalesce. The European Community provides a good example. In 1985 its members set the end of 1992 as a target date to eliminate trade and financial barriers among them. They developed a detailed set of programs to accomplish this. The goal is now nearing realization. The United States has successfully employed a similar technique to set goals for, and energize, the space program and environmental cleanup.

Agreement on a newly defined set of American economic goals, target dates to attain them and steps that must be taken by the public and private sectors to do so would serve as a benchmark—a standard of performance—to evaluate programs, policies and even political leaders. These goals should not be mandated by law nor devised by academicians or professional planners. They should be established through a dialogue between the president, Congress and the nation's governors, and after a focused public discussion involving the private sector. Congress engaged in thoughtful debate prior to the vote on whether to authorize the use of force to evict Iraq from Kuwait. Debate on a similarly high plane over the course of the next two years, especially during the 1992 political campaigns, would help to sort out the priorities for strengthening the U.S. economy.

The debate should address the major issues. What should be America's educational goals—for literacy, reduction of high school dropouts, preschool program participation—and what types of programs must be instituted to attain them? Should the nation aim to boost nondefense research and development as a percentage of GNP to its mid-1960s highs, to the level of a competitor nation such as Japan, or to some other target level? How should that target be reached? What are the consequences of success or failure? Should the United States seek to raise private investment in plant and equipment to the level of Japan or Germany, or to some other target; if so, what must the government and private sector do to attain that goal?

Achievement of the country's most vital priorities and goals will require new social, political and economic alliances in the 1990s. Older and younger Americans must forge a new alliance. Retirees will need to invest more time and effort to educate younger people, and thus improve their productivity. This, in turn, will allow younger people to generate the tax revenues and provide political support for programs that benefit the elderly. Businesses and the economic underclass must forge a new alliance as well. The corporate sector will need to help train and improve the relevance of education for poorer and minority Americans. In turn, their future productivity will increase, as will their contribution to the competitiveness of U.S. industry.

Political leaders and their constituents will also need to form a new alliance. Leaders must be more willing to convey tough economic messages to constituents; constituents must be more willing to judge leaders on their long-term policies rather than their immediate gratification of political pressures. Taxpayers and government must forge a new alliance. Government must demonstrate that federal revenues are being used wisely and that government services are being efficiently delivered. It must reduce taxpayer burdens by finding new ways of encouraging private financing for infrastructure, limit tax subsidies that encourage personal borrowing and corporate debt-financing and introduce new tax devices to stimulate savings and investment. Taxpayers, in turn, must be willing to provide additional funds when required to meet national priorities such as education, certain essential infrastructure projects and research in critical technologies.

Preoccupation with whether the United States is slipping vis-à-vis Japan and Germany has diverted attention from a more fundamental issue—the nation's failure to live up to its own past record of high economic performance. Even if the United States did not face intense competition from other nations, if the economic challenge of Japan and Germany were to collapse tomorrow, American living standards, international competitiveness and global influence would still be weakened if the nation's economy continues to underperform.

The opportunities before the United States in the late twentieth century are enormous. This country has more inherent human, entrepreneurial, natural resource and governmental strengths than any other nation—by a substantial margin. Its ability to maintain an unchallengeable defense capability, fulfill its global responsibilities and achieve its purposes in the fast changing world environment likely to confront it in coming years will require it to make the most of these strengths. The nation's capacity to maintain a strong economy and a healthy society will be critical to its global prospects—and will be severely tested. To succeed, the United States will require not only vision but also more investment, more savings, more emphasis on education and more ambitious goals for research, development and health care. It will require stronger, more purposeful economic leadership at all levels.

During the 1980 presidential campaign, candidate Ronald Reagan asked Americans to consider whether they were better off than they had been four years earlier. Now the country must consider whether, if it continues on its present course, it will be better off at the end of this decade than it is today.